D0875872

The SATURATED World

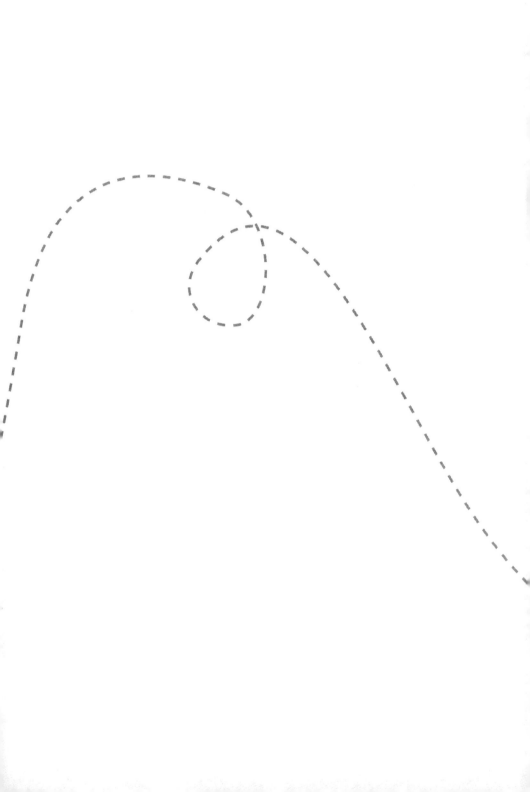

The SATURATED World

Aesthetic Meaning,
Intimate Objects,
Women's Lives,
1890–1940

BEVERLY GORDON

The University of Tennessee Press / Knoxville

Copyright © 2006 by The University of Tennessee Press / Knoxville.
All Rights Reserved. Manufactured in the United States of America.
First Edition.

This book is printed on acid-free paper.

Library of Congress Cataloging-in-Publication Data

Gordon, Beverly.
The saturated world : aesthetic meaning, intimate objects, women's lives, 1890–1940 /
Beverly Gordon.—1st ed.
    p. cm.
Includes bibliographical references and index.
ISBN-13: 978-1-57233-542-4 (hardcover : alk. paper)
ISBN-10: 1-57233-542-4 (hardcover)

1. Women—United States—Social life and customs—19th century. 2. Women—United
States—Social life and customs—20th century. 3. Women—Recreation—United
States—History—19th century. 4. Women—Recreation—United States—History—
20th century. 5. Amusements—United States—History—19th century. 6. Amusements—
United States—History—20th century. 7. Handicraft—United States—History—19th
century. 8. Handicraft—United States—History—20th century. I. Title.

HQ1419.G67 2006
305.40973'0904—dc22   2006004333

CONTENTS

ILLUSTRATIONS

ACKNOWLEDGMENTS

Many individuals and institutions have been instrumental in the completion of this manuscript. I am grateful to the University of Wisconsin–Madison for awarding me a Vilas Fellowship that helped with the research process and a Kellett Award that assisted with photograph expenses. In addition I received a Winterthur-Hagley Research Award (sponsored by the Winterthur and Hagley museums) that was invaluable in allowing me to find some of the seminal material that helped formulate my ideas.

I was assisted by tireless helpers at various archives and collections, including Neville Thompson, Pat Elliott, Mary-Elyse Haug, Gail Stanislow, Heather Clewell, Richard McKinstry and others, Winterthur Museum; Roger Horowitz, Carol Lockman, and Lynn Catanese, Hagley Museum and Library; the late Rodris Roth, Division of Domestic Life, National Museum of American History, Smithsonian Institution; Celia Oliver, Shelburne Museum; Leslie Bellais and Andy Kraushaar, Wisconsin Historical Society; Suzanne Flynt, Historic Deerfield; Ruta Saliklis, Allentown Art Museum; Mary Ellen Perry, Margaret Woodbury Strong Museum; Susan Tucker, Newcomb Library, Tulane University; Susan Sinclair and Dusty Logan, Isabella Stewart Gardner Museum; Joanne Hohler, Museum of Fine Arts, Boston; Dilys Blum, Philadelphia Museum of Art; Janet Dykema, Chippewa Valley Historical Society. In addition I have been helped by conversations and feedback from Ann Higonnet, Kasey Grier, Mia Boynton, Nadine Marks, Karen Goebel, Kathy Pickett, Danielle Devereaux-Weber, and members of the Walrus Club in Madison. I also thank Emily Auerbach and Norman Gilliland for featuring this work on their "University of the Air" radio program. I appreciate the many years of encouragement from Scot Danforth and others at the University of Tennessee Press, who have believed in this project from the beginning.

Chapter One

THE MEANING OF
THE SATURATED WORLD

Introduction:
About This Book and the Saturated World

This is a book about the way American women in the late nineteenth and early twentieth centuries enriched and added meaning to their lives through their "domestic amusements"—leisure pursuits that took place in and were largely focused on the home. They cultivated what I call a "saturated" quality, a kind of heightened experience (state, reality) that was aesthetically and sensually charged and full. These women created self-contained, enchanted "worlds" that helped feed or sustain them, usually by elaborating on their everyday tasks and responsibilities, "making them special" and transforming them into something playful and socially and emotionally satisfying. The story of their activities is in itself quite compelling, abounding with evocative images that push the imagination into high gear. The story is also a largely forgotten part of women's history, worth reclaiming because it helps us understand our foremothers' lives and teaches us to appreciate their intelligence, creativity, and agency. It is my intention to bring these ideas to the fore.

The book is an articulation of my ideas about this purposefully cultivated state or experience that I call "the saturated world." I believe such cultivation is a profoundly important part of the way we create meaning and personal sustenance, and the more we understand both the need for and the components of the experience, the better we are able to effect it. In some cultures, such as in Bali, everyone lives in a relatively saturated environment. In Western culture the saturated state has been disproportionately gender-linked; now, as a hundred years

2 ago, it is predominantly associated with and cultivated by women. It has been largely devalued because it is seen as "feminine" and "childish" and is aligned with the domestic. By making the elements of saturation more transparent, we can illuminate and thus disempower the stereotypes that make it seem unimportant or irrelevant and help bring its rich qualities to everyone. While most of the book consists of stories of the past, I use these as a *way in,* a means of understanding a universal human need or propensity. Looking through this lens at what happened a century ago, I believe, gives us a viewfinder or window into a part of ourselves.

I use this first chapter to explore the interrelated qualities of the saturated world in depth and thus frame or set the stage for the individual case studies that follow. The time is ripe for this discussion. We seem to be at a cultural turning point, when voices from many quarters are insisting on the importance of saturated qualities such as embodiment, aesthetic meaning, and a greater appreciation for the senses. While no one else has used my organizing image of saturation, I find support in diverse scholarly disciplines and a surprisingly wide range of popular sources. I draw on and synthesize these writings into what I hope is a thoughtful examination of a complex topic. The subject under examination involves passion, pleasure, and even spiritual meaning. It is my goal to insert these qualities into the theoretical discussion, thus enlivening and enriching it and keeping it tied to real people's lives. Again, I am concerned with all of us being able to learn about making life meaningful, and finding joy and satisfaction in our everyday activities.

I realize *The Saturated World* title might at first seem odd or even confusing; without explanation it might in fact lead one to imagine this to be a book about a soggy or waterlogged planet. I choose to keep the phrase despite its potential to mislead, however, because it so perfectly expresses what I am talking about. My choice of the saturation metaphor stems from my visual arts training: I first think of saturation in relation to color, where its synonym is "intensity." A saturated hue is at its brightest, most intense level and is in its purest form. Something that is saturated, be it color, water, or anything else, is in its most fully loaded or charged state; it has absorbed the ultimate amount of its medium. A "saturated world" is thus a full, rich one—sensually charged, bright, and intense. Everything in it seems extra alive.

At those times when I am able to step into this heightened state, I feel charged and happy. Things around me seem changed. Both the natural world and human-made objects may look especially bright, with intense color and sharpened edges— forms literally stand out more, with a greater contrast between foreground and background. Smells are stronger as well, taking on an extra poignancy and evoca-tiveness. Textures are more distinct and rich. I feel as if I have stepped into a poem, or somehow even *become* a poem; I am experiencing things with the senses and extra awareness of a poet. Others before me have struggled to find words to describe this same feeling or state of consciousness. The poet Rainer Maria Rilke talked about "living in the poetic image." The French philosopher Gaston Bachelard wrote about "being touched by the grace of super-imagination . . . through which the exterior world deposits virtual elements of highly coloured space in the heart of our being." The geographer Yi-Fu Tuan described the feeling of magic, when something seems "more real than real." The psychologist/theolo-gian Thomas Moore wrote about a more imaginative, "soulful," "hyper-aware" way of knowing and experiencing in his bestseller, *The Re-Enchantment of Every-day Life.*[1]

I have identified a number of interrelated qualities of the saturated world, and, while they will be explored in greater depth below, I summarize them here in order to help the reader understand what follows. As indicated, aesthetic intensity is a primary characteristic. This usually involves stimulation of multiple senses; sound, smell, touch, and taste are at least as important as sight. Related to this is a quality of embodiment, where the consciousness is grounded in the body, rather than the mind, and where abstract ideas may be given corporeal, animated form. A quality of childlike openness or wonder is also part of it, as is an attitude of playfulness, expressiveness, and creativity. In the domestic amuse-ments I focus on here and in other saturated women's activities I have observed, there is also a valuing of interconnectedness and community—connectedness with other people, certainly, but also connectedness and even intimacy with things. Objects are in a sense brought into the body boundary and used as an extension of self. Everyday, useful things are embraced and valued and further used to fos-ter connection with others. "Gift relations" prevail; objects are linked to human interactions and do not function as "property" or commodities.[2] Process, in effect, is more important than product: even when something concrete is constructed, it is the creative experience that matters more than what has been created.

In the period I focus on in this book, women's culture was characterized by a particularly high degree of aesthetic saturation. To some extent this was true of American culture as a whole. The wealth of newly available consumer goods had stimulated a kind of sensual excitement that filtered through to people on all levels of society. The novelist Theodore Dreiser expressed this quality when writ-ing in his 1902 diary about the impact of the display windows of the new depart-ment stores. "What a stinging quivering zest they display," he exulted; "[they]

4   taste of a vibrating presence." William Leach wrote of newly arrived immigrant women going to stand before such windows, taking in the heady mix of color, glass, and light that seemed to infuse the highlighted products. No longer limited by their Old World identities, the women were able to "re-imagine" themselves as people who could use such goods. Stuart Culin specifically labeled stores full of tantalizing merchandise the "aesthetic centers" of urban communities,[3] and Jean-Christophe Agnew coined the term "commodity aesthetic" to describe the way Americans channeled their aesthetic desires into goods. Their appetites were whetted—for more and more goods, but also for new levels of entertainment and other forms of sensual satisfaction.[4]

At the same time, new printing technologies had made it possible to reproduce images with intense color, and sensually rich pictorial imagery became ubiquitous. Consumer products came in packaging with bright labels, for example, and advertisements with saturated hues (the kind seen in Maxfield Parrish paintings) flooded the market in magazines, broadsides, and posters. Such pictures often portrayed a dreamy, fairylike scene that approximated the hyper-real poetic image I earlier equated with the saturated world. Similar images were depicted in the immensely popular storybooks of the English artists Kate Greenaway and Walter Crane, who drew innocent, picturesque children dressed in old-fashioned garments or rendered as sensually redolent flowers. The sweet child motif was reproduced ad infinitum on manufactured goods and women's handwork, and it was even acted out or embodied in stage tableaux, masquerade parties, and other entertainments. The turn-of-the-century period was also characterized by a series of overlapping "movements" (Aesthetic, Decorative Arts, Arts and Crafts, Art Nouveau), which resulted in a great outpouring of saturated products such as Tiffany Studios' stained glass. Aesthetic issues were part of popular discourse, so much so that when aesthete par excellence Oscar Wilde toured North America in 1882, he was met by exuberant crowds at every one of his lectures.[5]

While aesthetic awareness may have permeated the culture as a whole, it was a particular concern of women. They were disproportionately involved with the aesthetic movements and were generally identified with a kind of inherent artistic sensibility. Contemporary rhetoric maintained that the "fair sex" was innately attuned to the aesthetic realm (they were the "sensitive" ones) and bore the responsibility for creating the environments that would uplift their own and future generations.[6] A well-educated woman was expected to be familiar with the principles of art and design. Some took formal classes, especially in the decorative and "household" arts, but aesthetic training was also spread through informal channels including the women's press and women's club programs.

It is not surprising, then, that women cultivated the saturated quality in their   5
leisure activities that primarily took place in the home and involved a community of other women. In creating a theme luncheon, for example, they would
carefully plan and coordinate every element so as to provide maximum sensual
stimulation for all participants. The individual who organized an 1897 "Pink Tea"
in Milwaukee for a small group of friends, as a case in point, covered her table,
mirrors, and windowsills with fragrant, thematically colored blossoms, and softened the atmosphere by fitting handmade pink shades over her candelabra. She
glided through the scented space in a matching gown. She served refreshments
including rose-flavored ice cream and tinted bonbons, presenting them in handmade satin boxes that guests were to take home as souvenir favors. She also
"served up" lighthearted and amusing guessing games about the color pink.[7]

FIG. 1.1.
Suggestions for teas or other entertainments were presented in an aestheticized manner.
Drawings of this type appeared on every page of *Day Entertainments and Other Functions,*
a book put out by Butterick Publishing in 1896.

This event had all the qualities I have included in my profile of the saturated
world. It was a treat for the senses. The air was fragrant, and the ice cream both
smelled and tasted like roses, creating a kind of synesthesia. Eating the dessert
involved a cool, creamy sensation on the tongue and the feeling of satin on one's
fingertips. It was an embodied event, not only because of this insistence on sensual experience, but also because the participants were themselves a piece of the
whole, dressed as part of the environment, and interacting with it physically. It
was a playful and amusing event as well, designed to create good feeling and a
sense of happy surprise. Making all the elements pink helped transform them,
making them "special"; even something as ordinary as a source of light could be
seen through new eyes. The entertainment was based on—indeed elaborated
on—everyday household tasks such as cooking, decorating, and making clothes,

FIG. 1.2.
While this illustration of a "Days of the Week Social" features young people, many similar entertainments were exclusively for adults. Individuals are dressed up to personify domestic tasks such as washing and sweeping. From Nellie Mustain, *Popular Amusements for Indoors and Out-of-Doors* (1902).

FIG. 1.3.
The Party Book (1926) featured a vignette—a costumed doll, working at a toy spinning wheel—as the centerpiece of a luncheon table. Other features that added to the festivity included paper flowers and leaves, and tiny toy candles at each place setting.

but those tasks were transformed into something more significant. Each of their elements was experienced intensely and became the source of pleasure. Finally, the specialness and good feeling of the event was inclusive; everyone who was present was equally a part of the experience, even to the point of being given something to remember it by. Participants were meant to enjoy the experience as part of a community.

Pink teas and similar entertainments were predominantly women-only events. Most women still saw their primary arena of activity and strength as the home and were unashamed of its domestic values.[8] In this more private realm, the women felt free to engage in aesthetic elaboration, to embrace the sensual, and to be playful; as I see it, they had the gift of time and space in which to engage in the saturated world. Such parties helped conflate the realms of work and play; the activities involved work but were simultaneously amusements. Sometimes domestic tasks were even made the focus of play. Figure 1.2 illustrates a recommended "home sociable" where housewifely tasks were dramatized in a light-heartedly mocking manner; individuals literally *played on* or *played with* their usual roles. At some coeducational parties, women devised games where gender roles were humorously reversed, and men had to do woman-identified tasks. For example, at a "gingham party" described in *Ladies' Home Journal* in March 1908, men were asked to find a female partner in a matching apron. They then had to demonstrate their sewing skills by hemming the apron while the woman was wearing it.[9]

I discuss women's entertainments like this in chapter 3, treating them as one type of domestic amusement in which saturated experience was purposely cultivated. Each of the other chapters explores a different type of amusement, treating it as another case study. Each is self-contained and may stand alone. However, the chapters also fit together, like separate beads on a multifaceted necklace. Taken as a whole, the interconnected stories provide a holistic overview of late-nineteenth and early-twentieth-century women's saturated world. Chapter 2 focuses on "scrapbook houses," collage albums ostensibly made as homes for paper dolls. Women and girls spent countless hours finding, cutting, and pasting pictures into scrapbooks, creating detailed imaginary living environments from readily available materials such as advertising images and wallpaper samples. Each album represented a complete house, with successive double-page spreads serving as particular rooms. These were a feast for the senses and imagination; they were typically made with a riot of color, texture, and pattern with joyous attention to tiny detail. They illustrated domestic activities and reinforced girls' housewifely training, but their primary function was as an amusement, and their primary appeal was the opportunity they afforded for aesthetic expression and elaboration. They were embodied spaces: they included literal representations of women's bodies in the form of paper "people," and more abstractly they served as embodied realizations of an imagined environment and self. They were intimate miniature worlds

8 that helped reinforce female bonding and sense of connection. Some were made by girls—often one or two friends would work on them together—but others were made by grown women and given to girls as tokens of love and affection.

FIG. 1.4.
The two-dimensional tableau created on the page of a "paper doll house" collage comprising a world of women and children. Unidentified maker, 1880s. Courtesy, The Winterthur Library: Joseph Downs Collection of Manuscripts and Printed Ephemera, Folio 145.

No. 6   No. 7   No. 8

FIG. 1.5.
These figures—"Lily," "Sweet Pea," and "Jonquil"—appeared in *How to Make Paper Costumes* (Dennison Manufacturing, ca. 1920). They illustrated the kind of picturesque floral costumes that could be made with crepe paper.

Costumes of the Elements

No. 21 Rainbow A series of ruffles, each quite full, makes the rainbow skirt, while the waist of violet completes the scheme. Red, orange, yellow, green, blue, violet,—a "bow" at the waist line and one for the hair help make this costume a beautiful one. Maline ribbon and the little bouquet are quite in keeping.

The same design, if carried out entirely in yellow, will represent "Day" or "Sunbeam."

The head dress and waist decoration should be made of gold paper. The addition of a little gold tinsel, if it is obtainable, will be attractive.

No. 21

No. 22 Breeze Although this costume has been definitely named, if made in other colors it might be called "Fire," "Dawn" or "Rain." It is simply a series of narrow streamers or fringe sewed into place over a soft foundation slip. A tape from shoulder to wrist tied in place above the elbow and again at the wrist forms the foundation from which long streamers float.

From the head band other streamers float, the whole resulting in a graceful swinging costume that represents the elements well.

The colors of crepe paper which should be used for "Fire" or "Flame" are: No. 81 Red; No. 65 Orange; No. 64 Light Orange; No. 63 Dark Amber.

The soft pastel shades will represent "Dawn": No. 21 Heliotrope; No. 51 Light Blush Pink; No. 61 Light Amber; No. 51 Celestial Blue. "Rain" or "Mist" will require but one color, No. 13 Gray.

No. 22

FIG. 1.6.
"Rainbow" and "Breeze" were also featured in *How to Make Paper Costumes*. (Depending on the colors of the streamers, the "Breeze" outfit could instead represent another "costume of the elements," such as "Fire," "Dawn," or "Rain.")

Chapter 4 looks closely at women's dress-up activities, sometimes undertaken in the context of the entertainments explored earlier. Dressed-up women were literal embodiments—they appeared as imagined "fairyland" characters such as "Lady Spring," or the kind of personified flowers represented in Walter Crane illustrations (figs. 1.5, 1.6). Sometimes they dressed as colonial "foremothers" engaged in domestic activities such as spinning or quilting. Effectively they were domesticating history, understanding it through everyday objects and rendering it in their own image. Alternatively they dressed as European peasants or Japanese maidens, thus literally "incorporating" the wider world by identifying with it bodily. Dress-up too was a multisensory experience, as it involved elements such as colorful crepe paper or silk streamers that not only looked sumptuous, but tickled the body and rustled with every step (fig. 1.6). Sensual elaboration was perhaps the main appeal of this kind of activity, and the source of its greatest pleasure.

Chapter 5 focuses on "intimate companions"—iconic dolls that women made as miniaturized, costumed representations of themselves. Most of these conflated the realms of work and play. The earliest examples typically functioned as aesthetically elaborated domestic tools such as pincushions and penwipers. Their bodies might thus be stuffed so as to hold needles and pins, or they might wear voluminous skirts that could be used to wipe off excess fountain pen ink. In the twentieth century, iconic dolls were more often made as party decorations or favors or as "helper" dolls that helped make light of housework. Women made wedding shower gift dolls, for example, from housekeeping tools (see fig. 1.7) or packaged laundry necessities as female forms with names such as "Bridget." Also popular were anthropomorphized fruits and vegetable dolls that sometimes functioned as potholders. Others served as imaginary companions. Ethel von Bachellé made "Vegetable Folk" dolls, for example, to bring to life her storybook about a

FIG. 1.7.
"Anna" was made for a bridal shower in the 1930s. Anna's face is made from a wooden spoon, and her hair is a mop. She carries a biscuit-cutter bouquet. "Household helper dolls" made light of household tasks and women's domestic roles, and this one came with a typewritten note that assured the bride, "Her dress will make your tumblers shine / Her veil will make a duster fine." Courtesy, the Behring Center, National Museum of American History, Smithsonian Institution, AH2003-12545, photo 97-3605.

FIG. 1.8.
These elaborate outfits made from bright crepe paper were intended for paper dolls. The checks were in red and blue, and the hat included tiny artificial flowers. Collected by Elinor Kent Wyatt and later donated to the Joseph Downs Collection of Manuscripts and Printed Ephemera, Henry Francis DuPont Winterthur Museum and Library Collection 221. (Photo by the author.)

garden-party wedding. Von Bachellé's saturated world involved a domestic scene in which a community was brought together to celebrate in a sensual setting. Her dolls, like the household helpers, represented an aestheticized idealized self.

The last chapter explores women's collecting activities in this period. I demonstrate how women were disproportionately drawn to objects that had to do with the everyday and domestic—they typically collected useful items such as china or costume and accessories; ephemeral or miniature items (including dolls); or items characterized by intricacy of detail and texture, such as textiles. Interest in these objects certainly emanated from women's childhood training and social roles, but even more salient to our understanding of the saturated world, these were intimate and personal items. Women sought out sensory engagement with their collections, and their approach was especially embodied. Not only did many of their items relate to the body, but women generally cared about the very bodies (individuals) connected with those items. In contrast to male collectors, they typically took a personal interest in the people who made or formerly owned them. Their approach also differed from men's in that they were generally less concerned with "trophies" and objects' inherent value. Rather, they cared about context and connection—they wanted to know where an object fit (its setting was what gave it meaning), and were drawn to items that brought them closer to other people. Many even collected *with* others, forming deep bonds through their mutual passion.

Previous Dismissals of Domestic Amusements and What We Can Learn from Them

The domestic amusements I am concerned with are, as indicated earlier, largely forgotten today. When they are remembered, they are generally thought of as trivial pastimes that seem almost embarrassing. Sometimes they are cited as evidence of the oppressive or diminished quality of turn-of-the-century women's lives. Women were "limited" to the domestic arena, the argument goes, because society still generally "kept" them from "important" pursuits such as being a doctor, lawyer, or scientist. The contemporary bias toward professionalism and working outside the home colors the way activities like pink teas are seen at all; they are generally regarded as a frivolous waste of time.[10] The general stereotype is that the women did not really have enough to do at home and were thus reduced to filling their lives with silly, nonproductive activities. They subjected themselves to a kind of domestic brainwashing. The phenomenon of the scrapbook house, for example, has been discussed as a means of keeping girls busy and training them to fulfill and find satisfaction in their expected (limited) roles as housekeepers and consumers.[11] Discomfort with adult women's domestic amusements also stems from the fact that in today's terms they appear childish. The assumption is that activities such as doll making, party games, and dress-up should have been outgrown and that the women who engaged in them were somehow juvenilized or not allowed to act as autonomous grown-ups. I do not argue with the idea that women in the Victorian and early modern periods operated under significant social constraints, and I certainly do not advocate a return to keeping women "in their place." At the same time, I do not fully accept the idea that women were silenced by men and could only speak to their female peers through their domestic achievements.[12] I believe we should look closely at what those living under constraints actually did, and learn from that examination. I also want to restore women's agency—to stop accepting the idea that they were passive pawns who acted only out of lack of choice or power. Those who amused themselves in these ways may have operated within a given social sphere, but they still did what they did for reasons of their own. They acted "childishly" because they remained in touch with their sense of playfulness and wonder, not because they were not fully functioning adults. Their seemingly wasteful activities often brought satisfaction and pleasure into their lives. As I shall shortly explain, they were operating out of a different paradigm, based on domestic rather than workplace values, but this did not in any way diminish them.

Another reason that amusements such as these are negatively received is that they are typically thought of as activities of well-off or privileged women. In a time when we are trying to build an inclusive, nuanced history that recognizes the experience of the disenfranchised, it seems especially frivolous, even politically incorrect, to focus on those who enjoyed the benefits of money or leisure time. This idea can be challenged in itself, but it is also important to understand that the people I am concerned with were not just women of privilege. While some of the literature about domestic amusements was targeted at the upper class, most of it was aimed at a much broader populist or middle-class audience. Amusements were discussed in magazines such as *Ladies' Home Journal* and the *Delineator,* and in women's columns in publications such as *Farmer's Advocate and Home Journal.* Many of the articles were addressed to housewives operating on tight budgets who were concerned with saving pennies. Previous scholars have demonstrated that "middle class" was a very broad category by the late nineteenth century; it was a mind set as much as an identifiable income level. Middle class mores and expectations were widely understood (an increasingly literate population was able to learn about them through the burgeoning popular press), and most of the public was well steeped in its conventions. Furthermore, an abundance of manufactured goods in all price ranges meant that even those at modest economic levels could achieve a modicum of the middle class ideal in their homes, personal appearance, and activities.[13] Some poor women were probably exposed to these amusements through the work of turn-of-the-century social reformers, who organized handicraft projects and recreational activities to help raise the "aesthetic taste" of the "underprivileged." Others who worked as domestics may have been involved with their employers' activities. When a well-off woman gave a theme party for her friends, for example, she would rely on her maid or cook to help prepare the decorations or refreshments. It would be condescending for us to assume that the servants were not active players in what transpired or that they did not themselves experience some aesthetic satisfaction from the preparatory activities.[14] It is also important to understand that there was an increasing democratization of these amusements during the period under consideration. Some of the party-giving or entertaining ideas that in the 1880s might have been largely limited to the financially comfortable were, by about World War I, embraced by large segments of the population.

My insistence that these pastimes could hold deep satisfaction stems in part from my personal experience. While my first interest in activities such as theme teas and dress-up parties was "academic," I was from the start well aware of what must have gone into them. Having spent many hours myself working on creative projects such as dioramas and costume making, I appreciated the enormous amount of time, energy, and attention individuals needed to devote to these endeavors, as well as the rewards they would have yielded. To more fully appreciate this—to get closer to the qualitative experience the historical amusements afforded—I tried to reproduce some of them. I decided to stage a thematic entertainment, for example, and chose to play with the idea of the "Lemon Party." After inviting a group of eight women to my home on an appointed date, I got to work. Although mine was a simplified version, I still worked on it for weeks, trying out recipes, working on table and room decorations, and preparing party favors. Every part of the experience was pleasurable. Kneading and sculpting marzipan into miniature lemon-shaped edibles, for instance, was a treat for my hands, and then my eyes feasted on the concentrated yellow of the food coloring I was using to dye the perfect "rind." Everything I did was also heightened by an anticipation of my guests' reactions; delightedly I imagined their appreciation of the many details I had included and the way I had put everything together. During this preparation period, my mind often wandered to the party; even in the midst of other activities, I would be suddenly inspired with an idea for the invitation or another thematic favor. This experience not only reinforced my ideas, but made it quite clear to me why women of earlier generations expended so much effort on such activities. Their endeavors brightened up their world for a time, giving it an increased intensity and emotional charge.

I also know about the deep meanings of these activities because they are closely related to other topics I have studied in the past. Much of my professional career has been devoted to subjects that others dismiss as trivial or even find distasteful; I have encountered such reactions to my studies of needlework and other forms of domestic textiles, body adornment, charity bazaars, and Indian beaded "whimsies." These topics share common themes: all include aesthetic elaboration, and all relate to daily, ordinary things and the most intimate levels of life. All involve interpersonal relationship and embodiment. I have, in other words, been building my understanding of the saturated world for many years, but this is the first time I have fully put the pieces together and identified it as such.

My delineation of the saturated world builds on and adds another component to an organizing concept I articulated in previous writings—that is, I have been engaged in building a kind of "background history." To summarize briefly, the background framework was introduced by the feminist philosopher Mary Daly, who posited it as a domestic, female-oriented arena that can be contrasted against the more public foreground within which Western culture usually operates. Daly speaks of the background as the arena in which the deep rhythms of life are affirmed and where memory, connectedness, and wholeness are valued. It involves a consciousness that "would replace conquest with interaction and the hunger to own with the lust to create." Foreground culture is characterized by a sense of hierarchy, competition, and obsession with dominance and control. It values "work," which can be defined as something productive that leaves a permanent mark. Traditional or foreground history thus focuses on the unusual, on power relationships, hierarchies, and heroic deeds. It tends to look at the "important" work of exceptional people—the ones who are thought to have "created" history—and it demands a grand scale, a narrative voice, and a sense of narrative time. In contrast, background history is nonlinear, often even cyclic. It is concerned with everyday life, cooperative interactions, and the small things that prove satisfying and quietly meaningful on a repeated basis. It is focused on process rather than product, and it values play as well as work. Work may even be defined differently in the background: it is likely to be made up of repetitious acts instead of isolated achievements and, as in the case of a well-cooked dinner, it may leave no traces.[15] I believe the articulation of the saturated world adds even more to our understanding of the background, as it focuses on aesthetic elaboration and meaning and highlights the interconnection of work and play and the holistic gestalt of the different background elements.[16]

To reinforce the idea that different understandings emerge when one is using a background filter and applying the principles of the saturated world, I can compare my approach and that of Steven Gelber, who recently wrote a book entitled

Hobbies: Leisure and the Culture of Work in America. The periods we write about and many of our concerns (for example, collecting, craft activities) are similar, but what we pay attention to—and what we conclude—differ significantly. Gelber looks at hobbies as an expression of workplace values; "as a particular form of productive leisure," he argues, hobbies "expressed the deeper meaning of the work ethic and the free market." Gelber's research is excellent. He discusses both men's and women's activities and does try to grapple with the issue of the gendered hobby or object. Nevertheless he is steeped in the foreground perspective and, however inadvertently, looks through a viewfinder colored by its assumptions. Not only is the greater proportion of his attention given to male pursuits, but he dismisses or discounts much of what he sees about women's activities. He does not stop to ask what he might learn from data that does not quite fit his paradigm. For example, Gelber essentially defines collecting as "completing a set." This parameter might work in the case of a stamp or other collection that involves finite items in a series and would apply where there are strictly cognitive criteria for what does and does not belong. However, the types of collections that are disproportionately identified with women typically do not involve sets at all; they are open-ended and are likely to be based primarily on affective criteria. Items in a collection of stuffed animals, as a case in point, might be chosen because they are aesthetically and emotionally pleasing. Such a collection could never be considered truly completed, because one might always find another animal that evokes the desired response. Gelber talks about girls being taught to value the decorative and pretty. He readily admits they often collected "for aesthetic and sentimental reasons" and were likely to display their objects "as expressions of beauty" rather than wealth. However, he does not really seem to take these reasons seriously; he implies that sentiment and beauty are not in themselves legitimate reasons for wanting to amass or curatorially work with a collection. Whether consciously or not, he presents girls' collections as less meaningful than boys'.[17] Since I am using a background perspective that takes sensual and aesthetic pleasure seriously and looks beyond workplace values (as discussed below), I am able to honor and legitimate girls' motivations and experiences. This means I am working with a widened historical lens, one that I believe ultimately can break new conceptual ground and allow the past to shimmer with a new, broad-spectrum light.

A Deeper Look at the Qualities of the Saturated World
Aesthetic Experience and Sensory Saturation

It is important to clarify what I mean when I talk about aesthetically charged experience, since our culture uses the word "aesthetic" in multiple ways. Many people associate aesthetics with fine art, with abstract concepts about art, or with

16 highly refined, learned people—intellectuals spouting philosophy, for example, or art critics standing back from paintings in order to judge them. This is not really surprising, since the study of aesthetics functions as a branch of philosophy, and Western philosophy has been particularly concerned with the sublime, an abstract ideal of beauty. In his *Discourses on Art,* Sir Joshua Reynolds stated that true beauty must be above singular, natural forms; a work of art is an "idea of perfection." This is a cognitive or intellectual approach rather than an emotional one, and it demands a "psychic distance." Philosophers such as Emmanuel Kant and Edward Bullough talked about "aesthetic interest" in terms of an observer, who would attend to an object with a quality of "disinterestedness." Aesthetic pleasure would relate, therefore, only to elevated, near-perfect forms of art, and it would take place primarily in the mind, not the body.[18] This removed, antisensual attitude is not what I am talking about when I talk of aesthetic experience; it is not at all a background, female approach. (By virtue of their biology, women are particularly involved with the body and the corporeal realms. Cultural attitudes that dismiss or devalue the concrete, natural world implicitly devalue women's expressive forms and experiences.)[19] Again, I believe on the contrary that aesthetic experience is emotional and inseparable from the body and its multiple senses—it is about our experience in this material world and the pleasure and meaning we can take from it. My argument makes sense when we realize that the opposite of "aesthetic" is "anaesthetic"—defined as a deadening of the senses, or a substance that blocks sensation.

Happily, the idea that humans are really "aesthetic beings" is now more widely accepted. The philosopher Robert Ginsberg, who used the phrase in a recent book, argues that aesthetic experience fills us with joy and a sense of wholeness and is part of what makes life meaningful. It is an organic process, he tells us, that is commonly experienced by all.[20] This "democratic" attitude is exciting, as it overturns the classical art theory model, which held that such experience was available only in relation to "high" art and was limited to those educated in its conventions.[21] Mike Featherstone, author of *Consumer Culture and Postmodernism,* goes so far as to say that our postliterate, postmodern culture follows an "aesthetic paradigm," and Yi-Fu Tuan, a cultural geographer who has written intriguingly on a wide range of subjects, also unabashedly insists on the primacy of the aesthetic realm. His 1993 book, *Passing Strange and Wonderful: Aesthetics, Nature and Culture,* was written to demonstrate that the aesthetic is not just an extra, dispensable part of human experience, but its very "emotional-aspirational core." Tuan defines the aesthetic impulse as "the senses come to life." Because we experience everything through our senses, he maintains, everything can have aesthetic potential or significance. We can find aesthetic meaning in the most mundane daily tasks, such as the pleasure we take in the "neat swathes of flattened fibers" we create when vacuuming a carpet. Notable for my discussion of the meanings in domestic amusements, Tuan believes that aesthetic experiences are most common in the home. Our engagement with the environment is least self-conscious there, for that is where more of our nonvisual senses are engaged.[22]

The folklorist Michael Owen Jones also insists that aesthetic experience informs everyday activities. Jones had tried for several decades to reconcile the discrepancy between aesthetic theory and his own sense of people's response to the world around them. Drawing on his observations and the writings of the anthropologist Franz Boas, who argued that all human activities might be experienced with "aesthetic values," Jones eventually dismissed standard theoretical ideas such as psychic distance. Even when people do not have "*an* aesthetic" or a clear vocabulary to express what they feel, he found, they do have aesthetic experience. This could be true even in the most unlikely setting, including a repetitive job on a factory assembly line. He marveled at the worker in an Oregon tuna plant who stated, "I had no idea of the sensuous things I would feel just from cleaning fish." She was deeply engaged—even transfixed—by the colors and textures she was working with and especially loved the way she could transform the materials before her. Engrossed in her experience, she would often not notice the passage of time. The tuna processor had learned to play with her task to make it more sensually rich. (To use my central metaphor, she had saturated her small corner of the world of work.) Jones found that individuals often make their work lives more meaningful through many such small aesthetic details. They take time to make a pleasing arrangement of notes on an office bulletin board, for example, or take pleasure in certain ways of fastening or using paper clips.[23] Crispin Sartwell, who is concerned about spiritual wholeness, writes about this same phenomenon using slightly different terms. He also insists that the Western dichotomy between the aesthetic and the practical is a false one and that our main goal is to concretely bring our sense of "inherent artistry" (our aesthetic consciousness) into every aspect of our lives. By doing this, we are better able to experience a sense of oneness with everything around us.[24]

Yet another theorist who insists on the primacy of aesthetic experience is Ellen Dissanayake. In two recent books, *What Is Art For?* and *Homo Aestheticus: Where Art Comes from and Why*, she argues that the impulse to make art is an actual biological need; it is not something we pick up or add, like language, but is a fundamental part of what and who we are. It literally helps us survive. Dissanayake uses the phrase "making special" to describe our impulse to add order and (sensual or aesthetic) intensity to our world. Like others we have been discussing, she says that making special helps us heighten our reality, and through it we move into a greater sense of aliveness. Interestingly, she uses terms that are very close to Tuan's: echoing his statement that the aesthetic is the "emotional-aspirational core" of human experience, she calls making special the "biological core of art." It is important to note that while Dissanayake writes about art, she is not really concerned with finished products; almost any activity can be experienced in this way, and it is the artistic impulse she is most focused on. She ties making special to both ritual and play, which are universal in all human cultures (I will return to the subject of play shortly). In much the same way that others talk about aesthetic experience, Dissanayake claims that making special creates a sense of total involvement, effortlessness, and loss of time and it leads to a state that seems "less real or more real than ordinary reality."[25]

Recently there have also been many writers who have focused specifically on the importance—even the reawakening—of the senses. One compelling work with this perspective is Diane Ackerman's *A Natural History of the Senses*. Written almost as a prose poem, this 1991 book delves deeply into the qualities of touch, taste, and the other senses, explaining the way each operates and affects us. Ackerman proudly calls herself a "sensuist," "someone who rejoices in sensory experience," and her discussion is clearly intended to help others do the same. She states that "we need to return to feeling the textures of life" and promises us a richer, more charged existence if we do. "The senses don't just make sense of life," she says; "they tear it apart into vibrant morsels and reassemble it."[26] I have encountered many others taking this same sensuist stance. As I was working on an early draft of this chapter, for example, I happened to listen to Ira Glass's innovative National Public Radio program, "This American Life." The edition that was airing focused on individuals who were mapping and making sense of the world through their different senses. Glass found people to represent each of them—one was mapping the tastes of his city, for example; another was concerned with the tactile sensations of her body. The idea must have been "in the air," because shortly after, Jeremy Podeswa's film *The Five Senses* opened to strong reviews. It too centered around five characters who each represent a particular sense—the cleaner with an acute sense of smell, the eye doctor who is going deaf, and so on. While browsing in the new arrivals section of the library, I then came upon a book entitled *Interior Designing for All Five Senses*. Its author, Catherine Bailly Dunne, insisted that someone putting a room together should not only consider the way things look, but the impact on every one of the senses. A sensually rich, tantalizing environment, she said, satisfies deep emotional needs; it "fuels your dreams, grati-

fies your soul, and energizes your days." Soon thereafter I came upon a kind of   *19*
self-help book called *Senses Wide Open: The Art and Practice of Living in Your
Body.* Finally, I was drawn to a cover of *Utne Reader,* a magazine that reprints
material published in a variety of small publications and purports to have its
finger on the pulse of contemporary issues. "Born Sensuous," read the headline of
the November–December 2001 issue, "Recharge your life by coming back to your
senses." Inside, a highlighted phrase echoed the very words I used in my introduction to my concept of the saturated world: "Breathing in life through my
senses, not just my mind, changed the way I experienced the world. I saw brighter
colors, had stronger memories, became more receptive to other people."[27]

It is significant that all five of the senses were stressed in these works, for the
sense of sight has been privileged in Western culture for centuries. Sight is in fact
the most distant or disembodied sense, and it leads us away from our emotions.
The anthropologist Edward Hall first introduced this idea nearly fifty years ago,
when he pioneered "proxemics," the study of people and their culturally influenced use of space. Hall observed that people interact from different "distance
zones," each of which involves different kinds of sensory input and response and
in turn corresponds to different kinds of behavior. In the near zones (labeled
"intimate" and "personal," they are up to eighteen inches and four feet from the
body, respectively), there is a particularly strong reliance on the proximate senses
of touch, taste, and smell. These are the zones where people experience a high
degree of emotional involvement and intimacy. In the farther "social" and "public" zones that are dominated by the visual sense, behavior is more detached. We
can understand this because sight (and to a lesser degree, hearing) allows us to
be "out there," away, in a sense, from our own skin; it allows the most abstraction.
The proximate senses are literally experienced from "within" our bodies and thus
do not allow such distance.[28]

Our most primal reactions are body-based and involve all of the senses. The
proximate senses are of course what a baby first experiences (Ackerman even states
that synesthesia, or the mixing of the senses, is our natural, first state).[29] Taste, smell,
and touch represent very definite ways of knowing. Decades ago, the anthropologist Ashley Montagu argued in *Touching: The Human Significance of the Skin* that
all experience starts in the body rather than the mind—that in a very literal sense,
the skin has a "mind," or consciousness, of its own. As one review phrased it, his
study provided "an appreciation of the role of touch as the basic organ of contact
with the world and of the sense of one's identity."[30] Children continue to revel in
tactile sensation and other forms of nonvisual input, even after they have developed visual orientation and language. A child will jump in a pile of fallen leaves,

20 allowing herself to feel their papery texture and breathe in their earthy odor. At least in our culture, she will generally stop this as she becomes an adult. She will learn to step back and take the leaves in visually—she will learn to rely primarily on the sense of sight. Small wonder that theme teas and similar domestic amusements, which are by definition overloaded with multisensory stimulation, are so typically judged childish. Although we speak admiringly of children's sense of wonder and magic and their innate openness to the world and we decry the loss of this openness in adults, our culture has until recently devalued the kind of sensuality that makes this possible. The rationalist philosophy that has prevailed in Western culture since the Enlightenment—the same philosophy that posited an aesthetic of psychic distance—is made possible by this privileging of the mind and the sense of sight.

Scholars in many fields are beginning to argue for a more sensually based approach. I have already mentioned some anthropologists moving in this direction. More recently, Paul Stoller has expressly been insisting on "sensuous" anthropological scholarship based on "tasteful fieldwork." Stoller contends that "visualism" is "a Eurocentric mistake" that has impeded ethnographic inquiry. Many non-Western cultures elaborate on and experience the world much more through senses other than sight, he maintains, so effective ethnographers must become multisensorily attuned and rely equally on other means of taking in information. Those who simply stand back and observe (that is, without also smelling, touching, and so on) miss a great deal. Stoller states in his 1997 work *Sensuous Scholarship* that his intention is "to reawaken profoundly the scholar's body." Similar ideas are arising in other fields. The art historian Henry Drewal, who apprenticed with sculptors in Africa, insists on the value of multisensory experience in understanding the arts and coined the word "sensiotics" to describe his fully integrated approach. The historian Peter Charles Hoffer, author of *Sensory Worlds in Early America,* also maintains that his field has been limited by Western culture's overemphasis on the visual. He not only believes it is important to consider the sensory quality of historical events and encounters, but feels it is possible to reevaluate historical events by reconsidering sensory input. The way to tell the most compelling history, he states, "is to recover the intimate sensory details of the past."[31]

Clearly this is what I am trying to do. I want to add yet another consideration to this discourse, however, by pointing to the gendered dimension of the issue. "Visualism" is not just a Eurocentric bias, but a phallocentric one as well. Even within European-based cultures, women have tended to be disproportionately attuned to alternate kinds of sensory input. In my earlier article "Intimacy and Objects: A Proxemic Analysis of Gender-Based Response to the Material World," I built upon Hall's framework to offer another explanation for the cultural devaluing of women's experience and perception. I suggested that, due to different socialization practices, women in our culture are often more comfortable than men in the nearer distance zones, where the proximate senses are most salient. I also showed that individuals interact with objects at different distances, and this has ramifications for the ways those objects and interactions are viewed. It is the nearer, emotionally charged zones that are filled with the most intimate, detailed objects, and those are the ones our culture tends to characterize, often deprecatingly, as fussy and feminine.[32] A few other theorists have also referenced gender differences in sensory orientation. The folklorist Jane Przybysz, for example, claimed that visual pleasure is stereotypically associated with men, while tactile pleasure is associated with women. The physicist Evelyn Fox Keller argued that the culturally dominant "objective model" of truth is primarily a visual one that implies distance, but the model more often favored by women relates to listening, or hearing, which is experienced closer into the body zone.[33] We are brought back to the divergent values of the background and the saturated world, and we can see how at least some gender prejudices or stereotypes arise from other kinds of unconscious cultural biases.

Embodiment

Our culture's growing appreciation of the full range of senses is part of its gradual reacceptance of the body and corporeal experience. Once again, this attitude is being expressed on many fronts—by theorists, artists, and the public at large. It was in the 1950s that the French phenomenologist Maurice Merleau-Ponty first insisted on locating consciousness in the body. He argued that we think and perceive with the whole body, not just the eye or brain. It is impossible to know the world by disengaging ourselves from the body; any time we try to objectify or rationalize our understanding, in fact, we are in danger of distortion. We cannot be outside that which we are considering, because our body is always our entry point to the world. Merleau-Ponty was especially concerned with our apprehension or perception of art, and he unequivocally refuted the idea of psychic distance. Given the centrality of the body in his philosophy, it is sometimes referred to as "somatic aesthetics."[34]

The concept of embodiment soon made its way into diverse academic discourse. It was, for example, explored by scholars interested in information processing, such as psychologists working in cognition and learning theory and neurophysiologists. Those interested in the nature and expression of culture have also begun to acknowledge that physical form mediates all individual and cultural experience (the body, in turn, is understood as a biological entity that is affected by cultural phenomena). The concept is discussed by philosophers and students

22 of religion, media, and art and is filtering into other fields. An insistence on body-centered analysis was cropping up so much among folklorists that in 1989 Katherine Young coined the word "bodylore" to give a name to a new area of folkloric inquiry. As she expressed it, the "sense of corporeality . . . serves as a benchmark, a common frame through which people seek to understand themselves and the world in which they move." Notably, most of the folklorists involved in the first discussions of bodylore were women. Embodiment has also become a central tenet of feminist (and cultural) studies, as women have been "reclaiming" the female body and its ways of being and knowing.[35]

Contemporary artists are equally insistent on reinserting the body and the senses into their work. The growing prevalence of the body in this realm is perhaps most blatantly represented by the upsurge in the area of performance art, where the body *becomes* the art, and the epidemic popularity of tattooing, where the body literally *is* the art. Artworks are also often more tactile, in part because artists insist on evoking a kind of bodily response from the viewer. In writing about fiber art, Polly Ullrich explains the dynamic: "Bodily oriented art uses its visceral qualities, either literally or metaphorically, to engage our total being, not just our mental consciousness, in building a sensuous, evocative statement. This is art that is more than language; . . . its transcendent ideas are intermixed with the fabric of the world. We are touched by [it] not only because we understand it cognitively, but because we 'feel' it." Dissanayake, too, remarked that art is increasingly turning from representation to the realm of "felt experience."[36]

A review of definitions may help clarify why I insist that embodiment is characteristic of the saturated world and why I claim that the domestic amusements presented in this book were embodied experiences. We have already established that the term is related to embodied consciousness, that is, taking in and expressing information through the body rather than the mind. *The Oxford English Dictionary* further tells us that to embody is to give concrete form to something that is otherwise only abstract or ideal; it means "clothing" something evanescent with a body. Secondary definitions include imparting "a material, . . . sensual character to"; coalescing, uniting, or forming into one body; and giving life to, as in painting with a full body of color.[37] All these definitions relate to the amusements I deal with here. The decorated scrapbook pages or party spaces, iconic dolls, and collections of familiar domestic objects all served as concrete expressions of women's experiences and sense of self. They were, certainly, "alive" and sensually and aesthetically rich (I am delighted that the *OED* uses a saturation metaphor to explain the quality of aliveness). With their emphasis on the proximate senses and literal clothing or costuming, the experience of these amusements was often particularly corporeal. While the women I am writing about

often presented themselves in an idealized form, they still embraced their physi-
cality unequivocally.

I also take the concept of embodiment in a new direction, applying it not just
to people, but to their (human-altered) spaces and objects. These artifacts mirror
the people who make and use them, but beyond that they become extensions of
those people; they not only function as the stages they project themselves on, but
also take on "bodies" of their own. I began to explore this idea in my 1997 article,
"Woman's Domestic Body: The Conceptual Conflation of Women and Interiors
in the Industrial Age." I cited turn-of-the-century authors who talked about the
home as the "impersonation" of the woman who was responsible for it or who
pointed out that rooms, like faces, have "countenances" or "personalities." Like
individuals, rooms could be "dressed up" for special occasions or "freshened up"
with "make-overs." "When your home looks colorless and drab," wrote adviser
Ethel Seal in 1921, "perhaps what it needs is a tonic." In her treatise called *Woman
as Decoration,* Emily Burbank wrote about "animated" interior decoration, provided through women's "vital spark." Furnishings could be pretty or elegant, and
they too could be dressed. Tired sofas could "slip into quaintly patterned chintz,"
for example, and be energized "with a perky ruffle." Many words used to describe
the adornment of women's bodies were also used to describe the adornment of
the home. Windows and furniture were, like women, "draped" with fabric, and
"festooned" with ribbons or cloth, and their legs were modestly covered with
"skirts." Emily Post's 1930 advice book about home decoration even talked about
oil cloth "night clothes" one might make for bedroom window curtains. I also
remarked in this article on the abundance of biological metaphors applied to
homes. The image of flavorfulness was used particularly often for inanimate
things. Ornaments were described as "tasty" objects, for example, and the title of
Elsie de Wolfe's popular 1914 decorating book, *The House in Good Taste,* implied
the house was *wearing* its taste, almost like a costume. Words such as "delicate"
and "dainty," so closely associated in the last few centuries with the feminine and
so common in turn-of-the-century writings about houses and women-identified
things, also originally related to tastiness and food.[38]

I will extend my exploration of embodied artifacts below, in the section on
intimacy with objects, and will demonstrate in subsequent chapters how objects
may become "enlivened" by virtue of the attention that is paid to them.

Playfulness and Humor, Childlike Wonder, and Creativity

Many of those who discuss what I call the saturated state write about it in terms
of play. Several years after Diane Ackerman explored the senses, for example, she
wrote *Deep Play.* She refers to play as a "refuge from ordinary life"; it happens in

a "special mental place" with its own rules and qualities. Ackerman is most interested in the "transcendent" dimension of adult play, which she likens to rapture and ecstasy. It is a state so utterly absorbing that, when we are in it, time seems to disappear. We constantly long to experience it; we "relish or even require it to feel whole." What she describes is very close to the tuna processor's experience, and it recalls the state of spiritual wholeness that Sartwell talks about in terms of aesthetic consciousness, as well as the qualities Dissanayake attributes to "making special." Tellingly, Ackerman claims that art making is likely to lead us into the state of deep play, and we have established that art making is, broadly defined, the heart of the making special impulse. Many of the qualities of deep play are achieved or exaggerated by sensory stimulation and elaboration. Others, such as the elements of surprise, illusion, make-believe, and fantasy, are often part of the aesthetic experience as well.[39] When the Milwaukee women arrived at the Pink Tea I described earlier, they were surprised with a saturated, rosy space. The transformed environment helped them enter a make-believe, set-apart play world, where they could enjoy a feeling of aliveness. The woman who put together the tea was playing when she organized and carried out the details, and her guests joined the play-state when they came to her party.

Other theorists echo the idea that play is akin to art making or making special and that it is a universal human need. Dissanayake points to the many languages that use the same word for art and play, and in fact she plays with this relationship with the title of her second book. *Homo Aestheticus* ("Man the Aesthetic Being") is a takeoff on—and kind of homage to—Johan Huizinga's 1944 classic, *Homo Ludens* ("Man the Player"). The importance of play had been understood for some time. The nineteenth-century philosopher Friedrich Schiller talked about play as an instinct, for example, and Ernst Grosse linked play and art as long ago as 1897. In the twentieth century, more emphasis was placed on the importance of play to the human spirit. The educator/philosopher John Dewey took this position, as did the psychiatrist Austen Riggs, who in 1935 argued that play helps us develop and maintain a sense of emotional satisfaction; we need it to keep alive what we would today call the "inner child" of our being. Using language remarkably like Tuan's pronouncements about the aesthetic a half century later, Huizinga talked of play as one of the main bases of civilization.[40]

Almost everyone writing about play remarks on its absorbing quality and its ability to put us in an altered state. Huizinga says that it casts a spell—it is an enchantment—and it can belong to the sacred sphere. Rebecca Abrams talks about the focused attention and sense of self-transcendence play engenders. Gene Quarrick writes of the trancelike state that lies at the heart of adult play—a state that fulfills the human longing for greater aliveness and expands people beyond

their usual boundaries by allowing them to lose themselves in a different identity.
Play helps us reorganize our experience, almost creating a figure-ground reversal
of our usual state.[41]

With all this positive theoretical discussion of play, we might expect that play
and playfulness would be wholeheartedly embraced in our culture. At least until
recently, this has generally not been the case. We have been steeped in the mind
set of the industrial age, based on a work ethic that identified play as "not-work,"
and thus saw it as inherently suspect. If work was considered serious and "important," then play was by definition not important; if work was productive, then
play was wasteful or inconsequential. Children could play with impunity because
their time did not yet count and thus could not be wasted, although it would be
best if their play, too, was relatively goal oriented. Adults who put too much energy
into playful pursuits were looked down upon as nonproductive or, at best, as
childish.[42] An expression of this attitude or belief system was the Recreation movement, a loosely organized confederation of governmental, private, and voluntary
agencies that peaked during the years I am writing about, roughly 1885–1930.
Fearing that people would use their increasing amount of leisure time un-wisely
(that is, they would be wasteful or, worse yet, go astray), these agencies worked to
structure leisure activities for both children and adults. Recreation leaders were
not overly concerned with exploratory play; their endeavors centered around
purposeful pursuits, as their goal was to build "good character" and ultimately
the development of good public citizens.[43] Since, in contrast, the amusements I
am concerned with in this book were not typically "productive,"[44] we can see yet
another reason why they have been dismissed as childish and unimportant.

There is a curious irony and paradox in this idea that women's amusements
were childish and outside the work ethic mentality. As we have seen, turn-of-the-
century women's play was often not far removed from work; domestic amusements involved elaboration of everyday tasks and were based on women's household skills. The overlay of work and play was learned in childhood, as is evident
in the case of the scrapbook house.[45] I am not implying that women's play was in
any way diminished by this overlay; on the contrary, I think it must have made it
easier to move into a playful state, even in the midst of workaday tasks. The point
is that these women, who for the most part remained outside of the workplace
economy, never had to "count" their time and thus never felt the need to relin-
quish or outgrow their childhood pleasures. Just as they had played dress-up as
children, they felt free to delight in the same kind of activity as adults. They could
work on scrapbook houses, even though making the albums was touted primarily as a girl's pastime, because most had never graduated into "serious" working
women. They could unself-consciously cultivate the same kind of fairyland world

26 they had known in childhood because they were less tied to the rules of the real businessman's world. This attitude shifted somewhat as the majority of women became more fully integrated into the paid workforce and took on career as well as household responsibilities. By 1997 Rebecca Abrams was writing a book entitled *The Playful Self: Why Women Need Play in Their Lives,* arguing that women do not feel themselves entitled to play because they have so much to do and rarely put their needs first. Interestingly, however, Abrams admitted that women's play is different than men's and is often not recognized as such because play is conceived in male terms and spoken about in male language. "While much of the thinking and writing on the subject has assumed that it encompasses women's experience," she says, "its fundamental male bias, both linguistically and historically, has meant that the specific role of [women's play] has been consistently neglected." Women's play may be less identifiable—women do not necessarily "go out" to play or join formal leagues or games; their play may be embedded in or part of their daily activities.[46] Perhaps the kind of work/play dichotomy that has led to this unequal situation is lessening now as we move into the post–industrial age, but we still must learn to recognize and differentiate the more female approach to play before we can expect it to be fully appreciated.

A playful attitude and the quality of spontaneity are well recognized as components of the creative process, and it is important to credit the creativity of the women engaged in these playful domestic pastimes. They were continually looking for new ways to stimulate the senses, new ways to make use of the materials they had at hand (from advertising images to kitchen staples), and new ways to play upon a thematic idea. New linkages or connections—new juxtapositions of ideas, things, or images that were never put together before—are also understood to be central to creativity, so much so that many define creativeness in these very terms.[47] Involvement in a project like putting together a household helper doll would in itself stimulate new ideas; one would begin to look at pastry brushes and other cooking and cleaning tools with a new eye—with an expansive vision that could take in new possibilities. I had this experience when I was preparing my lemon party. I was scanning the environment for things made of deep yellow, but because I was also looking for other hues that would make the lemon imagery have the maximum impact, colors of all kinds would literally leap out at me. I thought broadly about concepts such as "sour" or "fruit," looking for ways I could incorporate new conceptual puns. The project gave shape to my everyday experience, in other words, and gave it a creative spark. Moreover, once I staged the party, my guests were stimulated to see things in new ways as well. One told me later that she had begun to look differently at fruits and other objects in her kitchen, wondering what else she might "turn them into." She was delighted with the fresh (saturated) view of her long-familiar environment.

Interpersonal Connection and Community

When I was working on my historical study of American bazaars (charity fairs), I kept asking myself why the institution persisted for over 150 years. A bazaar involved an enormous amount of work, and especially when the labor time that went into it was considered, it usually yielded only minimal profit. Bazaars were criticized, ridiculed, and constantly complained about, and yet they kept reappearing in different places and different forms or permutations. I eventually concluded that they could not be suppressed because they provided important opportunities for social interaction and experiencing a sense of community.[48] Women enjoyed their time working together—making sale items, decorating booths, or completing other tasks; in today's terms we would say they liked "hanging out" together in a relaxed, supportive atmosphere. This same feeling was evident in many other instances where women got together. Joyce Ice reported on a Texas quilting club, for example, whose members proclaimed their meetings primarily represented "a day of fun," a chance for "just gettin' together and bein' with your friends." Ice observed that their conversations were highly participatory; everyone was given a chance to speak and to be heard. Even less skilled stitchers were included in the group, as they were recognized for their other contributions. These women also extended their sense of inclusiveness and community to customers; when they completed quilt tops for others, for example, they liked to learn something about those individuals. I documented a similar cultivation of community and fellowship in "Restroom World," a small bathroom at the University of Wisconsin that was transformed by its users into a distinctive women's environment. Always catering to women's needs, it included a comfortable lounge area with a stock of reading material, candy and other giveaway items, and a guest book for patron commentary. It featured changing displays relating to women's shared history and experience.[49]

Earlier in this discussion, I identified the sense of connection and cooperative interaction as one of the features Mary Daly associated with her concept of the background. Other theorists have also identified it as a strong part of the way women negotiate their lives. The psychologists Carol Gilligan and Jean Miller have become particularly well known for the argument that men and women in our culture have distinctly different experiences of the world as they are growing up. Girls tend to construct their social reality—indeed define themselves—in terms of social relationships and connections; they value and seek out intimate

28   friendships and find strength less through competition than cooperation and the empowerment of others. This "relational theory" suggests that these childhood experiences set the pattern for adult behavior and ways of thinking. Consequently, connection, empathy, and intersubjectivity are the central organizing concepts of women's lives.[50]

The findings of folklorists and others who have looked at patterns in girls' and boys' play largely support Gilligan's picture of childhood. In 1988 Linda Hughes summarized studies of gender differences in children's games. It had been previously found that where boys tended to be competitive, girls tended to be cooperative and "turn-taking" (their competition tended to be more indirect and to occur between individuals rather than groups). The girls were more likely to play indoors, in small spaces, and they liked small, intimate groups, where all participants were active players. Their play could have multiple, well-defined stages, including periods of in-game waiting. Hughes also conducted her own comparative study of boys and girls playing the ball game foursquare. She too concluded that girls used a more cooperative mode, although she refuted the idea that they were in any way passive or unable to negotiate; they could vie for position within their cooperative groups. Marjorie Goodwin watched children at play a few years later and came to similar conclusions. She too found that girls had less structured rules and created egalitarian social structures to accomplish play tasks (the contraction they used, "let's," sets an inclusive, noncontrolling tone). Boys, on the other hand, usually took directives from a self-appointed leader. Girls did have disagreements and could be temporarily competitive and hierarchical when engaged in pretend games (they displayed shifting internal alliances), but they were less insulting to one another.[51]

Hughes points out that the language of corporate America is gendered play language; references to "remaining competitive" or being a "team player" or "good sport" represent a male paradigm and are based on games that men and boys are most likely to engage in. Once again, it is my intention in this book to elucidate a different model of adult play, where cooperation and aesthetic satisfaction are paramount. Women are far from powerless or passive in this cooperative mode, but their power comes from interpersonal connection more than control or authority over others.[52]

One last point I would like to make related to the theme of community concerns the strong presence of seasonal and holiday references in women's domestic amusements. Many of the entertainments discussed in chapter 3, for example, were based around seasonal celebrations. Even where the references were not obvious, they might be implicit; Bachellé's "Vegetable Folk" dolls, as a case in point, were given the setting of a summer garden party. Jack Santino has argued that attunement to and involvement in the seasonal cycle is very much a part of women's culture, and the celebration of annual calendrical festivals (holidays) can be thought of as "part of the domestic cultural property of women." He maintains that holidays help build community by giving us a language to communicate with others and involve them in a shared experience. When we decorate the outside of our houses for Halloween or Christmas, for example, we are extending our sense of community beyond the immediate family to passers-by.[53]

Intimacy with Everyday Objects

There is a growing body of literature about the ways people find sustenance and meaning in objects—not in the sense of materialistic greed, but as avenues of expression and reflections of themselves. Michael Owen Jones uses the term "material behavior" for the ways we express our ideas and beliefs through objects, and he says we use them in a kind of symbolic performance. Other scholars talk about the "psychic charge" that things may come to hold; they maintain that when we invest time and attention in a thing, it takes on some of that energy. As one of the Texas quilters whom Joyce Ice observed phrased it, "quilting is what makes a quilt." A textile "grew on" her as she spent time and worked it; it was transformed into something more beautiful and precious.[54] Another way of phrasing this would be to say that the love put into something is what makes it special. There are psychics who are able to pick up this energy from objects; when they are given a piece of jewelry that an individual has worn regularly, for example, they receive impressions or information about that person (this ability, called "psychometry," is sometimes called on by police looking for missing persons). Although they were talking more generally and not referring directly to this particular skill, Mihaly Csikszentmihalyi and Eugene Rochberg-Halton introduced the "psychic charge" phrase in their groundbreaking study, *The Meaning of Things: Domestic Symbols and the Self*. After querying multiple generations of Chicago-area families about the objects they were most attached to, the researchers found that it was the attention placed on an object that made it meaningful—what counted most was what the object reminded the owner of, or what it enabled him or her to do. Russell Belk and his colleagues in the "Consumer Behavior Odyssey" project similarly concluded after interviewing hundreds of individuals that objects hold "deep meanings," primarily as extensions of self. Even "trifling" things like souvenir programs or Mickey Mouse toys can be held "sacred" if they are particularly charged with personal memory. Significantly researchers in both of these studies found gender-differentiated patterns in relationships with objects. Women

30 in the Chicago study were far more likely than men to value objects for their associational meanings; they treasured photographs that helped them feel connected with others, for example, or appreciated jewelry because it had been given to them as an expression of affection. Men often valued objects for instrumental purposes or as symbols of personal achievement. When Belk and Wallendorf looked specifically at collecting behavior, they concluded that women use objects to "represent achievement in the feminine world of connection to other people— achievement of sentiment." In contrast, men's collections represented the achievement of control.[55]

Gaston Bachelard wrote about our engagement with things in his 1958 book, *The Poetics of Space*. When we attend to an object with poetic consciousness, he said—the specific example he gave was waxing a table—it can become something new; it awakens and "attains a higher degree of reality." This brings us back to the idea of saturation, of course, but it is also interesting because it refers to objects in animate terms. Several contemporary authors interested in spiritual meaning hold this view as well. In *A Home for the Soul: A Guide for Dwelling with Spirit and Imagination*, Anthony Lawlor writes of ways we can translate common spaces and things into "symbols of the inner workings of the spirit." He would like us to be able to see such ordinary objects as stoves and bathtubs as "symbols of nourishment and transformation," thereby expanding the usual "limiting or rigid boundaries that trap our hearts and minds." Shaun McNiff expresses similar ideas. "When we give sustained [and sensual] attention to the particulars of a thing," he maintains, it helps open the soul. We become more enriched and alive when we consciously engage with the energy (he calls it a spirit) that any given object holds.[56]

Whether or not they specifically saw them as nourishing or enlivening, it is clear that turn-of-the-century women appreciated ordinary, useful objects; they embraced rather than dismissed or overlooked them. This is very different from the long-dominant foreground perspective, where objects considered important would be those that were extra-ordinary. In reviewing an exhibition of Navajo woven blankets, the critic Ralph Pomeroy inadvertently expressed the idea that familiarity and usefulness rendered objects almost invisible. "*In order to really see them*," he said, "I am going to forget, that [these are blankets] . . . I am going to look at them as paintings . . . by . . . masters of modern art" (italics added).[57] The women I am writing about liked to understand how objects actually functioned or how they served people in their daily lives. They also liked to know an object's historical or social context, which made it even more meaningful. I think of this attitude as "context counts," and I will cite numerous examples in subsequent chapters.

The "context counts" preference makes sense in light of relational theory. As Belenky explains it, women's way of knowing and constructing knowledge is emotional and empathetic; women "enter into a union with what is known," and become part of it.[58] Union extends to objects as well as people. Women's particularly intimate relationships with objects are affected by their comfort with the nearer proxemic distances that I discussed above, and they relate to the subject of miniaturization. Once again, it is in the intimate distance zones that we find the little things—the small scale objects that must be held up close to the body to be seen and otherwise comprehended—that are so important in domestic amusements. Diminutive size affects emotion as well. Several scholars have argued that when we deal with miniatures, we enter a different emotional state: we feel a sense of reverie and timelessness and a comforting feeling of mastery and control. Bachelard likened little spaces to "daydreams of intimacy" that attract us almost as part of our primal well being. The miniature, as Susan Stewart explains, "makes its context remarkable" and transforms everything around it; it creates a particularly heightened kind of reality, a type of magic. Stewart says it puts us into a reverie because it seems to compress time as well as space, so that each moment seems suspended and especially significant. Bachelard insists we go into miniaturized space in order to see a vastness, a deeper reality that is not the world of representation, but imagination. When we enter the miniature world, images grow before us; the "large issues from the small." (The magic moves especially strongly only in this one direction; "a bit of moss may well [seem like] a pine, but a pine will never be a bit of moss.") One must give "unflagging attention" to all the details in a miniature, but the rewards are great, for through it even a grown person is able to experience the "enlarging gaze" of a child. The experience yields a sense of greatness and even personal power: when we miniaturize a world, Bachelard says, we are able to possess it. A miniature seems cute and evokes a sense of protectiveness; the person looking at or holding it feels powerful in relationship to it. Miniature items take on what Stewart calls an "intimate immensity." To use the word in a different sense, these small objects even *become* intimates, and emotional connection and satisfaction is heightened even further. Interestingly, Stewart identifies the miniature with the feminine and the female domain. It is not a narrative form, she says; because it represents a continual present, it tends to "erase" history. The gigantic, on the other hand, is in her mind an integral part of the historical stream and is identified with the male.[59]

Non-Workplace Values and Gift Relations

I have argued that the domestic amusements I am writing about do not reflect the same workplace values as the hobbies Steven Gelber was concerned with.[60]

32 Men's amusements often tended (and still tend) toward achievement of some kind—sports and gambling had winners and desired outcomes, for example, and even stamp collecting was, as explained previously, working to complete a series. The women involved with domestic amusements, on the other hand, were generally focused more on process than on product or outcome; in other words, they took an experiential rather than productive approach to leisure. Theirs were not goal-oriented and rule-bound or prepackaged entertainments, but activities that demanded creative participation and a spontaneous, playful attitude. They generally took place away from public view. This different—domestic, or background—profile accounts not only for their devaluation, but their relative invisibility in the historical record.

Most historians concerned with amusements or pastimes have thought in terms of the work/play dichotomy that so colored twentieth-century industrial-era attitudes; we might say they looked through the viewfinder of the Recreation movement. Books with titles such as *Leisure and Entertainment in America* focus on activities that took place in public settings such as churches and grange or lodge halls. Moreover, if one does a bibliographic or keyword search using the terms "amusements" or "entertainments," what shows up are references to organized entertainments such as theatrical performances or commercial ventures such as amusement parks. A typical attitude was expressed by Foster Rhea Dulles, author of the 1940 work *America Learns to Play*. Dulles acknowledged that most leisure in earlier eras consisted of simple, informal activities, but those would remain "hidden in the obscurity that shrouds private lives," and historical works on the subject would by definition have to focus on organized public recreation. In the same vein, he also stated that what a nation does with its leisure is important for civic life—as important as its government or economy.[61] While there is no clear dividing line between the public and private realms and some of the entertainments I discuss actually took place in public spaces, most domestic amusements centered on the home and were sponsored by individuals or small, often ad hoc groups rather than structured organizations. They tell us little about institutions of any kind, much less governments or nations. They do, however, show us what individuals found nourishing.

It is interesting to note how closely the dominant definition of leisure follows the workplace model. Kathy Peiss, who wrote about working women's entertainments at the turn of the century, distinguished between the kind of activities that married and unmarried working women were engaged in. Young, unattached, wage-earning women often spent their nonworking hours in dance halls and other commercial venues. They were part of the workplace world, and their amusements conformed more closely to the industrial era male model. Once married, however—usually meaning, in that period, being outside the wage economy—a woman's leisure and work activities could not really be differentiated. Even Peiss was defining leisure pastimes primarily in terms of organized recreation, and unfortunately she did not look closely at what those married women actually did.[62]

Some observers claim that in our postindustrial era, where we are less bound by the work ethic and its insistence on linear time, the work/play dichotomy is "flattening out." Quarrick points to the new phrases in our language that conflate the words or even reverse their original meanings: we speak of "extreme play," for example, or of "mild work."[63] While this idea is compelling, many of our new forms of play still seem to be based on workplace values. The image that comes to mind with the extreme play epithet is a thrill-filled activity such as bungee jumping or surfing an enormous wave—it still involves proving something; it is goal oriented and thus productive. This seems fundamentally different to me than the lighthearted, saturated quality cultivated in domestic amusements. They involved less adrenaline and showmanship, and they brought work and play together in a natural manner. Once again, their emphasis on aesthetic elaboration and collaborative experience represented background ideas.

The other aspect of domestic amusements that lies outside workplace values can be understood through "gift theory," a framework established in the anthropological and material culture literature concerned with objects and interpersonal relations. "Gift relations" are contrasted with "commodity relations." In a gift transaction, an object seems personal because it is conceptually linked to the giver, the recipient, and the bond between them. In a commodity transaction, an object remains impersonal "property"; it is not significantly linked to any human relationship and is thus alienated, or unconnected. Even a mass-produced, purchased object may lose its commodity status, but it must be appropriated, or converted into a possession. A sweater sitting on a store shelf remains a commodity, for example, until it is purchased by an individual, who invests energy in it. It then becomes identified with that person. If given as a gift, the sweater loses its alienated commodity past completely, for it is subordinated to the emotions and intentions of the giver and to the relationship between the giver and receiver. It is also in the private sphere, which is still disproportionately associated with women, where relationships of reciprocity and generosity are strongest and gift relations prevail. James Carrier argues that women in our culture have primary responsibility for the appropriation or conversion of commodities because they are most strongly identified with nurturing interpersonal relationships.[64]

Gift relations certainly prevailed in turn-of-the-century domestic amusements. Objects were sometimes given as literal gifts—we have mentioned scrapbook houses and party favors in this regard—but much else was given to others: the

34   *experience* of a sensually decorated environment at a women's tea, for example, or the pleasure of encountering an amusing household helper doll. The women involved in these activities were more likely to make their own objects or environments than to purchase them ready-made, but even when they bought commercial goods, they appropriated them. Consumer products such as strainers and pastry brushes were recast, for example—they were turned from work tools into play objects and recontextualized into something outside the rules of the workday world. Sometimes the very detritus of the consumer society was recycled, as when advertising imagery was turned into raw material for the scrapbook houses. Even purposefully collected (purchased) objects were often recast into relationship-oriented possessions, chosen as they were for the sense of connection they engendered, and then set up in tableauxlike, storytelling displays. In saturating or aestheticizing these objects, the women imbued them with the qualities of their private realm of gift relations.

Saturation in Our Postmodern World

It is exciting to note the major attitudinal shifts in our culture and to listen to the many voices trying to express what is happening. Some speak of the diminishing hold of the work ethic that insists on productive time use; some challenge long-held beliefs about art and the way it can be appreciated. Many count themselves as "sensuists," insisting on the importance of the body and a more playful reality. Several theorists tie these changes to our postmodern sensibility, which is less bound and defined by literacy and linearity and more open to sensory input. Significantly, some are talking about these changes in the same kind of aesthetic terms that were applied to the culture of the late nineteenth century. Mike Featherstone, for example, speaks of an emerging "aesthetic paradigm." Edwin Wade claims we are now beginning to understand that all "aesthetic inspiration has a common core" and to accept the inextricable overlay between art and everyday life.[65] These voices mingle with and often echo those of feminists working to articulate the background perspective. For instance, in talking about women's writing, the literary critic Rachel Blau Du Plessis says it is directly reflective of the "dailiness and repetitiveness" of their lives. She describes it as nonhierarchic, multicentered, and without climactic place or moment. These same terms and concepts also used to describe postmodern society; such qualities are the very hallmarks of postmodernism.[66] Our more rootless, postindustrial sensibility seems to be moving us closer to the background and pushing us once again in the direction of greater saturation. As the great success of popular books and programs about infusing our lives with soulfulness and enchantment indicates, our culture is clearly longing for deeper, more embodied experience. Thus, the time seems right for us to reevaluate the kind of domestic amusements I write about in this book and to look at the overall significance of the saturated world.

I remind my readers that while the domestic amusements I focus on have been largely dismissed in the last century, the women involved in them did not find their activities demeaning. On the contrary, they were the heroines of their own domain and were able to express their own values and way of doing things. It is true that most of these amusements referenced and helped sustain culturally dominant gender roles and divisions, but the women treated these as a strength rather than a weakness; their activities still had positive meaning. These pastimes led the women inward, to a sense of self, and helped them give shape to their lives. It is my hope that *The Saturated World* will help further this kind of consciousness. I expect it to stimulate a discussion of aesthetic meaning; push material culture discourse to a more intimate, personal, and contextual level; and contribute to the growing literature on the personal arena and everyday life of the background. Even more immediately and most importantly, however, I hope the book will help individual readers see the historic activities I write about—and everything else—through a different, more saturated lens. The stories in the subsequent chapters tell us about the pleasures of the sensory world and the ways joy and depth can be found in the seemingly mundane details of life. They are about what holds people's passion. Living as we do in our bodies, on this material plane, we can all learn to better enjoy, appreciate, and interact with it. Living as we are in a transitional time where the attitudes and values of the modern world are being left behind, we have the opportunity to take stock and make conscious choices about the way we live. I hope we, like the women who cultivated these intimate, embodied, playful, and connected experiences, will choose to live more and more in the "poetic image" of the saturated world.

Chapter Two

THE PAPER DOLL HOUSE

There I stood—dumbstruck and greedy in front of [pages taken from Victorian scrapbook albums (paper doll houses)]. The collages had cast their spell. Their array of domestic and decorative detail was dizzying, while their flirtation with scale, space, texture and pattern was disarmingly picturesque. . . . As an ensemble [they were] tantalizing. . . . They pointed to a scissor-happy, scissor-sure marriage between hand and imagination. . . . The sheer thrill of that first encounter will always reverberate for me.

—LINDA ROSCOE HARTIGAN,
"THE HOUSE THAT COLLAGE BUILT"

Introduction

I had a similar reaction when I first came upon a "paper doll house" scrapbook in the archives of the Winterthur Museum library.[1] I had never seen anything quite like it, and was immediately drawn to the rich world that lay before me.[2] I could identify with the house maker—the woman (or girl) who had so painstakingly attended to all the tiny details; I could almost feel in my own fingers the pleasure of handling and arranging the many differently textured papers and sense the "aha" that came with finding the just-right tiny accessories that would make the rooms come alive. Like Hartigan, I was thrilled by the dance of color and pattern. I was also delighted by the "context counts" idea, or the fact that the book functioned as a complete world, a fully realized, animated house with a personality or character of its own. I especially loved the sewing room, with its pasted-in furniture that seemed to float on a sea of shiny blue paper, and its window (large enough to let in adequate sewing light) of blue-lined notebook paper outfitted with gauzy tissue paper drapes. The house maker must have been pleased with the window too, for she made others like it for different spaces,

FIG. 2.1.
This double-page spread comes from a paper doll house given to nine-year-old Edith Washburn of Thomaston, Maine in 1892. Her nurse, "Miss Scanison," made it for her when she was suffering from a prolonged illness. The album was fashioned in an old account book, seemingly dating from the 1840s. Miss Scanison pasted different wallpapers in the album to represent the walls and floor, and then she added a variety of furniture and other accoutrements to each page. Courtesy, the Behring Center, National Museum of American History, Smithsonian Institution, Accession number 58-23, photo 79-11536.

continually experimenting with new arrangements. I marveled at the perfect symmetry of the sitting room—the furnishings, but also the accessories, such as the individually cut-out pieces of bric-a-brac arranged in descending size order on the mantel. The particularity of the furnishings enchanted me as well. The library was outfitted with a copy of *Webster's* and a complete set of books by Charles Dickens, for example, and the smoking room had antlered trophies mounted on the wall and the pistols positioned over the doorway. The album was a creative labor of love that could still speak to me after more than one hundred years.

I determined to learn more about scrapbooks of this type. Other than Hartigan's article that looked at decontextualized paper doll house pages as a form of collage and a 1992 lecture by Rodris Roth that treated paper doll house making as a part of household training, I found no scholarly references to the genre.[3] The story I have put together here comes from references in period women's magazines and advice books and, most importantly, from the artifacts themselves. I was able to locate about twenty complete albums and an assortment of miscellaneous pages in archives and museum collections, and I have spent many hours poring over them. Over time I was able to formulate a general chronology and sense of the paper doll house phenomenon.[4]

The Saturated World of the Paper Doll House

The paper doll house was a form of amusement popular in America between approximately 1875 and 1920.[5] As indicated in chapter 1, house making was purportedly a girl's pastime, but evidence indicates that grown women often put the albums together and gave them to girls as gifts. If we consider then that this genre came into prominence early in the period under consideration, was based on iconic images of houses, and involved "girls" of all ages, it emerges as particularly fitting topic for the first in-depth discussion in this book. By examining this genre, furthermore, we are allowed a glimpse of the kind of childhood training and experience that predisposed girls to a saturated consciousness. (It is intriguing to realize, in fact, that some of the women I write about in subsequent chapters might possibly have had or worked on a paper doll house album when they were young.) Scrapbook house making was an elaboration of the domestic skill of decorating; it brought the activity to an intense, concentrated level. Interacting with a paper doll house would have been a pleasurable activity that heightened sensory awareness and sensibility, and it provided opportunities for imaginative fantasy. It was also an activity that reinforced the importance of the domestic domain, a sense of community, and background rather than workplace values.

As even this brief introduction indicates, these albums are known by a variety of names. In their own time, they were called "houses for paper dolls," "doll house scrapbooks," "house albums," "scrapbook houses," or "book houses." More recently they have also been descriptively referred to as "collage albums."[6] They can be considered a subset of the scrapbook. Scrapbooks came into being during the Victorian era—they were so popular that commentators spoke of the "scrapbook mania" that took hold in the latter part of the nineteenth century—and reflected the astonishing new abundance of available goods. With industrial production turning out thousands of new items every day, people were for the first time concerned with managing the abundance. A scrapbook was a collection of images, objects, or ideas that were organized and arranged in a particular way. Many kinds of collections were housed in scrapbook albums. Familiar examples include photographs and autographs, but with the veritable explosion of printed matter, including mass-market magazines, greeting cards, trade catalogs, and other advertising material, many albums were exclusively devoted to paper items.[7]

40   Scholars have shown us that scrapbook making was popular with both sexes, but men and boys tended to keep books of informational clippings and were particularly likely to arrange them according to topical ideas. An interest in classification may have been a natural male predilection, but it was also the general thrust of the advice about scrapbooks that was given to boys; they were encouraged to save didactic material and organize their albums in a rational manner. In contrast, women and girls tended and were advised to focus their albums on attractive imagery. They often filled albums with commercial trade or greeting cards or literal scraps—that is, the small paper cut-outs that were given away by manufacturers. These were brilliantly colored images, illustrating everything from flowers to religious figures. Most female scrapbook makers were not content to simply secure the images on the album pages; typically they ordered them carefully into pleasing arrangements. In the attributed albums I have seen, women and girls were much more likely to treat each page or double-page spread as a compositional unit and focus on juxtaposition of color, pattern, and form.[8] It is easy to understand the paper doll house, then, as an elaborated type of scrapbook, filled with specific types of images and saturated in a particularly contextualized manner.

      In the first chapter I used the word "fairyland" to describe the particular saturated quality that pervaded these books and other domestic amusements. Before I continue my examination of the paper doll house, I wish to expand on the meanings of that term. The word was in common use by the 1870s; the fairyland idea was so much of a leitmotif in the second half of the nineteenth century, in fact, that "fairyland" functioned as a code word, implying something appealing and magically transformed. Any event, object, or space felt to be aesthetically charged, enchanted, and otherworldly could hold the fairyland association. Fairyland was a quality, but it was spoken of and sometimes understood as a beautiful, ideal place—a dreamland or wonderland that existed far away, apart from any painful realities or practicalities. It was a brightly colored, sensually rich, happy world. Visually it was represented in the images mentioned in the introductory chapter, including the drawings of Walter Crane and Kate Greenaway or the expressive, saturated hues of Maxfield Parrish chromolithographs. It was also evident in the dreamy paintings of individuals associated with the Pre-Raphaelite and Aesthetic art movements. Crane referred to the fairyland quality when he wrote about creating "ideal beauty rather than literal fact," and the painter Edward Burne-Jones expressed it eloquently when he described the kind of art he wanted to make: "a beautiful romantic dream of something that never was, never will be—in a light better than any light that ever shone—in a land no one can define or remember, only desire."[9] One was transported to fairyland and, once there, fell under a kind of enchantment. Esther Singleton talked about it as a beguiling realm where one was charmed. Her description of "an imaginative Pleasure Ground, a kind of Lotus-land" alluded to both its dreamlike state and sensual qualities.[10] Fairyland was inevitably associated with the unsullied innocence of childhood. This was evident in the ubiquitous popular images of picturesque children and was symbolized in the Neverland of *Peter Pan*—a place where one did not have to grow up.

As early as the mid-nineteenth century, appealing environments were described as "veritable fairylands" or places that "looked as if a thousand fairies had been at work." Queen Victoria, entranced by the sight of fluttering banners and reflective glass at the 1851 Crystal Palace Exhibition, proclaimed it had the "effect of fairyland." Similar proclamations continued for decades; the press routinely referred to halls and public spaces that were transformatively decorated for fairs or parties in this way, for example, and the White City created for the 1893 World's Columbian Exposition was repeatedly described this way. There were diverse attempts to consciously create fairyland environments. Tableaux with titles such as "Undine's Vision in Fairyland" or "Around the World in Search of Fairyland" dramatized the vision, as did popular books such as *The Wizard of Oz.*[11] Girls were particularly encouraged to cultivate the sentimental fairyland ideal, and it seems to have pervaded their image of the world. Scrapbook house making can be understood as an expression of this highly saturated vision.

The first paper doll house I encountered at Winterthur was worked in what had once been a saloon account book; new paper was pasted over the no-longer-needed records, and cut-out images were applied to the blank sheets. Based on the street names in the original account listings, the album probably came from the Boston area, and based on the clothing styles in the cut-outs, it was probably made about 1880. Recycling of ledgers or account books was common in the earlier years of the genre. The first article I know of that gave instructions for making paper doll houses, written in1880, indicated "any convenient blank book with pages of at least 8"x9" would be suitable."[12] Later examples were more often made in new books, some of which were expressly sold as scrapbook albums.

Fashioning a paper doll house was a long-term process, akin in many ways to the process of outfitting and arranging a real house. The house maker first had to collect the materials for the interior settings (for example, foil, crepe paper, wallpaper samples), as well as hundreds of suitable pictures of household furnishings. The advice literature seemed to presume that most makers would amass quantities of these images ahead of time, cut them out, sort them by category or

42   room, and carefully store them for future use. I have seen a few extant books with envelopes of just such unused cut-outs tucked into them.[13] The pictures were taken from the commercial sources mentioned above—primarily magazines, trade catalogs, and advertisements—although some house makers augmented the cut-outs with hand-drawn or -painted details (fig. 2.2). It may have been a challenge to find this visual material in the earlier decades of the paper doll house's popularity, but by 1920 the advice-giver Maude Nash claimed that "any furniture store of a large city [would] send a catalogue upon request," and its "page after page of pictures" would adequately fill the rooms of a given book. In any case, the search for appropriate materials could engender an almost obsessive excitement. Carolyn Wells commented in 1901, "if you . . . begin to make paper doll houses, you will soon find yourself pouncing on pictures suitable for your use wherever you happen to run across them—and running across them everywhere."[14]

Once the house maker was ready to start, she had to organize the house—decide what would be included on each page and what would follow what. As indicated, the usual convention was to treat each double-page spread as a single

FIG. 2.2.
The maker of this paper doll house, Harriet Brown, was trained in perspective drawing, as is evident from the stairway she added to this scene. Note the children playing hide-and-seek around the bench on the right, and the cat eyeing a tiny mouse in front of the door. Courtesy, the Behring Center, National Museum of American History, Smithsonian Institution, Accession number 301846.1, photo 79-11523.

room and to set up successive spreads as if one were moving further and further into the house. The cover or first page was thus usually made to represent the porch, front door, or entryway, the next set of pages the front hall, and so on. The more public rooms were therefore positioned near the front of the book, and the more private spaces further toward the back. This conceptual layout seems to have already been familiar by 1880, when the first instructional article by Jessie Ringwalt appeared, and it was to stay popular for generations. Every house scrapbook I have seen included rooms such as parlors, bedrooms, and kitchens, which together seem to have made up a template for the "oneiric" or internal image of the house in this period. Some, however, went well beyond this, ending up with more than forty use-specific spaces, such as pantries, dressing rooms, music or art rooms, schoolrooms, gymnasiums, ballrooms, and, in one remarkable example, a home theater. A few examples extended as well into the backyard, incorporating gardens and even outdoor cottages. Specialized spaces called for targeted cut-outs—pianos and harps for the music room, for example, and desks and blackboards for the schoolroom. A house maker might have decided to include such rooms only if she already had the requisite images on hand, but she was in any case involved in a dynamic interplay among idea, image, and construction.

Before she could arrange any of the furnishings, the house maker would, like anyone moving into a new home, have to prepare the interior space. She would usually first divide each page set into three or four horizontal bands, respectively representing the floor, walls, ceiling, and other architectural features of the room. She would typically delineate each area with fancy papers of different patterns, textures, or colors and then superimpose and arrange the decorative features such as windows and doors (these were usually cut-outs but could also be drawn in). When this was complete, she could add furniture and accessories (I think of this as the fun part; unlike moving furniture in a three-dimensional house, it involved no heavy lifting). Actual arrangement of the room—decisions about what would be in the foreground, what would overlap or be superimposed with what to effect the right kind of three dimensional space, and what would sit on the table or the mantel—offered many opportunities for experimentation. Emily Hoffman instructed *Harper's Bazar* (later *Harper's Bazaar*) readers that it was best to first make the corners of the rooms and later fill in the center, putting images down first without pasting so that they could be moved around for a more pleasing effect.[15]

After the room was outfitted with objects, most house makers added "people." Some used actual freestanding paper dolls. I have seen extant albums with dolls tucked into them and albums with slits or pockets in cut-out beds or other

FIG. 2.3.
The narrative quality that paper doll house pages could hold is evident in this scene where women are engaged in a tête-à-tête. The maker of the album was clearly familiar with the qualities of the latest "Aesthetic" interior, as she included iconic images such as water lilies and owls, and an Eastlake-style bed. She also incorporated saturated touches—bed furnishings made from textured paper doilies, for example, and a floor treatment made from a fine-checked tissue paper. Other pages in the album feature hand-colored objects and details such as a pasted-in mica mirror. Unidentified maker, ca. 1875–85. Courtesy, The Winterthur Library, Joseph Downs Collection of Manuscripts and Printed Ephemera, Folio 252.

furnishings that flat figures were designed to slide into. Far above the freestanding dolls in importance, however, are the pasted-in images of people engaged in domestic activities included in most albums (I have seen relatively few completely "uninhabited" houses). The fixed figures are arranged in vignettes. They literally enliven the books, making them embodied, animate entities that could thus function as intimate companions. Even though the book houses were referred to as homes for paper dolls, there is almost a double level of embodiment, for, with the pasted-in figures, they are complete unto themselves.

Each of the rooms in these houses functions as a self-contained, "readable" dramatic story, and even Ringwalt's early *Godey's Lady's Book* article alluded to a theatrical model. She said the paper doll house should be presented as if it were "being viewed by a guest"; the maker should fashion each room as a perfect vignette. Ringwalt's descriptive details all support the idea that the pages were thought of as minidramas; for example, she suggested that a "pretty little girl-doll" cut-out be placed so "she seems just ready to spring upon the [dining room]

table" or that the doors of a pasted sideboard should remain half open so as "to   *45*
suggest a meal in progress."[16] The presentation device illustrated in figure 2.4,
where a bedroom is flanked on either side by a drawn curtain, indicates the house
makers took this theatrical model to heart; each page became a stage set, reveal-
ing an ongoing play.

Creating these perfect vignettes called for—and allowed the makers to engage
in—an intensely saturated experience. Ringwalt spoke of the importance of adding fanciful, textural details, for they would make the pages "come alive" (note the
embodied imagery in her statement). Her descriptions, filled as they are with
saturated language and loaded adjectives, imply a physical and emotional engagement with materials and process. She dwelled on different kinds of textures and
colors, explaining for example that curtains might be made of bits of lace or net
and that gilt or silver paper might be found for door knobs and mirrors. "Highly-
colored pictures" might adorn the walls, she noted; "gorgeous flowers" might rest
upon a golden table. Even the cut-out characters were described in sensually
appealing terms—a figure in the front hall, for example, appeared in a "fanciful

FIG. 2.4.
The maker of this dramatically presented album conceived of it as a grand house she dubbed the "Kenilworth Inn."
Bright-red crepe paper curtains are highlighted with metallic paper stars. The frame on the print at the top has
been carefully cut in a zigzag shape. Unidentified maker, possibly from Chicago, 1903. Courtesy, The Winterthur
Library, Joseph Downs Collection of Manuscripts and Printed Ephemera, Folio 36.

46 costume, well bedizened with buttons."[17] Tactility and fancifulness are certainly evident in most extant house books. The previously mentioned bedroom curtains were made with a particularly pleasing textured tissue paper, far more interesting than any paper on the market today.[18] Floor and wall coverings seem to have been selected in many cases for their visual intensity rather than their suitability as backgrounds; their patterns are rarely in proportion to that of the furnishings, and their colors overwhelm some of the monochromatic cut-outs. Even without the furnishings and accessories, they create fantastic interior spaces that often literally dance on the page.[19]

Some house makers seemed to revel in these details. They pieced in mica inserts or hand-colored panes of "stained glass" on closet doors, for example, or pieced "parquet" floors of bits of wood-grained wallpaper; they painstakingly fringed the edges of paper rugs, and fashioned picture frames out of embossed gold foil or braid. To make the spaces come alive, they also cut out individual fish to outfit inch-wide aquaria or placed tiny shoes by the side of a bed, as if waiting for the owner to wake up and put them on. They positioned paper cats as if they were chasing mice. In one startling example now in the Margaret Woodbury Strong Museum, the artist went so far as to cut out small shapes from one patterned paper and paste them at odd angles onto another to form the background effect she desired.[20] Often house makers added watercolor to the black and white engraved images they had cut from magazines, modifying them to suit particular rooms or, as indicated above, they drew in details to tie their compositions together.

House makers also liked to play with layering and did so in several ways. For example, with multiple layers of paper superimposed over one another, it was easy to create the kind of openable doors that Ringwalt referred to in 1880. Many houses include furnishings that open to reveal something hidden inside—a nicely browned roast in the oven, a closet full of crepe paper dresses, even a potty chair secreted in a convertible chair. These items were essentially built-in and would remain part of the house permanently, but Ringwalt also wrote about fashioning covers for other bare "wood" furnishings that would be attached with the sort of folding tabs that fastened dresses on paper dolls.[21] I have not seen any tabbed covers, but these would easily have been lost over time. Some book houses also include a type of layering involving pasted-in people, many of whom were reconfigured for the roles they were to play. For example, Louise Hovey transformed cut-out magazine figures into the characters she wanted by taking them apart, adding additional details, and repositioning them. In order to transform a fashion figure into a maid, for instance, she repositioned the arms so they would fit neatly over a newly created apron (see fig. 2.5). Some of the most skillfully done houses include a very sophisticated layering between sequential pages. "Kenilworth

Inn," an album made in 1903 that is now in the Winterthur Library (its name is proclaimed on the first page, that is, the front door), has several pages with cut-out windows that allow the viewer to see into the next room. A remarkable album in the Strong Museum carries the idea even further. Not only can one look through an artfully cut-out section on many of the pages into the next vignette, but the revealed section helps create the story on the previous page as well. For instance, the ballroom is constructed of two layers, consisting of an indoor vignette on one page and an adjacent outdoor patio scene on the one behind it. Indoor dancers seem to be watching what is going on outside and wondering about the interactions going on there.[22] This type of house would have required particularly careful planning.

FIG. 2.5.
The exuberant effects created by the juxtaposition of differently scaled images is apparent in this page from an album made by Louise Hovey (later Mrs. Austin Kautz) in the 1880s, but the effect is even stronger when the element of color is visible. Hovey consistently used a "horror vacuii" approach—that is, she left no empty space on her pages. Here she created a "maid" by cutting out a picture of a woman in fashionable dress, covering her clothes with a handmade apron and cap, and repositioning her hand so it could go over the apron. She also painted in the details on the folding screen at the lower left. Courtesy, the Behring Center, National Museum of American History, Smithsonian Institution, Accession number 232.559, Catalogue number 61.293, photo 79-11535.

On a more abstract level, the houses often evidence a kind of conceptual layering, where different realities are freely juxtaposed. Some of the vignettes feature individuals in eighteenth-century dress interacting with others in contemporary styles; a man in a powdered wig and breeches, for example, is seen gesturing to a woman in an Edwardian hat. These details afford continual surprises and are part of the dizzying enchantment of the paper doll house compositions.

Surely the people who were creating these vignettes were "making special," adding intensity to their world through what Bachelard called a "hallucination of detail." In chapter 1, I cited contemporary writers who talk about enriching our lives by engaging deeply with the particulars of the everyday things around us and treating them as symbols and embodiments of our inner lives.[23] The house makers were doing this instinctively. Their deep engagement with the material world in which they lived, coupled with their cultivation of sensory stimulation and delight, still calls to us from the pages of these books.

All of the fantastic and saturated qualities of the paper doll houses were heightened by the fact that they were self-contained miniature worlds. Miniature things of all kinds, as we have seen, give us a sense of power and protectiveness, magic and delight. As described in chapter 1, they change our sense of time and space, creating and allowing us to experience the wide-eyed wonder of a child. When the miniature is a space that can be entered, at least in the imagination, its power is particularly potent. Many writers remark on the hold that miniature environments have on us; they make such an impression, in fact, that stories about them are often included in autobiographies. Edith Nesbitt, the famed English author of children's books who charmed turn-of-the-century audiences with her miniature "magic cities" (cardboard dioramas), said she never met a child who did not like building tiny places, and few grown ups could resist them either. Nesbitt explained that the enchantment did not stop even after the miniature was constructed, for makers would keep making up stories about it, imagining "how splendid it would be" if they were small enough to walk into it.[24] I see this kind of projection into the space as another kind of embodiment; we literally imagine our bodies at a different scale and imagine going into the minuscule space in a kinetic and tactile manner.

The power of the paper doll house was magnified even further by the fact that it was a house. Bachelard is helpful in explaining the particular pull of the house form. He likens a house to a large cradle, and he claims each of us has a "house of dream memory" that may be much like the house we were born in. We relate to this internal template, as to all houses, as a place—or a metaphor—for personal integration. We like corners and niches (and there were many of them in the paper doll houses) because they function as "chambers of our being." Emily Hoffman, another author who gave suggestions about making paper doll houses, wrote in 1904 of the huge pleasure involved in fashioning them. She alluded to the opportunity they presented for creating one's own integrated, personal environment and thereby feeling a sense of personal power.[25]

Ringwalt demonstrated how strong the appeal of the miniature could be when she indicated that her ideal book house included an even smaller space within it.

She described the "very heart" of one of the albums she was discussing as a play-room with *its* own doll house (the "most minute of miniature houses"). The power was compounded; not only was this a miniature within a miniature, but a house within a house. More recent commentators have reiterated the universal appeal of this combination. It was singled out in a 1964 essay called "The Doll-house Multiplied," for example. "*Everyone* wants a dollhouse within a dollhouse," noted author Eloise Kruger. Susan Stewart similarly argued that this is what we look for when we encounter a doll house—we search for another inside it, the "within within within."[26]

Those who made these houses were in effect making an entire world—they were fashioning a complete and unified, living entity out of literal scraps and organizing it according to their own fantasies and ideas. "Imagination ruled" in this world, Hoffman said, where every girl could be "her own architect." Wells, too, stated that one of the "major charms" of the scrapbook was that it allowed the imagination to expand. This meant entering Ackerman's state of "deep play," where one was absorbed and focused and lost track of time. The process required ongoing thought and hours of intense, concentrated activity. It generated a tran-scendent, "enchanted" feeling. When a girl spent time with these books, Hoffman claimed, "ennui [wa]s forgotten."[27] When a grown woman did so, she probably felt even more permission to act playful—she was literally constructing and playing with a toy—and indulge and express her childlike self. House making was an ulti-mately creative pastime, based on making something orderly, whole, and new out of disparate pieces. If we use the theatrical metaphor mentioned earlier, we can think of the house maker as the director, set designer, costumer, and stage manager of the dramatic scene. If she later played with the album, she was also the author and producer of ongoing or ever-changing plays. Most examples show enough wear to indicate that they were indeed pored over and played with repeatedly.

Every house reflected an idiosyncratic personal vision. A sense of individual style and preference was evident in each example I examined, as was the personal involvement and attachment the maker felt toward it. Some house makers liked to fill the space completely, indicating a kind of *horror vacuii* (figs. 2.5, 2.6); oth-ers liked more free-floating figures and minimal furniture. Some seemed to care more than others about linear perspective. Some favored a high degree of catego-rization and organization—they not only divided the house into many function-specific rooms, but even divided the space within a room into separate areas. A few preferred to leave their houses unpopulated and allow the furnishings to take on a life of their own (figs. 2.1, 2.6, 2.7). Some included commentary in their vignettes. The maker of Kenilworth Inn not only named her house, but included handwritten homilies such as "Too many cooks spoil the broth" in the kitchen.

FIG. 2.6.
The unidentified maker of this seventeen-room album marked this page "Summer Kitchen." Presumably because she could not find suitable cut-outs, she drew a sink and cabinet door on notebook paper and placed them among the commercial images. The cabinet door opened to reveal stored foodstuffs or dishes (they are now missing). This paper doll house was made in an account book from a saloon, which, based on the street names that appear on the records, was in eastern Massachusetts. The last date cited in the accounts is 1872, and judging from the outfits on the cut-out people on some of the other pages, the collages were made several years later. Courtesy, The Winterthur Library, Joseph Downs Collection of Manuscripts and Printed Ephemera, Folio 144.

FIG. 2.7.
The maker of this album grouped the furnishings precisely and relied on overlapping images to get a good sense of perspective. Nevertheless, the different scales of the cut-outs give the image an informal, dizzying quality. The maker is unidentified. Courtesy, The Winterthur Library, Joseph Downs Collection of Manuscripts and Printed Ephemera, Folio 252.

An unidentified house maker from Bennington, Vermont, similarly pasted pre-printed mottos in several places, including, in a well-appointed music room, "Let the sound of music creep into our ears." Personal connection to the houses is also demonstrated by the fact that owners often conceived of the rooms as belonging to particular individuals. Pages are tagged "Laura's room," "David's room," and the like, and some of the inserted paper dolls bear names to match. If, as the advice literature implies, girls sometimes carried these book houses to friends' houses or took them on journeys, it would have been like taking a companion (an embodied "friend") along. Marian Dudley Richards wrote that as a child she was particularly attached to one of her paper dolls and felt that "block houses were not good enough for her." She demonstrated her great affection for that doll by making her a book house, into which she poured a huge amount of love and attention.[28]

The Paper Doll House as Part of a Female Community

It is a child who would have been likely to bring a scrapbook house with her when she went to visit a friend, and I have stated that the advice literature spoke of making paper doll houses as a girl's pastime. Ringwalt's original article appeared in *Godey's Lady's Book* as a "help to mother," implying a rather young audience, but house making was really too demanding for small children. Some books bear sure signs of a child's hand; one at the Smithsonian Institution, for example, has pages marked with the backward letters of a young person learning to write. However, the arrangement of that house is too sophisticated to have been made by a child of about five or six. She must have added her letters to an already-completed composition. Mary White included a photograph of three girls "planning a book house" in her 1905 *Child's Rainy Day Book,* and they appear to be about ten to thirteen years old. I believe that it would have been children of this age (perhaps a bit old for playing with paper dolls) who were most often creating these albums. I have two other indications that this may have been the case. From Marian Richards's reminiscence about making book houses when she was young, I surmise she would have been about twelve, and from information provided by Christine Ruth Grier's granddaughter, I know that Grier and her friend Martha Ross collaborated on an album when they were eleven or twelve.[29]

Documentation with many other extant houses indicates that they were made by grown women and then given to girls as expressions of affection. Another Smithsonian book house (fig. 2.1) bears a childishly penciled inscription by Edith E. Washburn of Thomaston, Maine, who wrote, "Miss Scanison (my nurse) made this when I was sick in 1892. I am always going to keep it to remember her by." Other books were given to children by their parents. Harriet Green Brown of Mystic, Connecticut, made one for her children in the 1880s, and a Chicago girl

52   received not one but two books from her family in the next decade. One is inscribed, "Painted for Anita C. Blair . . . by the Baltimore Decorative Arts Society. A gift from her mother and father, Mrs. and Mrs. Henry A. Blair." The second of Anita's books was prepared, or at least painted, by Miss Jenks, a student at the Art Institute of Chicago. It was clearly made with Anita specifically in mind, for it includes an image of Ceylon Court, a building said to have been moved from the Columbian Exposition in Chicago to Williams Bay, Wisconsin, by a friend of the Blairs. The Kenilworth Inn looks as if it, too, may have been made by an art student, as its fine construction and self-conscious presentation implies a maker who was formally trained in composition. ("Kenilworth" is a Chicago-area street name, and I have wondered if this might have been made by an Art Institute student as well; perhaps Miss Jenks and the Kenilworth Inn maker were even asked to make these houses as part of a class project.)[30] There are also several books that appear to have been made by different hands, some surer and more accomplished than others, leading me to believe that girls may have received scrapbook houses as presents and then added rooms of their own. Fifteen of the rooms in Anita Blair's first album appear to have been worked by the trained person from the Decorative Arts Society, but three are cruder, suggesting they might have been worked by Anita herself. Similarly, the backgrounds in Emilie Hickey's book appear to have been worked by a skilled adult, but the furnishings were filled in by someone else, probably Emilie herself. It is likely that many of the books represented collaborative efforts. When Christine Grier and Martha Ross worked on their book in Lebanon, Pennsylvania, each contributed what they could. Ross was skilled at drawing and actually rendered the settings, but Grier helped to paint them in.[31]

Such gift giving and collaborations between girls and their mothers, relatives, or friends are certainly qualities of the interconnected, or "relational," woman's community. There are many other ways, also, in which the scrapbook house genre represented the female world. Women were the major players in this genre, and their values predominated, as the houses celebrated the domestic ideal. They were, to begin with, only made by girls or women. We have seen that boys and men kept scrapbooks, but they do not seem to have made scrapbook *houses* and certainly not scrapbooks that were specifically (or even only ostensibly) made for dolls. Some of the materials commonly used in the paper doll houses were also strongly gender linked at the time; crepe paper was so clearly thought of as a woman's material, for example, that the Dennison crepe paper company hired two sisters as craft specialists to teach women how to use their product. Wallpaper was similarly identified.[32] The houses replicated and reinforced the nineteenth-century

conceptual dichotomy that associated the inside (private) with the female and   *53*
the outside (public) with the male. First, females were the ones who were making
and using the books (interior spaces). Moreover, the spatial arrangement was
telling; gardens and other exterior settings were placed in the back pages—beyond
the back door, or outside the boundaries of the house itself. Even within the
home, the pasted-in characters were placed in gender-specific rooms; male figures might appear in the library or music room, for example, but were rarely
placed in the nursery or kitchen. They were sometimes given their own, distinctly
masculine spaces, such as dens or smoking rooms that were filled with gender-
linked objects like spittoons, walking canes, and trophy heads.[33] One book house
has a man's dressing room, complete with all the necessary outfits. Furnishings
for these rooms were equally gender-appropriate; a page marked "John's bedroom" would not have been outfitted with lacy curtains or pillowcases. Even cut-
out cats were frequently placed near women, while dogs were placed near men.

To return to the theatrical metaphor, the books played out a kind of domestic
drama—both a household theater and a theater *of* the household—and women
were its unquestioned stars. While men were given a place in most houses, they
were heavily outnumbered and overshadowed. Not only were more pages devoted
to women's activities than to men's, but most houses included a disproportionate
number of female figures (for example, eleven to one), even on a single representative page. Cut-out women were often positioned together, sometimes in intense-
looking tête-à-têtes. I am reminded of Buckler and Leeper's remarks on the way
nineteenth-century scrapbooks reflected themes of women's magazines. Middle-
class women, they say, "were portrayed . . . as true heroines of unparalleled, unno-
ticed dignity and virtue" when situated within the context of the domestic sphere.[34]
Paper doll houses were scrapbooks that took this general presentation to an extreme: they represented the very spaces those heroines inhabited.

The themes of interconnection, interdependence, and family harmony were
also stressed in the pages of the house books. One extant example now in the
Strong Museum collection literally references these ideas on the walls of its well-
appointed nursery: pasted-in mottos with messages such as "Help One Another"
and "Love One Another" remind the children to cultivate "family values" and en-
courage them to grow up to be nurturing adults. Many book houses include
collages of families sitting on comfortable chairs and sofas, cheerfully sharing
each other's company, and some even include miniature portraits of supposed
family "ancestors," or framed pictures representing happy domestic scenes (see
figs. 2.1, 2.2, 2.7). Ruutz Rees wrote in 1883 that boys turned to their scrapbooks
as a place for their "quaint oddities" while girls used them to preserve sentimental

54   items, and we can see how the scrapbook house took the preoccupation with sentimentality to its ultimate conclusion.[35] Making a scrapbook house may have sometimes been a solitary occupation, but as the photo in Mary White's book makes clear, even that activity could be shared with friends. When we couple this with the fact that they were often shared across generations and that they were miniaturized artifacts that were by definition (at least in Susan Stewart's terms) feminine, we see how profoundly the books were grounded in the female world.

Rodris Roth, a curator in the Smithsonian Institution who was the first scholar to look at paper doll houses, focused on the way they introduced girls to their expected social roles. The emphasis on nurturance would certainly have been part of this, but there were other aspects as well. Roth felt the time spent with advertisements and trade catalogs would have taught the girls to become good consumers; they were literally immersed in commercial products, and paper doll house making was a kind of training in purchasing. There is no question that making a scrapbook of this type would inculcate familiarity with trade material (see fig. 2.6), and the houses certainly reinforced the contemporary consumer landscape. They featured the most up-to-date products. "There will be a telephone of course, and a phonograph, and possibly . . . a typewriter," noted Hoffman in her 1904 "Homes for Paper Dolls." Even today, we can date some of the extant houses because they include images of specific brands and products. The Strong Museum has a book with scenes fashioned from cut-outs from Ivory Soap advertisements, for example, that can be definitively dated to 1886, when the ads appeared in *Ladies' Home Journal.*[36] The houses were often also outfitted with a battery of servants—not only cooks and maids, but governesses and gardeners. These helpers were never surly or undependable; they were perpetually cheerful and ready to offer assistance. As Hoffman put it in a tongue-in-cheek fashion, "the most delectable serving-maids are to be had for the cutting out. [They] are always irreproachably capped and aproned, and offer chocolate or steaming soup with an ingratiating smile and a small tray."[37] Servants and spaces such as billiard rooms, conservatories, and wine cellars showed girls what they might be aspired to, but these were made-up dream houses that did not necessarily represent an expectation or even a hunger for such luxuries in real life. One did not have to be well off to make a house like this; several of the descriptive articles stressed, in fact, that all one needed to make book houses were scraps or advertising materials and flour paste or a jar of mucilage. Endless rooms did not so much represent a longing for consumer goods as they represented a *play* with luxury—as Hoffman wrote in *Harper's Bazar,* the paper doll family and its pampered pets could revel in such splendor.[38] Additional rooms meant more opportunities for cut-out tableaux and thus more opportunities for a house maker to order and elaborate a world of her own creation. They provided more of the sensual, aesthetic pleasure that came from handling the books and the scraps within them. Marian Richards noted, in fact, that some makers would keep adding to their house books because blank pages represented additional avenues for creative expression: "If pages still remain, they may be devoted to . . . an art museum, a 'zoo', stores, theatres, boat landings and railway stations..[or] views of the countryside. . . . A child may play so entirely in [a] book that there is no place she can devise that has not some page devoted to it."[39]

If we couple this with the understanding that the house makers were often not children at all, we see that consumer training was not a primary function of the paper doll houses. I would argue, in fact, that in some senses the books even subverted the consumer model. The objects of the consumer world (and simultaneously, images of them) were used as raw materials—as fodder for the creative imagination. They came in a free, or give-away, form, and then they were further decontextualized and recycled into something else. The Ivory soap characters described above, for example, were removed from their advertising context and repositioned into new, imaginary settings that had nothing to do with product recognition or association and everything to do with composition, arrangement of pictorial elements, and creation of an emotionally satisfying story. In addition, the completed albums were not thought of in terms of inherent value and were never part of the marketplace; rather, they were made and given as gifts. In the terms of the gift relations theory outlined in the introductory chapter, they could not be considered commodities because they were imbued with personal associations and the psychic energy that had gone into them.

Roth also stressed the idea that scrapbook houses were an ideal medium to introduce young girls to their future roles as wives, mothers, and homemakers. I do not disagree, but neither do I believe that was their primary purpose, and I think she was ignoring the positive aspects of those roles that the houses stressed. Learning to fashion a "proper" house would certainly have fit with prevailing beliefs about housewifely training. According to nineteenth-century ideology, women were responsible for the moral well-being of their families, and a properly appointed home was critical because well-designed and outfitted environments would in and of themselves exert a positive influence on those who lived in them. However, rhetoric about social and moral training did not appear in any of the writings about paper doll houses. On the contrary, magazine articles stressed the pleasure of making them. The very first published discussion of the houses appeared in a column called "Fun for the Fireside," and the word "fun"

56 was repeated in almost every treatment of them thereafter. The fact that various authors applied it to different aspects of the experience—Wells wrote of the fun of openable doors; Mary White spoke of the fun of "house hunting," or first finding an appropriate blank book—indicates how satisfying each step in the process might actually be.[40] Women's social roles were certainly reinforced through these paper vignettes—the importance of caring for a house and developing values related to nurturing and social bonding was evident on every page—but the household focus of the activity made its pleasurable quality more acceptable. The author of *Home Amusements,* a book published at approximately the same time that album making became popular, remarked that indulgence in pleasurable pursuits was "ennobled [or made] unselfish if it added to the cheerfulness of a home." Domestic training may have been part of paper doll house making, then, but it was overshadowed and shaped by its joyous, fun context.[41]

I think that the most important kind of training the paper doll houses furthered must have been aesthetic. The advice literature did stress the idea that house making would help develop artistic skill and foster aesthetic sensibility. Richards wrote of the excellent training with perspective that making a book would afford, for example, and Nash and Hoffman both spoke of house making as a way of developing good taste.[42] Extant books indicate that makers did concern themselves with drafting skills and artistic principles. In some, hand-drawn lines are carefully rendered in one- or two-point perspective (fig. 2.2), and obvious effort is made toward effecting pleasing color harmonies. Most houses also reflected the very latest design styles and ideas; early examples (1870s–early 1880s) are filled with Eastlake-style furniture, Japanese fans, and other accessories associated with the Aesthetic movement, and later the 1903 Kenilworth Inn and Christine Grier's 1905 book both have a sparer look, with up-to-date Arts and Crafts style furniture. To some extent this would reflect the imagery that was available—the latest trade catalogs would have featured the latest furniture—but the changing approach to space and design also suggests an informed or aesthetically trained eye. My earlier speculation that paper doll house making might have been an assigned art school project comes from the sophisticated designs I have seen, coupled with the evidence that some makers were associated with the Art Institute or the Decorative Arts Society. Whether or not this was so, the aesthetic sophistication of so many of the books reflected well-learned design lessons. Because aesthetic sensibility and training were so deeply intertwined in this period with female identity, the success of these albums would have added to the sense of personal competency and mastery that their makers felt.[43]

I offer one last speculation that, if accurate, would indicate how much pleasure the scrapbook houses afforded their makers—how powerful a hold they had on their imaginations. It is possible that girls who had made such albums when they were children in the 1880s and 1890s returned to the same occupation when they were grown women after the turn of the century; as adults they would have given finished books to a new set of youngsters. This hypothesis is based on diverse evidence. Most straightforwardly, we see that Marian Richards, who wrote in 1902 about the book house she had made as a child, was instructing adults who were interested in making them for little girls.[44] There was also a long hiatus after the first flurry of magazine features on paper doll houses were published around 1880; the next group of articles (including Richards's) only appeared after 1900. I have also seen an example in the Strong Museum that, based on the furnishings and clothing of the pasted-in figures, was made in the 1880s but has tucked-in paper dolls dressed in the style of the teens. Conceivably it was played with by more than one generation of girls. Whether or not the book house idea was resurrected for a second generation and the same individuals were involved in different phases of their lives, it is true that the genre stayed remarkably consistent for nearly fifty years. Flora Gill Jacobs, who made a paper doll house for a cousin two years her junior, remarked that "such residences were as cheerfully gaudy in the 1920s as in the nineties."[45] The style of the furnishings and clothing of the cut-out people was updated and the size of the books tended to get a little larger over time, but the type of represented rooms, the layout, and the general concept of the houses remained quite the same.

Commercial Book Houses

One indication of the popularity of the paper doll house genre is the fact that commercial versions were on the market by the early twentieth century. The idea of making a structure for paper dolls was not completely new when the book houses were introduced; one hundred years earlier, German children had already been able to buy sheets of pasteboard with printed images of furniture and people. The idea was that they would cut out the figures and arrange them on their own painted backgrounds. Similar sheet sets were available in the United States by the mid-nineteenth century. A series dubbed "The Girl's Delight," available for sale about 1850, included furniture, dolls, and the ceiling, floors and walls for stylish rooms. In 1910 Raphael Tuck, the famous manufacturer of colorful paper dolls, advertised a "Home Sweet Home for Dainty Dollies"—a flat printed sheet with twenty-two pieces of furniture that, when cut out and folded, would furnish two rooms. None of this preprinted imagery corresponded to the book format, although Mcloughlin Brothers, a New York company that patented a lithographed folding dollhouse in 1894, was clearly familiar with the conventions of the scrapbook house genre. Its printed images included details such as pasted-in homilies on the

58 wall and the same kind of twin pillow arrangement that appears in almost every house album. At about this same time, newspapers sometimes included art supplements with paper furniture that looked like it might fit into a scrapbook house—the *Boston Sunday Globe* printed one with parlor furniture in 1895, for example, and another named "At School" in 1896. The latter included rows of children at desks, a blackboard, and a prominent globe.[46]

It was after the turn of the century that a handful of published books expressly reproduced the paper doll house format. *The House That Glue Built,* written by Clara Andrews Williams and illustrated by her husband, George, included seven rooms of Arts and Crafts–style furniture, each of which came with a story about its inhabitants. *A Paper Home for Paper People,* published in 1909, included nine rooms of furniture and cut-out figures. All of the conventions of this so-called luxurious home followed the paper doll house model. There was a maid and a "mammy" figure (presumably the cook) and an idealized family consisting of a mother and father, boy and girl, and cat and dog. Interestingly, author Edith A. Root indicated that "Mr. and Mrs. Cut Paper" needed more than the basic furnishings she had provided. "It will be found that there are not nearly enough [articles] for the house," she wrote, and "the real pleasure will be found when magazines, catalogs and even the daily newspaper are searched to supply vases, pictures, books, rugs, hangings, etc. to complete the . . . home." Root's comment underlines the idea that the fascination in a house like this lay in working with its details. It implies, too, that individuals who received other such houses may also have personalized them by adding their own tiny accessories.[47]

I surmise that commercially published book houses like this followed upon and took advantage of the popularity of handmade paper doll houses; we might say that the authors hoped to capitalize on the folk genre and provide ready-made books for those who did not want to make their own. The last one I have found came out in 1921 in England, about the time the paper doll house phenomenon was fading (at least in America). *My Dolly's Home,* written by Doris Davey, is a brightly colored book that came with an envelope of paper dolls and a separate storybook called *Biddie's Adventure: The Story of My Dolly's Home.* Davey's book is printed in glossy, bright colors and is laid out like a prototypical handmade scrapbook house; its double-page spreads begin at the front gate, progress up to the bedrooms, down the back stairs to the kitchen, and out to a garden, orchard, and garage. Almost every room has some sort of openable door. The story is about a girl who receives a paper doll as a present and magically finds she has become small enough to follow the doll into her miniaturized world. The girl explores the doll's house, including looking into cupboards and joining a tea party in the garden. She later discovers her visit had just been a dream, but her parents give her a picture book where the same happy house is represented. *My Dolly's Home* repeats the house-within-a-house theme discussed above, and it underlines once again how much of the attraction of a scrapbook house was the aesthetic pleasure it afforded. The girl was entranced by the doll world because of its aesthetically saturated details such as rich color, enticing pictures and evocative descriptions (for example, "sky scooter" clouds, a fountain where the dolls "kept their own rainbows"). She pronounced it a pretty, happy place, "just like fairyland."[48]

The preprinted, or commercial, book house seems not to have been a long-lived phenomenon, but it is significant that it appeared when it did. By about 1910 American culture was undergoing monumental change. The wealth of consumer available products was no longer a novelty, and citizens were becoming more and more accustomed to having things made for them instead of making them themselves (for example, they were buying ready-to-wear clothes more routinely). Women were increasingly clamoring for a greater presence in public life, from the right to vote to paid positions in the corporate workplace, and were in turn functioning more and more in the world of "workplace values." The modernist aesthetic was beginning to take hold—an aesthetic that favored a sparer, less "cluttered" look, with less of the rich detail that had so characterized the Victorian era. Beginning at this time, in sum, there was less physical and symbolic separation of the public and private, more mixing between men and women, and an ever-greater involvement on the part of women in the marketplace mentality. The highly saturated, female world that the paper doll house represented was no longer as dominant. The commercial book houses seem to have come on the market during this transitional time, when that saturated world was still strong enough that the publishers assumed an interested audience, but when manufactured products—including prepackaged amusements—were already taken for granted. The new book houses were commodities. They might be made less "alienated" through the addition of additional personalized components, but they could not hold the psychic charge or deeply satisfying pleasure of the laboriously created handmade ones, because they represented a more generic, stranger's vision.

An Undervalued Artifact

If paper doll houses were so entrancing and were popular enough to convince commercial publishers that they might profitably bring out ready-made versions of their own, why has the genre been so little known? I have partially addressed this issue in the first chapter but will recap the explanations here in order to

60   reinforce how insidious and mutually reinforcing they are. The albums were, first
of all, made of fragile, throwaway materials. As Ringwalt put it in 1880, they were
put together with the "many unconsidered trifles [such as scraps of paper] that
constitute the treasured wealth of children." As Hoffman noted, furthermore,
they were made for plain handmade paper dolls. Hoffman believed these unas-
suming dolls held a "special corner in every girl's heart," but the very ordinariness
of the paper they were made of led to their dismissal in future generations. Paper,
especially lightweight, ephemeral varieties such as tissue and notebook paper, is
taken for granted and, to most, seems inherently valueless. (The very definition
of ephemera found on the *Merriam Webster-Online* site is "something of no lasting significance.")[49]

In addition to their ephemeral materials, the scrapbook houses have not been
taken seriously because they functioned, at least some of the time, as toys. Toys,
too, are generally thought of as "things of no value"—a definition that appears in
The Oxford English Dictionary. The dismissal goes beyond the identification of
toys with children. As described by Sidney Brower in a typology of the basic
human purposes of artifacts, a toy is meant to "titillate, but never tax" our minds
and senses; it is related to immediate satisfaction rather than anything lasting,
and it is not itself meant to last. Brower contrasts toys with *important* objects,
which he refers to as "masterpieces."[50] There are certainly individuals who understand this as a false dichotomy—the poet Baudelaire, for example, stated, "The
toy is the child's initiation into [the application of] art . . . , and when he has come
into man's estate no perfect work of art will ever arouse in him the same warmth,
or the same enthusiasm, or the same confidence."[51] The dominant paradigm has
not yet fully shifted, however, and the understanding of objects such as the paper
doll house is not yet generally filtered through the poet's eyes. The scrapbook
house is still more typically associated with trivial "girlish pastimes" that are eventually outgrown.

Finally, the domestic imagery of the scrapbook houses has been a major
strike against them. They were not only made in and for the home; they were
about the home, and since the prevailing culture undervalues that domain, anything with such subject matter remains relatively invisible. The book houses
were, as we know, *collage* albums, and although art historians have judged collage
to be one of the most important categories of twentieth-century art, these domestic colleges were not even perceived as part of the genre until very recently. The
accepted story had been that collage was "discovered" or "invented" by twentieth-
century male artists such as Picasso and Joseph Cornell. Some authors had
acknowledged that nineteenth-century women and girls worked in a collagelike

fashion, but dismissed their efforts as "household art" fashioned by mere "amateurs." Harriet Janis wrote of nineteenth-century "folk collage," for example, as a "simple pastime" that was "no concern of serious artists."[52] Diane Waldman argued that the special appeal of collage is the way it brings "the incongruous into meaningful congress with the ordinary and gives the uneventful, the commonplace, the ordinary a magic of its own," but she did not appreciate the commonplace imagery of the household or see the magic it had been put to. Although she argued that collage is a form that emphasizes process as much as end product, she only saw the process of making a paper doll house as busywork. Linda Hartigan was the first to recognize the artistic significance of the women's collage albums, in 1993. She not only argued that the collage form was already well established in these women's pastimes, but demonstrated that Cornell himself collected and was undoubtedly influenced by collage-filled scrapbook albums. She pointed out that many of the qualities that Cornell is known for, including intimate scale and love of detail; contradictions of scale, material, and idea; and the transformation of the imagery of mass production, were long evident in the paper doll house genre.[53]

This inability to appreciate images of and work emanating from the home is a part of the devaluing of the background—of women's lives and work—that I hope to rectify. It is time that the inexorable fascination, the pleasure, and indeed the magic of these albums be fully recognized, just as it is time to acknowledge the creativity and artistic exploration of the house makers. I do not to mean to imply that the paper doll house should be looked at apart from its social context and its function as a conceptual house; I find, in fact, that laudatory as it is, Hartigan's treatment of isolated pages as collage compositions does not tell the whole story. The scrapbook house can be simultaneously understood as an early and underappreciated form of collage, a vehicle through which girls were socialized into their culturally accepted roles, a theatrical form of personal expression and aesthetic exploration, and a means of feeling intense pleasure and satisfaction. We must recognize the intimacy and everydayness of the book house as its *strength* and understand that the home and its activities—the domestic context—was its source of creative imagery and expression.

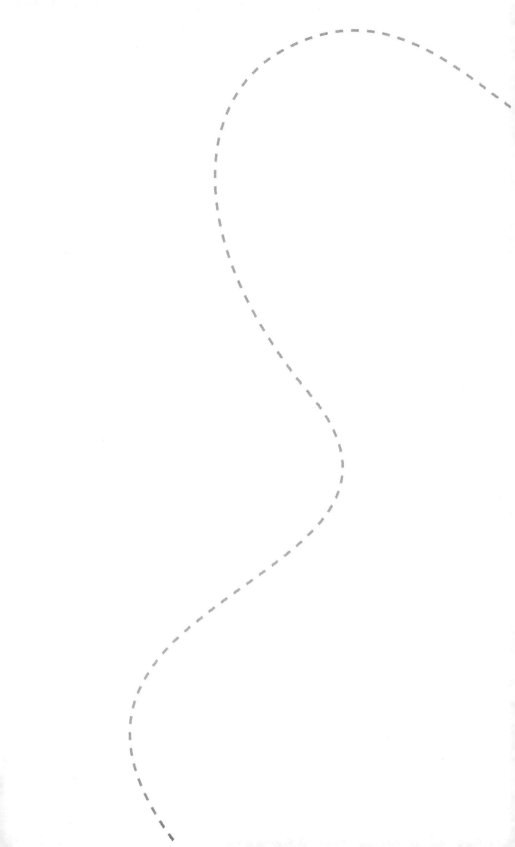

Chapter Three

PARTIES AND PARTY GIVERS

The rooms should be decorated to represent the frozen northland. . . . Use draperies of soft white cheesecloth and cotton, over which silver dust has been sprinkled. Grasses and leaves may be crystallized by suspending them in a strong solution of alum and water; these much resemble icy formations. The lights should be shaded in silvery white paper. The refreshments may consist of ices, ice cream, silver cake and bon-bons wrapped in silver paper.

—FROM NELLIE MUSTAIN,
POPULAR AMUSEMENTS FOR INDOORS AND OUT-OF-DOORS, 1902

Introduction

This chapter explores the conventions and meanings of the luncheons, teas, showers, and other small-scale entertainments that women staged from about 1890 to 1930. I am most concerned with the parties or entertainments that women gave for each other in their own homes, although there was no clear demarcation between those events and the ones they organized for coeducational groups or fund raising purposes in more public spaces. The same lemon-theme party might be used, for example, at a private tea, a bazaar or supper designed to help pay off church debts, or a program for a YMCA youth group. Would-be up-to-date hostesses could consult books such as *"Dame Curtsey's" Art of Entertaining for All Occasions,* which was filled with "novel schemes" adaptable for "old and young, at home, church, club and school." Author Ellye Howell Glover (also known as "Madame Merri" and "Dame Curtsey") introduced this volume with an acknowledgment of the importance of "the social side of life," stating that "every mother, teacher, club-woman, or guild-worker" would sooner or later confront the problem of "what to do and how to do it" for entertaining. Her book was offered as a "collection of ideas which [might] be enlarged upon or curtailed to suit the requirements and ingenuity of the individual."[1]

Much of the advice literature stressed this kind of adaptation. For example, a simple get-together where women spent time knitting and sharing lunch or tea could be easily transformed into a fund-raising event suitable for a woman's club or church society if the knitters met in a clubroom or church parlor and paid a small admission fee and/or donated their knitted objects to charity. It could also be turned into a "yarn party" if the ladies brought their husbands or male friends to provide entertainment. As the women worked at their knitting, the men would compete for prizes by telling their best stories.[2] While there were general norms or conventions for different types of entertainments, there were no hard and fast rules. An entertainment with a butterfly or flower theme, for example, usually implied a women's dress-up party, and bridal showers were usually female-only affairs, but even here there were exceptions.

Despite the permeability of these categories, a quick review of the conventions and terms in common use at the turn of the century should still be helpful. A "social" or "sociable" generally implied a coeducational get-together, usually held at a school, church, or clubhouse. "Stunt parties" could take place either in a public space or in the home, but they typically had male performers and also involved both men and women. When the gathering involved festivities such as music and dancing, it might be dubbed a "frolic" or "fete." However, "fete" also functioned as another word for "party" or served as a synonym for "festival" or "fair." The latter word implied an array of booths or separate attractions. Fairs often included goods for sale and were frequently held for fund-raising purposes—the word "bazaar," which was frequently substituted for fair by the late nineteenth century, is more familiar to us today. Some fairs or bazaars were so elaborate that they incorporated dramatic performances, parades, concerts, or dances, and most included costumed salespeople, decorated booths, and fortune-tellers. (At the other extreme, some were small-scale sales or only slight variations of the familiar church supper.) Other public events that specifically implied live music and dancing included "germans" [sic], "cotillions," and "kermisses."[3]

At-home events ran the gamut from formal dinner parties to relatively casual teas. The dinner party, a nineteenth-century phenomenon, was a social ritual characterized by a display of goods, including abundant food, elegant and function-specific dishes, glassware, and table linen. By the end of the century, even families of relatively modest means could occasionally afford to give such parties, and doing so became an important part of a family's set of social obligations. While women were the ones who organized and prepared them, they were not really women's events; rather, with their emphasis on conspicuous consumption and competitive display, they were expressions of the more dominant "workplace" or foreground values discussed in chapter 1. The irony of the dinner party, according to Katherine Grier, is that although it "seemed to be a sensual call to physical pleasure," it was actually a constrained event with strict rules.[4]

By the turn of the century, however, the formal multicourse dinner party was often supplanted by a lighter meal. "Suppers" also took place in the evening, but they were not major repasts. They might be scheduled on a Sunday after a substantial midday meal or either before or after a theatrical performance. A "collation" was a "little supper" of this sort. "Chafing dish suppers," where a simple one-pot dish such as curried eggs could be placed at the table, became popular soon after the turn of the century. "Breakfasts" were morning entertainments, although they were often held late enough in the day that we would now refer to them as "brunches," and the foods were often indistinguishable from what was served at lunch. The food was simpler and more limited at these events. These were most popular before World War I. There were also an increasing number of the female-oriented entertainments examined in this chapter, characterized less by a display of abundance than by an emphasis on amusing and entertaining presentation. "Luncheons" became very popular. The diminutive ending of the word (that is, it was a luncheon rather than a lunch) was a clue that this was a ladies' event. In the parlance of the day, a luncheon featured "dainty dining." "Dainty" food was "refined" and nonfilling, and it tended toward a miniaturized scale. It often included what we would now call finger foods, such as crustless sandwiches. Visual appearance counted more than sustenance. The "suggestions for luncheons" section of *Hints on Entertaining*, published by the Minneapolis YWCA in 1897, for example, described "a dainty arrangement in the way of fruit" that consisted of hollowed-out orange skins filled with fruit jelly and decorated with artificial orange blossoms.[5] (I discuss such refreshments in more detail below.)

"Teas" were perhaps the most common of the women-only entertainments. A tea was usually an afternoon event (times varied, but 4:00 or 5:00 was typical) that rarely involved more than twelve guests. The idea of the "tea party" seems to have gained favor in America during the Centennial era (that is, around 1876), when it was linked with patriotism and democracy. Although the phrase might be associated with a Revolutionary political act involving tea dumping, these parties were domestic pastimes built around tea drinking, which was perceived as a quintessentially colonial activity. There was a spate of "Martha Washington Teas" in this period, in fact, that essentially functioned as costumed colonial reenactments. After the Centennial, teas were based on other themes, but dress-up remained a common element. Afternoon tea parties were certainly not unique to America—they had long been popular in England, for example, and are rightfully

66   thought of as an English import. Nevertheless they seem to have had a different trajectory in this country and often a more playful tone. English teas held more distinct class associations; as one nineteenth-century source explained it, the custom began there "as a needed refreshment [for the upper class] after a day's hunting ... or out-of-door exercise, before dressing for [a late] dinner."[6] Teas in English country houses involved both men and women, and they were not costumed theme events, although well-heeled turn-of-the-century Englishwomen did sometimes change into "tea gowns," which were relatively informal, almost boudoir-like garments. Tea gowns were also occasionally worn in America, although I have not seen them mentioned in any American advice book.

In this country, teas were usually known by their theme or purpose—for example, "pink tea," "rosebud tea," "musical tea," "sorority tea"—but there were other event names, such as "kettle drum," that essentially referred to teas as well. The origin of the latter title is a bit obscure, although it was clearly English. It is variously reported as relating to the tea kettle, referring to a London tea at which people spoke so fast and loud as to suggest the noise of a rattling drum, or stemming from the at-home afternoon receptions given for one another by officers' wives in India where light refreshments were served on a drum head.[7] The term was popular in the late nineteenth century, but it subsequently seems to have fallen out of common use.

By the second decade of the twentieth century, there were even more occasions for women's entertainments. The new popularity of bridge and related games led to an enthusiasm for card parties. These were often folded into the ladies' luncheon or tea (the favored time was between 3:00 and 6:00 P.M.) and could feature the same kind of thematic decorations and foodstuffs as these other entertainments. Suggestions also abounded for the increasingly expected "announcement party" (announcing an engagement) or wedding "shower party," which was a special variation of the familiar luncheon or tea. According to the advice giver Emily Burt, the announcement party was hostessed by the engaged girl herself or by her mother or sister; in contrast, the shower party was usually given by a nonrelative. Centered as they were around the transition into marriage, these conceptually related events were in a sense the most feminized of the women's entertainments. There were also parties held to honor girls making their social debut, graduating from high school or college, or embarking on long trips. Summer entertainments such as lawn or garden parties could be coed but were particularly popular among women. "Porch parties," held outdoors on presumably hot days, were typically similarly informal female get-togethers.[8]

The rise of homosocial entertainments of this sort corresponded with the rise and popularity of homosocial organizations. Women's clubs and associations exploded at the turn of the century; the National Federation of Women's Clubs, as a case in point, counted approximately one hundred thousand members by 1896, ten years after its founding, and nearly a million by 1912. Groups had various purposes, ranging from ethnic or religious affiliation (the National Association of Colored Women), to shared interest (a literary society), to furthering social change (the National Consumer League, the Women's Christian Temperance Union), or establishing hereditary pedigrees (the Daughters of the American Revolution). This was also the period in which the National Home Economics Association was founded, leading to an institutionalized gender-specific high school and college curriculum based on "domestic science." (Cooking schools loosely affiliated with this association were largely responsible for the rise in "dainty dining" cuisine.)[9] At the same time, men also joined together in record numbers in gender-based fraternal organizations and benevolent associations. The turn of the century was also the peak of the fraternal movement in America; one source claims that in 1897 more than one in four men belonged to such an order.[10] Membership in fraternal organizations and women's clubs dropped considerably after World War I, and many more social activities involved mixed groups of men and women, but women-only parties remained normative until World War II.[11]

Who were the women involved in these entertainments? What was the audience for the rash of magazine articles and books filled with suggestions for the up-to-date hostess? The picture may seem confusing because references to social debuts or embarking on long trips would imply a relatively elite or upper-class group of women, but my assertion about "democratic" tea parties and reference to an instruction book published by the YWCA indicate something else. As mentioned in chapter 1, the profile did change over time; the entertainments became increasingly populist, particularly after World War I. Even at the turn of the century, however, this was not an exclusively upper-class phenomenon. Just as the paper doll house or collage album discussed in the last chapter might represent a luxurious house with many servants even though it was made by someone without a great deal of money, so too was the *image* of the party of this era cast in elite terms, even though actual events were often staged by middle-class individuals. The broad audience and class permeability was tacitly acknowledged in the 1897 *Hints on Entertaining*. The unnamed author included instructions for a coming-out tea and more than once intimated that servants were necessary for successful parties, but spoke of the relatively undeveloped state of entertainment in America (I interpret this as a less-rigid class code) and discussed ways that people without very much money might manage dinner parties of their own. Books such as *Indoor Merrymaking and Table Decorations* included "party stories of society matrons," but once these appeared in print, any woman could effectively create a similar party of her own. Grier points out that while most turn-of-the-century cookbooks and household manuals were directed to women who could afford a full-time servant, that demographic in reality accounted for only about 15 percent of American households. She feels we can understand the advice literature as a "collective representation" of prevailing social ideals.[12]

Much of the party-giving advice first appeared in women's general-interest or "service" magazines, which burgeoned in popularity and influence in the 1880s. These had a combined circulation in the millions and were generally aimed at women of modest income (as *Ladies' Home Journal* put it, its readers were concerned with "plain living and high thinking"). Their articles related to various aspects of homemaking and women's lives.[13] All included regular helpful features on parties and entertaining, treating them as an expected and accepted part of community life. Beginning in the 1890s, for example, *Ladies' Home Journal* included a monthly column called "Pleasant Evenings at Home," and it soon added another, "The Minister's Social Helper," which offered instructions on church suppers, parties for young people, bazaars, and other such activities. *Woman's Home Companion* ran a similar column about entertainments entitled "How to Pay Off Church Debts." By the early 1900s, *Good Housekeeping* introduced a regular section called "The Hostess," which featured up to eight or nine kinds of events in each issue. Readers generally felt these were "their" magazines. Tellingly, they were encouraged to write in to these columns, describing innovative ways in which they had recently entertained. They could earn a few dollars ("pin money") for published descriptions, and as many of the winning entries talked about pinching pennies, this seems to have been an attractive proposition.[14] While a certain amount of cash was necessary to host a party, ingenuity could go a long way in coming up with less costly attractions. Clearly it was not just the wealthy who were concerned or involved with these entertainments.

I believe that the prevailing American ideals embedded in these entertainments had as much or more to do with cultural sophistication as it did with money. Party-giving instructions were directed to an audience of well-educated individuals, who, especially in the prewar period, were conversant with literary conventions and the canon of important writers and philosophical ideas. Whole parties or fundraising events could be built around literary themes. There were "Dickens Bazaars," for example, where booths would represent various novels by the English writer, and there were fairs dubbed "Fete of the Heroines," where saleswomen would dress as Becky Sharp, Juliet, Alice in Wonderland, or other characters from popular literature. At-home parties followed the same trajectory. The "Literary Leaves

Tea" featured in the 1896 volume *Day Entertainments*, for example, was conceived of as a seasonal entertainment. Punning on the idea of leaves, it mixed autumnal and bookish references. It was assumed that guests had at least a passing knowledge of literary figures that would equip them to participate in party games. "Conundrums," in which guests were asked to solve riddles, were a popular pastime. At the Literary Leaves Tea, they had to come up with an author's name that matched a humorous description. For example, "Bunyan" was the solution to the phrase, "A disagreeable fellow to have on your foot"; "Pope" was the correct author for "Many pilgrims have knelt to him." Another entertainment mentioned in the same book was a "Poet's Tea," in which guests were required to write a poem with a particular meter and rhyme.[15] This, of course, was a demanding skill. Another common practice at late-nineteenth-century entertainments was to write the luncheon or dinner menu with lines of poetry or quotations that metaphorically referred to the proffered dish. A suitable epigraph for the menu as a whole might be a line from *The Taming of the Shrew*, "Feast with the best, and welcome to my house." Tag lines for specific menu items would follow. Asparagus would be accompanied with the line, "Fingers were made before forks" (Jonathan Swift, *Polite Conversations*); "chicken halibut" with the phrase, "From the rude sea's enraged and foamy mouth" (*Twelfth Night*); sorbet with "So coldly sweet" (Byron, "Giaour"). I think of this practice as akin to citing biblical verses in support of various political or moral agendas. In both cases, the person coming up with the verses had to have a strong command of the source material. While there were reference works in print that could be consulted for this type of annotation, the very fact that these literary references were expected and included underlines how much cultural weight they carried.[16]

Some of the entertainments were expressly organized for groups that came together for intellectual improvement. For example, when "conversation clubs," whose members were expected to share ideas and present topics of interest to one another, met at one another's homes for luncheon, dainty food and table decorations might make the conversations seem more lively. In her 1891 book *Home Games and Parties*, Mrs. Hamilton Mott spoke of utilizing the "Fairy Folk Frolic" idea for a "literary society session." Members would offer moon-theme presentations at this event, such as a scientific talk about the tides or lunar eclipses or a biography of Dr. Moon, who "gave light to the blind" by developing the Braille system.[17]

Another indication of the educated ideal that shaped these parties is that there were many references in the women's magazines—including in the entertainment columns—to prestigious colleges. As I explained in my book *Bazaars*

70   *and Fair Ladies,* entertainments could include college-related themes or products, with decorations or sale objects such as picture frames in "Harvard Green"
or "Princeton Red." Those sponsoring or enjoying the entertainment need not
have had any personal connection with the Ivy League. In its list of suggested
themes, *Entertainment for All Seasons* (1904) included a college fair, with each
booth representing a different university. The college theme was an organizing
idea, no different from others that sparked the imagination, such as "Japan" or
"Gypsy Encampment," but this does demonstrate that institutions of higher
learning resonated with the popular imagination.[18]

The prevailing ideals that both shaped and were represented in the entertainment literature did not include ethnic diversity; a white, Christian audience was
presumed. As indicated, many of the entertainments took place in and were associated with the social life of the church, and suggestions for seasonal entertainments routinely included celebrations of Christian holidays such as Easter. Moreover, the entertainments not only reinforced prevailing racist stereotypes, but
routinely incorporated them into the amusement. *Parties* magazine described a
"Plantation Party" in 1927, for example, that included costumed "picaninnies"
and other slaves, and "little piccaninny dolls" were suggested in 1926 as suitable
place card holders for a Lincoln's Birthday party. It was not uncommon for participants to come to a party in blackface or to dress as Indian maids or warriors
(see chapter 4). My impression is that this kind of racially based dress-up occurred
especially often at coeducational events, but women were certainly fully com-
plicit in hegemonic stereotyping.[19]

As indicated, there was over time an increasingly informal quality to women's
entertainments. The discussions in the late-nineteenth-century advice literature
often spoke of reciprocal social obligations, but the emphasis shifted by the teens
to "having fun." The shift reflected the general democratization of American culture, as well as the general increase in available or leisure time.[20] Entertainment
advice literature peaked in the "Jazz Age" (1920s), a period often associated with
hedonism and abandon. More suggestions for entertaining were carried in the
regular monthly magazines in this decade than at any other time, and two new
magazines appeared which were devoted exclusively to this subject. The *Hostess,*
"A Magazine of Inspiration and Suggestion" that was launched in 1922, claimed
its appeal was "neither to the rich nor the poor. If we were to indicate our field in
a phrase . . . [it would be] the gentlewoman who entertains." *Dennison's Party
Magazine* (later simply called *Parties*) was launched in 1927. This was published
by the Dennison crepe paper company, which was suggesting ways its product
could be used. In the first issue the editor claimed, "We will show [the general

public] how to create the real party spirit . . . how to make the occasion gay and 71 colorful." Crepe paper was relatively inexpensive, and the targeted audience was decidedly middle class. While the life of the proverbial average American was hardly hedonistic, leisure activities *were* of popular concern. This postwar period was the heyday of the Recreation movement described in chapter 1, and many of those who gave suggestions for parties worked as recreation leaders with church or school groups or organizations such as the YMCA. Recreation workers were disproportionately female.[21]

Many Jazz Age parties actually stressed the *idea* of leisure. They might be based on a theme such as golf, for example, or be staged as a mock resort. Again, while these topics might seem to refer to upper-class pastimes, even formerly elitist activities had filtered down to the middle class, and anyone could play with them as imaginative fantasy. The wealthy themselves were actually less likely to entertain at home by the 1920s—increasingly, they took guests to a restaurant or club—so that even the dinner party, which had once been so much a matter of conspicuous display, had largely shifted to a more informal amusement.[22]

Because it was assumed that the hostess would be doing all of the work herself at most Jazz Age entertainments, contemporary books such as Edna Tipton's *Table Service for the Hostess* featured "easy entertainments" such as picnics, card parties, or afternoon teas where all refreshments could be placed on a portable tea wagon. Instructions increasingly focused on amusing activities or decorations rather than proper form or complex repasts. In her 1921 book, *Entertainment for All Occasions,* Corinne Wentworth described an up-to-date dinner party exclusively in terms of the enticing miniature scene—a kind of diorama or tableau—that would dominate the table. This tableau was so much the main attraction that Wentworth did not even discuss the menu; instead she wrote at length about creating a farm effect with rows of sand and a stick-candy rail fence and procuring toys and dolls to populate the landscape.[23] This model was particularly important at women-only entertainments such as wedding showers and announcement parties that were increasingly popular and prevalent in the 1920s and 1930s. They emphasized picturesque, charming presentation above all else.[24]

As references to golf parties imply, the thematic content of parties often drew from what we would generally think of as popular culture. Topics were often timely, but always lighthearted and nonpolitical—an entertainment was essentially an escape, and thus it had to be noncontroversial and amusing. There was a spate of suffragette and "New Woman" parties at the turn of the century, for example, but they were humorous—they played with the idea of liberated women and tended to exaggerate elements of reform dress.[25] Popular imagery could also

72 come from the latest technology. Turn-of-the-century parties often incorporated imagery or ideas from the railroad, but by the 1920s, "Automobile Lunches" (the auto was a leitmotif, not a location), or "aeroplane" decorations were more au courant.

In keeping with the emphasis on escapism, many other themes were based on a generalized sense of nostalgia ("Ye Olde Fashioned Hearte Partie") or a more timeless idea such as a "Sweet Pea Tea" or "Springtime." Such conventions would now be associated with children's entertainments, but it was not until after World War I that fairyland themes began to seem inappropriate for adults. As the Recreation movement grew stronger and youth programming was of increasing concern, such themes tended to move further down the age scale. Formerly adult pastimes began to be recommended for school and playground groups, and what had been considered suitable for older teenagers—girls coming of age and just entering womanhood—were suggested primarily for younger children.[26] The kind of "calendar party" *Good Housekeeping* magazine suggested as a girl's entertainment in 1930, for example, was essentially a recycled version of a party thought to be suitable for grown women a few decades before. The changing demographic and juvenilization was strengthened even further after World War II. We must remember that this kind of play did not imply childishness or a lack of intelligence or choice. Rather, it was evidence of the fact that these party givers were unafraid of acting childlike.

The Advice Literature

I will return to the conventions and qualities of women's parties shortly, but first I need to say more about the advice literature I have been referring to. As stated, party-giving advice began to proliferate in America in the 1890s, especially in popular women's magazines. It can be considered a subset of domestic advice literature, which was itself an increasingly important phenomenon in the later nineteenth century. Sarah Leavitt explored this subject in *From Catharine Beecher to Martha Stewart: A Cultural History of Domestic Advice*. She pointed out that the roots of the genre lay in etiquette manuals, and much of the early advice carried a rather moralistic overlay. This receded with time, but even in the 1920s and 1930s the genre was associated with wholesomeness and goodness, and the things that its spokeswomen advocated were associated with a happy home life. Who were these spokeswomen—individuals who would seem to have been in a position of some influence since, sooner or later, most women found themselves concerned with entertaining? The majority of advice givers were professional writers who essentially specialized in subjects of interest to women. Some also wrote fiction or poetry and/or wrote about gender-identified topics such as interior design, decorative arts, or antiques collecting. A few had regular editorial jobs with the women's magazines, while others worked on a freelance basis. In the case of the party-giving advice, some were particularly aligned with Christian organizations (groups such as Bible House, the Epworth League, and the YWCA effectively functioned as women's publishers).[27]

I have tried to track down information on the women who were particularly associated with party-giving advice and have found (to the extent that I could find information at all) that they fit the profile that Leavitt outlines; they were, in fact, often the same women who gave advice about other matters. Emily Rose Burt, who published four books about entertaining and bazaar giving between 1919 and 1928, graduated from Mt. Holyoke in 1909 and, after working as a teacher, held editorial positions at *Women's Home Companion, Good Housekeeping,* and *The Designer.* She also wrote children's stories. Louise Dew, author of the 1904 book *Entertainments for All Seasons,* was a journalist who wrote for outlets like the *Detroit Tribune* and the *Michigan Christian Advocate,* but was especially identified with women's magazines. Over time, she was on the staff of *Ladies' Illustrated Journal, Smart Styles, Woman's Home Companion,* and *Lady's World.* She also wrote books on horticulture and pets and was known for her charitable work. Winnifred Fales, co-author with Mary Northend of *The Party Book,* published books on home decoration, housekeeping, and cooking and short stories with homey titles such as "The Fire on the Hearth." Northend herself was a consummate writer who published eleven books and hundreds of articles in periodicals such as *McCall's, Outlook, Modern Priscilla, Good Housekeeping,* and *Century.* She specialized in design subjects and promoted the Colonial Revival style, in part through her photographs of old New England homes. Between 1906 and 1936 Northend took more than thirty-five thousand images. Ella Shannon Bowles, author of *Practical Parties,* also published cookbooks, travel articles, and volumes on antiques and crafts. Her books included *Handmade Rugs* and *Homespun Handicrafts* (see fig. 6.2). Alice Bradley, whose entertainment advice appeared in *Parties* magazine and *Women's Home Companion,* was a cooking specialist associated with the Fanny Farmer cooking school. Alice Crowell Hoffman, another frequent contributor to *Parties,* was known as a writer of children's books and juvenile poetry (her poems bore titles such as "A Pumpkin Seed" and "Crocus Children") and Marie Irish, author of *Novel Notions for Nifty Entertainments,* was known as a poet of seasonal verse. In sum, entertainment advice was an arena for some of the most prolific female writers of the day.[28]

Women's voices so far outnumbered men's in the entertainment advice field that it was clearly accepted as a female bailiwick. In the three years that *Parties* magazine was published, for example, it included bylined articles by forty-nine

74 women (many of whom contributed multiple times) and five men. Some male Recreation movement leaders wrote on programming ideas, but their contributions were relatively sparse. Where men did publish suggestion books, they tended to be about stunts and games or about ways individuals might become "the life of the party." Women's advice centered on creating the festive atmosphere that would make everyone feel included and amused. Given the fact that the female advice givers were well educated (some went to college; all were well-read and articulate), it is not surprising that the entertainment advice genre was aligned with women's education, and both spoke to and encouraged a literate and cultured public.[29]

These advice givers must have had a strong role in shaping the entertainments of the era. Many individuals wrote over a long period of time, and their suggestions appeared and were marketed in multiple formats. Party-giving advice columns often first appeared in periodicals, and then the same suggestions were later collected into books. The features in the 1896 volume *Day Entertainments* had all originated in the *Delineator* magazine, for example, and Theresa Wolcott's 1911 book, *The Minister's Social Helper,* consisted of reprints from her writings in *Ladies' Home Journal.* Wolcott's name began appearing with entertainment advice as early as 1906, and it still appeared in *Parties* magazine in the late 1920s. Emily Rose Burt wrote on these same topics from about 1911 to the early 1930s, and she too published books based on articles she had written while entertainment editor of *Good Housekeeping.* Several women's magazines also sold copies of particular suggestions well after they originally appeared or packaged previously published advice columns into thematic booklets that could be purchased separately. For example, *Good Housekeeping* noted in April 1925 that the "hearts of lettuce party" it had suggested for the previous Valentine's Day was so successful that they would send out the instructions for ten cents. The magazine boasted that the party was a highly adaptable affair that "could work equally well as a luncheon, tea, home affair, school or class party, or social." Upon request, the same magazine also sent out booklets with targeted themes, including "Around the Year in Holidays" and "For the Engaged Girl and Her Friends."

Since many of the same party suggestions were in circulation for a long time, ideas were continually recycled, and one can speak only of a general evolution rather than a strictly linear progression of the genre. The advice offered in the periodicals was the freshest and can thus be read as the most immediate expression of the popular culture. It is also important to remember that, influential advice givers notwithstanding, this was in many ways a highly interactive phenomenon. Magazine writers and editors were always looking for new ideas—the word "novelty" was almost a trope in the advice columns—and, as indicated, actively solicited ideas from readers. It is sometimes difficult to determine if an idea was sent in by a reader or was really the contribution of the editor, for many of the party features were presented as journalistic reports of what was going on around the country. In the "Home Entertainments" section of *Goodform: A Magazine for the People* in January 1893, for example, Carrie May Ashton began descriptions of various events with introductory lines such as "At a recent tea given by a leader in society. . . ," "A Violet Tea was recently given by a circle of Kings' Daughters . . . ," "A pleasing feature of a recent dinner was . . . ," or "A forget-me-not luncheon was recently given in honor of a prospective bride."[30] Although there was no specificity as to time and place, the implication was that these were actual entertainments. The impression was furthered by the fact that some magazines, notably *Ladies' Home Journal,* often included photographs with party descriptions. I believe there was a dynamic feedback loop with this kind of advice. Readers must have perused it hungrily and adopted it for their own ends, and then their events were in turn reported on and further modified by others. In a sense this may have functioned almost as a national "folk" tradition, using the women's press as a medium of transmission.[31]

There were conventions in the way the advice was presented. The idea of looking for something novel was used almost as a contrivance. Ashton's description of a "sachet souvenir supper" begins with a familiar, almost formulaic litany: "The entertainment committee of a young ladies' society had racked their brains in vain for something new and novel. Kaffee klatches, crazy socials, Japanese and pink teas . . . candy folics and conundrum socials had all been given, and were fairly successful. At last a bright idea struck one of the girls, and she was heard to exclaim, 'Why not have a sachet party?'"[32] The suggestions had a particularly literary quality in the period before World War I. Some descriptions included poems, as in Adele Mendel's *Indoor Merrymaking and Table Decorations.* Some were written as stories. *Day Entertainments and Other Functions* (1896) began many of its features with a bit of dialogue:

> "Do let me give them a tea," pleaded Annie earnestly.
> "I must think the matter over a little," answered her mother. "It would be very pleasant, I admit."
> "There are just twelve of us girls in the graduating class," continued Annie, "and that is such a convenient number to arrange for."

The agreed-upon event was a "Rosebud Tea," suitable for these girls "just budding into womanhood."[33]

A well-crafted description of an entertainment was itself highly saturated. It would have brought the reader into the rich space of the event, allowing her to

76 taste, feel, smell and otherwise experience the party in advance. I know many people today who read cookbooks in this way, perusing them for the sheer pleasure of imagining what is described. Sarah Leavitt explained the popularity of Martha Stewart advice columns similarly. She classified Stewart's output as a kind of "domestic fantasy literature," noting that the very act of reading Stewart's magazine or watching her television program helped people project themselves into a "dream." In Leavitt's words, Stewart helped make "their lives, or at least their day-dreams, more delicious, more unique, more decadent, more inviting."[34] The advice givers of the past, like Stewart, were able to write in such a way as to help create and maintain these dreams and good feelings.

Qualities and Conventions

Let's turn now to a closer look at the conventions of these women's entertainments to see how they functioned as a means of cultivating a saturated world. First we must understand the importance of the theme. An entertainment of this type ideally functioned as a time apart, a holistic, self-contained experience in which each element was embellished and made special; a party was a well-choreographed production, where every element, from the invitation to the table decorations to the party favors, was coordinated. Planning the event around an overriding theme was a good way to make this work, as it helped the hostess come up with creative ideas and make the details come alive. A party giver working with the construct of a "Fan Tea," for example, could play with the fan *shape*—fan-shaped pieces of cake, fan-shaped almond and flower holders, napkins folded as fans (fig. 3.1); fan *imagery*—pictures of fans mounted on the walls, painted on party favors, or pinned to the hostess' dress; fan-related *stories;* and *words* that might contain the word "fan" within them. She could incorporate fans of different types of materials and wildly different scales—from tiny plaited colored paper decorations on the dinner plate to huge fans positioned over the central chandelier.

FIG. 3.1.
Fanciful folded napkins were a relatively simple and inexpensive way of dressing up one's table. The swan-shaped image appeared in *Godey's Lady's Book,* November, 1873. Similar elaborate designs were still popular in the next century, as seen in the rose and fan shapes from the 1923 book *The Art of the Table.*

In the course of this discussion I have already mentioned a range of different themes—parties based on literary references; on foods such as lemons, oranges, or lettuce hearts; on the image of the plantation or the character of Martha Washington; and on fairyland or its components. Other themes focused on the seasons and holiday celebrations (there were countless ideas based around hearts for Valentine's Day—see fig. 3.2); exotic places (Japan, Cuba, Hawaii); or characters (Alice in Wonderland, gypsies, and so on). Historical or patriotic themes were popular, with variations ranging from Colonial and Quaker teas to Washington's Birthday parties. Themes might also re-

FIG. 3.2.
The idea that women would dress to match the rest of the decor at their parties is clear in this image representing a Valentine's Day party. The illustration is from Lilian Day's *Social Entertainments*, 1914.

volve around particular pastimes, such as crossword puzzles or canoeing, or around conceits, such as a letter of the alphabet, "the spinster," "poverty," "The Five Senses," or "The Seven Ages of Woman." Color was such an important organizing device that there were also many events based either primarily on a single hue (orange or violet were common, as they could also allude to fruits or flowers) or on the entire rainbow. At a rainbow party the color-matching idea was taken through every hue—violet foods, decorations, and favors would predominate in one area, for example, blue in another, and yellow in a third. Every element was considered; if a table were devoted to the color yellow, for example, the menu might consist of such foods as custards or other egg dishes and angel and sponge cakes, all set out amid daffodils under a sunny umbrella. Another broad theme was "work": there were "spring-cleaning parties" and "house-cleaning luncheons" that turned icons of women's labor into child's play. The table centerpiece of one such luncheon consisted of toy brooms and brushes; the favors consisted of feather dusters; and decorations included scattered camphor balls.[35]

A house-cleaning luncheon stands as an overt or explicit expression of the way these entertainments transformed women's ordinary work into a heightened experience. The hostess was in a sense the primary player, but when she invited other women to join her, they too entered the inversion of ordinary reality where work became play. Such entertainments stimulated humor, creativity, and a

78

FIG. 3.3.
The decorations for an April Fool's party described in *Social Entertainments* included a topiary tree made of cauliflower, a feather-duster palm tree, and "fruits" made of garlic cloves.

childlike fun. While they were often built around intellectually interesting, abstract concepts and drew on awareness of world events for their panoply of puns and associative games, these events allowed participants to leave their troubles and serious concerns behind.[36]

In addition to their emphasis on playfulness, the entertainments engendered good feelings through other "saturated" qualities. Sensual stimulation was all-important. The visual sense was obviously heightened through an imaginative use of shape, color (at the Literary Leaves Tea, each guest found a rose at her place setting that was particularly keyed to her individual facial tones), texture and scale. The foods were a taste treat as well as a visual delight, and they might provide varied textural experiences as well—a custard would slide over the diner's tongue, a cake would seem to melt in the mouth, and so on. Touch, or tactile sensation, was catered to in many ways, as at a "Snow Fete" party, where featured textures ranged from fur to powdered mica. There was even an emphasis in the party descriptions on kinetic sensation. The hostess of the Snow Fete wore stars that "quivered and twinkled" as she moved, for example, and, at the Literary Leaves Tea, an oak bough was set up to sway "as if caressed by a wandering zephyr." The sense of hearing was also involved through the rustling or tinkling sounds of costumes, and hostesses commonly offered musical interludes. The Fan Tea featured music from *The Mikado*, with some of the guests acting as the Three Little Maids from School (they waved their oversized fans in choreographed motion). The sense of smell was ideally engaged as well through an emphasis on aromatic foods and perfumes.[37]

Women's parties were inclusive (at least for those invited) and fostered a sense of community. Wealth was generally not on display as much as creativity; rivalry did not usually revolve around lavishness or expense, but around who could come up with the most interesting and novel event. Games were participatory and designed to keep everyone amused. Lizzie Stocking expressed this principle in the preface to her 1903 manual, *How to Entertain:* "It is not the elaborateness of the affair that counts so much, as it is to know that each guest goes . . .

home feeling that the [time] has passed all too quickly, and to know that an invitation . . . to your home is a delight to the recipient."[38]

I see these entertainments functioning as a kind of domesticated pageantry. They represented "tamed," private, scaled-down, and amusing versions of what had once been public activities tied to great political and economic power. Thematic, coordinated decorations and food displays, allegorical costumes, and dramatized table tableaux had all originally developed as part of the pageantry and ritualized power plays of the courts of Europe; kings such as Henry VIII used them to demonstrate their influence and authority. In the industrial age, such aesthetically elaborated display passed largely into the domestic or woman's domain. With this shift, and certainly by the turn of the twentieth century, it was the "play" rather than the "power" that became significant. Instead of trying to best political rivals with their entertainments, women amused one another, turning what had been a serious contest into a kind of game. They transformed the social context of obligation into an aesthetically satisfying experience where playfulness could be allowed full expression. The inclusive nature of these parties is

FIG. 3.4.
This illustration accompanied an article about a "Christmas Announcement Party" featured in the *Hostess Magazine*, December 1925. The women each hold a streamer attached to a suspended "wedding bell," and they are asked to pull them at an appointed time. "From the bell comes a shower of tiny cards," explains the article, "each bearing the names of the engaged pair."

FIG. 3.5.
Even at a simple tea or luncheon, guests might be given small favors. Objects made from ribbon and paper were represented in *Day Entertainments and Other Functions* in 1896. The round favor consisted of petals from artificial roses, glued around a pocket mirror. The ribbon loop at the top allowed it to be fastened to the guest's coat. The rosette was suggested for a card party as a consolation prize for the person who did not win the game.

symbolized for me by the image of the circular table at an announcement party, where guests all participate in the primary dramatic moment. They simultaneously pull streamers that will release the name of a new fiancé (fig. 3.4). No one is at the head of the table or in a place of honor, and everyone has an equally important role in effecting the surprise. The idea of the party favor also shows this same domestication and democratization. Favors had once been bestowed only on certain individuals, again as an expression of power. Here, favors were pleasing trifles given to everyone present (fig. 3.5).[39]

These gatherings also fostered a sense of belonging with the broader, national community. Not only did they refer to cultural elements such as literary references, "New Women," or trains or automobiles, but many were organized around seasonal holidays. As shown in chapter 1, such "calendar customs" provided opportunities for bonding with others.[40]

The language used at women's parties helped set the transformative mood. Written materials such as invitations and place cards carried a particularly upbeat, lighthearted rhetoric, and they were often put in rhyme. An invitation to the 1914 "Snow Fete" (written on a mica-covered cardboard "icicle"), read:

> Come over the snow. . .
> On iceberg and floe. . .
> Join our merry band
> And we will all go
> To the frigid land
> Of the Esquimeau.
> Wear white—Saturday night.[41]

An invitation to a "Mystical Party" published in 1905 followed essentially the same format. In easy cadences, it also promised a happy, out-of-the-ordinary experience and assured the recipient that her presence mattered:

> The Y.W.C.T.U
> Has cordially invited you
> To the Mystery Reception,
> Strange and weird beyond conception.

> At seven-thirty o'clock night fall
> We will welcome one and all;
> With solemn rites and grewsome [sic] sights,
> We'll meet you all on Monday night.[42]

Literal and conceptual puns were also often involved in party rhetoric. The invitation to a St. Patrick's Day event planned for a church club not only used rhyme, but repeatedly emphasized the letters "P-a-t."

> Please *pat*rol the club-house *pat*h
> Or you will incur our wrath:
> Never mind a rain or *pat*ter
> There'll be pork upon the platter!
> *Pat*rick will be auctioneer,
> *Pat*ronize him, never fear . . .[43]

Invitations often came in unusual shapes or materials that gave a flavor of the event to come. Teepee or tomahawk shapes and strips of birch bark were suggested for an Indian theme party, for example, and toy slates or heart-shaped paper were recommended for a Valentine's party. An "Amateur Decorators' Luncheon" was to be announced with notepaper outfitted with crepe paper moldings and chintz panels. The general idea was to build interest and enthusiasm. As Florence Winterburn put it in *Novel Ways of Entertaining,* "to untwine the meaning of an invitation is often a delicious species of excitement, like finding the path of a labyrinth."[44]

The play with language and use of puns extended far beyond the invitations. Foods at the Snow Fete were purposely "cold"—not just to the touch (as in iced punch), but also in terms of reference, as in "iced" or "frosted" cakes, or "crystallized" ginger. Conceptual puns could relate to the overall theme of the entertainment or to individual elements. The whole conceit of the Literary Leaves event, as indicated, revolved around a conflation of autumn leaves and the pages of a book, and the featured conundrums involved puns with authors' names. There were also many word games that played with suffixes or parts of words. "A Family of Kates" was a game based on words with the suffix "cate." The solution to "the prophetic Kate," for instance, was "prognosticate"; the solution to "Kate just left" was "vacate." I previously described menu tag lines in the forms of poetic citations, but sometimes the whole menu appeared as a series of riddles. A meat listed as an "unruly member," for example, was in fact tongue; a vegetable identified as the "result of a tight shoe" was corn; a relish identified as "a noisy supper" was catsup; and a bread listed as "fruit of the spinning wheel" was a roll. By today's standards, some of these puzzles seem intellectually sophisticated—the answers were not always self-evident, and a good vocabulary was assumed. Again,

82   this speaks to the idea that the parties were aimed at an educated audience. At the same time, these word games were never exclusive; everyone could be an equal part of the joke. Female party advice givers never suggested tricks or stunts that poked fun at anyone present or made any one person stand out from the rest.[45]

In addition to riddles and literary conundrums, some entertainments featured other kinds of participatory games. At a "five senses" party, blindfolded guests were asked to identify various substances by touch, taste, or smell and to identify specific sounds. (Prizes included a magnifying glass or tin trumpet.) Some contests had participants making thematic drawings or three-dimensional creations such as "potato animals" outfitted with toothpicks. Prizes were given for the funniest entries. The Snow Fete included games such as "Biting the [popcorn] Snowball," "Shooting Polar Bears"—tossing marbles at a precariously positioned white Teddy bear (fig. 3.6), and "Digging the Drift"—using a toy spade to unearth little favors from "drifts" of confetti or table salt.[46]

Shooting Polar Bears

" Tossing Marbles at a white Teddy Bear posed precariously on a Parrots perch."

manship were required to knock Teddy from his perch, but when he toppled over, the successful "big-game hunter" who scored highest in bringing Bruin low, was awarded an air-rifle for his skill; or if "he" happened to be a girl, she was presented with a Cupid's-bow-and-arrow calendar.

FIG. 3.6.
The "Snow Fete" party described in Lillian Pascal Day's 1914 book, *Social Entertainments: A Book of Practical Suggestions for Entertaining,* included a silly game called "Shooting Polar Bears," which consisted of throwing marbles at a white teddy bear.

The Snow Fete games were funny in part because of their reliance on miniatures and children's toys; they made the big people playing with them seem not only childlike, but relatively large or powerful. Miniaturization, which I think of as a kind of visual pun, akin in a sense to word play, was a salient feature of many of these entertainments. I have mentioned "dainty," miniaturized food and tiny table decorations. Favors were usually miniatures as well; there were the just-mentioned little treasures hidden in confetti snow, for example, or "tiny boxes in exact imitations of books" given out at the Literary Leaves Tea. Small pocket mirrors decorated with artificial rose petals were suggested favors for teas or card parties in 1896, and "wee" fans or baskets were suggested favors for a wedding breakfast in 1919. At a 1925 announcement party, favors consisted of lipsticks fashioned as dolls, with skirts of pink crepe paper and gumdrop heads. Hostesses could paint faces on these characters with melted chocolate.[47] The word "little" appeared as an adjective in a great many of the descriptions of these entertainments, to the point that it seemed to automatically imply charm.

Occasionally, party givers played with scale at the other extreme, including some elements in exaggerated scale. Room decorations might for example include blown-up versions of everyday objects such as candy baskets, bells, vegetables, or flowers, and, as noted, people sometimes dressed as oversize vegetables or flowers. At turn-of-the-century "doll parties," they even dressed *as* dolls (see chapter 4). Here, too, exaggeration would create surprise and delight.

Ideally, a guest would feel a sense of magic as soon as she entered the space where a party was taking place. *Day Entertainments'* description of the Literary Leaves Tea gives a sense of the sensually saturated quality that was aimed for: "The hallway of Mrs. Toff's house glowed under the cheery light of crimson shaded lamps, while oak and maple . . . flamed along the wall as a frieze of gorgeous [autumn] color. Against the brilliant foliage . . . a table was set, and from the ruby depths of a great bowl placed thereon, two leaf-crowned girls ladled delicious punch for the arriving guests."[48]

Similarly, the description of the Snow Fete alludes to a living room transformed into a frozen bower, filled with shrubs and tree branches "a-glitter" with artificial hoarfrost. Guests were greeted by a hostess in a white crepe paper costume, "pasted thickly with silver stars and magnified snowflakes," her powdered hair capped with a tinsel crown (I will further discuss the conventions of thematic costume in chapter 4). Later, the guests entered a cotton-covered igloo with stalactite icicles. At a "Spinning Party," which had a literal spinning contest as its central conceit, several rooms were outfitted with knotted threads that "looked like the work of a giant spider." They were "ingeniously twisted together and wound around pictures, bric-a-brac, and table legs," and actually formed the basis of one of the party games: individuals had to follow a thread to its end, untying all the knots on the way. At the end of the thread, each found the name of their partner for the ensuing amusements.[49]

This degree of elaboration was probably not typical and might in fact have been most often seen at larger coed events ("partners" typically implied a male-female pair), but even simpler parties invariably involved some form of transformative decoration. An apple-blossom luncheon called for masses of blooms throughout the dining room, for example, and an Indian-theme party called for a "wigwam made of blankets" in an out-of-the-way corner. Ordinary draperies might be replaced or transformed: rose-colored tarlatan might be hung instead

84   of heavy velvets for a rose luncheon, for instance, or sheer lace curtains might be
lined with purple cloth for a violet theme tea. For Valentine's Day, one might
transform the doorways with wire hearts. One element that was frequently played
with was the lighting; many suggestions were made for the kind of colored shades
used at the Literary Leaves Tea. Candles were also used to cast a romantic glow.
This was important at colonial theme parties, but it could be worked into any
occasion. A suggestion for a corn supper included candle-filled jack-o-lanterns.
Candles and candlesticks could themselves become part of the decor. At a 1914
Easter luncheon with a violet theme, it was suggested that purple ribbons cover
the candlesticks to "reflect" the violet color, for example, and candles were marked
out in squares with black sealing wax at a crossword puzzle party a few years later
(see fig. 3.8). Those who "cared to take the trouble" could even fashion candle
shades from half-turned leaves for an autumn theme tea.[50]

   The table functioned as the heart of the entertainment and was invariably
"dressed." It was usually covered with fine linens, although, by the early twentieth
century, paper table coverings often replaced cloth and made entertaining much
less labor intensive. Starting about 1900, the Dennison company offered printed

FIG. 3.7.
At an unidentified party in southeastern Wisconsin about 1900, the decorations were simple but nevertheless
transformative. Crepe paper streamers were hung from the central chandelier, setting off the table with a canopylike feeling. Paper or cloth was also festooned over horizontal architectural panels, and the table was covered
with a white cloth. Photograph by Henry F. Bergmann, Courtesy, the Wisconsin Historical Society, WHI-33712,
(B61) 162.

FIG. 3.8.
A "Cross Word Puzzle Party" described in the *Hostess* in January 1925 included white candles marked off in squares with black sealing wax, creating a checkerboard look. The table centerpiece was a large dictionary. Author Mary Elizabeth Ford suggested "inducing" one's friends to come in costume. All they would have to do to effect the proper look was to wear black and white squares.

crepe paper napkins and lunch sets, with a range of seasonal or holiday designs (holly, shamrocks, flags, flowers, and so on). These were clothlike, with damask or "linen-weave" effects and scalloped edges or borders that imitated the effect of hemstitching.[51] The linens, too, were expected to be color coordinated, although a colored accent such as a band of ribbon could substitute for a mass of cloth. At informal luncheons and teas with "light" menus, fancy mats and doilies were often used in place of full table covers. Doilies could be made to reflect a particular occasion—they could be cut in the shape of a valentine or flower basket, for example, or adorned with appropriate motifs. By the early twentieth century, the increased popularity of these informal entertainments was reflected in an abundance of patterns in the women's press for embroidered, crocheted, and cutwork doilies. They were easy to make at home, and added a touch of color, up-to-date imagery and graciousness to even a modest table (see fig. 3.9). Napkins were also made more visually interesting through folding. They were worked into a wide range of shapes, including rosebuds and other flowers, boats, and caps (see fig. 3.1).[52]

Every table had a centerpiece. At the turn of the century, these usually consisted primarily of flowers and foliage. (Sara Sedgwick, writing in *Goodform* magazine in 1893, even spoke of growing ferns specifically for table decorations.)

FIG. 3.9.
Handmade doilies, used to make the dining table even more festive, were very popular in the early twentieth century. A small round plate could be placed on top of a circular doily such as this one made about 1900. Courtesy, The Helen Louise Allen Textile Collection, School of Human Ecology, University of Wisconsin–Madison, E.A.U.S. 1023.

Commonly, such arrangements would be placed on top of a mirror that was either edged in smilax or surrounded by attractive cloths. Ideally, the flora was thematically appropriate. At a 1905 snow-theme luncheon, "a long low snowbank formed of white sweet peas" was mixed with sprays of other white blooms "to give the soft feathery appearance of wind-blown snow." At an Indian-theme party, the hostess was advised to feature an Indian basket filled with red and yellow flowers over a leather "skin." Sometimes the floral centerpiece was in an unusual shape, such as a wishbone, and sometimes it could function as a pun. The "bouquet" at a "Vegetable Garden Party" consisted of a scooped-out cabbage filled with carrots, beets, parsley, and ears of corn.[53]

By the World War I era, thematic objects often replaced the flowers in the central place of honor. These might be single items; a clever hostess might position a harp on a green cloth for St. Patrick's Day, for example, or feature a toy windmill for a Dutch supper. Sometimes the food itself was the centerpiece, as at a Valentine's Day event where a large heart-shaped cake dominated the table. As the earlier description of the Landscape Dinner Party with its stick-candy rail fence implies, however, tables were increasingly dominated by dramatic vignettes. The centerpiece at a 1913 Mother Goose theme party, for example, consisted of "the largest available shoe" arranged with little dolls tumbling out of it. The central mirror that had first simply reflected attractive flowers was transformed by 1915 into a "lake" in a Japanese garden. This was surrounded by paper "grass," and topped with a small bridge with two figures looking musingly over the scene. Glover described a "dream-like table" at a prenuptial luncheon where white swans "floated" on a similar mirror-lake, and a table at a spring party "laid out like a formal garden." Miniature trees and toy wheelbarrows completed the latter tableau. A "charming" scene set in a forest was described in *How to Entertain at Home* in 1928. It too featured paper grass and toy trees, as well as a small settee with seated boy and girl dolls. A "tiny deer" was "peering at them from the trees." In order to create the appropriate stage-lighting effect, a small Christmas tree bulb was hidden in front of the bench.[54]

FIG. 3.10.

This centerpiece featuring a chariot powered by two Cupid cut-outs was suggested in 1928 for a Valentine's Day party, but *Parties* magazine also indicated it would also be charming for a shower or announcement party. The chariot and base were made of cardboard covered with crushed gold paper.

insisted that everybody accept although they did not play.

The guests arrived on the specified evening wondering just what would be the nature of the entertainment.

It was an evening early in the spring when weather conditions had caused

When you're married it's Clubs."

"What's Trumps? When you're dead it's Spades."

The place cards were hand painted

The table centerpiece represented a bridge from which a small doll fished in the stream

many freshets, and the washing away of several bridges had been the subject of newspaper stories and of general conversation. One nearby had been washed out by high water and so

to discover these little couplets and they caused much merriment.

The rest of the "bridge" idea was taken up and soon the conversation turned to the fallen bridge in the town, the most picturesque ones, new ones, unusual ones and those seen during foreign trips.

While this chatter was going on the hostess served

It took a few minutes after the guests were seated for them

FIG. 3.11.

Parties magazine used visual and conceptual puns with this image of a table centerpiece in spring 1928. The doll standing on a bridge was featured at a "mock bridge party" that "bridged over a delightful evening."

FIG. 3.12.
Another elaborate table-top diorama was pictured for a "'Blue Monday' Shower" illustrated in the 1926 publication *The Book of Games and Parties*. A doll hanging tiny handkerchiefs on a clothesline was the central conceit, but other toys, including water pumps and miniature baskets, were also worked in.

Picturesque scenes made with toys and doll "actors" were commonly included in advice books of the 1920s. At a "stork party" for an expectant mother, the centerpiece contained a small wishing well with the "doll fairies of Health, Happiness and Beauty in gauzy raiment." At a luncheon or tea bridge party described in *Entertainments of All Occasions*, the center of attraction was a figure dressed as the Queen of Hearts. Surrounded by diamond-shaped rock candy and diamond-shaped fence, she was guarded by dolls dressed like the King of Diamonds. This same book recommended "Candy Island" as the centerpiece for a "Honeymoon Shower." The table was covered by a mirror functioning as the "Sea of Matrimony," and candies dressed in crepe paper bride and groom costumes were placed on one of its islands. There was a footbridge in this scene as well, also made with sticks of candy. The honeymoon itself was represented by a silver tinsel moon attached to another candy stick. Today we still expect dressed bride and groom dolls on wedding cakes, but we have for the most part lost the rest of this diorama tradition.[55]

Again, one can understand these scenes as tamed or domesticated versions of what had been displays of social power in the preindustrial period. At a Medici family wedding of the sixteenth century, each banquet course appeared as a hunting scene that read as a metaphor for humankind's ability to overcome the physical world. Miniature tabletop landscapes or gardens were common at elite entertainments by the turn of the eighteenth century. There had been lakes made of small mirrors at those events as well, along with sugar or porcelain cottages, almond-paste cattle, and even miniature fountains. In some cases, Turkish carpet patterns were emulated on the table in sand or sugar.[56]

The centerpiece at a women's entertainment was usually surrounded by other thematic tabletop touches, including items arranged at each place setting. These might be merely decorative, but they often served an ostensibly practical function. Place and menu cards marked individual places. Place cards ranged from simple Bristol-board markers to fanciful ornaments; an enterprising hostess could cut them out of wallpaper or paper napkins or combine them with artificial flowers or miniature favors. Cutlery might be placed in some sort of thematic holder, as at a Golf Luncheon where small "caddy bags" held the guests' knives, forks, and spoons. At the Vegetable Party where a cabbage held the central bouquet, individuals found smaller hollowed-out cabbages at their plates. These were lined with paraffined paper and used to hold salad, nuts and candies. Other

FIG. 3.13.
The Party Book (1926) pictured festive "nut cups" with ribbed paper cups surrounded by elaborate paper or ribbon trim. Other condiment holders were made from hollowed-out oranges or small toys.

FIG. 3.14.
At each place setting at a Cinderella-theme party featured in *Parties* in fall 1929, there were slipper-shaped items and a clock pointing to the midnight hour.

FIGURE NO. 1.

FIG. 3.15.
Day Entertainments (1896) pictured a bonbon box that was elaborately decorated with ribbon and artificial flowers. The name of the guest was painted in gold on one of the ribbon streamers. Small candies would seem very special when presented in such containers.

foodstuffs such as hollowed-out orange or grapefruits skins were also used as condiment containers, but most often these "nut," "bonbon," or "ice" cups (the latter were used to serve sherbet) were made of nonedible materials. Touted as important "dainty accessories which add . . . color and charm to the party table," nut cups were usually made of fluted paper. Hostesses would buy them ready-made and then decorate them further. Fales and Northend gave instructions for fashioning cups as baskets, flowers, pumpkins, "St. Patrick's Day potatoes," and other shapes (see fig. 3.12). Condiment holders could also be made of other objects: a pair of wooden shoes served as holders at a Dutch party, for example. At a Post Office theme party, nuts, candies, and little cakes were placed in toy trains and stagecoaches, allowing the guests to have "great fun guiding the . . . conveyances around the table." Place settings also often included favors. Paul Pierce recommended a tiny bouquet of violets tied with a gauze ribbon at a festive breakfast, and *Day Entertainments* suggested a yellow satin bonboniere outfitted with a cloth butterfly (it was "trembling on its wire as if ready to take flight") for a luncheon.[57]

Specific types of dishes and cutlery were rarely mentioned in the advice literature, presumably because a hostess would use what she had on hand. One exception to this was the 1905 Snow Luncheon, where the theme necessitated an all-white table service. "The services of a caterer were not called upon" for this event, according to the *Good Housekeeping* report, but "it was necessary to rent from him" eggshell china and cutlery with white porcelain handles.[58]

One last aspect of decoration that was important at many of the entertainments was the addition of a canopylike feature over the dining table. A canopy was another feature of the triumphal Renaissance feast; it had been used to enclose and set apart the space beneath it. The central decoration over the table at the turn-of-the-century party served the same purpose, but rather than contributing a sense of grandeur, it was thought of as an airy "bower" that added to the fairyland quality of the event. The arrangement devised for a Valentine's Day event described in *The Party Book* consisted of a heart-shaped "cobweb" suspended over table. Made of heavy wire and wound with tinsel and artificial roses, this web belonged to a bisque or wax cupid rather than a spider, and it had already "caught" many cardboard hearts. A similar effect was suggested for "'A Little Bird Told Me' Announcement Luncheon": a gaily painted wooden parrot was positioned inside a wooden embroidery hoop that was hung over the centerpiece. Often the canopy featured streamers that billowed, Maypole-fashion, down to the table. Each streamer ended at an individual place setting, visually and symbolically tying the place and the person who occupied it into the tableau (see fig. 3.4). Streamers of this type often led to "surprises," such as tiny notes with the name of a newly engaged couple ("A little bird told me / A very nice thing, / That Randolph gave Sally / A diamond ring).[59]

Streamers were such an important party convention in the twentieth century that when there was no canopy, ribbons often fanned out from the center of the table. "From a centerpiece of paper roses formed in the shape of a heart," one author directed, "radiate streamers of crepe paper ending in place-cards inscribed with appropriate love couplets." In the previously mentioned Queen of Hearts tableau, narrow ribbons were brought from the central doll vignette to cards at each place. These included both the guest's name and verses about the Queen of Hearts. At an appointed time, the guests were told to pull the ribbons, which released "diamond" rock candy that could be used as a coffee sweetener.[60]

Streamers could also release other kinds of favors. At one party, they were attached to another "Sea of Matrimony," this time a central fish bowl containing celluloid fish and trinkets in the form of engagement rings, thimbles, pennies, and similar items supposedly symbolizing the guest's future (marriage, an old maid, and fortune, respectively). At a doll theme party intended for young girls, the ribbons released pieces of tiny furniture from a dollhouse centerpiece.[61] Sometimes the favors were released from "surprise pies" (also called "bird pies," "trick pies," or "Jack Horners"—the latter because Jack Horner had stuck his thumb in a pie). The surprise pie tradition was linked to the nursery rhyme "Sing a Song of Sixpence," in which four and twenty blackbirds were baked in a pie and set before the king. In these later versions, the pies were usually inedible, and the surprises were not birds, but written messages or prizes.[62] In Mott's 1891 guide, *Home Games and Parties,* for example, guests who reached into the pie at a Mother Goose party pulled out envelopes with amusing original verses. Burt's 1919 *Entertaining Made Easy* described a pie filled with pasteboard bluebirds (the bluebird was known as a symbol of happiness), each carrying an announcement

FIG. 3.15.
This "standard rose Jack Horner" centerpiece was illustrated in *The Party Book*. Although "Jack Horner" alluded to an actual pie shape, favor "pies" took many imaginative forms by the interwar era. The rose petals were made from crepe paper.

about the bride to be. It started with an adaptation of the "Sing a Song of Sixpence" rhyme: "When the pie was opened / The birds began to sing / About a certain couple here / who have some news to spring."[63]

In the interwar era, favor/surprise pies sometimes took more fanciful forms. Burt featured a daisy-shaped "pie" for "The One I Love Shower." It was made from a round basket covered with petals attached to streamers. When pulled at the appointed moment, these released tiny dolls dressed as various characters—rich man, poor man, beggar man, thief, and so on. Like the celluloid fish, these were supposed to represent each guest's future (the engaged girl was given a preassigned petal, with a doll matching her fiancé's profession). The 1926 *Party Book* featured a whole chapter on surprise pies (then generally called Jack Horners). The authors offered instructions for constructing them in the shape of flowers, a heart, muff, hat, firecracker, Easter egg, haystack, and snowball. *Parties* magazine illustrated "pies" in the shape of an American eagle and an ocean liner in 1930.[64]

It would have taken considerable time to make these elaborate devices; instructions for a flower-shaped pie, for example, involved cutting out and curling petals one at a time, winding wire stamens and stems, and individually wrapping the presents and attaching the ribbons. Hostesses could buy surprise pies ready-made, however; the Shackman Company *Catalogue of Favors* featured eight pages of them in 1910.[65] They seem to have been particularly prevalent in the twentieth century at announcement parties and showers, and for that purpose they were often shaped as wedding bells or hearts. As a variation on the theme, pies at announcement parties sometimes contained gifts for the bride to be rather than for the guests. A bride to be might even be asked to cut the cake, only to discover it was not the real thing—it was an icing-covered cheese box filled with gifts.

The mid-1920s seems to have represented the height of the Jack Horner craze, and after this time most such artifacts were made in a considerably simpler manner. One description called for a dishpan covered with white paper, which func-

tioned as a grab bag of commercial samples, such as tiny tubes of toothpaste.
Another, suggested for a "North Pole Party," consisted of a simple "pack" (bag)
arranged on a sled.[66]

I have introduced the idea of punning conceits and dramatic effects worked
into party refreshments, giving some examples of menus with riddles and puns.
A few more examples will give a deeper sense of the convention. At a Valentine's
party, for example, the "way to man's heart menu" included items such as "melt-
ing warmth" (hot bouillon), "soft speech" (tongue sandwiches), and "clinging
vines"(tomato pickle). At an announcement dinner, the soup course was listed as
"cream of love apples" (tomato), and the entree as "chickens that have lost their
hearts" (they had been processed into cutlets). The appetizer listed as "the drive
off" at a golf theme party turned out to be halved oysters. "Golf sticks" were
breadsticks at that event, and the "tee" was tea with lemon. A "spinster tea" menu
listed table items such as "always in pairs" (a cup and saucer), "courtship" (mush),
and "objects of envy" (pears [pairs]). Menu clues appeared as anagrams in one
case—DAKEB ANEBS unscrambled was baked beans, LODC ATEM was cold meat,
and OBWNR RABDE was brown bread. An entire menu (as indeed an entire party)
might be based on a particular letter. A "B" (or "beehive") theme party thus featured foods such as bread, beets, bananas, baked potatoes, boiled pudding, "barnyard beasts" (chicken), or "bewitched beverages" (frozen ices). Food puns might
also serve as the basis for conundrum games. A breakfast mentioned in 1907
included a game entitled "Who takes the cake?" There, the correct answer to the
"geologists cake" clue was "mountain"; an "advertiser's cake" was "puff"; and an
"idler's cake was "loaf."[67]

Sometimes food puns related to the form or presentation of the food. Especially at an April Fool's event, it might be "masqueraded." At one, potato salad
was arranged so as to look like cream puffs, and sandwiches were dressed as slices
of cake and vice versa. (There were some "false" treats at that event as well, such
as chocolate creams stuffed with cotton, and cakes that, like the Jack Horner pie
described above, were really only icing-covered boxes.) Another entertainment
for April 1 featured "chocolates" that were really coated oyster crackers, and baked
potatoes that had been hollowed out, lined with wax paper, and filled with vanilla
ice cream. Real food might be hidden in other ways, as at the party where sherbet
glasses full of ice cream were served inside of crepe paper bags. Food was also frequently shaped into a new form. At a "Captain Kidd Announcement Luncheon,"
mashed potatoes were sculpted into waves in order to effect the promised "stormy
seas," and cucumbers were hollowed out to form "canoes," then filled with peas
and pearl onions that functioned as "emerald and pearl cargo." "Cannon balls"

94   were made from cream cheese rolled in nuts; "treasure chests" were made from hollow bread loaves filled with carrots in white sauce. "Rice and rats," repeatedly mentioned for Chinese theme parties, consisted of molded cooked rice topped by a candy rat (this dish was served with cream and sugar). For Easter, cream cheese was molded into "ducklings" that floated on a pond of aspic jelly. For Halloween, cheese could be made into a cat shape and fitted with shredded wheat whiskers. A "vanity salad" suggested for another announcement party took the form of a female face. Made of a pear half placed upside down on a lettuce leaf, it was drizzled with dressing that simulated bobbed hair and given facial features made of maraschino cherries and nuts. "Porcupine salads" were similar tours de force, consisting of pear halves pierced with slivered almonds. A "pin party" featured long, narrow croquettes fitted with bits of macaroni at each end so that they looked like miniature clothespins, as well as cheeseballs on skewers that were designed to look like hat pins. Elsewhere lettuce leaves were pinned together with safety pins to form "cups" that held fruit salad. "Pigs in blankets," another popular new dish, consisted of oysters wrapped in bacon slices and fried in batter.[68]

Foods might also be presented in other unusual ways. A bridge luncheon might feature as many heart-shaped foods as possible, for example—sandwiches cut into hearts, biscuits baked in heart molds, heart-shaped fruit in a gelatin mold, and so on. Ice cream was sometimes served in spun-sugar "baskets" or "nests," and candy might be served in scooped-out carrots or hollow goose eggs (the latter were to be painted silver). A green pepper might function as a mustard holder.[69] Foods were also adorned with both edible and inedible decorations. The leaf theme at autumn parties was extended to the table, for example, with such touches as lettuce leaf "nests" under every dish, geranium leaves on teacup saucers, and colored leaves in the cake icing. The oyster bisque at the Captain Kidd party was served in cups with tiny pirate flags fastened to the handles, and the accompanying crackers had gold play money tied around them to resemble doubloons. "Sea rovers" were salmon croquettes in egg sauce, decorated with gilt cardboard pistols.[70]

Hostesses worked to make foods thematically appropriate. The fare at a plantation party, for example, consisted of hoe cake, corn pone, hominy, and syrup; rye bread, smoked herring, pickled beets, eggs, and onions were offered at a Dutch party. Standard items could also seem thematic when they were given new names. At the Indian theme party where the table was covered with leather, bouillon was entitled "squaw soup," and other courses bore names such as "Apache gravy," "Choctaw peas," "papoose rolls," and "Hiawatha cake." (The same dessert might be rechristened "Dolly Madison" or "Martha Washington" cake if the party theme were colonial.) Color, as we have seen, could also imbue ordinary items with a special quality, as when an entire menu consisted of yellow, green, or white foods. Color could equally transform a single dish. Red, white, and blue combinations were worked into many patriotic meals. A cake might be made in three colored layers, for example, and a "Yankee Doodle Salad" would consist of red items such as peppers and tomatoes and white pearl onions and celery served in a blue bowl. At a "Cornucopia Luncheon" with a two-color theme, the salad consisted of alternating layers of red cabbage and cubes of celery. "Light" menus emphasized salads and deemphasized meats.[71]

Vegetables at turn-of-the-century repasts were not typically served raw; on the contrary, they were heavily dressed and sweetened. A "vanity fruit salad" dressing, for example, combined pear juice, eggs, whipped cream, butter, and sugar. In her discussion of dainty dining, Laura Shapiro explains that the addition of dressings and sauces helped civilize or refine foods. Creamed dishes were very popular: there were creamed potatoes, crabmeat, salmon, sweetbreads, and chicken (this is when chicken a la king became popular). There was also a great use of gelatins, especially for raw foods such as cucumbers. Creamed cheeses, blended with walnuts, olives, chopped ginger, oranges, and the like, were popular as well, as were mixed or flavored butters. Paul Pierce recommended a wide range of flavorings, including everything from parsley or chives to paprika, sardines, lobster, salmon, or horseradish. He also approved of fruit (such as lemon, coconut, or peach) and flower butters (for example, mixed with rose or violet petals), calling them "delicate and attractive," although he noted that they found "little favor with the sterner sex." Condiments of this sort could be tinted and thus change the color tone of an entire dish—there was green mayonnaise, for example, or pink marshmallow cream or meringue. One refining sauce might be served with another, to a point we are likely to be uncomfortable with today. "Puff sandwiches" recommended by the *Hostess* in 1925, as an example, consisted of mayonnaised chicken salad spread on rounds of white bread, covered with whipped cream.[72]

In addition to white dressings that helped "lighten" foods, daintiness was characterized by diminutive size or "fineness." Tea sandwiches were usually crustless and were always sliced as thin as possible. Meats were preferably chopped, rather than sliced, and all fillings were finely processed. Pierce's recipe for an olive sandwich thus not only called for diced olives and mayonnaise, but "cracker dust." Chopped nuts might be spread between "thin wafers" for a particularly delicate repast. Small foods could themselves be stuffed with smaller items (stuffed dates were popular) or "crystallized" with bits of sugar (candied ginger slices were common). Even the daintiest item could be further transformed, as exemplified by a sandwich treatment suggested in 1897 in which the bread was rolled

96   and tied with a narrow yellow and lilac ribbon. Everything was made "prettier than life."[73]

Daintiness, as Shapiro explains, was valued because it seemed to embody femininity—the opposite of drudgery, or toil. It was implicitly about class, since it was the wealthy who could "afford to have dainty articles, daintily done."[74] When less wealthy women followed this tradition and created seemingly refined foods, they too were becoming "ladies" and participating in the good life. Small wonder that advice givers reminded hostesses to "make every dish as attractive to the eye as it is to the palate," for refined people would be concerned with appearance, even more than sustenance. Shapiro claims that the domestic scientists who advocated this dainty cooking were actually unconcerned with taste or the pleasures of eating. I disagree. Dainty food was certainly transformed and decorative, but it had flavor, and its proponents were suggesting not tastelessness, but a particular taste experience. Creams and sauces were smooth, and gelatins, meringues, and whipped creams felt light on the tongue; breadcrumbs and the sugar granules on crystallized fruit had a texture that teasingly stayed in the mouth. Ices or sherbets were almost always offered at the end of the meal (remember that they took much more work to prepare in the days before household freezers) and provided both a smooth texture and a startling sensation of cold. Candies and salted nuts were usually on the table, offering contrasting textures and tastes. Confections like walnut "kisses" offered the same the kind of textural contrast in

FIG. 3.17.
Food was often shaped into expressive forms, as these cream cheese Easter ducklings from *The Party Book* demonstrate. Kernels of unpopped corn were used for beaks and parsley for the eyes.

FIG. 3.18.
Sweet foods, including cakes, were an expected element of most entertainments. This "Barnard College Cake" illustrated in *The Party Book* was given an especially lovely presentation with ferns and paper doilies.

one bite, with a coating of soft, light meringue over a hard nutmeat. Sweetness was de rigueur in a dainty meal; in addition to sweetened salads, ices, stuffed dates, and the like, almost every menu included cakes. Sweetness might in a sense be considered a metaphor for daintiness—the women who prepared these things were themselves sweet—but it was also a pleasing taste or flavor. If parties of this type were, in Mendel's words, meant "to spread happiness," then it is unreasonable to maintain that the pleasure of eating was discounted.[75]

Conventions surrounding dainty food at women's entertainments also went back to the pageantry and conspicuous consumption of earlier aristocratic eras. From the time of ancient Rome, well-off people had been treated to elaborate food masquerades. Ice cream hiding in baked potatoes was, therefore, a vestigial version of the regal feasts where an alive-looking animal turned out to be cooked and edible.[76] The obvious forebear of the aforementioned "porcupine salad" was a European "conceit" that consisted of a pudding or marzipan hedgehog covered with sliced almond bristles. Marzipan and other moldable foodstuffs had been commonly used to impress guests at Renaissance and Baroque dinners; almonds were exotic foodstuffs at the time, and sugar was itself expensive. These substances were shaped as miniature animals or objects such as shoes, gloves, or knots. Like the women's conundrums, they frequently bore riddles, although theirs tended to be coded triumphal messages that regaled the host. The white, or refined, foods at women's parties, including crustless white bread and sugar (and, by extension, cream sauces), were no longer novel or expensive, but they still alluded to luxury and tasted like treats. What had once been the privilege of the wealthy was now available to everyone.[77]

One convention of women's entertainments that did not have its roots in earlier, male forms of pageantry was the importance of handcraft. As many of the illustrations and earlier descriptions make clear, a hostess might spend a great deal of time making decorations, centerpieces, or favors for her party, in addition to preparing all of the elaborated and highly crafted foods. Contemporary sources acknowledged that these preparations could be deeply satisfying; as advice-giver Mary Moxcey put it, "Making the decorations ... [for these parties] may often be the occasion for real jollification." There were also parties where the guests were involved in participatory "making" activities; participatory games might for example revolve around everyone's fashioning their own version of a specified item. A bottle-theme entertainment suggested in 1914 not only featured bottle decorations and puns, but a bottle-decorating contest. Guests were led to the kitchen where they found a play dough–like mixture with which they could encase a bottle, creating a figure to their liking. At a springtime party, guests were asked to fashion "daffodil crooks" or "fleur de lis wands" out of broom handles and crepe paper. As mentioned in chapter 1, handwork at coeducational parties was sometimes even used as an amusing gender play—that is, men were asked to do what were understood to be women's tasks, with humorous results. At a "Modern Sewing Bee" described in 1891, each man was required to make a bonnet for the woman with whom he had been paired off, and women were to make their partners smoking caps (millinery supplies had been provided in advance, so guests could settle right in to work). These had to be worn all evening. "Many of the productions were comical in the extreme," remarked chronicler Effie Merriam. This kind of inversion may even have functioned as a kind of courting ritual. Men who had to "get down on their knees" and hem the apron of a woman whose fabric scrap they had selected at the gingham party were not only placed in close proximity to their partners, but put in the iconic position of the marriage proposal.[78]

Handwork was most commonly featured at showers or related parties that featured a guest of honor, who would be presented with the freshly fashioned items at the end of the event. At a "stork party" given for a pregnant woman, for example, most of afternoon was spent in making a silk puff for the expected baby; every guest worked on a separate square that the hostess later put together. Each guest was similarly given a small doily to embroider at a German-theme bridal shower, and these were offered to the bride at the end of the day. At a "Cretonne Shower," guests worked on dress bags, coat hangers, and other practical items made from the cheerful material (they also broke into teams and tried to fashion the "most ideal husbands" out of clothespins, tissue paper, and paste).[79]

As these stories exemplify, many of the features of women's parties were most dramatically manifest at showers. Daintiness was all important at these events, which symbolically represented a woman's future. Florence Winterburn even remarked that a wedding breakfast "should be *super-dainty*" (italics mine). Gender roles were consciously played with at such entertainments as well. One shower featured in *Parties for the Bride-Elect* explicitly punned on the idea of a hen party. Each guest impersonated a hen (she was known as "Brown Leghorn," "Rhode Island Red," and so on) for the afternoon, which was spent doing fancy work and "cackling." Because showers and related parties were such "pure" expressions of the women's entertainments, they deserve even more focused discussion.[80]

A Further Exploration of Announcement Parties and Showers

A young woman might be the guest of honor at both an announcement party and a shower, for the events had different purposes. An announcement party was, as indicated earlier, usually given by the engaged girl or her family, and it functioned as an offering to her friends—it was a party for them, announcing her soon-to-be changed status. They were the ones who received gifts (in the form of favors) and treated to a pleasant afternoon. A suggestion that appeared often in the advice literature was that the real intent of the party should be kept from the guests; the invitation should imply it was just an ordinary event. Members of a card club might receive invitations to play hearts, for example, with no hint that the planned amusement was really a guessing game with love symbols. The true purpose of the gathering would become apparent as soon as the guests arrived and encountered props such as a wedding bell suspended over

Parties for the Bride-Elect

PRICE 25 CENTS
Published by The Priscilla Publishing Company, Boston, Mass.

FIG. 3.19.
The cover of this 1925 publication offered by *Modern Priscilla* magazine captured the romanticized image of the wedding shower. The costumed figure is in a colonial-looking outfit and stands in an April shower.

the table or place cards decorated with "Cupid blowing on a megaphone."[81] Then the excitement would build. The important moment of the announcement party was the literal release of the fiancé's name, worked into the type of contrivances we have previously discussed.

The bridal shower, according to an often-repeated myth, originated in a long-ago (preindustrial) European past. One version recounted in *Shower Parties for All Occasions* featured a Dutch girl who wanted to marry a generous man who had given his money away. Her father would not provide her with a dowry because the man was so poor. He was so beloved in the village, however, that the townspeople held a party and "showered" the maiden with gifts to help set up a future household. The father was won over.[82] The main event of any shower party was thus to give the bride presents that were in some way useful, and opening gifts was the central drama. The gifts were often made to be amusing as well as practical and were presented in the usual tour de force manner. They were not necessarily expensive; Burt made a point of the fact that gifts at one party could not cost over fifty cents. Showers also always featured amusing games, many of which played with the idea of marriage. "Making the Most of Matrimony" was one such game; another was a word contest entitled "Honeymoon Hurdles." Yet another was "Mail Order Marriage," where guests were able to write humorous descriptions of the ideal husband. Like announcement parties, showers acknowledged the rite of passage that was about to occur and sometimes played with the fact that the bride was in a liminal state. This was symbolically expressed in a shower that followed a sailing theme, which was appropriate for someone "embarking on sea of matrimony."[83]

Punning on the very idea of a shower, a number of these events were built around rainy day or "April showers" themes. (In one, gifts were hidden in a rain barrel.)[84] Others followed seasonal cues like any other kind of party or were based on something particularly relevant to the engaged girl. A woman who planned to furnish her new home in the colonial style, for example, was given a shower with an "Early American" theme. A "kitty shower," given for an engaged cat lover, featured pussy willow decorations, china cat favors, guessing games based on the word "cat," and a gift-release device based on the nursery rhyme "pull pussy out of the well." The gifts consisted of the "kits" that each guest had produced (a traveler's sewing kit, a boot-blacking kit, an emergency kit, and so on), and these were placed in a well-shaped container. A kitten-shaped doorstop and an apron decorated with cat motifs were also featured at this event. Another shower novelty was the pull, which was a Jack Horner–like container with ribbon streamers that caused presents to "shower down." At a shower based on a honeymoon theme, for example, the container was a round paper moon (worked over wire) that hung in the doorway. When its protruding ribbons were pulled at an appointed time, the paper broke open like a piñata, releasing gifts onto the bride.[85]

Many showers played with the idea of outfitting a house. "Linen" theme parties were built around linens as gifts, of course, although the women contrived many ways to make them feel special or exciting; as Burt put it, every event needed "an original touch somewhere." A "gypsy peddler" bearing a large basket might show up at a linen shower, for example, ready to sing the praises of her "wares," which were all intended for the bride. Another common ploy was to hide the gifts. The guest of honor was handed a string and had to follow it (she was "led up and downstairs, inside and out") to the secreted cache. Another way to add novelty was to embed the gifts in a giant cobweb and ask the bride to be to extricate each of them separately.[86]

Commonly linens were accompanied by a rhyme that helped make light of the labor the item was actually intended for. The textiles were thus "animated" and took on the role of humble but willing assistants who would add a touch of magic to the task ahead. Items taken from webs of pink twine might thus bear messages such as this:

> Unromantic dusters we
> A homely part we play.
> Little elves of shine and sheen
> To chase the dust away.

Other conceits suggested for linens included a laundry bag with the lines "I'll keep soiled clothes concealed from sight / Till wash day comes and makes them white"; potholders that said, "By using these for dish and pot / You'll save your hands when things are hot"; and a towel with the verse "I'm just a towel but still, you see / Devotion I don't lack / Quite gladly I will go for thee / Right straight upon the rack." All of these notes conveyed the idea that shower gifts were an expression of affection. *How to Entertain at Home* suggested this verse, suitable for "any small embroidered piece":

> The girl who made me for the bride
> Her very best has really tried
> To show how much love she could place
> In a tiny little space.

Loving words appropriate for specific types of linens were also offered. A pillow sham:

> It seems a shame
> To send a sham
> In friendship's name
> But here I am.

Here comes your raft a-drifting in,
And so you shall, at once, begin
To search its cargo through and through
And find the gifts it holds for you.

A raft centerpiece that
carries a cargo of linens
for the bride

JULY – AUGUST

FIG. 3.20.
Hostesses could symbolize a "raft of good wishes" for the bride with this shower centerpiece featured in *Parties* magazine in spring 1928. The raft carried a "cargo of linens" as bridal gifts.

A lunch table cover read,

> When you spread your luncheon table
> For those dearest to your heart
> May I add to all your pleasures
> By just doing my humble part?[87]

Kitchen showers were also popular, and they too included rhymes, games, and animations that lent a happy note to the housewifely tasks ahead. The "basket of cheer" presented to the bride at one such event was filled with cooking tools bearing messages. A dish mop not only offered help, but complemented the bride on her beauty:

> My lady's hands are lily white, and it would be distressing
> To soil their snow with kitchen work, and spoil them for caressing.
> Then take this mop and use it well on cups and plates and such.
> 'Twill make them shine and will not harm 'the skin he loves to touch.'

Another shower featured the game of "kitchen ears," where guests were asked to correctly identify the source of cooking-related sounds such as beating eggs, striking matches, and other kitchen chores. Kitchen items were worked into a more embodied game at a shower suggested in 1928. Guests received the following invitation:

You're invited to a kitchen shower
We'll change it to a show
And all the presents meant for dower
Are what will make it go!

You're asked to make a sort of hat
Just out of kitchen tools
A kitchen apron wear with that
(We'll look a bunch of fools!)

Inverted colanders might thus be trimmed with scrub brushes, or sieves with tea balls and dishcloths.[88]

Embodied kitchenware decorations were in fact suggested for many kitchen showers. The bride centerpiece at one party had a body made of a potato masher and a head made of a dish mop. Her gown and veil were made of cellophane. "Mirandy," proclaimed "a clever maid despite her wooden head," was a similar table centerpiece. She too had dish mop hair but was further outfitted with hands and feet (kitchen forks and spoons), and her clothes, made of tea and dish towels and dust cloths, were more functional.[89] Kitchen tools were also used to fashion freestanding helper dolls that were given as gifts by the shower guests. I will discuss these at more length in chapter 5.

Related to the idea of embodiment is the fact that other showers revolved around personal gifts for the bride herself—items that she would wear, often in intimate situations. Emily Burt included a "Lingerie and Hosiery" section in her *Shower Book,* but other wearables were popular as well. Glover suggested a cap shower, where gifts ranged from luxurious lace boudoir caps, or a perfumed cap "to be put on after a shampoo," to "sweeping or cleaning caps." (Sweet breads and ice cream were to be served in "hat-shaped cases" at this party.) Handkerchief showers, where each guest gave a handkerchief that she had personalized for the bride in advance of the party, were common. At one such event, the hostess hid the handkerchiefs in paper roses and gave the bride the full "bouquet." A somewhat similar presentation was featured at a hosiery shower. Guests provided stockings that the hostess rolled in crepe paper, fashioning them into "funny babies" positioned inside a large crepe paper shoe.[90]

As the title indicates, in 1949, when Webster published *Shower Parties for All Occasions,* she wrote of more than bridal showers. Hostesses might plan showers for graduations, for a coworker's promotion, or for a friend who was leaving to go somewhere else. As I see it, this extension of the tradition reinforces the idea that a shower marked a liminal period associated with a rite of passage, but it also indicates that the wedding was not the only such passage women were concerned with by the 1940s. While bridal showers have never gone out of fashion, their heyday was over long before World War II.

Summary: Saturated Entertainments

Women's entertainments were, in sum, full expressions of the saturated world. Of all the domestic amusements, thematic parties existed most entirely in a time apart. From the rhyming invitation that heralded the event, to the closing moments, when guests gathered up their favors to take home, the party was organized around making special.[91] In this atmosphere, even the most everyday activity or object could be transformed. Everything was given a greater aesthetic charge: the space itself, the table, the menu, the food, and the activities were all made to amuse, delight, and stimulate the senses—this was, in its ideal form, a kind of fairyland. The party world was also highly embodied. Like the space itself, the people who came were likely to be dressed up, and there were anthropomorphized refreshments, table decorations, games, and gifts. Objects were often animated or made to "speak" through place cards or little notes, offering their services as humble but amusing helpers. Many of these objects were miniaturized, and their tiny size added to the sense of intimacy and embodiment as they were effectively brought inside the body boundary.

Miniaturized objects were also an expression of playfulness and humor; they brought a kind of childlike wonder to these events. Inside the set-apart space and time, adults were able to play like children, using toy pails as props, throwing marbles at teddy bears, dressing dolls, and making diorama-like landscapes with miniature trees and mirror lakes. Today such activities are relegated to children's parties, but women of the early twentieth century were unafraid to bring out the unjaded part of themselves that responded to the same pleasures. "Making things," another childhood pastime, was also an important part of these events. Most often it was the hostess who was particularly caught up in the making process, but many party games involved making things as well, and handmade gifts were sometimes the very point of showers. The gifts were always made in a saturated fashion—they were pleasurable to look at, touch, and use—but the making process was in many senses equal to the product in this situation, and the recipients valued the gifts for the loving labor that had gone into them as much as for their practicality.

Women's entertainments helped build community and fostered a sense of connectedness and belonging. Games, table arrangements, and favors stressed inclusiveness and sharing, and participants appreciated one another's efforts to make them feel welcome and valued. In contrast to the kind of entertainments that had prevailed in earlier eras where the emphasis was on a display of wealth, authority, and importance, these "domesticated" entertainments were democratic. Their prevailing allegories or myths focused not on power, but on fairyland or the natural world and calendrical cycles. For all its childlike qualities and sensual delights, however, fairyland was still a place filled with sophisticated, intelligent people, and the women who designed and frequented these parties played with their own assigned social roles, with cultural conventions and expectations, and with ideas.

Chapter Four

DRESSING-UP AS EMBODIED AMUSEMENT

Human nature has a weakness for masquerading as somebody or something else, and struts its best in borrowed plumes.

—MARIE JONREAU,
"NOVELTIES IN FANCY DRESS," 1897

Introduction: The Appeal of Dressing Up

Dress-up is an inherently satisfying form of saturated play, a way of adding intensity and pleasure to almost any activity.[1] Recognizing this, turn-of-the-century advice givers told would-be hostesses that they could be assured of a successful party if they asked their guests to come in costume. While the greatest amusement might ensue when guests came "in the most grotesque costume possible," even a small dress-up element such as a flower lei could "excite much fun."[2]

The satisfactions were many. As the *Delineator* noted in 1881, dress-up "delights the eye and excites the curiosity." Putting on a costume delighted more than the eye, however—it was a multisensory pleasure. For example, the "quivering" butterflies mentioned in the previous chapter (they were attached to costumes on bobbing wires) brought kinetic excitement, as they responded to the slightest body motion and heightened wearers' awareness of their movements. A similar effect was achieved with crepe paper streamers, which were popular on dress-up outfits of the 1920s. Attached to a foundation slip, they would move with a wearer's every step, "resulting in a graceful swinging," according to *How to Make Paper Costumes*. The sense of motion engendered by such a costume was so strong that one variation was even recommended as a personification of "The Breeze" (fig. 1.6). Tactility—the feel of the costume on one's skin—was always an important part of the dress-up experience, so much so that many descriptions of

108   dress-up outfits dwelled lovingly on their tactile properties. Paper outfits also rustled and crinkled, bringing in the element of sound. In addition, they were exciting because their fragility (there was some concern that they might tear) made them seem a little risque.[3]

Putting on a costume also allowed grownups to experience the imaginative freedom of childhood; dress-up was a form of make-believe, which carried an expansive sense of possibility. This quality even extended to the act of preparing costumes. Ruth Champenois explained, "We made . . . [the] costumes rather carefully . . . they were such fun to make that our thoughts went back to little-girl days when making doll's clothes was the all-important business of life."[4] The childlike reverie was linked with the creative satisfaction of envisioning and then actually making the outfits. Probably because of this creative stimulation and the embodied nature of the experience, dress-up could almost by itself make adult work seem like play. Clara Hasseltine Fair wrote in *Modern Priscilla* of the "thrill" of dressing up as an ancestral seamstress at a 1902 "Quilt Make" party. Actual quilting did take place at this event, but it was the experience of coming in costume that was most memorable. Dress-up could also be used to make light of serious tasks and roles, as in the "Labor Party" described in *Day Entertainments,* or the mock wedding that Emily Burt recommended for an anniversary party in 1919. The humorous bride was to wear a veil made of mosquito netting with dried orange peel trim, carrying a bouquet of chicken feathers.[5]

Dress-up was used to make serious public programs *feel* like amusements. (While my focus is still on domestic pastimes, there was so much interpenetration between public and private in this arena that in this chapter I interweave discussion of various kinds of events.) Thus educational groups sometimes used costume to increase the appeal of their activities. For example, Canadian Women's Institute groups organized playful costume parades in the 1920s. In describing one that took place at an agricultural fair where marchers wore ancestral wedding dresses, *Farmer's Advocate* magazine likened it to "an animated edition of some old family album."[6] Similarly entrepreneurs used costume to add a playful touch to their commercial ventures. An acceptable way for women to make money in the early twentieth century, for example, was to open a tea room—a restaurant that catered primarily to female customers. In the 1920s, some tea room proprietors had their waitresses dress to match the "colonial" decor of their establishments. Those who worked for the "Martha Ann Tea Shop," for example, wore "becoming caps" and "gay little print gowns of colonial fashion"; in another establishment, servers wore "Puritan caps" and blue frocks with white aprons. There were also women who built businesses around the design and marketing of colonial-looking embroidery patterns and who took on colonial personas such as "Aunt Martha" and "Grandmother Clark." Quilt promoter Carrie Hall liked to dress as her character when she lectured in department stores and women's clubs and became known for her red moiré dress and net fichu. As we shall see, these same practices—and the same costume elements—were also used at home parties.[7]

Dressing up is a way of playing with ideas and identities through one's own body; it is an embodied way of relating to the world. The women discussed in this chapter embodied everything from historical characters to flowers and other elements of the natural world, literary heroines, abstract concepts, and artifacts of daily life. They were relating to other cultures and time periods in the most direct and personal way possible: they were *incorporating* them and in a sense taking them on as part of themselves. Often they even connected bodily with the spaces around them, as they dressed to match their environments and became part of the decoration. They also expressed an intimate relationship with objects that filled the environments. Sometimes they symbolically *became* those objects through their dress; other times they used them as personal adornments and props.[8]

The aestheticizing quality of dress-up was always well understood, and individuals were highly conscious of the effect their outfits created. Those giving costuming advice repeatedly stressed the idea that individuals could choose outfits to showcase their best features; a brunette might look particularly good in a red, white, and black Brittany peasant costume, for example, while a blond would look good as an "arctic maiden" or the impersonation of "Air" or "Canadian Snow." *Art, Society and Accomplishments* went on enthusiastically about the appealing costumes that sisters might wear; if they came together dressed as a "set" (apple and pear blossom, sovereign and shilling, orange and lemon, and the like), the effect would be especially charming. Descriptions of available materials also dwelled lovingly on color and texture. A *Good Housekeeping* feature on crepe paper costumes, for example, talked of "the subtle shades of flowers of dawn," and the brilliant colors of sunsets or birds of paradise.[9]

There was a close association, also, between turn-of-the-century costuming and the important aesthetic movements of the day. We shall discuss several individuals identified with the Aesthetic and Arts and Crafts movements who made illustrations or staged photographs, pageants, and other dress-up activities, influencing the iconic images that were considered appropriately picturesque. The costumes we are looking at here, in other words, were in no way marginal or of interest to only a small subset of the population. On the contrary, they were representative of the most up-to-date artistic attitudes and images of their day.

Many commentators have written about costuming as a kind of personal wish-fulfillment. Stevenson and Bennett, authors of *Van Dyck in Check Trousers: Fancy Dress in Art and Life 1700–1900*, claim that "people often dressed up in hopes they could take on reflected charm of a period or person they admired." This idea was expressed in 1930, when *Good Housekeeping* ran a piece entitled "Let Fancy Dress Release Your Dream and Be Just What You'd Like to Seem." "Perhaps you've never been yourself / 'Till someone says, 'Let's masquerade,'" wrote Caroline Grey in the same magazine.[10] Perhaps wish-fulfillment was significant at elite fancy dress balls held in the preindustrial era, when individuals were likely to impersonate specific kings, queens, or other historical figures, but I do not think those who attended the "Quilt Makes" and other events I am writing about were really concerned with taking on particular personas. Rather, dress-up helped create a certain *feeling* in a group, or communal, context. (Play-acting needed an audience—it had to be shared.) In turn, costume affected the shared experience of the group, furthering its sense of connectedness or social bonding. Moreover, dress-up projected more than individual personae: taken together, the costumes projected and actually helped manifest the aesthetically saturated reality this book is exploring. They portrayed a happy, conflict-free, rather magical world, and for a short time they helped create it. This aspect of dress-up has not been fully explored by previous scholars, but I believe it is the most interesting and most important aspect of all.

I explore historic dress-up in several ways in this chapter, always looking to the ways women used it to manifest their saturated vision. I offer a typology of costume categories and examine the many contexts in which dress-up was seen in the period under consideration. I also contrast the divergent way men used costume for their own somewhat different ends.

Types of Dress-Up: Women and Children

The range of possible costumes was, of course, vast, but I find it useful to group them into several categories. These groups overlap, and the classifications are primarily meaningful as organizational devices for discussion, but they do offer a point of entry to this complex topic. While every costume would ideally be considered "aesthetic," most outfits fell into one of three main categories: historical, exotic/international, and allegorical/fairyland.[11]

Historical costuming could theoretically draw from any era and presumably from any part of the world, but Americans generally thought of history in terms of their own country. Dress-up outfits occasionally represented European royalty, but by far the most common historical impersonations were colonial. (This term was loosely interpreted; it referred to a preindustrial past, ranging from the mid-seventeenth century to about 1840, and elements from the entire time were freely mixed together). As we shall soon see, colonial-theme dress-up was enormously popular from the time of the Civil War through the 1930s. In previous articles I have argued that the costumed colonial enactment was a vehicle through which women both "claimed" and "tamed" history. They cast the past through a domestic filter, playing up the importance of homey tasks such as spinning and cooking, and casting a romantic glow over historic events. When she dressed as Martha Washington or the iconic spinner, Priscilla Mullins (a historic character mythologized in Longfellow's exceedingly popular poem "The Courtship of Miles Standish"), a woman was in effect acting as a domestic heroine. She might do this as a means to an end, since women organized many costumed enactments in order to help civilize public institutions and public life, or she might do it simply for amusement. The character of colonial dress-up did change over time. From the Civil War period to about 1880, it was typically comical, but enactments often took on a more reverent and serious quality at the turn of the century, when women were especially active in reform-oriented social and artistic movements and patriotic/hereditary societies such as the Daughters of the American Revolution [DAR]. By the interwar period, the reverential quality gave way to a greater commercialism—it was in the 1920s that the colonial tea room was at its peak—and colonial costuming was at the same time reduced to a kind of seasonal platitude. Such outfits became an integral part of the calendrical cycle and were brought out for Washington's Birthday, July 4th, and Thanksgiving. Because they served as holiday markers in schools, they were increasingly identified with children.[12]

Colonial outfits always reflected the fashionable looks of their own day; in the 1880s "colonial dames" wore silhouettes that echoed the contemporary bustle, for example, while those of the 1920s wore short, waistless gowns. Charm or visual appeal was what mattered. *Dennison's Party Magazine* noted in 1927 that "the costumes of the guests [would] furnish the major part of the decorations" at a colonial tea, and the author asked rhetorically, "What woman can resist the thought of herself with snowy white hair curling over one shoulder? Or the appealing idea of a lacy kerchief folded around her throat?" (see fig. 3.19).[13] Even those who donned colonial dress because of their interest in ancestral pedigree or historic preservation were not particularly concerned with historical accuracy. Eliza Philbrick of Salem, Massachusetts, a member of several patriotic groups, made a costume that she first wore to an 1898 DAR party in Boston. It "felt" colonial because she made it from homespun cloth that had been saved in a trunk

112   for the past century and a crewel-embroidered panel that had probably been part
of a set of eighteenth-century bed hangings. Philbrick wore the dress repeatedly
but changed it slightly in subsequent years, probably in response to changing
styles in the fashions of the teens.[14]

FIG.4.1.
Members of the Mary Floyd Tallmadge Chapter of the Daughters of the American Revolution, Litchfield,
Connecticut, posed in costume shortly after their group was founded in 1899. Each of the women interpreted
colonial dress differently. The poster behind them announces a Colonial Tea and Loan Exhibition, which was
probably the event they were dressed for. Courtesy, the Litchfield Historical Society, Litchfield, Connecticut.

Women's insistence on the picturesque and their taming of the colonial era
was so pervasive that historic enactments were generally thought of as "feminine" by the turn of the century. Women participated in much greater numbers
than men, and many advice columns spoke of the difficulty of getting men to
take part. In her 1905 article, "The Church Sociable," Helen Landon proclaimed
that an event with a colonial theme was "warranted to be a success, since every
one is interested in it from the very start." Nevertheless she indicated that it would
be particularly charming "if the men *[could] be persuaded* to wear their grand-
father's knee-breeches, buckles and stocks" (italics added).[15]

Exotic dress is the second category of my costume typology. This is a broad,
inclusive idea, usually relating to international costume—that is, garments worn
in other parts of the world or by different kinds of people.[16] Exotic dress-up could
incorporate almost any kind of person that seemed "other" or different. (Even

FIG. 4.2.

Young women attending a Japanese-theme tea were fully dressed for the occasion. The illustration appeared in Nellie Mustain's 1902 volume, *Popular Amusements for Indoors and Out-of-Doors.*

FIG. 4.3.

This image was taken at a "Masonic party" held about the turn of the century. Men, women, and children all appear in blackface, although they wear a variety of different types of costumes. While the names of some of the individuals are identified in a handwritten note, the photographer, date, and location of the party are not indicated. Courtesy, the Wisconsin Historical Society, WHS classified file 895, WHi-33711.

114   colonial costume could in a sense be considered exotic, but those who adopted it thought of it as historical, so I treat it as a separate category.) Following the model established at the enormously popular and culturally resonant international fairs or expositions, individuals transformed themselves into would-be Brittany peasants, Dutch girls, Middle Eastern dancers, and Japanese or (American) Indian maidens. Just as it was in colonial attire, charm, rather than ethnographic accuracy, was the operative principle. "No one would probably view the national costumes [seen at dress-up events] with more curiosity than the peasantry they are intended to portray," stated *Art, Society and Accomplishments* in 1891. Exotic dress-up was especially common at women-run fairs—that is, at fundraising bazaars. A "Floral and Musical Charity Festival" held in Detroit in 1890, for example, included individuals in Dutch, German, Greek, Arabian, Japanese, Italian, Russian, French, Spanish, Scottish, and Scandinavian costume, in addition to the colonial-looking denizens of the "Log Cabin" booth. International or "Carnival of Nations" themes were also common at church socials and a variety of home entertainments, including card parties.[17] Exotic dress-up might also be based on a single theme or locale, meaning that everyone might come dressed as a gypsy.

Exotic dress was not really all-inclusive, since costumers generally chose to dress as familiar people they could identify with. European folk (understood as "peasant") outfits were most common, no doubt because those creating the costumes were usually of European ancestry themselves. Oriental costume was extremely popular, but the only parts of the Far East that were specifically represented were China and Japan. With the exception of light-skinned Egyptians,

FIG. 4.4.
"The Spirit of the Wheat" was photographed by Frances and Mary Allen at a pageant held in Deerfield, Massachusetts, about 1913. Courtesy, The Pocumtuck Valley Memorial Association, Memorial Hall Museum, Deerfield, Massachusetts (96.14.639).

people of African nations were not represented at all. White Americans *did* dress up as the dark-skinned people they knew best—that is, as African Americans—although they did not do so at international-theme events. "Blackface" dress-up was typically confined to special "plantation" or "minstrel" parties (fig. 4.3). Since the international expositions that gave rise to this type of dress-up were steeped in imperialistic assumptions and sensibility, one might argue that such costume reflected a supremacist, racist attitude. Unquestionably, dressing up as the other was a form of appropriation, and these exoticized others were largely presented as childlike (American "darkies" were painted as particularly comical). However, *all* types of dress-up portrayed the same romanticized quality, and this kind of appropriation did not involve conquest. I find it significant that it was based on acting-out or becoming—that is, *incorporating*

FIG. 4.5.
This figure, pictured in Lillian Pascal Day's *Social Entertainments: A Book of Practical Suggestions for Entertaining* (1914), represented a "Bird Woman." Paper birds were not only used on her headdress, but were pinned to her costume.

or embodying the other. I think it implied an imagined sense of connection with those others, and entering into a kind of community with them rather than expressing aggression or a power relationship. Significantly, given my argument that this was a female attitude, men did not generally like to don exotic costumes, as they too were seen as "feminine."

Allegorical or *fairyland* costume is the third of my dress-up categories. A broad range of outfits is included: imaginative symbolic impersonations such as "Autumn," "Liberty," "Night," "Stardust," or "The Spirit of Wheat" (fig. 4.4); classical-looking dress; personified images of nature, including birds, flowers, fruits and vegetables (figs. 4.5, 4.6); costumes based on fairytales or nursery rhymes, including representations of medieval ladies, forest sprites, or "BoPeep"; pastoral icons such as "dairymaids" and "farm lassies"; and fanciful holiday outfits such as Eastertime bunnies or Valentine's Day heart ladies (fig. 3.2). This category also incorporates a class of children's outfits, such as the "Little Lord Fauntleroy" suit, that were associated with "Aesthetic" dress.

I group all of these outfits together because they primarily functioned as picturesque icons. While it might seem reasonable to put medieval dress or representations of eighteenth-century dress such as the dairymaid in the historical costume category, they were adopted for their romantic qualities, not their historical
connotations. When *Good Housekeeping* described a costume of a lady of the
"Moyen Age" (middle ages), she was said to "spend her time making tapestry and
waiting for her lord to return from the wars"; she was an imaginary storybook
heroine rather than a real character. At a different time, the same magazine spoke
of a "Godey Girl" costume. The Godey reference was to the popular nineteenth-
century woman's magazine, but the impersonation had nothing to do with wom-
en's history. The Godey Girl was notable only for her "hoopskirts and tiers of
flounce," her parasol, and her bloomer bottoms.[18]

Allegorical/fairyland costume was perhaps the purest expression of the saturated world. As Theresa Wolcott explained in *Ladies' Home Journal* in 1916, fairyland was a place where nothing was "tawdry or gaudy"—it was a place where
people were "always doing something nice."[19] It was free of struggle and pain; it
created a sense of enchantment. "It is a wonderfully pretty picture to look at the
masquers as they promenade," exclaimed the *Delineator* in 1881.

> [One sees Queen] Elizabeth sociably chatting with a North American
> Indian...What a delicious contradiction it all is! . . . It is fairy-land, and
> one wants the masquers never to . . . come back to every-day life. . . . It
> brings to mind . . . [Moore's] poem that describes so well the delights of
> the Feast of Roses in the Valley of Cashmer . . .
> "And oh! if there be an elysium on earth,
> It is this, it is this!"[20]

While men hardly embraced historic and international dress-up, they had
almost *nothing* to do with allegorical and fairyland costume; this particularly
saturated category was exclusively identified with women and children. Not surprisingly, fairyland costumes *were* strongly linked with the young. The costumes
were very popular at the juvenile dress-up parties that began to come into fashion
in the 1890s; such events seem to have functioned, in fact, almost as animated
storybooks. Harriet Adams Ganahl, writing in 1901, noted that "some of the best
dresses worn by young people are suggested by illustrated books, fairy tales and
other [juvenile] fiction." Ruth Champenois echoed the idea in a *Good Housekeeping* feature called "Let's Dress Up." "There is all of Fairyland and the world of
Mother Goose to draw on for inspiration," she noted. Her suggestions were indeed
taken from contemporary literary references. She described a "Squash Blossom"
costume, for example, that made its wearer "look like the enchanting *Susan Blue*

or one of the beguiling little maids in 'Tip-a-Toe'" from 'Marigold Garden.'" Children dressed in sweet-looking dress of this sort seemed, as Barbara Baines put it, "quaint and dainty." I find this an interesting choice of words. Dainty dress, like the dainty food discussed in the previous chapter, was something that made life seem more refined; it was feminine, light, and delightful. Since daintiness implied miniaturization, it seemed naturally aligned with children.[21]

Ganahl claimed the Squash Blossom costume was based on a Kate Greenaway illustration, and she spoke of a "Greenaway party," which was the "newest idea in children's entertainments." Greenaway has already been mentioned as an icon of the saturated world. She was a British illustrator and children's author whose work was overwhelmingly popular in the last third of the nineteenth century. Bearing titles such as *Fairy Gift, The Toy Book,* and *The Language of Flowers,* her books portrayed a pastoral landscape filled with cherubs, birds, and dewy-eyed, innocent children in "old fashioned" clothes (typically, early-nineteenth-century styles with empire-waisted dresses and bonnets). Her images were rendered in a light, almost cartoonish style that was unusual for its time and was itself considered dainty and refreshing. The costume worn by Greenaway's sweet-looking children came to symbolize Aesthetic sensibility. In England, Liberty of London sold Greenaway-style frocks as "artistic dress"; in France, the Aesthetic dress style was referred to as "Greenawayisme." Americans who wanted to be in the vanguard of aesthetic taste were encouraged to play with such imagery at costume parties.[22]

The other British Aesthetic artist whose work influenced dress-up was Walter Crane. Crane also illustrated children's books and was concerned with "ideal beauty." He too used a lighter illustrative style to portray an innocent, happy world. Books such as *Flora's Feast: A Masque of Flowers* and *The Baby's Opera* were filled with images of fairies and other characters of the forest and garden characters such as "Daffodil," "Hollyhock," "Primrose," and "Poppy."[23] Many were rendered with upside-down flowers as hats and overlapping petals cascading from their bodies. It was just this type of figure that became popular in dress-up costume (see fig. 1.5). Partygoers were encouraged to "copy their dress from Crane" in order to create the kind of atmosphere that would feel like a "veritable scene from Fairyland" (fig. 4.6). Marie Jonreau wrote in the 1890s about the "wonderful possibilities" that tinted crepe paper afforded for making flower and vegetable costumes that looked just like Crane's illustrations. "Flowerland parties" were portrayed as quintessentially saturated experiences, as an 1892 feature in the *New York Home Journal* made clear. Even the very day of a party seemed to be under a spell:

The birds were carolling their merry lays. The blue sky was entirely free of clouds. The brooklets murmured gayly [*sic*] over the stones. . . . The Calla Lilies were robed in white satin and the Lilies-of-the-Valley in white silk. . . . The Misses Hyacinth wore exquisitely shaded silks which had a delicate, clinging perfume.[24]

FIG. 4.6.
"Chrysanthemum" was one of the characters suggested for an Eastertime bazaar in *Ladies' Home Journal* in April 1904. Her costume directly recalls the type of floral characters popularized by Walter Crane at the end of the nineteenth century (see also fig. 1.4).

It is important to remember that, despite their associations with children, fairyland costumes were also worn by adults. Childhood was idealized at the turn of the century. This is the time when *Peter Pan,* a play about refusing to grow up (1904), found great cultural resonance. The interest in holding on to youthful innocence is symbolized for me in the "Childhood Party for Grown-ups" that was described in *Bright Ideas for Entertaining* in 1905. Ladies' club members were to act like children for this event. In addition to coming in costume, each was expected to perform an appropriate stunt or recitation—for example, an individual dressed as a baby might sit in front of the others and wail. The picturesque quality of the juvenile costumes was much appreciated, and everyone participated in a "grand march" where they could be seen to advantage.[25] As we have seen, this kind of fairyland image pervaded contemporary popular culture. Theatrical productions with dancing bonbons and titles such as "The Butterflies' Ball" appeared on the New York stage, for example, and civic celebrations included fairyland-theme parade floats. Many communities held "Floral Fetes," which featured a range of costumed tableaux. In Saratoga, New York's 1898 production, "The Realm of the Rose," girls of about eight to ten years of age appeared in picturesque outfits such as "Silver Leaf" and "Hummingbird." Local productions of this type were in turn illustrated in the popular press. The *Puritan* magazine included many photographs of the Realm of the Rose, for example, encouraging readers to create similar enactments of their own. Photographs of these events also graced every issue of *Parties* magazine.[26]

FIG. 4.7.
"Butterfly Boy" was illustrated in *Ladies' Home Journal* in November 1919. Wings were much-beloved on early-twentieth-century costumes (see fig. 4.10), and this boy wears particularly large ones.

While most dress-up outfits fit into one of the three categories already mentioned, there were miscellaneous others that deserve mention as well. Some of the advice literature of the late nineteenth century specifically referred to a "fancy dress" category, for example, that included the types of costume associated with European masquerade parties, including Harlequin and Pierrot outfits. These never dominated the American imagination, but they were clearly understood as dress-up conventions. Another category relates directly to the theme of embodiment: women dressed up as images and objects that were iconic in contemporary culture. At fundraising fairs held about 1910, this even took the form of popular advertisements—saleswomen dressed as figures from the ads. Other examples were drawn from—and sometimes literally incorporated—fashionable artifacts. The "Lamp Shade Costume" described in the 1897 feature "Novelties in Fancy Dress" not only took the form of a contemporary lamp shade, but had small lamp shades attached at wrists. The wearer was also advised to fashion a hat in the same shape (it would be made with a wire frame and contain a glass chimney in the center) and carry another small, shaded lamp. The latter costume is even more intriguing when we remember the period fascination with lighting effects.[27]

Finally, there were *"inversion" costumes* that helped their wearers play with gender, class, and social role. Women enjoyed dressing as men, for example, and

FIG. 4.8.
Alice Austen took a photograph of herself and two of her friends dressed up as men in 1891. (Austen is at left.) "We look so funny with those mustaches on," she said when she saw the photograph sixty years later, "I can hardly tell which is which." Austen lived in Staten Island, New York. Courtesy, the Staten Island Historical Society.

FIG. 4.9.
This couple posed in "Hard Time Social" costumes were included in Mustain's *Popular Amusements for Indoors and Out-of-Doors.* "Poverty socials" (also called "rag" or "rag-tag" parties) were quite popular at the turn of the century, and they were one of the few types of costume parties that men liked to attend.

some party suggestions called for them to appear as Rough Riders or as male laborers (fig. 4.8). Judging from the descriptions of these entertainments, this was exciting for several reasons. Cross-dressing was appealing in itself, but the women also seem to have enjoyed the very feel on their bodies of work clothes such as flannel shirts and overalls. (Middle-class ladies would never have had this experience under ordinary circumstances.) At a time when looking prosperous was very important, furthermore, both men and women liked to dress "down" at "poverty socials" and "rag parties" (fig. 4.9). (While the racial stereotypes of blackface costuming were certainly most salient, I think "plantation" or "minstrel" parties also had a dressing-down, role-reversal element.)

There were also many entertainments where dress-up was used to play with gender expectations and other kinds of social roles. As mentioned in the previous chapter, at the turn of the century these were sometimes based around the New Woman idea. In 1905, for example, Linscott encouraged women coming to a party of this kind to dress in a mannish fashion and to bring an apron for their escorts to wear.[28]

Making Costumes

Those who went to fancy dress balls might rent their costumes or even have them made by dressmakers (significant sums could be spent on this),[29] but the dress-up outfits worn at domestic amusements or public enactments were usually made at home. The advice literature was filled with reassurances that costumes were easy to construct. "Any one possessed of a knowledge of sewing and a little cleverness can get up a[n] . . . attractive fancy dress herself," declared the *Puritan* magazine in 1897. In her 1901 article, "The Story of a Paper Ball," Harriet Ganahl told her readers that while every town was sure to have some genius in costume making, every "proud mamma" could "find a way to make her loved little one look captivating" at a dress-up party. Ardern Holt's *Fancy Dresses Described*, originally published in 1879, was so popular that it went through five more editions before the end of the century. (Its companion piece, *Gentlemen's Fancy Dress*, was reprinted twice.) Populist middle-class magazines such as the *Delineator* (published by the Butterick pattern company) also routinely described dress-up outfits that could be "easily gotten up at home." The conventions for costumes did become simpler over time, meaning that a greater and greater percentage of the population could be involved in dress-up. The "calico party" that was in vogue at the turn of the century emphasized costumes made from inexpensive cottons or other noncostly materials, for example, with wedding veils and other sheer fabrics made from cheesecloth. Simpler dress styles also prevailed in contemporary fashion by the teens, making costume construction even easier. As a result, women with less time, money, and skill were able to participate in these activities.[30]

Crepe paper, which was positioned as a cost-effective cloth substitute, was also introduced at this time. It was undoubtedly a real boon to dress-up. It was inexpensive but at the same time visually exciting. In describing the "new idea in children's entertainments," a Paper Ball, in 1901, Ganahl wrote of flower and butterfly costumes made from "the many beautiful and varied kinds of fancy papers the shops provide nowadays." The papers *were* in fact appealing and diverse; they had innovative designs and came in a wide array of saturated colors (the Dennison company listed thirty-one hues in 1906). Some had shaded effects; others were printed with plaids and other patterns (see fig. 1.8). There was also a wide range of paper lace and colorful foils that could be used in lieu of costly trims. When I first encountered these turn-of-the-century papers, I actually found myself gasping at their stunning quality. Paper materials were also easy to work with. Where fabric had to be stitched, paper could often be glued, meaning that costumes could be made with little if any sewing. Crepe paper did not fray and could be cut into ribbons, streamers, and other shapes. These properties also meant that there was more room for experimentation, resulting in new outfit types.[31]

The easiest way to build a costume was to work on top of existing garments. A mother making a picturesque boy's costume, for example, might just add a ruffled crepe paper "shirt front" to his suit jacket and then tie "immense bows and rosettes" at his knees and toes. Girl's outfits such as "Miss Holly Berry" and "Little Miss Rose" might similarly be made with tiers of paper flounces attached to cotton underclothes. Costume makers were advised to avoid fitted sleeves if at all possible, as they might not hold up to strenuous activity, but cap sleeves which

A BRILLIANT TISSUE
BUTTERFLY.

FIG. 4.10.
Instructions for creating different kinds of wings were included in Dennison's *How to Make Paper Costumes* (ca. 1920). The illustrations on the left represent (top to bottom) Cupid wings, butterfly wings, and angel wings. Smoother wings, such as those used on fairy and bee costumes, were also covered. The illustration on the right, showing a butterfly costume with large tissue paper wings, is from *Puritan* magazine, 1900. (See also fig. 4.7.)

covered the shoulders like little capes looked charming, particularly in flower   *123*
costumes. These same construction principles applied to adult outfits. The foundation garment might be an old dress or an appropriately colored blouse or skirt.
The foundation of a bat costume described in 1897 consisted of dusky grey garments covered with bat cut-outs that were brought to life with the addition of
dramatic wings. These were made from black silk fitted over rigid ribs, as in an
umbrella. They were attached to long black gloves and fastened over the shoulders like a cape.[32]

By the 1920s, when Dennison published its popular 32–page booklet, *How To
Make Paper Costumes,* current fashion favored straight, waistless dresses, and it
was easy to construct slip-over tunics that would fit, rather like an apron, over
adult women's garments. These were adaptable and formed the basis of outfits of
all kinds: exotic costumes such as "French Peasants" or "Scotch lassies"; floral
outfits and personifications of birds, butterflies, and vegetables; and allegorical
figures such as "Fire." (The fluttering streamers of the type described at the beginning of the chapter were attached to these tunics.) *How To Make Paper Costumes*
also featured a special section on fashioning wings, wands, and crowns that could
be used with a variety of costume styles (fig. 4.10).[33]

The Uses of Dress-Up

Having surveyed the appeal of dress-up and the general forms it took, let us turn
now to a discussion of the ways it was used and the roles it played in American
social life in the fifty-year period from 1880 to 1930. We will focus at first on the
highly visible public contexts in which it appeared. The overview will be roughly
chronological, although it will not be completely linear, since different forms
sometimes necessitate separate discussion.

We actually must begin in the middle of the nineteenth century, when costuming began to be an important element in American life. As we have seen,
industrialization had progressed by this time to the point that there was a growing middle class, meaning that increasing numbers of people had leisure time to
enjoy theatrical performances. They flocked to see costumed plays and "living
pictures," or tableaux, which were included with most dramatic shows. They also
began to stage entertainments at home. These activities became so popular that
guides such as *Hudson's Private Theatricals for Home Performances* were said to be
"pour[ing] off the American press" in the 1850s.[34] Women adapted this same
kind of theatrical vignette as part of their work for social good. To raise funds for
the YMCA in 1858, for example, Boston women offered a dramatized representation of Benjamin Franklin's birthplace, complete with costumed singers. A few

124   years later, women of many northern cities again staged historical tableaux at their Civil War "sanitary fairs," which were large scale fundraising bazaars organized in support of the Union cause. Among the most popular features of the fairs were their "New England Kitchens," which were in effect thematic restaurants representing country farmhouses, supposedly of the Pilgrim era. Visitors were served "olde time" foods by costumed waitresses, whose antique veneer lent further historical flavor. The women also reenacted domestic tasks in these settings, including spinning, quilting, and apple paring, and even held mock colonial weddings for which they charged an additional admission fee.[35]

Similar costumed portrayals exploded in the last quarter of the nineteenth century. One stimulus was patriotic sentiment in the Centennial era, which fueled interest in colonial costuming. There were Centennial Balls, where well-positioned individuals appeared in aristocratic-looking colonial attire (sometimes fancy dress and sometimes actual ancestral garments),[36] but there were also more theatrical dress-up events that were accessible to a much wider audience. "Centennial Teas" were popular. One held in Woonsocket, Rhode Island, and dubbed a "Martha Washington Reception" drew over two thousand participants and turned away another one thousand. Some of the teas functioned as continuations of the humorous New England kitchens, while others were more like bazaars; in either form, dress-up was central. Sale tables at the Philadelphia Centennial Tea were presided over by ladies arrayed in full "Martha Washington costume," five hundred of whom participated in an evening procession. A full-scale New England kitchen was also set up at the Centennial Exhibition in Philadelphia "to represent a backwoodman's cot[tage] in Vermont or Connecticut" from about 1776 and featured stock characters such as "Priscilla," "Mother," and "Obadiah." It was so popular that organizer Eliza Southwick kept it open for several years after the exhibition closed. She later staged additional kitchens in the 1880s to raise funds for a soldier's home, and in 1893 for the Columbian Exposition in Chicago.[37]

The proliferation of international expositions in the last quarter of the century also stimulated the appearance of exotic dress-up. Bazaars, which by then were a ubiquitous feature of the social landscape, often followed the exposition model, with international-theme sales booths. These could be general, following the "All Nations" theme, but they sometimes focused on a single ethnicity, especially if it were thematically appropriate to the cause at hand. A fair held to benefit a Swiss Benevolent Society was thus set up to look like an Alpine chalet, with costumed frauleins in attendance. By the 1890s, "Japanese maids," "gypsies," Italian "peasants," and wholesome "Dutch girls" could be seen in almost every community in the country. The exotic-looking, sometimes slightly titillating costume of these events was a major part of their appeal; newspapers referred to the plea- *125* sure of seeing the "fair women at the fairs" and wrote long descriptions of their appearance. Dress-up helped create the kind of atmosphere that helped everyone feel good, enough so that they cheerfully gave money to the cause at hand. Exotic dress-up was also central to a related type of fundraising scheme that swept the country at the end of the century, the kermiss (also spelled kirmesse, kirmess, or kyrmiss). This was a combination folk dance festival and fair, featuring food or sale articles from different countries. Professional managers sometimes came to a town for several weeks to teach dances to groups of young people, who would perform in costume at the actual event.[38]

Allegorical and fairyland outfits were equally seen at bazaars and other public events. Such costumes contributed to the desired "wilderness of beauty" that "looked as if a thousand fairies had been at work." The outfits designed for grown-up characters such as "Chrysanthemum" (fig. 4.6) and "Marsh Marigold" were just as picturesque as those worn by the children at the previously described Paper Ball.

Tableaux, drills, and costumed community sings were also integral to turn-of-the-century church and community life, and there was an abundance of advice books with step-by-step instructions for details such as choreographed drill formations, dialogue, and costume making. Here again, dress-up conformed to the expected categories. Historical dress-up was featured, for example, in *American Heroines* (1900), which offered "patriotic pictures" (tableaux) "suitable for entertainments at churches, secular societies and lodges." Exotic and allegorical/fairy-land dress-up was included in Edna J. Witherspoon's *Fancy Drills for Evening and Other Entertainments* (1894). The activities she recommended included a fan drill, in which lines of young women dressed in kimonos manipulated large folding fans in syncopated rhythm; a dairymaid drill, complete with polonaise costumes and decorated milking stools; and a broom drill. The latter functioned as an inversion of the male military parade, as the "broom brigaders" marched with brooms and mops in place of rifles, chanting lyrics such as "Our peace-loving weapons we only . . . wield. . . . We . . . brush away suff'ring and sorrow . . . and everything hurtful." Other drills involved floral costumes and "poetic empire gowns" (marchers carried shepherd's crooks) or props such as hoops, dumbbells, tambourines, or teacups. Witherspoon even wrote of a "fancy dress drill," where each person appeared in a different costume. Drills were frequently staged in schools and involved young people as well as adults.[39]

By the end of the nineteenth century, dress-up was incorporated into activities sponsored by church groups and social organizations. Masquerades had begun to lose their association with the wealthy; Kathy Peiss, author of *Cheap*

126 *Amusements: Working Women and Leisure in Turn of the Century New York,* even claims that costume balls were routinely held in working-class social clubs at the turn of the century in the winter months.[40] Balls were generally superceded, however, by more informal "masquerade parties" that did not necessarily include dancing. These parties were suitable for all ages, which explains the increasing popularity of children's dress-up. At this point the "calico party" often featured young costumed children, and the term "calico" was used to refer not just to inexpensive materials, but to costumes characterized by sweetness and innocence.[41]

Costumed impersonations were also used by individuals and groups for a variety of political, social, and artistic reform purposes in the early twentieth century. For example, members of the patriotic /hereditary societies that had been founded in the 1890s, including the DAR and the Colonial Dames of America, made great use of ancestral guise (see fig. 4.1). They staged costumed activities with colonial scenes that they felt would inspire a reverence for the past and help "Americanize" new immigrants. Some of their enactments were in essence variations of the New England kitchen, with proceeds going to historic preservation (often to save homes associated with Revolutionary heroes). Society members also posed in patriotic tableaux in parade floats and put on a variety of other animated historic programs. "The Days of Auld Lang Syne," a pageant staged jointly in 1896 by members of the DAR and Colonial Dames in Rhode Island, was an outdoor, scripted production that functioned as a series of tableaux. The scenes ranged from "signing deeds with the Indians" to the "Sewing Circle of 1812." This event helped initiate a national community pageant movement, and by 1912 *American Homes and Gardens* pronounced the country "pageant-mad." A professional organization, the American Pageant Association, was founded the next year. The movement remained strong into the 1920s.[42]

Where British pageant givers drew their primary imagery from the medieval era, Americans—even those who were not associated with the DAR and similar groups—recast the scene to the New World. Because the enactments focused on local history, reformers of various kinds embraced the pageant form as an educational opportunity for generating civic and national pride. Performers in a single pageant might number in the hundreds, even thousands, meaning that large percentages of given communities were often involved. Progressive reformers such as settlement house workers, like members of the patriotic societies, thought pageants a good mechanism for inculcating newcomers with democratic values (because many of the scenes had minimal dialogue, even immigrants with poor English could take part). Civic leaders felt they brought the citizenry into community life. Arts activists believed pageants could help raise the general level

of aesthetic sensibility and appreciated the fact that they brought visual imagery,   *127*
poetry, music, dance, and theater to broad audiences.[43]

While historical subjects were most common, the pageant form was highly
adaptable. During the teens there were pageants celebrating everything from
industry and education to the sea, and supporting causes ranging from foreign
missionary work (the "Pageant of Darkness and Light" in Chicago) to the promotion of fruit ("The Princess and the Magic Raisins" in Fresno). College productions often dramatized the liberal arts—at Mt. Holyoke in 1912, performers
pantomimed chemical elements, fruit flies (illustrating Mendel's genetic theories),
an array of plants and flowers, and Greek muses. Even ostensibly historical pageants incorporated allegorical imagery (see fig. 4.4). Historical scenes would be
punctuated by allegorical interludes (characters such as "Columbia" and "Liberty"
were popular) or would integrate allegory into the narrative. In Boston's 1910
"Cave Life to City Life" extravaganza, for example, dancers dressed as "Dust
Clouds" and "Disease Germs" attacked the city in an imaginative dramatization
of public health.[44]

Costume was critical to creating the right mood for scenes of any kind, and
pageant costumes followed the same conventions as dress-up for parties, drills,
socials, and bazaars. The same categories of dress were seen (admittedly there
were few exotic outfits, but some Indian maidens and recent "peasant" immigrants were worked in). As fig. 4.4 illustrates, pageant participants seem to have
enjoyed the same sensual and emotional satisfaction from their costumes as
those involved in domestic entertainments. The guiding vision of the pageants,
in fact—and the one played out in scene after scene—was domesticated and
saturated. This is not surprising, since women were key players in the pageant
movement. The underlying fairylike vision was evident even in the original "Auld
Lang Syne" pageant in Rhode Island. Its director, Margaret MacLaren Eager, had
previously published children's books with titles such as *Toyland; or, Nip and
Tuck, the Fairy Toymakers*.[45]

The aestheticizing function of costume was also put to use by groups such as
the Camp Fire Girls. That organization was created in 1910 through the collaboration of Luther and Charlotte Gulick (he was an official with the YMCA; she was
developing a girls' summer camp) and William Chancy Langdon, a pageant
movement leader. They envisioned the Camp Fire Girls as a counterpoint organization to the Boy Scouts, but rather than adopting the Scouts' quasi-military
uniform, they dressed the girls as picturesque Indian maidens, with fringed
dresses, headbands, and beads. The very first "Law of the Camp Fire" was to "seek
beauty," and this ceremonial attire was believed to embody that principle. It

128 would help infuse everything the girls did with a romantic quality. Similar costumes were sometimes used in the women's auxiliaries that grew up around turn-of-the-century fraternal organizations. Groups such as the Order of the Eastern Star, which was the female counterpart of the Masons, developed costumed rituals as part of their initiations. In that organization, the women achieved ranks based on the biblical heroines of Ruth and Esther. Like the Indian maidens, they dressed up as virtuous domestic heroines in sensual, flowing clothes.[46] (I will contrast this with men's dress-up in these fraternal orders below.)

The fact that picturesque costuming was used by entrepreneurs in the twentieth century has already been discussed; this was the time when tea-room operators and women promoting colonial needlework dressed in seemingly historic outfits. Commercialization crept into costuming in other ways as well, and many of these were relatively sensationalized. Event organizers were under such pressure to provide ever-greater novelty and grander scale, for example, that those sponsoring fundraising bazaars sometimes hired professional managers to stage theme events such as "The Streets of Paris." The costumed saleswomen wore slightly risqué outfits, sometimes "shamelessly" peddling their goods from the folds of their costumes. Expositions, which had become even more numerous, similarly became more titillating. They not only included extensive "native villages," but also featured commercial amusement areas with costumed actors. The most popular area at Chicago's 1893 Columbian Exposition was the Midway Plaisance, which included scantily clad women in animated tableaux such as "The Streets of Cairo" and "The Chinese Market." Later expositions followed suit, and permanent freestanding amusement parks that included costumed enactments soon opened to the public. Visitors to New York's Coney Island could thus engage with the "300 natives" (dressed-up individuals) at the Delhi marketplace, could visit the German or Eskimo village, or attend spectacular costumed dramatizations of events such as the fall of Pompei. Professional theatrical tableaux—the kind presented on the New York stage—also became more spectacular and fantastic. One example was "The Triumph of Epicuru," which featured eighty-five figures impersonating the elements of an eight-course banquet.[47]

Costume at Parties: Specific Conventions

Less sensational, but no less transformative, was the costume found at home parties. The overriding function of this kind of dress-up should be apparent. We have seen, for example, that outfits covered with quivering silver stars and powdered wigs were saturation devices that allowed partygoers to "make special" and enjoy themselves more fully. Let us look even further at the specific ways costume was put to use at these events.

One of dress-up's most important roles was a way of delineating who was hosting or serving the guests. At coeducational parties, it was not uncommon to find that the only ones in costume were the host and hostess. Their masquerade not only helped set the proper mood at these events, but set the party givers apart and established their "authority" for the evening. From a close reading of the descriptive literature, I have the impression that hostess costuming functioned slightly differently at women-only events. When the only ones who were dressed up at a woman's party were those who greeted the guests, their costume seems to have been chosen primarily for its saturated quality. This helps explain the earlier comment about women not being able to resist the thought of themselves with the snowy white hair or the lacy kerchief of a colonial costume: they would not only look attractive, but get a head start on establishing the transformative mood necessary for a successful party. Putting on a costume would also have helped the hostess lighten her workload, or at least make it seem more like play.

At other times, hostesses did not dress up themselves, but asked sweet-looking young people to don costumes and help them welcome new arrivals. Burt described a Japanese garden party in 1919, for example, where attendees were met by "cunning little girl friends" of the hostess dressed in kimonos, their "hair done high and stuck full of tiny fans or flowers." *Day Entertainments* described a "Ramona [the Indian/Mexican heroine of a popular novel] Luncheon" where a boy in Spanish costume served the same purpose and an Easter party where "rabbit sisters" received the guests. Servers were also delineated with dress-up, and here too it was often young people who filled this role. At a "Happiness Tea," the server was the hostess' younger sister, dressed up with decorative bows and a fanciful apron. Even symbolic dress-up elements such as a paper cap and apron could help transform an individual into a pseudo-servant. The costume functioned in one sense as a kind of livery, but connotations of class and power seem to have been less salient than the aesthetic pleasure provided by the sight of such a waitress. Dress-up added charm to a home-based entertainment in much the same way as it did in a tea room.[48]

Dress-up could also function as part of a courting ritual at young people's coeducational parties. One of the conventions of these events was to "match" males and females for the evening, and costume elements sometimes served as the mechanism that enabled them to find one another. Girls at an April Fool's Day party had to locate their partners, for example, by finding the boy with the same color dunce cap as their own. This idea, as well as the importance of dress-up for hostesses, was also demonstrated in the "Spring Cleaning Party" suggested in *Here's for a Good Time* in 1929. The party giver and her helpers were to be dressed in "bungalow aprons and dust caps" when they greeted the incoming

130   guests. They were to give each woman a rolled-up length of crepe paper and then pair her with a male guest. Each couple was to construct its own party costumes from this material—the woman was to make the man a dust cap, and he was to make her an apron.[49]

Because dust caps and aprons were associated with servants, we can see that even this kind of costume play could be linked with the inversion or "dressing down" phenomenon I described earlier. Putting on work clothes—even in symbolic form, such as a cap—must have brought on the same kind of titillating feeling that was activated by putting on an exotic or otherwise risqué outfit. Furthermore, males were more likely to agree to come in costume to a "tramp," "poverty," or "rag" party than they were to most other types; they seem to have been more comfortable appearing as raggedy than as picturesque (see fig. 4.9). Linscott described a "Tramp Poverty Party" for young people (it too featured a partner-matching ritual) where the "ruls and regulashuns" stipulated women "must ware a kaliko dress and apern, ore somethin ekally appropriate." Men were told to "ware there ole close and flannill shurts. Biled shurts and tanup dickys air prohibbitted onles there ole and rinkled."[50]

The Spring Cleaning Party illustrates the use of hats as symbolic costume elements at interwar-era affairs. Cecil Henry Bullivant included a whole chapter in *Home Fun* on the "universal hat" as an effective party device, and elsewhere he gave instructions for folding paper into amusing forms, including head coverings. Party hats could also be purchased inexpensively. *Novelties That Create Fun*, a catalog published by a Chicago company about 1925, featured hats ranging from turbans with crepe paper plumes to Martha Washington caps, sunbonnets, and assortments of patriotic red, white, and blue headdresses. These could be purchased singly or in bulk and were clearly geared to hostesses looking to create easy amusement.[51]

Staged Photographs as Domestic Amusements

Another costume-related activity that bears separate discussion was the production of staged photographs. Photographs of this type were popular throughout the period under discussion. They functioned both as parlor entertainments and a way of making money (in fact, they exemplify the difficulty in even defining what was and was not a domestic amusement, since they were used to both public and private ends). They also represented an overlay between amusement and work, amateur and professional.

The artistically staged photo can probably be traced to Julia Margaret Cameron, an Englishwoman integrally involved in that country's Aesthetic movement. Cameron began taking photographs in the 1860s. She created paintinglike dramatic compositions with biblical, allegorical, and mythological subjects, many of which functioned as book illustrations. These were populated with costumed women and children, posed in scenes such as "Madonna and Child," "Esther before Ahashueras," "Spring," "Pomona" (the Roman divinity of trees), "Venus and Cupid," and "Five Wise Virgins." True to the tastes of her Aesthetic contemporaries who looked to medieval art as inspiration, Cameron also staged fairytale images of kings and queens, capturing moments such as the "Parting of Sir Lancelot and Guinevere" (she posed Alfred, Lord Tennyson, and other poets in the mythic male roles). Her photographs had a dreamy, allusive quality, often achieved with a soft lens focus. Cameron was a paid professional, but, tellingly, given the public/private overlay described above, she operated in a domestic context. She not only created idealized images of home life, but worked from her own home, where she spent much of her time caring for her grandchildren, who often served as her models. Her vignettes helped set the stage for the kind of imagery seen in later photographs and in the many contemporary animated enactments we have been discussing.[52]

When the Kodak camera was introduced in 1888, it stimulated the movement for amateur photography. The equipment was relatively inexpensive and easy to set up and operate, and photograph taking became something that could easily fit into domestic routines. Sensing an enthusiastic market, Kodak directed much of its advertising at women. Women also accounted for a high percentage of the readers and contributors to a new magazine, *American Amateur Photographer* (they contributed nearly half the frontispieces published in the first four years, 1889–1892). The editor had suggested early on that "the ladies" would probably be especially interested in photographing interiors, and indeed many did turn their lenses on domestic scenes. According to Rosenblum's *History of Women Photographers*, in fact, one of the first of the new Kodak images was Catherine Barnes Ward's "Five o'Clock Tea," which featured dressed-up women posed around a beautifully appointed tea table. Ward became associate editor of *American Amateur Photographer*.[53]

The title of that publication may be misleading, for no distinction was made at the turn of the century between amateur and professional photographers. While the magazine was geared at recreational photographers, it nevertheless included articles about selling one's work. Barnes herself lectured on photography as a profession for women, and general publications ran articles with titles such as "Profitable Industries for Women—Photography" (*Woman's Magazine*, 1904). Photographs by "hobbyists" and "professionals" were also freely mixed by camera clubs and photography salons, and even the casual picture taker was encouraged to sell her images. She found many outlets, for the introduction of the Kodak was concurrent with an increase in printed matter, especially illustrated magazines.[54]

Sources such as *American Amateur Photographer* advised women to focus on architectural shots, portraits of individuals in their homes, images of domestic products, and "attractive women and children." Many specific features reinforced this message. In 1892, for example, Marie Kendall published "An Afternoon with Dolls," which described the day she took multiple images of her children with their playthings, resulting in a wonderful narrative series. Images of this type were known at the time as "genre scenes." In the spirit of Cameron's artistically posed compositions, they typically focused on rural life and/or children, and included costumed characters. They often used Cameron's soft focus techniques. Genre scenes were much in demand, as they were published as calendar and book illustrations. They were also commonly reproduced as postcards that were enthusiastically exchanged with friends and were given as gifts.[55]

The staged photographs functioned as two-dimensional versions of the tableaux, pageants, and other costumed enactments we have been discussing, and they followed many of the same conventions. Some images featured exotic-looking international "peasants" (these were not as common in photographs as in actual dress-up, but they did appear with regularity); others featured allegorical and fairyland characters. Mrs. N. Gray Bartlett was an early successful photographer who was known for her books of fairylandlike nursery-rhyme genre scenes. One of these, *Mother Goose of '93,* was sold as a souvenir of the World's Columbian Exposition in Chicago.[56]

Most common of all was the staged colonial photograph. Readers may be familiar with Wallace Nutting's images, since so many were in circulation (approximately ten million copies were sold in a twenty-five year period) and were displayed in homes throughout the country. Important to the discussion of the role of women and costumed photos, however, is the fact that it was Nutting's wife, Mariet, who suggested he include dressed-up people in his scenes. Mariet supervised the costuming and positioned the models and sometimes posed for the images herself.[57] Other women also specialized in creating similar two-dimensional tableaux. Mary Harrod Northend, described in chapter 3 as one of the successful advice writers of the early twentieth century, illustrated her books and articles with photographs of "colonial" women in domestic settings (spinning at the great wheel, drinking tea, and so on). Mary and Frances Allen of Deerfield, Massachusetts shot similar photographs of early American buildings, peaceful pastoral scenes, and imagined historic vignettes. All had a romantic quality, and were bathed in soft, dreamy light. The 1904 composition "The Question" (fig. 4.11) even focused on the ultimate romantic moment: the wedding proposal.

The Allen sisters presented themselves as social and artistic reformers and consciously aligned with the Arts and Crafts movement in Deerfield. Their obituaries referred to them as "artistic amateur photographers." In reality, they had run a business for years—they published an annual catalog of their images from 1904 to 1920 —and relied on income from their photographs. Staged photographs were also made by reformer/artists in other summer-season art colonies. Emma Coleman and Mary Coolidge Perkins staged photographs of agricultural

FIG. 4.11.
"The Question" was a staged photograph taken by Frances and Mary Allen of Deerfield, Massachusetts, in 1904. The figures in colonial dress were reenacting a wedding proposal. Courtesy, the Pocumtuck Valley Memorial Association, Memorial Hall Museum, Deerfield, Massachusetts (96.14.292).

and handcraft activities in the Piscataqua region (York, Maine, and environs), for example, many of which also had colonial settings. Additionally, they produced picturesque fairylike images with subjects such as "wood sprites."[58]

There were many levels of interpenetration between the live enactments and the staged photographs. They looked similar, and they served similar ends. In addition, they often even involved the same individuals. For example, Mary Coolidge Perkins was a playwright as well as a photographer, and she helped stage pageants in the Piscataqua area. The settings for many staged photographs, furthermore, were actual pageants and other enactments. The Allen sisters shot scenes at Deerfield pageants, for example (see fig. 4.4), and some of the Piscataqua photographers documented costumed events at the York's "Old Gaol" historic site. The complex interrelationships among photograph, enactment, and historic site is exemplified for me in an image of an 1899 colonial dress-up garden party that appears in the book about the Piscataqua area, *A Noble and Dignified Stream*. The party, which was itself immortalized in a posed photograph, was held to raise funds for the restoration of the Old Gaol—a place where costumed dress-up events took place regularly.[59]

Dress-up parties that took place in private homes and were held with no overriding purpose other than amusement were also extensively photographed.

134

FIG. 4.12.
Amateur photographer Annie Sievers Schildhauer photographed her friends in Madison, Wisconsin, in 1899, when they were dressed up and striking "Grecian poses." Courtesy, the Wisconsin Historical Society, PH 2775, WHi-33716.

The images not only documented the events but, by dint of the fact that they helped keep those fleeting moments alive, allowed their pleasure to remain intact for a long time. Looking at the images today, one gets the feeling that mugging for the camera was much the point of many of these masquerades. Annie Schildauer's friends in "Grecian" outfits in Madison, Wisconsin in the 1890s, for example, seemed delighted to pose for posterity (fig. 4.12). Books such as Nellie Mustain's *Popular Amusements for Indoors and Out-of-Doors* (1902) included photographs of individuals dressed as bluebirds, Bo-Peep, Cupid, or Miss Columbia, all of whom seemed to be enjoying themselves immensely. The fact that photography could be an integral part of home parties is also evident from the "Kodak Social" and a "Kodak Meet" suggested in *Popular Amusements.* Amateur photographers were to bring both cameras and samples of their work to the former (fig. 4.13).

FIG. 4.13.
Popular Amusements for Indoors and Out-of-Doors (1904) included suggestions for a "Kodak Meet" party, where the main entertainment consisted of taking photographs.

There would be a contest for the best photo display (nonphotographers would do the judging), but the primary amusement of the evening would be setting up and posing for new images. The meet was set up as a country picnic, with participants shooting "pretty nooks and corners" (essentially, they were composing genre scenes). The illustrations in Mustain's book are themselves self-consciously posed to be amusing and picturesque.[60]

Many posed photographs carried comic overtones because they were based on social inversions such as the tramp or poverty party. There are many examples of young women dressing up as men, for example, and taking pictures of their transformed visages. Alice Austen, who posed in this way with two friends in 1891, claimed they "did it just for fun" (fig. 4.8). Turn-of-the-century partygoers who frequented "Plantation" or "Darky Parties" also liked to have pictures taken of themselves in blackface (fig. 4.3). While we now look at them as permanent records of their embedded racist attitudes, they saw these pictures as records of their lighthearted leisure-time amusements.[61]

All the photographs of dressed up individuals projected a happy, pretty reality, filled with sensual pleasure. Whether they were made to somehow affect or improve the world—for example, to help inculcate foreigners with seemingly American values or bring them an appreciation and hunger for the arts; whether they were to help sell products for personal profit or for charitable causes; or whether they were "just" an amusement with no greater goal than creating good feeling, they always presented and helped create an alternative, highly saturated world.

Men's Dress-Up

As indicated, men liked to participate in dress-up parties only under certain conditions. They were willing to wear inversion outfits that allowed them to look "sloppy" or to put on simple symbolic costume elements such as hats. Most did not like to be bothered with making or otherwise procuring elaborate outfits, and most did not enjoy the kind of self-consciousness display that the women so delighted in. When they were persuaded to dress up most fully, they typically preferred to portray powerful, swashbuckling heroes or, alternatively, to use costume as a kind of comic horseplay or burlesque. The divergent profile is well illustrated in Emily Burt's description of a 1927 May Day party, where the women appeared in Greenaway dresses and milkmaid costumes while the males dressed as Robin Hood or as chimney sweeps with blackened faces. It is also evident in the adjectives used in a *Good Housekeeping* article that gave suggestions for "dashing" Cossack outfits for the males, contrasted with "demure" Bretonne dresses. Such polarized types embodied what Cynthia Cooper and Linda Welters referred to as "the familiar gender dichotomy of 'doing' versus being.'"[62]

Such male preferences had remained consistent in both public and private contexts since the middle of the nineteenth century. The handful of men who put on costumes for the New England Kitchens usually took on comic roles such as "Brother Jonathan," who was presented as a country rube, or they appeared in positions of authority such as a minister officiating at a reenacted colonial wedding. In the Centennial era they participated in satirical street theater such as "Antiques and Horribles" parades, which were "full of the most ludicrous presentations," or comical reenactments that mockingly alluded to authority and importance. In Amherst, Massachusetts, for example, there was a staging of a mock court "presided over by Judge Biging," who, according to the tongue-in-cheek report in the local newspaper, "sat on Mr. Naugherty, the accused." They also portrayed Revolutionary heroes such as Lafayette and Washington in more serious tableaux or appeared in reenactments of pivotal historic actions such as the Boston Tea Party or the Battle of Bunker Hill. They marched in military uniforms in parades and drills that celebrated hierarchy and authority, where, in contrast to the domesticating brooms at comparable women's events, they carried real weapons.[63]

The same pattern prevailed at the turn of the century. Men of means were sometimes willing to dress up for fancy dress balls, because those were social occasions where one would be seen—they were opportunities to demonstrate one's position and importance.[64] Few men dressed up to work at bazaar sales booths, but those who could be persuaded to do so appeared in costumes that presented an aggressive front or embodied wealth or power. At the 1896 Bazar of All Nations in Milwaukee, for example, the German village featured "frauleins" in folk dress surrounded by "fierce-looking . . . ancient warriors." In the Polish and Irish displays, male minuet dancers appeared in elaborate historical court costume, but more of the women appeared as romantic-looking peasants.[65]

Men's preferred approach to costumes at private parties is epitomized for me in a description of a colonial-theme party that appeared in *Entertaining with Cards,* a suggestion-filled volume reprinted in several editions around 1900. The assembled guests at this party were gathered around the usual "spinning wheel manipulated by a lady in colonial costume," when they were startled by a "warwhoop on the outside. The doors burst open, and men dressed up as Indians came trooping in."[66] Whooping Indians embodied what we would now call macho personas, and the situation was comical. Men were also generally willing to dress up when they would be appearing specifically as entertainers (that is, at the center of attention), especially in a burlesque context. Cecil H. Bullivant's *Home Fun* was one of many books written by and for men that focused on such amusements as "bunkum entertainments," and he included costume elements as part of many of suggested "tricks." (Racist dressing-down outfits were included in Bullivant's chapter "Nigger Minstrelsy.")[67]

The most important context in which men used costuming in this era was the all-male world of the fraternal lodge meeting. The turn of the century was the peak of the fraternal movement in America; according to one source, in fact, as many as one in four men belonged to a fraternal organization. While camaraderie and mutual aid were part of the appeal of these groups, the heart of the fraternal experience was ritual initiation and enactment—a kind of participatory theater. The men used costume for this experience in a scripted, formal manner. The ritual premise was that the initiates were choosing a new life by entering into a new, male society. They proceeded through a series of ranks, each of which involved a ceremonial drama to enact the metaphoric rebirth.[68] The costumed characters of these dramas embodied the same masculine ideal we have been discussing, and for the most part they lived in a seemingly more "primitive" past. Sometimes, echoing those who let out "war whoops" at the colonial-theme card party, the initiates represented "red men" (Indians). More typically, they embodied biblical patriarchs or exotic Persian kings, gladiators, knights, or warriorlike Crusaders. Descriptive text in the catalogs put out by those who supplied these outfits gives a sense of the "ancient glory and glamor" they were trying to portray. The Ihling Brothers Everard Company, for example, boasted its guard costumes "depict[ed] the warrior ever-ready to protect and defend" and "always ready for action"; though these guards had seen "considerable rough duty," they were still "ready to devote 'Sword, Heart and Life itself'" to their tasks. Armor, helmets, and spears were included with most outfits, and historical references were intermingled freely.[69] As Foster Dulles put it,

> [The appeal of the] elaborate ceremony and ritual of the lodge . . . could hardly be withstood. . . . Any one might find himself a Most Illustrious Grand Potentate, Supreme Kahalijah . . . or Imperial Prince on Lodge night. In gorgeous robes of state, jeweled collars, imposing helmets or high-crowned fezzes; carrying the swords, lances, and axes that constituted the impressive symbols of their office, [ordinary men] strutted for a brief hour . . . in all the magnificence of the borrowed plumes.[70]

Fraternal brothers never wore their ritual costume outside the privacy of their halls, but they did march publicly in militaristic regalia. At the Masonic Fair held in Atlanta in 1900, for example, different fraternal groups paraded on subsequent evenings. A procession of 700 Odd Fellows marched in with "bright new uniforms" on December 10, and on the eleventh, the scarlet dress suits and fezzes of the Shriners "were everywhere." At the Bazar of All Nations in Milwaukee, fraternal groups were joined by "boys in scarlet military uniforms beating toy drums."[71] Those boys were probably about ten years old, and parading with the lodge members was part of their socialization into the world of men. It was younger boys who were dressed as flowers, forest sprites, and other picturesque characters at entertainments like the Paper Ball (fig. 4.9) or whose mothers had "colonial suits" made for them to wear at costume parties. Small boys were still understood to be part of their mothers' domain; as they had not yet taken on the qualities of the adult male, they could still be made to look "pretty."

Conclusions: Deep Saturation

Women embraced costume for its very saturated qualities; they found delight in the magical, romantic qualities that dress-up helped engender. Costume provided sensual stimulation and delight and contributed to a sense of childlike playfulness. The preparation of dress-up outfits offered creative satisfaction as well, for it was almost limitless in its possibility. Costuming also furthered a sense of connectivity or community, as dress-up activities involved play-acting with others and had to be shared. At the same time, this type of social bonding was highly personal. The women were playing with ideas and identities through their own bodies—they embodied everything from historical characters to elements of the natural world or abstract concepts. They related to other cultures and time periods, to objects, and even to the environments around them in an intimate manner, symbolically becoming them or using them as personal adornments and props. Dress-up was a way of making special and charging everyday experience.

Women's dress-up was for the most part not concerned with rank, power, authority, or control over others; women used costume for amusement rather than conspicuous display. Returning to the idea of the nonconsumerist ethos described in chapter 1, most women were happy to make their costumes from inexpensive or recycled materials. In offering the dress-up for others to enjoy, furthermore, they treated it as a gift rather than a commodity.

Dress-up can actually be seen as a multifaceted phenomenon. We saw in the previous chapter the way a dressed-up environment could build excitement and delight. In this chapter, we focused on the ways that individuals dressed up their own bodies. In the following chapter, we will look at the way women found pleasure through creating and dressing dolls, treating them almost as icons of themselves.

Chapter Five

ICONIC DOLLS AND HOUSEHOLD HELPERS

Introduction

This chapter expands upon ideas we have already been exploring—embodiment and miniaturization, for example, and dress-up and making special. We link dolls with playfulness as well, of course, and while dolls are specifically associated with little girls, we have already seen that they were also a part of adults' amusements. Two-dimensional dolls were the raison d'être, if not exactly the focus, of the book houses discussed in chapter 2. Three-dimensional figures were an integral part of bridal showers and other women's parties. They functioned as decorations, positioned atop cakes and in table-top dioramas, or as centerpieces from which streamers radiated out to each place setting, and they were given as gifts and favors. We will look more closely at some of the handmade gift dolls in this chapter, particularly those that functioned as "household helpers," and will expand outward to a broader consideration of the iconic dolls that women made as miniaturized, costumed representations of a projected self. The dolls functioned as intimate companions that helped increase the saturated quality of the women's experience. They were emotionally satisfying to make, see, and handle. Symbolically, they also often helped turn work into play and further erased the boundary between work and personal self. They stand in direct counterpoint to the polarizations of workplace values discussed in Chapter 1.

I begin the discussion by looking at the "making and doing" sections of women's manuals and instruction books of the nineteenth century, highlighting the way needlework could function as an amusement and examining the fancywork that literally incorporated dolls or was given animated, dolllike qualities. To further set the stage for the iconic dolls of the twentieth century that are the primary focus of the chapter, I also describe the way turn-of-the-century advice literature on children's amusements stressed making dolls out of plants, vegetables, and other natural or man-made materials. These same ideas resurfaced in new forms in the interwar era, when many of the dolls we are concerned with were made. The adults of the 1920s had been children at the turn of the century. They were the very ones who were encouraged to dress up as flowers or turn actual flowers into playthings, and they had been surrounded by saturated anthropomorphic objects such as dolllike pincushions. We can thus easily understand interwar era amusements as part of a continuum where the same impulses were packaged into new, contemporary forms.

Embodied Fancywork and Dressed-Up Dolls

We have stressed the close relationship of women's work and play, an idea that was built into childhood socialization. As Emma Churchman Hewitt wrote in her 1889 book *Queen of the Home,* "So closely are the subjects of home training and home amusements connected, that it seems almost useless to try to separate them."[1] Home manuals such as Hewitt's gave distinctly different advice for boys and girls. The "making and doing" sections of these books directed boys in the construction of action toys, while girls were directed to sewing and needlework projects revolving around household objects. The creation of ornamental needlework, or fancywork, operated much the same way for grown women. Fancywork projects appeared in women's magazines under the heading "work," but the adjectives used to describe them indicated that making them was also a leisuretime pursuit. The contradictions ran deep. The very act of doing fancywork was simultaneously seen as a sign of industry and gentility (the woman who did it was not idle, but neither was she a laborer). Objects such as pincushions, wall pockets, and penwipers (used to wipe excess ink off fountain pens) were also understood to be at once useful and ornamental. They were ostensibly practical but were still mostly "little nothings," particularly appreciated for their decorative, pretty qualities. They could be made for sale at fundraising fairs or bazaars, and thus they were a vehicle for women to support causes they believed in. They were also considered suitable for gifts ("there cannot be a more appropriate or gratifying souvenir of affection," noted *Ornamental Toys and How to Make Them*). Even when they were simply made for display in the home, however, these fancywork objects helped women show off their skill and good taste and fulfill their socially prescribed mission of creating a beautiful and morally uplifting environment for their families. Nevertheless, as I argued in "Victorian Fancywork in the American Home," making these "ornamental toys" was also a source of pleasure. The making process could itself be soothing, and it functioned as a creative outlet and an opportunity to add a bit of levity into one's day. This idea is even embedded in the "fancywork" term. The first definition given by *The Oxford English Dictionary* for the word "fancy" is a "fantasy or illusion of the senses"; in early use, in fact, "fancy" was synonymous with the word imagination. Fancy is also defined as a whim, an invention or transformation, and something that entertains or pleases.[2]

FIG. 5.1.
The "Little Companion" sewing accessory was featured in *Peterson's Magazine* in January 1865. Made from a small, commercially produced wooden doll, this object allowed the maker to create a fashionably dressed figure in her own image. Making such iconic "companions" was a form of amusement for Victorian women.

From about the middle to the latter part of the nineteenth century, pincushions and related fancywork objects were often made as miniature tours de force. They were themselves "dressed-up" as representations of other objects, such as cottages, drums, and sheaves of wheat, or they were given animated forms. A pen wiper might be made to look like an animal, for example, such as a rat, mouse, pussycat, or butterfly; a match holder might be made in the shape of a pig; a pincushion might be made to resemble a beetle or fish. Many of the objects were dolllike, looking like miniature people. Others implied people by metonymic

FIG. 5.2.
This diminutive (four-inch-high) penwiper was made from a china doll covered with absorbent cloth. It was probably made by women in a Shaker community, possibly Sabbathday Lake, Maine, in the early twentieth century. Private collection.

reference, for they were made in the form of pieces of clothing or accessories such as boots, hats, and parasols.

In this era when more and more commercially produced dolls were on the market, actual playthings were also incorporated into some of the animated figures. Jane Weaver's design for a doll pincushion featured in *Peterson's Magazine* in 1865 instructed women to "get a small china doll [and] break off the legs" (the remaining torso was to be inserted into a cushionlike skirt). Weaver also published instructions for a "Little Companion" the same year. This was little more than a five-inch high wooden doll outfitted as a sewing accessory, complete with pincushion, scissors scabbard, and needle holder (fig 5.1). *Godey's Lady's Book* also featured dressed-up doll pincushions in the 1860s; one of its examples was dressed as Queen Elizabeth sporting a stiff ruff. A "very pretty pincushion made with dolls" was featured in the *American Home Book of Indoor Games, Recreations and Occupations* a few years later. Here, the maker was encouraged to dress the bran-stuffed character "in any fancy style desired"—as a nun, for example, or as an old woman. Toilet table cushions, which held hat and straight pins, could also be fashioned as dolls with cheerful skirts. (The pins might be inserted in grouped clusters that looked like dressy spangles.) Pin holders with "tiny bisque doll heads" and flannel skirts were still suggested as appropriate gifts for women at the end of the century; in fact, ceramic dolls with voluminous skirts were turned into different types of fancy items, including pen wipers (fig. 5.2) and perfume bottles. *Ladies' Home Journal* suggested one of the latter in 1896 where the doll's head replaced the regular bottle stopper. Instructions indicated a skirt over the bottle itself and an additional "red riding-hood cloak" that could be draped over the head and torso.[3]

The association with play and amusement was explicit in a fancywork suggestion submitted to the *Ladies Floral Cabinet and Pictorial Home Companion* in 1874 (this magazine was "geared to the lady who wants to make her home beautiful and meaningful"). The contributor alluded to a nursery rhyme when she suggested a "very comical looking" fancy pincushion representing the "Old Woman Who Lived in a Shoe." An actual old child's shoe would serve as the base, and a stuffed cushion representing the "body of a fat old woman in sitting posture" would be positioned inside it. Her face would be made from a hickory nut (see fig. 6.1). A "witch penwiper" suggested in *Ornamental Toys and How To Make Them* also incorporated a doll with an old woman's face; ideally, she would be made to look as if she were stooping over. The witch and the old woman were lighthearted objects that would bring a smile to anyone's face and were suggested as suitable bazaar or Christmas presents as well as household display.[4] They were useful dolls that functioned as direct antecedents to the shower gifts that became popular in the twentieth century.

Fancy objects made in the shape of garments usually referenced women's dress. There were many pincushions fashioned as high-heeled slippers or boots, for example, and items such as the wall pocket illustrated in *The Dictionary of Needlework* (1887) that echoed the shape of a woman's bodice (fig. 5.3). These objects totemically referred to the bodies of their makers, and notably they were referred to in the advice literature as effective vehicles for "dressing-up" the domestic environment. The 1888 manual *Our Homes: How To Beautify Them* insisted that a simple rocking chair could be improved with a bandolier-like ribbon draped across its back, for example, or that an easily procured peach basket could be transformed into "a thing of beauty" if it were fitted with "six lush lappels" [*sic*] that adorned it "like a fancy collar."[5] Once again, we see multiple levels of conflation: not only was it impossible to separate women's work and play, but women's work could not even be fully separated from their bodily selves.

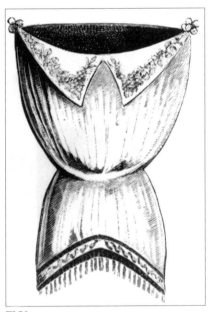

FIG. 5.3.

This wall pocket featured in *The Dictionary of Needlework* in 1887 echoed the shape of a woman's bodice. Pockets of this sort were made to hold small household items such as combs and whisk brooms. This example totemically referred to the body of the maker, and it "dressed up" the home.

It is worth mentioning here that nineteenth-century dolls of all kinds, like real people, often wore dress-up costume. The *American Home Book of Indoor Games, Recreations and Occupations* noted in 1872 that it was "amusing to dress dolls in the costumes peculiar to each nation," and it described appropriate outfits for "foreign dolls" impersonating European peasants. Instructions for outfitting paper dolls also mentioned dancers in Egyptian and Turkish costume and in unspecified "fancy dress." Fanciful doll attire was very common by the 1890s, especially after the World's Columbian Exposition. One could purchase a doll that was already dressed—there were commemorative dolls from the exposition itself, and the Raphael Tuck company published a "Races of Mankind" series in women's magazines, for example—but more often women made the costumes themselves. (Much of the advice about dressing dolls was aimed at young people, but as in the case of the paper doll houses, adults were probably responsible for much of the costuming.) Adults also participated in "doll shows" ("doll fairs"), which were popular entertainments at the end of the nineteenth century. These featured tableaux of dressed-up dollies, such as miniaturize "peasant booths" with dolls in ethnic costumes, vignettes of dolls impersonating storybook characters, doll versions of the New England Kitchens, and even doll "weddings."[6]

Nature Dolls and "The Garden Party of the Vegetable Folks"

One part of what some have called the "doll craze" that took hold at the end of the century was the interest in making dolls out of natural materials such as flowers, plants, and other vegetables. These were ephemeral creatures, of course, and highly picturesque. Some looked much like small versions of the flower people in the Walter Crane illustrations discussed in the last chapter—the ones that were so often imitated in life-size dress-up.[7] The first reference I have found to a nature doll is from 1872, in the *American Home Book of Indoor Games, Recreations and Occupations*. The author explained that German children were making dolls out of flowers and suggested it was such a delightful pastime that their American counterparts might like to follow suit. They might enjoy dressing poppy seed pods in leaf skirts or turning fallen fuchsia blossoms into "people" by inking in facial features and adding wire arms. They might also fit flower-

FIG. 5.4.
"Cornelia Shucks," the "Corn Husk Lady," was pictured in Margaret Walker's *Lady Hollyhock and Her Friends: A Book of Nature Dolls and Others* (1906).

petal skirts over clothespins, especially the round-headed type, which had built-
in faces. The press also routinely carried features on characters such as "Rose
Girl," who was made out of flowers and toothpicks.[8]

Vegetables provided even more possibilities for doll making. "Radish babies"
were for example simple to make; one only had to turn their leaves upside down
and fasten them around the radish with blades of grass—their radish heads
would look out proudly over the leafy garments. Corn husks also made wonderful dolls, as they came complete with "silken" hair and easily accepted inked-on
faces (fig. 5.4).[9] One might also find inspiration for vegetable dolls while in the
kitchen. It was easy to look at an unusually shaped potato, for example, and revi-
sualize it as a human face or an animal. Substantial vegetables—turnips, beets,
carrots, and pumpkins—were sometimes carved out, but the more common
treatment was to insert toothpicks and lengths of wire into whole vegetables, thus
creating creatures such as the "potato turkey." When the *Puritan* magazine featured a "Child's Garden of Vegetables" in 1900, complete with photographs of
completed characters such as "Maizie Tendercorn," it included a happy rhyme:

> Molly Cabbage went to town
> Taking Piggy Tater Brown
> Tater Brown and Cabby Green
> Later in the day were seen
> Dressed as Fine as they were able
> At the evening dinner table.[10]

The idea of "vegetable people" was resonant in the popular imagination at the
turn of the century. As early as 1885, Jerome B. Rice Seed Company had advertised its products in personified form, with Mr. Turnip, Mr. and Mrs. Radish, and
their counterparts appearing on brightly colored trade cards. The vegetables
looked temptingly healthy, and the realistic-looking faces that emerged from
their tops would have helped would-be customers remember the product fondly.
Postcards with vegetable people were also in circulation in the latter part of the
century. Similar characters appeared in popular literature. At the turn of the century, they were sometimes rather sinister. In chapter 6 of Frank Baum's 1900
novel, *Dorothy and the Wizard in Oz* (this was one of many sequels to the original
Oz book), Dorothy, the Wizard, and their companions found themselves in the
Land of the Mangaboos. "I don't like these veg'table people," said Dorothy. "They're
cold and flabby, like cabbages, in spite of their prettiness." Her distrust was warranted, for the Mangaboos threatened to throw the interlopers into the "Garden
of the Twining Vines." The Wizard outwitted them in the end. Vegetable characters similarly appeared in the 1897 story, *The Vege-Men's Revenge*, written by
Bertha Upton, who also penned the very popular "Golliwog" books. The heroine

of *The Vege-Men's Revenge,* Miss Poppy Cornflower, was taken into the vegetable kingdom by residents of her garden, Harry Carrot and Don Tomato. There they had to contend with King Murphy (a potato), who was irate about the way people routinely torture vegetables (for example, boil them in fat). Here the heroine did not escape. "Without a sigh," the king ordered that Poppy be planted and grown as food for a royal banquet.[11]

While some of the fictional vegetable people were not friendly, the general sense of such imaginary creatures was still positive, and their main appeal seems to have been that they brought one into an altered reality. Nature dolls, in any case, never seem to have had negative connotations, and the practice of making them was described as a way of entering into the poetic or saturated state. Bertha Johnston, author of *Home Occupations for Boys and Girls,* claimed that anyone who had become "accustomed to looking upon odds and ends of wire, paper, weeds, seeds and grasses as hiding delightful secrets" was likely to gain a lively, "inventive imagination."[12]

A volume devoted to these figures, Margaret Walker's *Lady Hollyhock and Her Friends: A Book of Nature Dolls and Others,* was *itself* structured in an inventive, imaginary way. It was presented as a big storybook, with each of its dolls introduced by an elaborate tale told to the children of "Hollyhock Place." The story about the "Clothes-Pin Tribe," for example, followed a group of corn husk–covered pin people living in burdock-leaf teepees. The static, tableauxlike appearance of these "pygmy" characters, the children were told, could be explained by the fact that they had been put under a spell by a giant. In fact, the theme of enchantment was repeatedly stressed in this book. The final chapter was written as a letter to the children from "Uncle John," a frequent visitor to Hollyhock Place. He sent them a doll made of kelp, but, more to the point, he told them how spending time with them as they made their nature dolls had transformed him. His vision had become so saturated that he was starting to see the world differently:

> Half the things I see turn into dolls as I look at them, and I immediately begin to make songs or jingles about them. As I sit at the table the dishes even, take doll form in my mind. The plates seem to have great moon faces, while the sugar bowl seems to stand with shoulders thrown up and arms akimbo like an awkward china washerwoman. The knives, forks and spoons are almost human with their shining faces. . . . This morning as I passed a bake-shop and glanced in at the window, the cakes and buns seemed to laugh and wink at me with the fat faces of their bakers.[13]

While Walker insisted on the sheer delight of nature doll making, she also indicated there might be other benefits. In addition to her fictional tales, she told the story of a "crippled girl on a Nebraska farm" who had begun making corn-husk dolls for her own amusement but became so good at fashioning lively look-ing characters that she found she could sell them for profit. "Cornelia Shucks" was one of her successful creations (fig. 5.4). This reminds us of the multivalent nature of these activities. *American Home Book of Indoor Games* spoke of the play value of vegetable characters, but it also noted that the creations could help "beautify your houses, however poor or humble your lot."[14]

This discussion of animated turn-of-the-century vegetables sets the stage for the story of Ethel von Bachellé, who created a different kind of vegetable doll a few decades later. Von Bachellé's Depression-era creations functioned as an aes-thetic outlet and amusement, but she also hoped to earn some much-needed cash through them. She was born about 1885[15] in Chicago in a relatively prosper-ous household; her father was a German-born physician, and the family owned property about a hundred miles north in Delavan, Wisconsin. While little is known about her childhood, turn-of-the-century Chicago was an exciting place to be. The 1893 World's Columbian Exposition was generally experienced as "an astonishing sight," and it brought an abundance of intellectual, architectural, and artistic wonders to the city. Chicago women were particularly active in the cre-ation of new societies and organizations designed to institute social and artistic reform. For example, Bertha Palmer mobilized a strong woman's community to work with the Woman's Building at the Exposition. Jane Adams and Ellen Gates Starr drew supporters and public attention to their progressive settlement, Hull House. The city was also a primary center of the Aesthetic and Arts and Crafts movements, and many of its women were involved in organizations such as the Decorative Arts Society, which was intent upon raising the general level of aes-thetic taste.[16] Von Bachellé not only grew up in this milieu, but attended the Art Institute of Chicago and became an art teacher herself (her active teaching years were 1910–1914). We will be looking at work she produced in the 1930s, but understanding her background is important: she was one of the children who had grown up at the turn of the century who, as an adult, still reproduced the same kind of charming fairyland world familiar from Kate Greenaway and Walter Crane illustrations, book houses, and theme parties.

By 1930 von Bachellé was living an isolated life at the family home in Wisconsin. Heavily overweight and quite poor (the family money seems to have been gone, since she was receiving welfare), she turned to her artistic skills to bring in in-come. She worked on several books for children, including an alphabet primer and *The Garden Party of the Vegetable Folks.* The latter was a beautiful storybook describing an outdoor party and dinner dance given for Blanch White Celery, who was soon to leave home to get married. Blanch, like all of the thirty-four

148   party guests, was an animated vegetable character. In addition to painting beautiful watercolor illustrations, von Bachellé also fashioned her characters as three-
dimensional dolls and then had them photographed in picturesque tableaux
(figs. 5.5, 5.6, 5.7). It was her hope that these stuffed figures would serve as proto-
types—they would be put into production and sold along with the book (rather
like the *American Girl* series today). That does not seem to have happened. Nevertheless, the garden party and its characters are excellent examples of the kind of
domestic amusement I am concerned with in this chapter. The fact that the book
was made to come alive with three-dimensional, tactile figures illustrates how
iconic dolls functioned as intimate companions in an idealized, saturated world.
For von Bachellé, they functioned as both work and play, and as a way of extending a happy vision out into the world. Her book dedication expressed both her
delight and her offering to others. It was written for "all who have the spirit of
youth, whether few in years or full of years . . . may it give as much happiness to
you all as I have had doing it."

Blanch, the bride to be in von Bachellé's story, wears a "celery colored" silk
gown that would have been stylish in the late 1920s or early 1930s. She sports a
veil, implying her bridal status. As her name implies, Blanch is very white and has
blond hair and blue eyes. Her (light green) bridesmaids are the "Lettuce cousins,"
Leticia Leaf and Henriette Head. Leticia is dressed rather like a European peasant,
with a lace-up bodice, full skirt and puff sleeves (she wears the miniature equiv-

FIG. 5.5.
"Rose Pink T-Rose" and "Parcival Parsnip" were
two of the guests at Ethel von Bachellé's "Garden
Party of the Vegetable Folks." The dolls were three-
dimensional versions of the illustrations in von
Bachellé's hand-painted storybook. Both the figures
and book are in the collection of the Wisconsin
Historical Society (accession 1989.216).

FIG. 5.6.
"John Corn Cob" and "Mexican Blue Corn" were
among the other Vegetable Folk invited to von
Bachellé's party. Each figure represented a real
vegetable as well as a distinct character.

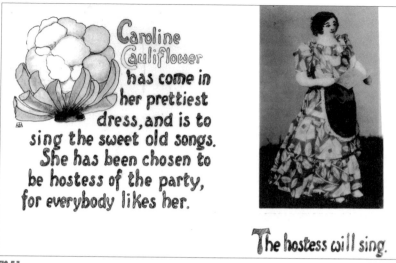

FIG. 5.7.

Von Bachellé had photographs of the Vegetable Folk taken by Burke and Koretke of Chicago, and she featured them with her hand-painted text. This page features "Caroline Cauliflower" singing from miniature sheet music. The book, dated 1936, was never actually published. Courtesy, the Wisconsin Historical Society, PH 3932.10, Whi-33719.

alent of the peasant-girl outfit popular at parties at this same time). Von Bachellé remarks in the storybook that unlike her larger cousin Henriette, Leticia has "kept her delicate daintiness." Other party guests also wear representations of folk dress—Hans Red Cabbage is conceived of as a "constantly blushing" Dutch youth with breeches and wooden shoes, for example; sweet Ruby Bell Pepper is dressed for a Spanish dance; and Mexican Blue Corn sports a sombrero. Some party guests, including Parsival Parsnip and Charles C. Carrot, wear stem caps that both recall Crane's nineteenth-century flower people and reference Colonial Revival dress-up preferences of their own era, as they are "interested in dancing the minuet" and wear colonial-looking fancy outfits with breeches and ruffled cravats. Several of the female characters also wear eighteenth-century attire; Rose-pink T-Rose has the requisite mob cap, and her dress is stitched over a full pannier underskirt. Still other guests wear approximations of other types of full-scale fancy dress: William Winning Grapevine is dressed in a Pierrot-like outfit with multicolor patches, and Robert Rhubarb wears an oversize Cavalier-style hat. There are also picturesque children, appearing here in radish form. One of them wears a leaf top.

This garden world also reflects prevalent stereotypes and class, racial and ethnic divisions. Some characters have not actually been invited to the party and have to watch it longingly through the fence. Timothy Turnip, who appears in

150 farmer-type overalls with a darned handkerchief sticking out of his back pocket, is a neighbor who looks out over the goings-on. Becky and Ruddy Sunflower[17] are black-skinned and are portrayed as both childish and uncouth. Ruddy's trouser legs are of different lengths, for example, and the top is missing from his braided straw hat. Becky seems to be in a house dress and wears a scarf tied around her pickaninny-type braids. The Sunflowers' clothes are made from felt and inexpensive cotton rather than the silks of Blanch and her attendants. Patrick and Katie, the brownish Irish potatoes who are allowed into the party because they have come to see their Idaho relatives, are also presented as slightly comical. Von Bachellé notes that they have "eyes to see everywhere, even on the back of their heads," but there is some sense of embarrassment about that—Katie has to "keep her head discreetly covered." She is also said to be plagued with weak ankles because of her excess weight.

Stereotypes aside, von Bachellé was able to play with contemporary culture in this story; much of the text draws upon or provides cheerful commentary on the world around her. In addition to demonstrating her familiarity with dress-up costumes seen at contemporary entertainments, her vegetable folk often reflected up-to-date fashions and stock character types. Gypsy Egyptian Red Beet, for example, is referred to as an "athletic young lady," and her clothes reflect what would have been the most fashionable gym clothes in the late 1920s. The puppy, Pumpkin Vine, who is said to be often underfoot and so rambunctious that he may knock the Radish children down, is made with a polka-dot fabric and has one ear up and one ear down. He brings to mind "Pete the Pup," the beloved dog in the *Our Gang* comedies that were among the most popular film shorts of the interwar years. Working within her storybook fantasy format and her use of a kind of charming double entendre, Von Bachellé also demonstrated her awareness of woman-identified activities such as cooking. For example, her commentary indicates she knew of the latest trends in preparing vegetables. She remarks that Winningstadt Winnie Cabbage feels neglected because of the "new seven minute idea for [cooking] young cabbage" (with her "solid heart," Winnie is one of the bigger vegetables and presumably not young enough to know such things). Archibald Artichoke, a Frenchman, is yet poorly known here. Ruby Bell Pepper, on the other hand, is becoming a favorite. Von Bachellé's descriptions also reflect a knowledge of the garden. Comments about characters such as Angeline Fern Asparagus (so tall that some are saying she is "going to seed"), Connie Morning Glory (wild enough to choke others), and Gran'pa Crookneck Squash (he needs a cane from William Grapevine) reference the way that plants grow and interact. Gardening, too, was accepted as a quintessentially female endeavor.

The happiness that von Bachellé experienced in making the garden party is evident in every detail, from the play with these elements of everyday life, to the play with language, to the sensually satisfying qualities of the dolls themselves. Each is fashioned in just the right shape—party hostess Caroline Cauliflower, for example, wears multiple petticoats and bloomers that give her a round silhouette; Gran'pa Crookneck has a rounded tummy and a thin, twisted neck. The dolls are also made with appropriate fabrics to reflect their social position and personalities, as well as their individual vegetable natures. Winnie Cabbage wears a dress of a leaflike, iridescent green, but her plaid shawl is reminiscent of Ireland; it is the same fabric, in fact, that is worn by the Potatoes. Blanch Celery's dress includes chiffon overlays, much like real celery leaves, and is made with a graceful handkerchief hemline, befitting a fashionable bride of some means. Von Bachellé's sense of delight with miniature detail and the "within within within" mentioned in chapter 2 is evident on Caroline Cauliflower, who has a tiny book tucked into her apron. Labeled "Loves the Old Sweet Song," it includes actual sheet music—if inspired, one could follow its notes and burst into song. Indicating even more of the play with double entendre and miniaturized world-within-world is the fact that this book lists a publisher, "B&K," on its cover. The dolls had been photographed in suitable poses by Burke and Koretke of Chicago, presumably for publication along with the full-scale *Garden Party* volume (fig. 5.7).

These vegetable folk probably served as a comfort and perhaps an escape for an apparently lonely woman in the Depression era. The world von Bachellé created was a fairyland kind of place, with pretty, romantically inclined characters. More than a reference back to the sweetness and innocence of childhood, this seems to have represented an alternative vision to the kind of bleak and hard-edged world seen in much of contemporary culture. Von Bachellé's saturated world was not unique, however. The whole idea of a "Vegetable Garden Party" may have been something that von Bachellé picked up in the popular media. Her vegetable characters not only perpetuated imagery that had been seen for over fifty years, but drew on or at least paralleled suggestions in some of the women's press of her own day. Hilda Linscott suggested a vegetable party in 1924 in *Up-To-Date Social Affairs*, with thematic games, decorations, and costumes. Even if von Bachellé was unfamiliar with that, she may have encountered *Needlecraft's* 1931 advertisement for a stamped pattern of a stuffed "Farmer Boy" doll that was quite similar to Timothy Turnip or that magazine's articles about stuffed dolls such as "Tillie Tomato" and "Ollie Onion." (Von Bachellé's characters were much more elaborated and lovingly conceived than these; her Olive Onion had not only the right "oniony" look, but a complete personal history.) *Ladies' Home*

Journal similarly featured patterns for personified stuffed animals such as "Porko Pig" and "Puffo Rabbit" in 1938.[18]

Most of the projects in the needlework press in the 1930s projected the same kind of dreamy, happy world; the magazines were replete with literal images of "dream cottages" and happy homes. Some of the projects hearkened back to the fancywork toys of the nineteenth century, as they consisted of dressed-up sewing tools, such as a "bunny pincushion" featured in *Needlecraft* in 1933. Other toys helped women make light of different kinds of household labor. A bunny suggested as an "Easter gift whimsy" in *Needlecraft* in1933, for example, was really a potholder that would add whimsy to the kitchen. This is the phenomenon I refer to as "household helper dolls." We will turn now to a closer exploration of their role in the creation of a happy home and, even more pointedly, their role in bridal showers and other domestic amusements.[19]

Dolls as Household Helpers

The idea of a helper doll seems to have been part of the popular imagination for a long time. *The Only True Mother Goose,* published in Boston in 1833, included a poem about such an imaginary friend:

> I had a little Doll
> > The prettiest ever seen.
> She washed me the dishes
> > And kept the house clean.
> She went to the mill
> > To fetch me some flour,
> And always got it home
> > In less than an hour;
> She baked me my bread,
> > She brewed me my ale,
> She sat by the fire
> > And told many a fine tale.[20]

The fact that this ditty appeared in a collection of nursery rhymes reminds us that social expectations were inculcated through childhood play; girls—the ones most likely to play with dolls—were made to laugh about their expected adult roles. At the same time, the rhyme seems to have been written as much for the grown women who would read it to those girls as it was for the children. By associating their own kind of adult responsibilities with dolls, their work was able to seem more playful and less onerous.

The tasks these dolls actually helped with reflected the demands of their respective eras. In 1833 this included milling flour and brewing ale, but, later in the

nineteenth century, the focus was on sewing and needlework. In the twentieth *153*
century, cooking and cleaning tasks came to the fore once again. The bunny potholder alluded to above, for example, reminds us that by the interwar years,
middle-class women were typically expected to do their own cooking and entertaining.[21] Kitchen helpers abounded at that time. There were also helpers for
cleaning and keeping the house tidy and for hiding toiletries and other signs of
the backstage labor that went into making the house (and its housekeeper) look
presentable.

Let us begin with a discussion of the toiletry covers. By the 1920s, women
were using increasing numbers of cosmetics, but they preferred to keep them out
of sight. Interestingly, they covered up these items with *personified* household
helpers—with iconic dolls. Like animated Victorian pincushions, these picturesque companions wore voluminous dresses. Despite the fact that women's fashion in this era followed an almost abstract, modernist silhouette (dresses were
short, and cut straight), these dressed-up miniature ladies wore long, ruffled, and
flounced outfits—wide enough to cover a jar. They too projected a familiar saturated image, for their costume had a vaguely colonial reference and in that sense
fit into one of the dress-up categories discussed in the previous chapter.

One could purchase toiletry covers ready-made for a dollar or two, but they
were also easy to make. The example illustrated in fig. 5.8 required almost no
sewing; one merely had to buy a "piquant doll" and add lengths of braid and wide
taffeta ribbon. (The ribbon was gathered in three tiers around the jar, and the
trim attached to the hems.) Construction of a similar "crinolined doll" featured
in the Canadian publication the *Farmer's Advocate* was equally simple, as crepe
paper simply had to be wrapped around a squat round "salve jar" and gathered
at the neck. This "dignified" figure was also outfitted with a colonial-looking cap.
Readers were assured that friends would be happy to receive her as a gift. Another

FIG. 5.8.

This "piquant doll" pictured in *Good Housekeeping* in February 1923 was designed to cover a jar of cotton balls.
Toiletry items were often covered so as to represent "entire" women.

FIG. 5.9.
The modern technology of the telephone was hidden by a colonially dressed female figure in this illustration from *Needlecraft*, February 1923.

doll featured in *Good Housekeeping* in 1925 that was said to make a good present was not exactly a toiletry cover, but still related to a woman's intimate toilette. This was a handkerchief holder, also made from a purchased doll with a minimum of construction. The maker could dress her by draping two linen handkerchiefs around her body, forming a bell-shaped dress, and then wrapping other handkerchiefs around her head and shoulders. (The shoulder wrap formed a fichulike "modesty scarf" of the type worn in the eighteenth century, so she too looked appropriately colonial.) Handkerchiefs were usable intimate items, particularly important in an era before disposable tissues were common.[22]

The toiletry covers were related to personal hygiene and projected a sense of femininity in the bedroom. Other household helper dolls assisted in public spaces such as the foyer or parlor. For example, *Needlecraft* gave instructions in 1923 for a "telephone screen" that also carried a colonial ambiance. This woman-shaped form functioned in much the same way as the jar covers, as her skirts hid a full-size telephone and thus softened that form of modern technology (fig. 5.9). Very often, the helper dolls made for public areas projected a kind of wishful thinking on the part of the white, middle-class housewife; they were fashioned as black or Irish helpers—that is, as servants. They were used to hold open doors, feed out balls of string, and decorate whiskbrooms, and they embodied the same kind of stereotypes and assumptions as von Bachellé's potato and sunflower dolls. The first reference I have found to this particular type of working toy was in the *Puritan* magazine in 1900. Suggested as part of a feature on Christmas presents that children might make themselves, this "funny gift" was described as a "whisk broom dressed up to represent an old colored 'mammy.'" The child was to dress a purchased broom by padding the handle with black cotton cloth and giving it a face with "red silk lips and shoe button eyes." She would then add a Mother Hubbard gown, neck kerchief, and "gay turban." (The skirt was short enough so the broom corn could do its work without being impeded by the cloth.) When one used this whiskbroom, in other words, she would have her fingers around the doll itself.

This supposedly amusing item was recommended at a time when mammy images were becoming common in American popular culture. According to Patricia A. Turner in *Ceramic Uncles and Celluloid Mammies: Black Images and Their Influence on Culture*, the now-familiar Aunt Jemima image was first seen at the 1893 Columbian Exposition, when an African American woman was hired to impersonate a mammy character as a sales gimmick for the pancake mix. The image was soon seen on a variety of commercial products and made its way into popular literature. "Implicit in each rendition," comments Turner, "was the notion that these thick-waisted women were happy with their lot, honored to spend their days and nights caring for white benefactors."[23]

The National Museum of American History at the Smithsonian Institution has in its collection a disturbing example of this type of mammy figure. It is a stuffed cushion, almost five inches high, whose printed fabric bears the image of a winking, uncouth-looking black woman in an apron, fichu, and headscarf. "DO YOU'S WANT ANY HELP?" is printed across the apron. She is also accompanied by a printed mailing tag that says,

High Class Help Furnished, City or Country
Our Servants are Guaranteed
 To remain where sent.
 To answer truthfully or remain silent.
 To not break dishes.
 To be content with small wages.
N.B. Any servant not satisfactory can be returned to us at our expense.
If I don't make a good servant, use me for a pincushion.

This was a commercial novelty (the patent was applied for by Art Fabric Mills, New York), meant to be sent as a gag gift, and the Smithsonian example had actually gone through the mail with a penny stamp. It was sent to Miss Mary Marshall of Ulysses, Kansas, from her "Aunt Mattie," about 1900. Mary used it before donating it to the museum.[24] The fact that this servant was to be used as a pincushion (the implied cruelty and mistreatment of African Americans is duly noted) implies a continuation of the fancywork doll of the past, but the fact that she was not handmade reminds us that that kind of fancywork had gone out of style.

It was in the interwar years that the fashion for household helper dolls dressed as ethnic stereotypes was particularly strong. Some mammy figures functioned as string dispensers: their large cloth dresses easily kept hidden the ball of twine or string, and the end of the string would usually feed out of the mammy's big, round lips. Other helpers of this era appeared as "pickaninnies." The *Hostess* magazine described a dressed-up doorstop in this form in 1924, for example, and

156 *Dennison's Party Magazine* included a pickaninny lantern cover named "Topsy" in 1927.[25]

Ethnic stereotypes were also very common in figures that helped with cooking and washing tasks. In *Needlecraft* in 1923, Anna G. Bailey wrote about a "Bridget" figure that would provide "first aid in the laundry." Echoing the attitude attached to the mammy-shaped pincushion of over twenty years before, Bailey commented, "We enjoy 'joke gifts' at our house, and this is one of the cutest, and useful, as well." "Miss Bridget's" body was made from a purchased laundry tool—a cake of wax already outfitted with a wooden handle. The woman making this doll was to paint the handle as a face, and make a full skirt to cover the ball of wax. Once outfitted with a "quaint little bonnet" (Bailey's was made from raffia), Bridget was "ready to help with ironing." Given the fact that the faces were hand painted and the outfits could vary greatly, dolls of this sort would each be unique. They were recommended as appealing bazaar sales items as well as personal gifts.[26] I have seen one doll in the shape of a Chinese laundryman, but, in keeping with the idea that these tasks were most often done in the home, laundry dolls were almost always female. Since washing and ironing were particularly arduous activities, it is unsurprising that homemakers who had no one to work for them would have been likely to make them look like surrogate maids.

Fig. 5.10 illustrates another maid, fashioned as an African American mammy, with the stereotypical big eyes and lips, and Aunt Jemima–style head-scarf. She represents the most common type of helper doll—a kitchen helper,

FIG. 5.10.
This laundry doll appeared in *Needlecraft* in November 1923. Her features imply a "mammy" figure, who was a wished-for servant of the presumed owner.

FIG. 5.11.
Marilyn De Long received a mammy-shaped kitchen helper doll at her wedding shower in Ohio in 1939. The doll's body is made from a whiskbroom, and her head consists of a wire mesh strainer, covered by a hand-crocheted potholder. Author's collection.

whose body is made from cooking utensils. In this particular example, the doll's trunk is made from a whiskbroom, and her head is made from a round-topped strainer covered with a potholder. Her clothes are fashioned from a dishcloth, tea towel, and handkerchief, and peeking out of them are her arms, made of pastry brushes. With the exception of the potholder, which was hand crocheted and embroidered, these items were purchased. This particular doll belonged to Marian DeLong Merrill, who lived in Cleveland Heights, Ohio. She was a schoolteacher, and it was one of many such presents she received from the coworkers who gave her a "dolly" wedding shower in 1940 (each of the teachers made a different doll). It is the only gift that remains intact; the rest were taken apart, piece by piece, as each tool was put to use. When asked to provide information about this figure, Merrill was rather apologetic about the racial stereotype that was embedded within it, pointing out that "no one thought anything" of such a portrayal at the time it was made.[27] I find it interesting, however, that of all the household helpers her fellow teachers made, this is the one that was saved. There could be any number of reasons for this, but it is possible that she was the one who best seemed to embody the "servant" and was kept as the most appropriate shower souvenir. In any case, the fact that she was considered a suitable gift for a well-educated, middle-class woman shows us that these stereotypes and assumptions were indeed pervasive. It also reminds us that a woman about to get married and take on the role of housekeeper (she was to give up teaching) appreciated a gift that poked fun of her new status. Iconic household helper dolls were integrated into bridal showers of all kinds, although they were most frequently suggested as gifts for those with kitchen themes (there were even a few of these that were dubbed "dolly showers").

The "Mirandy" centerpiece mentioned in chapter 3, which was to be made of "kitchen helps" such as a dish mop and wooden spoon, also functioned as a gift doll, because in addition to her decorating function, she was to go home with the bride when the party was over. With her "capable hands" made of forks and other helpful features, Mirandy was described by her creator as "a clever maid" who would be the "'life of the party,' especially when she presented her application for employment." This came in the form of a lighthearted poem that detailed her usefulness:

> I'm looking for a place to stay
> And so am headed out your way;
> I hope that I have not delayed
> Too long to be your kitchen maid.
>
> They call me Miss Mirandy-Ann
> Who works as hard as any man.

Although I may not look so smart
I know right well each kitchen art.

To scour and scrub, alas! 'tis true
That all good housewives this must do;
I'll spare you, lady, all this work,
Be your staunch friend and never shirk.

When things "burn on" you need not fret;
My bandeau stands the worst gas jet—
Just keep it in the kitchen-kit
My able helper, mystic-mitt.

My gown will wipe things shiny bright;
I'll polish up with all my might—
You'll never say, "Oh, what a pity!
You can't keep clean in this blame city."

And, oh, I'll dust so thoroughly
That not a black speck will there be;
You'll find that ne'er will I demur
At polishing the furniture.

I hope that I will make the grade
And be your little kitchen maid.
I know you'll find me *awfully* handy.
    Your ever faithful friend,
    Mirandy.[28]

The imagined helper of the Mother Goose storybook written in the early nineteenth century was brought to life by and for twentieth-century women. In her new guise, she was more accommodating than ever.

    Kitchen helper dolls had made their appearance before World War I and remained popular until about World War II. Ellye Glover's book on entertaining that first appeared in 1913 included a poem much like Mirandy's:

I am a bride, not bride-to-be,
And that I'm useful you'll agree
Of kitchen utensils I am made—
From the ten-cent store—the highest grade.

Behold my face—'tis but a fake;
But comes in fine for mixing cake.
My hair you'll think an ugly crop;
In fact, it's only a nice dish mop.

A potato masher I have for feet
(And potatoes mashed are good to eat).

Instead of arms two forks you'll find
(They will not bend, but I don't mind).

Last, but not least, my draperies white
For drying dishes will prove all right.
Therefore as bride I come to you—
I'll prove your faithful servant too.[29]

Adele Mendel described another kitchen servant in 1915. This too was a "comical figure called Dinah," but she was a little bigger, with what seems to have been a full-size broom for a body, and wooden-spoon arms large enough to hold pails. She sported a teaspoon necklace.[30]

By the 1930s some kitchen helper dolls were fashioned as brides, rather than servants. One of these, now in the collection of the American Museum of National History at the Smithsonian Institution, was discovered at an antiques store in Kensington, Maryland. "Anna" is complete with a cheesecloth veil and a biscuit-cutter bridal bouquet (fig. 1.7). The typewritten poem that accompanies her is written in the third, rather than first person, but she too makes it clear that getting married will entail new responsibilities:

This is Anna in miniature
Armed for new duties to be sure
Her dress will make your tumblers shine
Her veil will make a duster fine."[31]

In 1949 *Shower Parties for All Occasions*, which was published by the YWCA, featured a "kitchenware bride" dressed in a cellophane gown and veil. Although this is the last historic reference I have found for a helper doll, the idea did not fully die out; in fact, it seems an almost irrepressible idea. Appearing on a web site devoted to "practical and unusual bridal shower gifts" in December 2001 was a "cute bride doll" with copper-scrubber hair and a lace veil. Her body reflected the availability of new materials, as it was to be made of Styrofoam and newspaper-filled trash bags, but her white wedding dress was still made from useful dishcloths and kitchen towels.[32]

Other Iconic Dolls

Iconic doll figures were also sometimes offered as other types of table decorations and as party favors. These too were made in the now-expected forms: dressed in historic, exotic, or fairyland attire or as slightly comic ethnic stereotypes. Place cards often appeared as "dainty girlish figures" outfitted in dairymaid and Dutch costumes, for example, or as characters such as the Queen of Hearts. Personified menu or candy holders were dressed similarly. Many of these decorations were,

FIG. 5.12.
This table decoration with a crepe paper costume could represent either Martha Washington or Betsy Ross. She appeared in a feature called "Table Decorations in Red, White and Blue," in *Parties*, Spring 1929.

like Mirandy, made to be take-home souvenirs. Decorative favors at a "Plantation Party" suggested in *Dennison's Party Magazine* in 1927, for example, included a "Mammy Doll made of licorice gum drops" and a "lolly-pop disguised as Aunt Dinah." The next year the same magazine featured a variation on the theme—the licorice doll would appear as a pickaninny with red bows on her stuck-out pigtails. Favors could be more substantial as well. The pickaninny-shaped doorstop mentioned above was actually suggested as a table favor in 1924. There were also favors that paralleled or at least related to the bridal shower dolls. At the same shower where the large-scale Dinah was the center of attraction, each guest was given a bridesmaid doll to take home. Her special surprise was that she held small candies under her skirts. Another simple favor at a St. Patrick's Day theme party was an "Irish Girl" figure made from a lollipop.[33]

Doll favors were so popular that commercial party supply companies began to sell them ready-made. Dennison, best known for its fine crepe paper, featured jointed cardboard dolls in its 1896 catalog. Some were unadorned, ready to be dressed as the purchaser saw fit, while others were already outfitted. These included dancers in Egyptian and Turkish costume, figures in bicycle and bloomer outfits, and figures in unspecified fancy dress. Dennison also sold dressed-up "Gaiety Girls," fashioned over wooden clothespins, which the company touted as effective party favors. Slack Manufacturing Company's *Let's Make Whoopie!* catalog, published sometime in the mid-1920s, included celluloid favor dolls, and *Shackman's Favors* (1910) and *Novelties That Create Fun* (1925) offered similar figures.[34]

Let us return for a moment to the subject of table decorations and the important role that iconic dolls had in tabletop tableaux. While the suggestion about pickaninny-shaped doorstop favors did not indicate how they were to be displayed, they might very well have been placed at individual place settings. A circle of such figures would have created a striking vignette that would help saturate the event for all concerned. As we learned in chapter 4, doll-based centerpieces were often quite elaborate. The following description of the table at an April Showers party (remember that this was a popular bridal shower theme) indicates how much these centerpieces might contribute to the magical effect. The table at this party was said to be dominated by a "fairly large" doll dressed in a slicker and cap. She was carrying an umbrella "to protect her[self] from the shimmering raindrops. . . . falling all about her," but many of the "tiny drops" nevertheless glistened on her coat. The falling rain shower had been created through an arrangement of "fine threads with wee, clear glass and occasional iridescent glass beads, strung and knotted on them," all of which were illuminated by an over-head electric light. In the words of the author, the light "scintillated" on the beads, creating the shimmery effect. "Raindrop chains" of iridescent beads also led from this central figure to each place setting, where they connected with tiny paper umbrellas. The description of this party does not indicate what happened to the raincoated doll after the party, but it is likely that she was a favor for the bride.[35]

Interpretations

If domestic amusements as a whole are generally considered trivial in our culture, the subject of dolls tends to evoke a particularly rapid dismissal. As Elisabeth Cameron points out in *Isn't S/he a Doll? Play and Ritual in African Sculpture,* dolls fall at the bottom of a long hierarchy of art forms. They have two counts against them: they are primarily associated with girls, thus engendering little interest among male art historians and other scholars, and they are thought of as children's playthings, items that are soon outgrown and certainly not serious objects of study. Even though dolls come in many forms, the stereotypical image that comes to mind in America is usually an object of the nursery—a helpless baby doll that has little personality or power of its own. Cameron demonstrates that dolls are sometimes taken more seriously in other cultural contexts where they are used to express honor or serve as mediating devices between seen and unseen worlds, but she argues that even when they serve as playthings, they help people realize their humanness. They "transport the user into an extraordinary world, suggesting rich parallels between imagination and spiritual agency."[36]

The importance of this "extraordinary world" is, of course, what I have been arguing throughout this book. Dolls were a wonderful vehicle through which to saturate daily life: they helped turn ordinary activities into something extraordinary; they made things special and added aesthetic intensity and a sense of magic. Through these embodied figures, women turned everyday functional objects such as pen wipers, sewing tools, and doorstops into playthings and made even routine, tedious tasks seem more pleasurable. Simply adding a dressed-up doll to a cake or a tabletop, in fact, would help it seem extraordinary; it would thus take on aspects of a theatrical production or a play.

Women projected iconic images of themselves through these dolls. On one hand they presented an especially charming, beautiful and magical self; one that was "perfect" and perfectly content, and that retained the innocence of childhood. (This projection recalls Huizinga's characterization of the play world as one with a kind of "limited perfection" that was superior to everyday reality.)[37] On the other hand, they projected a perpetually positive imagined helper or servant—a willing assistant who would take on the drudgery of daily life. In both manifestations, the women used the miniatures to represent themselves and to express their embodied experience of the world. Their symbolic bodies matched (became one with) their tasks and their environment; they put themselves *into* what was around them and imaginatively and emotionally merged with it.

No matter what their forms, these dolls were perpetually available. As the rhymes that accompanied the household helper shower gifts made clear, the dolls functioned as characters that would always be there for their owners as trustworthy and loyal friends. They would work "as hard as a man," without complaint, but they would also help keep things beautiful and in control. Some held personal products such as facial creams or the cotton balls used to apply or take off makeup—the products that helped a woman maintain a beautiful face and body. The dolls were made in the shape of women because they functioned in a sense as alter egos—the ones who kept the backstage labor of the woman's toilet secret or hid unsightly items such as big black telephones or the weights used to prop open doors.[38] As befitted their pleasant dispositions, they also hid treats such as candies or other confections. This was, in effect, their "life's purpose": to add a sense of joy, delight, and further sweetness to any occasion and to project that sense of sweetness into the lives of the women who handled or experienced them.

Perhaps we can go so far as to say that these iconic dolls epitomized an alternative vision to the seemingly harsh (male) world of the "foreground." It is well known that, in the nineteenth century, the domestic domain was posited as a comforting, more wholesome counterpoint to the public, or "outside," world; the idea was the very basis, in fact, of the so-called cult of domesticity that dominated Victorian rhetoric. This juxtaposition remained intact at the turn of the century, for, as the term "municipal housekeeping" succinctly infers, reformers of that time also hoped to transform public discourse and institutions according to a domestic model. The alternative vision was still expressed in the early twentieth century, even when greater numbers of women were out in the workforce and the male and female spheres were less distinct. The women's press continued to focus on ways of bringing a sense of respite and good feeling into the home (the overwhelming popularity of colonial-looking objects and imagery in the interwar era was based on the idea that they carried these qualities). Amidst the relentless hardships of the Depression years, in particular, designs for women's handwork—for products that would appear in the home—had a self-consciously saccharine quality, with images of protected cottages and bonneted figures posing with flower baskets in hollyhock gardens. Furthermore, the women's magazines of the time were filled with adjectives such as "gay," "cozy," and "demure," adding to the respite from breadlines, labor unions, political upheavals, and other realities of the modern world. It is not hard to understand why a *Needlecraft* article that suggested embroidered samplers might be given as bridal shower gifts boasted that they could help raise morale. "Surely the 'heart of the house' should be uplifted from drudgery to delight with such a cheery legend on the wall," remarked Grace Noll Crowell, who provided the sampler verses.[39] Ethel von Bachellé, who herself knew the difficulties of poverty and loneliness, similarly created a pretty garden party world that could bring her out of her travails. Characters such as Charles C. Carrot and Ruby Bell Pepper provided a comfort of their own.

Despite my discussion of the racism embedded in the "ethnic" servant dolls, I feel that when women made these figures in such a playful form, they must have felt a sense of connection with them.[40] I stand by the arguments I made in chapter 4 about exotic dress-up, and I still see the dolls as a form of alter ego. Certainly their feelings of superiority and entitlement meant that white, Anglo-Saxon doll makers were connecting to a stereotype and an "other" rather than any kind of real person. Nevertheless, iconic dolls were almost always adult figures rather than babies, and they implied grown-up relationships.

Cameron tells us that in Renaissance Italy and France, dolls were often given to brides as symbols of their future children. In Italy the doll was typically part of the dowry, and the bride was encouraged to bathe, feed, and cuddle it; the idea was that by thus playing with this symbolic icon, she would bear a happy child.[41] It is intriguing to think of the servant dolls given to the guest of honor at twentieth-century wedding showers as a vestigial expression of this custom. The doll was still an iconic representative of the future (and future self), but motherhood was no longer the salient identity the bride would have to take on; rather, she was looking forward to a life of household labor. The irony, certainly, is that the projected servant would not really take on any housewifely duties. She provided the tools, but it was the bride who would have to do the scrubbing and polishing; she herself would have to step into the role (the part of herself) that the household helper doll was representing.

Iconic dolls also contributed in other ways to the creation of the saturated world outlined in chapter 1. We can begin with they way they furthered the women's sense of connection and community. When used as gifts or party favors, for example, they served as tangible symbols of friendship and affection. Because they were made in the shape of other women, they represented a kind of sister-hood and reinforced a sense of female bonding. Iconic dolls were also often made as bazaar sales items. A bazaar was itself a kind of party and helped build fellow-ship and community. Those who worked together to make bazaar items forged strong relationships, but even if a woman was alone when she made a doll, she could feel connected to the imagined person who would eventually take delight in it. This must have been true, also, for von Bachellé, who worked in isolation on her vegetable dolls. The inscription of her book, indicating she hoped others would take pleasure in her creation, makes it clear that she was thinking of a broader community. The very setting of the book was an affirmation of commu-nity; she was writing about a gathering, a party that "folks" naturally gravitated to. Even though she was alone and nearly destitute, von Bachellé fashioned an imaginary fellowship with many characters who expressed care for one another.

The fact that most of the iconic dolls were handmade is also significant. Those who received them as gifts found them especially meaningful because of the time and energy that had gone into them, but, beyond the labor, they also appreciated the way the dolls expressed their makers' creativity. A fancy pen wiper or kitchen helper was always most special when it bore evidence of the person who had made it. At the same time, the creator also found pleasure in the making process. Doll making was an expressive outlet, a chance to put together materials and ideas in novel and creative ways. Many of these figures are humorous precisely because of their unexpected juxtapositions, such as pastry brushes serving as arms or children's shoes serving as pincushions. It is easy to understand why a hostess would want to spend hours stringing beads to represent raindrops around a doll centerpiece; imagine how intently someone who had to make a kitchen doll for a bridal shower would walk through the aisles of the Woolworth store, looking at everyday implements with fresh eyes. These are compelling, involving activities that engage one's creative interest. The fact that the final product was a doll, moreover, made this creative work seem even more like play. Everyone who was involved with the dolls—makers, receivers, and anyone else who interacted with them—was better able to step into a happy, childlike state because of them.[42]

Despite the fact that they often relied on purchased products, handmade iconic dolls also expressed a distinctly nonconsumerist ethos. We are brought back to the discussion of gift relations and the understanding that consumer goods can be appropriated, or transformed, from commodities to seemingly personal items. Even in the 1860s, when manufactured products were much more of a novelty than they later became, magazine writers felt free, as previously mentioned, to instruct readers to break the legs off an existing doll in order to make a fancywork pincushion. Consumer goods were thus recast and transformed so that they became raw materials in their own right. In the interwar years, when sewing skills had become less universal, shower guests still usually embellished store-bought gifts. They might embroider a set of linens with the bride's initials, for example, or make linens "speak" with typewritten verses. Perhaps the most powerful way to personalize a gift, however, was to literally make it in embodied form—to *personify* it. (By virtue of the fact that dolls seem to have personalities, the doll form was likely to seem personal even when it was not handmade, but the handmade version was likely to seem especially full of this quality.) When given as a gift, a doll represented a kind of human bond between the giver and recipient, which distanced it even further from an "alienated" piece of property.

We can probably all agree that these iconic dolls did not project what is generally thought of as an empowered image.[43] The primary asset of the dolls was their prettiness and charm. While the household helpers promised to assist with the drudgery, they could not really do so; they represented a fantasy rather than anything that would come to pass, and, in order to be of any assistance at all, they had to be dismantled—literally taken apart to the point that they would be unrecognizable. Other types of dolls stayed intact, but many of them functioned as hiders of things that should not be seen. The dolls *did* have power, but it lay in another direction: they had the power of "enchantment." They not only projected happiness and good feeling, but "magically" brought those qualities into the daily life of the those who made or interacted with them. Because women made dolls in their own image, I think we can ultimately conclude that they expressed a positive sense of self. Cameron writes of doll-based ritual as a context in which the play world and real world intersect; by creating something in one world, she argues, its qualities seem to become tangible in the other.[44] Those who created rituals around iconic dolls did not think they would change the outward reality of their lives, but they knew they could infuse a different feeling into it, at least for a time. These figures expressed friendship, affection, and a sense of community. They were intimate companions that elicited sensual pleasure and infused everyday responsibilities with a quality of delight. They allowed grown women to relive the happy moments of childhood and the imaginative parts of themselves. We must see them as life-affirming amusements that played their part in the creation of a more saturated world.

Chapter Six

COLLECTING

I wish I could take [my collection of paper dolls] with me when I die. . . . I honestly mean it. . . . I love the smell, the feel, the colors, the care with which they were done, just *everything* about them.

—MRS. WILLIE ARMSTRONG,
QUOTED IN A LETTER FROM MARIAN HOWARD
TO MAXINE WALDRON, NOVEMBER 10, 1959

Introduction

An exploration of women's collecting seems a fitting conclusion to this volume on domestic amusements. It brings us back full circle to the discussion of Steven Gelber's book, *Hobbies,* and the different approach to leisure activities taken by men and women at the turn of the twentieth century. It is related, too, to the amusements discussed in other chapters. A scrapbook house functioned as a kind of collection, for example, but, even beyond that, many of its qualities matched those that characterized the types of objects women liked to collect. Dress-up and iconic dolls are relevant because women frequently collected costumes or dolls (and dolls dressed in exotic costume). Furthermore, they often arranged their dolls in animated, tableauxlike vignettes that were akin to the animated party table decorations and staged photographs discussed in chapters 3 and 4. The interpenetrating quality of these subjects is symbolized for me in a 1919 *Good Housekeeping* feature I found in the papers of Maxine Maxson Waldron, a passionate collector of paper dolls and related ephemera. The magazine illustrated a group of paper dolls with a caption indicating they were "holding a fancy dress party." Here, the "denizens" of the scrapbook houses—the focus of women's collections—were both "hostessing" and dressing up.[1]

The period under discussion in this chapter is roughly 1890–1950, although there is a particular emphasis on the teens and the interwar years.[2] This was an era, again, of increasing democratization and relative prosperity, meaning that greater numbers of women had money to spend on collecting activities. It is the period when community pageants, home parties, and elaborate wedding showers were also at their peak, and many collectors were involved in those activities as well. The idea that these were overlapping arenas is demonstrated by the fact that many advice givers covered both collecting and entertaining. Ella Shannon Bowles, for example, authored both *About Antiques* and *Practical Parties*.[3] The audience for the books on collecting was thus the same predominately well-educated, white, and Protestant population we have been considering. The literature was aimed at the middle class as well as the wealthy, and it included many references to counting pennies.

Collecting was a pastime that filled leisure hours, and collecting was identified as a hobby. Most of the sought-after items were thought of as antiques or curios,[4] but whatever the objects, collecting was seen as a form of entertainment. This was made explicit in one of the first books chronicling collecting pursuits, Annie Trumbull Slosson's *The China Hunter's Club* (1878). Slosson explained that the people of her town were wondering what they were going to do in the upcoming winter because they "were so tired of Lady Washington tea parties . . . [and] historic tableaux." As an alternative amusement, they organized a club. Members pooled their money to buy reference works on ceramics and soon ventured out into the nearby countryside to look for pottery. "We were none of us very rich . . . we were not great travellers; some of [us] never went five miles from home," claimed Slosson, "but we were indefatigable in our narrow sphere." Members entertained one another at their meetings with stories of collecting exploits.[5] The overlay between collecting and entertainment remained strong fifty years later, toward the end of the period under consideration. In 1925 Edna Greenwood (1888–1972), a collector of colonial artifacts, gave up modern conveniences such as gas and electricity in order to live in an ongoing tableau—a kind of living history experiment that she dubbed "Timestone Farm." Soon after she moved in, she invited guests to parties where they were provided with period costumes and were served period-specific meals. These were elaborate versions of the colonial theme party, and the guests essentially became characters in her fanciful "historic" play.[6]

The Emergence of American Collecting and Children's Collecting Patterns

While wealthy individuals had been able to fill "cabinets of curiosity" with natural and human-made artifacts since the Renaissance, hobby collecting—that is, collecting as a popular leisure pastime—only became possible with the abundance of goods engendered by industrialization. In the industrialized environment of the mid-nineteenth century, formerly precious objects became commonplace, and new items appeared constantly. Amassing goods and arranging them in various kinds of groupings made sense in this context. We have previously mentioned stamp collecting, which was made possible by the issuance of the first official government stamps and became popular in the 1870s, and we have discussed the popularity of scrapbook albums brought on by the explosion of printed matter at approximately the same time. Moreover, when everyday items such as textiles, dishes, and furniture could be made by mechanical means, individuals began to look at the handmade objects of previous generations with new appreciation. An excitement about "antiques" (that is, anything old and handmade) thus also began to take hold of the public in the 1870s—the time when the China Hunter's Club came into being. The first books on collecting ceramics and furniture appeared in the 1870s, and the first store featuring American antiques opened in that decade as well. *Godey's Lady's Book* referred to antiquing as the "latest mania" in 1878. The interest in antiques was spurred on by patriotic sentiment and United States Centennial celebrations and by the fact that American objects were particularly affordable—one could simply go into people's houses and ask to buy the old things that they no longer cared about. Collecting Americana was thus not limited to people of great means or social connection (although, again, collectors tended to be educated).[7]

The real explosion of collecting occurred at the turn of the century, when it was promoted as an uplifting activity that anyone could master. Aesthetic reformers advocated collecting American antiques as a way of building good taste. Clarence Cook wrote about collecting in this way in *The House Beautiful,* for example, and Arts and Crafts movement leader Gustav Stickley referred to the colonial style as one that would help create harmony, as it offered refreshing "old-time quiet . . . in a breathless age." The individuals who staged the photographs discussed in chapter 4, including Mary Northend and Mary and Frances Allen, were involved with collecting as well as the promotion of good taste. They used antiques as aesthetic props. The Allen sisters set up many of their images in the Deerfield home of their friend C. Alice Baker, who is credited as one of the first to restore a colonial house and fill it with a collection of antiques.[8]

In this period, antiques also took on associations with a kind of nobility. There was a profusion of books with titles such as *Colonial Dames and Good Wives* that painted a romantic picture of women of the past and stirred up excitement about the kinds of items they had lived with. Old objects were thus valued because they had been used by forebears engaged in "heroic" domestic activities.

170   With encouragement of this sort, more and more middle class women caught the collecting bug in the new century. Advice volumes such as *The Charm of the Antique* soon proliferated. These were aimed at the novice collector, and offered assurance that anyone could succeed at the delightful pastime of collecting.[9]

Collecting was such a widespread activity at the turn of the century that the popular press was referring to it as an instinct, and several scholars became interested in young people's collecting behavior. Caroline Frear Burk studied 1,214 California children, ages six to seventeen, in 1900. She found interest in collecting to be nearly universal, but boys and girls had different attitudes and collecting practices. Girls were most likely to collect beautiful objects or objects with sentimental associations; among their favorites were pictorial images, buttons, textiles, and dolls, followed by natural specimens such as seaweed and flowers. About half of them collected chromolithographs (brightly colored picture cards). Only about 9 percent of the boys collected picture cards and pretty things; they favored cigar tags, stamps, and marbles. When they collected natural materials, furthermore, they were disproportionately interested in animal products such as bird's eggs (and beaks, claws, and wings), skeletons, and rabbit's ears.[10] We can see then that both genders favored items that alluded to their eventual adult roles; cigar bands were products of the male-identified activity of smoking, for example, and buttons related to the clothing women were ultimately responsible for.

Young children were not yet interested in classification, Burk said, but young boys already gravitated toward products that appeared in sets and could be organized according to intellectual criteria. Boys expressed a full-blown concern with classification by about age fourteen. Girls of the same age were less likely to care about classification; rather, they "exceeded in decorative arrangements." The importance of personal relationships also showed up more in the girls' collections. Almost twice as often as the boys, their collected objects had been received as gifts. (Burk described one nine-year-old girl who fit this pattern perfectly. She referenced many relatives in her collection description: "My cousin gave me my paper dolls. My aunt gave me my box of shells. My papa and mamma gave me my picture-cards and scrap-books. And my grandma sent me my rocks." She also indicated the importance of the aesthetic dimension when she added, "Whenever I find a pretty rock I take it home.") The boys generally approached their collections more aggressively than the girls; they were interested in the products of the "hunt," as we have seen, but, in addition, they were particularly interested in marketable items that could be sold or traded.[11]

Other reports confirmed these findings and reinforced the idea that boys' collecting conformed more closely to Gelber's "workplace values." Girls were said to collect books more often than boys, for example, apparently for sentimental rather than economic value. A 1928 Kansas study found boys from ages nine to sixteen were twice as likely as girls to collect things that might eventually be sold. Another study correlated boys' hobbies with success in school, since their aggressive, systematic, market-oriented approach "reproduced attitudes valuable for schoolwork."[12]

The advice literature aimed at children reinforced and inculcated these same gendered values at the turn of the century. In *Every Boys Book of Handicraft, Sports and Amusements,* for example, Chelsea Curtis Fraser impressed upon his readers that besides being fun, collecting was educational and good training for the competitive adult world. Many of the world's "greatest and most honored" men had been collectors when they were young, he said, and some had "learned [such] great secrets" through their activities that "the world was better for these discoveries." Fraser wrote about tasks such as preserving skeletons and mounting natural specimens that furthered the image of man the hunter, and he addressed coin and stamp collecting in language that reiterated the importance of the market. The assumption that boys would collect animal specimens was so widespread, in fact, that Janet E. Ruutz-Rees wrote, "In every home where there are boys, the value of a collection of birds' eggs is well known." In contrast, advice given to girls always stressed the aesthetic. If girls were to hunt anything, it was imagery. While Lina and Adelia D. Beard mentioned nature collections in *New Ideas for Work and Play: What a Girl Can Make and Do,* they spent much more time discussing how one might collect "art pictures" from magazines, and then spend time mounting and displaying them to great advantage. Mackarness's *The Young Ladies' Book* similarly passed quickly from discussing collecting natural items to suggesting that girls collect "church prints" and other pictorial images. The Beards also referred to autograph books, diaries, and calendars as "collections" that indicated "the importance of associative, emotional emblems in girls' lives."[13]

These instructions relate, of course, to other aspects of childhood training. We have touched on this topic in previous chapters, but a further comparison of messages given to girls and boys about amusements will bring us even closer to understanding gendered collecting patterns. As noted, girls were told that work could be play and play could be work, but they were not taught to hone skills for the competitive workplace. Boys were. *The Boy's Own Toymaker* proclaimed as early as 1859 that "a boy engaged in making a toy-house becomes half an architect. . . . he who makes a toy boat learns skills that may be handy when he is a man." The companion book, *The Girl's Own Toymaker,* did not have the girls making toy houses at all—rather, they were given suggestions for decorating

172   them with pretty tables and stoves. They were taught that amusements should involve relationships with others. Many of their toys were human shaped and either represented everyday people or picturesque characters such as the "fate lady" (fortune teller). The boys might play with human figures, but only in contexts that related more to individual, outside, sporting activities—they cut out cardboard horses and jockeys, for example, or individuals outfitted for a fox hunt. Such gendered instruction was still fully intact in 1916, when Edna A. Foster published a set of books entitled *Something to Do—Girls!* and *Something to Do— Boys!* The foreword of her girls' volume began, "Have you ever seen a little girl sitting by her mother's sewing table and learning to take the first stitches? How happy she look[s]. . . . here are things to learn. . . . your finger fairies will do your bidding and they will help you to make beautiful gifts for those you love." The boys' manual began, "Do you like to watch a great piece of machinery? Whirr sings the big wheel. . . . each [part] moves with perfect accuracy and power. . . . Did you ever think that your mind is a machine? . . . All boys like to create something to work out problems."[14]

Collecting Patterns among Adult Men and Women

Not surprisingly, adults reiterated these same patterns in their approaches to collecting. We shall look at the ways in which this was manifest, with the caveat that we are talking about overall trends and proclivities rather than actual individuals and with the understanding that these contrasts paint a somewhat oversimplified picture. The contrasts nevertheless provide a framework for making sense of the kind of collecting advice written by men and women and the collecting activities and interests of actual individuals.

    Men's collecting in the early twentieth century led outward, away from the self and toward the workplace reality and broader world. Men often gravitated to objects that related to industry. In *Antique Collecting for Men,* Louis H. Hertz remarked that men are interested in machines, in how things work, and how they are made. They like the "workings of the internal mechanism, and the business around it," he proclaimed; they are drawn to machine-made, "substantial" objects. China and glass could be suitable men's collectibles due to their industrial history. Major H. Byng Hall concurred. He claimed china collecting was a worthwhile pursuit because china showed both "genius and practical skill" and united art and science. Henry Chapman Mercer, who amassed a huge collection of twenty-five thousand tools at the turn of the century, was even more adamant about linking collecting with science, and created an elaborate classificatory scheme for the products of human industry. Mercer was literally hostile to those who collected strictly out of aesthetic interest. Writing in 1897 about the meaning of a collection such as his own, he intoned, "We are out of mantel decoration and bric-a-brac, and knee deep in science . . . looking at tools by which man conquers nature, eats, lives and enjoys life." Industrial magnate Henry Ford visited Mercer's museum in 1922 and was so impressed that he started his own collection of objects that represented the history of tools and industry. It was a grand-scale tribute to the power of man over nature. Ford's collection was eventually also opened to the public as the Ford Museum and Greenfield Village.[15]

Men also tended to collect in order to increase their personal power or importance—in a sense, to achieve a kind of immortality. Individuals such as Charles Pendleton, a Providence lawyer who willed his collection to the Rhode Island School of Design in 1904, were concerned that their names live on through such legacies. Collections could serve as trophies; Major Hall even likened the Sevres china cups he had collected to the scalps an Indian warrior had won in battle. This kind of rhetoric was not uncommon; men of this period frequently used words such as "trophies" and "pedigrees" to describe their collections. (It is still not uncommon. Werner Muensterberger used the latter term in a 1994 book, even likening objects' "bloodlines" to those of racehorses). The insistence on pedigree also meant men tended to be highly concerned with authentication. This was evident even in the story of the China Hunter's Club which, as we have seen, was one of the earliest collectors' groups. The group fell apart, according to Slosson, when two of the male members got into a fight about the authenticity of a particular object. Their heated feelings created so much rancor, she said, that the "spell [of the group was] broken."[16]

The same concern for pedigree and authentication was evident in 1933, when Henry Francis du Pont described a set of his furniture to fellow members of the exclusive collector's club, the Walpole Society. Du Pont first demonstrated the importance of the family of the former owner, Rebecca Gratz, by establishing its ties to a range of American heroes. Gratz's brother Benjamin married a "granddaughter of an intimate friend of Washington," du Pont noted, and the daughter of that marriage was also related by marriage to a grandson of Henry Clay. He also emphasized the family's influence (they "must have been a fine, sturdy set of characters," he argued, since they owned land and had connections in multiple states) and the idea that Gratz herself was said to have inspired a character in Sir Walter Scott's *Ivanhoe*. The Walpole Society was made up of elite men. Its original members had displayed their antique collections in the Hudson-Fulton Exhibition of 1909, and later recruits such as du Pont were admitted only after they had demonstrated their "distinction in collecting" as well as the right ancestry

174   and loyalties. In other words, the club required two types of pedigree: appropriate social class and a collection of rare and expensive pieces. (Interestingly, some of the members, including du Pont and Charles Hitchcock Tyler, were animal breeders who were particularly concerned with bloodlines.)[17]

Men who could not join an exclusive organization such as the Walpole Society could still hope to collect rare objects that would by association help them seem important. George Blake Dexter, author of the 1923 book *The Lure of Amateur Collecting* wrote of seeking unusual souvenirs in Europe, such as an Iron Cross medal or a letter that had been written by Napoleon Bonaparte. Dexter's self-aggrandizing exploits did not end with procuring these exotic items; he seems to have made a career of speaking about his adventures at places such as the National Arts Club and war charity benefits. C. R. Clifford's *The Junk Snupper: The Adventures of an Antique Collector* was written at about the same time. Clifford was particularly interested in getting good deals on rare items and boasted about the many times he turned down a family's "treasure" because it was not worth enough money. He mocked the unsophisticated who did not know what was really valuable, and he went on about the danger of fakes or reproductions. The idea that collecting was a competitive game was also particularly prevalent in men's writing. "It is always fair to take advantage of the other fellow's mistake," claimed collector John Ramsey, and J. W. Mackail went so far as to say that stealing was "not a breach of the rules."[18]

The hunt metaphor was salient in men's discussion of collecting. *St. Nicholas* magazine published a collecting reminiscence in 1925 that referred to the sought-after objects as "prey" and "big game." Gelber commented that "the image of the hunt as both a search for game and a form of game imbued collecting with an air of masculinity that legitimated it as an expression of superiority in a Darwinian world." Gelber further linked the kind of aggressiveness common to hunting and competitive games to the qualities that led to success in the marketplace (this concept was hinted at by Gabriel Wells in 1920, when he commented, "collecting stands midway between sport and trade"). Gelber wrote of the obsessive and possessive quality that men often exhibited and cited two book collectors who verbalized this tendency. One claimed the desire to collect really rested on "the privilege of possessing something that your neighbor has not." The other claimed the possession of a rare item, "coveted by all the world, perhaps supplies a something that is lacking even in the successful merger of great industrial organizations."[19]

Collecting in order to complete a series was also a way of winning a game. We usually think of series in terms of collectibles such as stamps and coins, but other, more surprising items might also be approached this way. A 1994 *New York Times* article illustrated this with a report of a "major gender gap" in the way that men and women buy classical music recordings. Women buy albums because they want to hear the music, according to the marketing survey, but men buy them in order to own recording sets. As author Diana Jean Schemo explained, "Many men who collect records . . . describe their quest for every known recording of a given composer, conductor, or musician as an urge not just to listen to the music, but to possess it as well." These same impulses have clearly been operative for more than a hundred years.[20]

A characterization of the qualities of adult women's collecting not only echoes what we have talked about in relation to girls' pastimes, but sounds remarkably like the a list of the qualities I have used to characterize the saturated world itself. I will begin with a brief overview—really a listing—of these qualities, and I will then explore them individually in greater detail (because I am writing about women in this book, they get more "air time" than men do).

Perhaps the most salient characteristic of women's collecting was its aestheticized nature. Women's collecting also led inward, to both the self and the home environment, and it served as an extension of their domestic training and roles. Women tended to gravitate toward objects that were part of, rather than apart from, daily life. They not only considered useful items to be as good as those that were strictly decorative, but in many cases preferred them. Furthermore, many women *used* their collected objects, integrating them into everyday experience. In a variety of ways, women's collections also helped further a sense of relationship. Collectors felt connected to their objects and generally also liked objects that helped them feel connected to other people. Moreover, the collecting process itself often involved relationships with others (that is, collecting *with* others or connecting with the people who made or previously owned their objects), so the relationships and collecting experience were valued as much as the collected items. This is not to say that women never "hunted" for their objects—many did, but their hunts were typically less predatory, as they focused more on the experience of the hunt than on the prey.[21] Since women on the whole were concerned less about authenticity and pedigree, they were able to treat both the collecting process and the collections themselves as play. Many used their objects to create dioramas or contextual displays, as we have seen, or, like Edna Greenwood, used them as part of enactments. (Here again, the objects helped them relate to others.) Women also tended to favor intimate items, often made of soft or even ephemeral materials. Their collected items were often home-related or were related to—and reflections of—the women themselves. This helps explain the many embodied items in women's collections, including dolls and elements of clothing.

FIG. 6.1.
This "Old Woman in the Shoe" pincushion was collected by Electra Havemeyer Webb, who, like many women of her generation, was drawn to amusing objects that evoked happy childhood memories and included representations of women. Photograph courtesy of Shelburne Museum, Shelburne, Vermont.

FIG. 6.2.
Cheerful hooked rugs were among the items that interested women collectors of the early twentieth century. This illustration is from Ella Shannon Bowles's *Handmade Rugs* (1927). Bowles not only wrote books about antiques and collecting, but about entertaining. She was the author of *Practical Parties*.

We have already mentioned many of the specific items women were espe- cially interested in; in addition to dolls, textiles, and costumes, we have discussed china and ephemera, including paper dolls, valentines, and trade or picture cards. Other items included glass; personal accessories such as fans, jewelry, and hats; decorative and simultaneously functional small household items such as cookie cutters and butter molds; silhouettes; and wallpaper and related printed or sten- ciled items such as bandboxes. They were also disproportionately drawn to Ameri- can Indian art, including baskets, pottery, and other functional items; and to so-called peasant and folk art.[22] This list brings us back to the idea that, in keep- ing with their training, women were interested in outfitting the home and in small or miniature things. They paid attention to the little details—the curtains in a home, the table accoutrements, the curios on the shelves, or the objects that provided comfort and filled practical needs in the bedrooms and children's rooms. They also paid attention to the things that extended or represented the body, and they collected the very kind of iconic dolls—including sewing tools—that we discussed in the last chapter as embodied images of self (fig. 6.1).

My overview of men's and women's collecting in the period under consider- ation is admittedly painted with a broad brush, and it presents a highly polarized picture. Certainly historical reality was more nuanced. Nevertheless, when we look at the words women wrote about collecting and track the collecting experi- ences of actual women, the picture comes alive and tells a compelling story.

Women's Attitudes and Experiences: A Closer Look
Aesthetic Elaboration and Personal Connection

Aesthetic elaboration and pleasure seemed to be infused in almost all of women's collecting pursuits. "To arrange a collection of stamps to be attractive, as well as valuable, takes the fertile mind of a woman," boasted Mame A. Keene in an 1893 commentary. Collector Maud Charlotte Bingham demonstrated just this kind of mind. Rather than arranging her stamps in straight rows, she grouped them in shapes appropriate to their categories. Stamps relating to agriculture took on the outline of a plow, for example, and those issued by the Department of War were grouped into the shape of a "monster siege gun." Fay Jordan, who collected in the 1940s, filled her albums exclusively with purple stamps. Women's button collec- tions, too, were often organized according to idiosyncratic rather than "scientific" categories. Some were grouped according to materials, such as glass or mother of pearl; others by subject (all buttons with a face), and some by whimsical categories.[23]

Male commentators typically cited this emphasis on prettiness as evidence of the women's less-developed understanding of the world around them,[24] and

178 there were certainly some instances in which women's advice literature treated collecting as little more than a fashionable facade. In 1939, for example, the beauty editor for *Ladies' Home Journal* advocated that women take up hobbies as a way of becoming more appealing—they might collect objects that would be charming to contemplate, such as theater programs, bells, buttons, maps, and historical dresses. For the most part, however, women's writings about collecting stressed the way that aesthetic experience deepened one's experience of the world. For example, when Ruutz-Rees spoke about fossil collectors (referring to both boys and girls), she stated, "a collector of fossils is like a person with second-sight. To him every particle of the earth's surface is fraught with meaning, and his senses once fully awakened, new facts dawn upon him like a continuous revelation." When Helen Bowen wrote about collecting old quilted textiles, she lovingly described the way the low relief of the quilting would have been enhanced by soft firelight in a colonial home, and pointed out how lighting conditions change what we see.[25] Close identification with aesthetic detail and saturated experience was rare in men's writings on collecting.

Women's comments make it clear how the magic of saturated childhood pastimes often lingered into adulthood. Isabella Stewart Gardner, creator of the famous Fenway Court (Gardner Museum) in Boston, said her husband "accused" her of acting like a little girl who never grew up; when she was collecting, she was "playing" with things, he said, much as she had in her youth. Electra Havemeyer Webb, whose objects now fill dozens of buildings at Vermont's Shelburne Museum, stated that her first hobby was collecting dolls, and she never really got out of the habit. Margaret Woodbury Strong, who obsessively amassed the "objects of fascination" that are now seen in the Strong Museum in Rochester, New York, similarly spoke longingly of the dolls that were her companions as a child. She kept voluminous scrapbooks in her youth, as well, and then later collected much the same sort of paper material that they had been filled with. Some commentators expressly referred to the fairyland quality of childhood pleasures. Ella Shannon Bowles related it to adult collecting interests in her 1919 book, *About Antiques*, particularly mentioning the long-lasting pull of remembered storybook characters. Paper doll collector Frieda Smith reminisced about such characters in 1962. In a letter to a fellow collector, she wrote of the countless hours she and a childhood friend had spent recreating a village of log cabins for "Judith of the Cumberlands," as well as making paper dolls based on fairy tale princesses, Greek gods and goddesses, and characters from "boarding school stories." Her descriptions are full of almost dreamy aesthetic detail. The idea that grown-up women prized their child-like delight was summarized in a statement Catherine

Collison made at a doll collector's club meeting: "Never believe the song, 'When You Grow Too Old to Dream!' For doll collectors are little girls grown up, and little girls never outgrow their dreaming."[26]

Judging from women's writing about collecting quests, the same saturated quality was sometimes infused into the collecting process itself. The expeditions seemed delicious; not only was there a sense of excitement about what one might find, but just being outdoors or off on a country trip could in itself bring pleasure. Alice Kent Trimpey intoned, "Who can describe the blissful anticipation that warms the heart of a collector! With a well-filled lunch basket and a tankful of gasoline, and imbued with the keenest spirit of adventure, he is off at sunrise. The dew is on the grass, the wild flowers nod by the wayside. . . .The millionaire who passes him in his powerful limousine creates not one particle of envy." Alice Van Leer Carrick began her book *Collector's Luck* with the statement, "If I were a physician prescribing for the ills of the body and mind, I know I should have one sovereign remedy . . . collect!" She referred to her collecting trips as "happy pleasures." "'L' and I go together through storm and sun, dusty and muddy, sunrise to sunset," she noted, "[and some of the country we go through] is so beautiful that to drive through it is a joy all by itself."[27]

Once they got to their destinations, they were equally delighted with what they saw. "Oh what a visual feast!" remarked Alberta Anderson on seeing photographs of newly collected dolls. "I got my magnifying glass out and . . . they're simply out of this world." Carrick referred to the treasures she picked up at an auction as "captured dreams." Even the most humble item might fill the collector with joy because of its sensual quality. In a 1925 article describing her antiquing experience in a Canadian farmhouse, Amy Lyman Phillips explained her reaction to what she and her companion saw in the kitchen. "There, on the table crowded with . . . [cooking paraphernalia] were three pickle bottles of a beauty and rarity that makes one gasp."[28]

In an unpublished manuscript, "Hunting for Antiques," Mary Harrod Northend wrote about collecting as an activity that raised artistic awareness, and her writings, like those just quoted, were filled with poetic, saturated language. "The sweetness of [the item's] contours suggest the drift of snow under the wind or the ripples along the ocean beach," Northend noted. The literature also drew on the same kind of alliteration von Bachellé used to name her dolls; chapter titles in Georgia Dickinson Wardlaw's *The Old and Quaint in Virginia,* for example, included "Silhouettes: A Study in Shadows" and "The Vogue of the Valentine." Metaphoric literary conceits were also common. Virginia Robie's 1912 work *Bypaths in Collecting* was built around the idea of highways and by-paths: the

180   well-traveled, main collecting roads might lead to objects such as colonial furniture, Robie explained, but she favored the "little roads off the beaten path" such as "Staffordshire Lanes." Even the most prosaic topic could take on an evocative, romantic quality when presented in this aestheticized manner, and aesthetically rich experience was always linked with—or even considered synonymous with—romance. In *The Quest of the Antique,* Mrs. Willoughby Hodgson wrote about filling one's life with the fascinating objects of the past —objects like shoes, wigs, and corsets— whose "histories teem with romance." By definition, these would "call forth an imaginative vision."[29]

Most women appreciated objects they could relate to sensually. Avis Gardiner told Waldron that she could "still smell the flour and water paste" used on the paper dolls she had worked with as a child, and it was one of the reasons she felt so viscerally connected to these objects. Many collectors spoke of just "taking in" their pieces and relating to their unique qualities; as Elizabeth Day McCormick wrote of her collection of costumes and accessories, they fulfilled a longing for "beauty to contemplate." The joy this kind of sight provided was expressed by Marian Howard: "I received a gorgeous scrapbook . . . yesterday. The cover is worn, but the cutouts are so beautifully arranged and pasted on only the right hand pages so I can add my own to the left hand sides. I just oh'ed and ah'ed as I went through the ones in the book. Perfectly beautiful!"[30]

FIG. 6.3.
Margaret Woodbury Strong collected this English collage. The heavy relief is worked against a sandpaper background. The highly textural image of the house evokes coziness and cheer. Courtesy, the Strong Museum, Rochester, New York, 79.5161.

The ideal object created a feeling of well-being; as Robie explained, it was the "coziness and cheer" of teapots that explained their popularity with collectors. Ultimately, what many women wanted was a sense of being taken to another place—taken to fairyland. This longing was made explicit. Webb explained that she hoped to create something with her collection that "put her in a different world," and she called the idiosyncratic museum she created a "dreamland." Other collectors used terms alluding to enchantment. Dolls have a fairy quality, noted Zona Gale, and "have a hold on us." McCormick described a set of costume prints as "so teeming with charm . . . they bewitch me." (We tend to think of "charm" as prettiness, but remember that it also implies magic.) Robert and Elizabeth Shackleton used the idea of charm as an organizing device in their book, *The Charm of the Antique* (every chapter begins with "the charm of . . ."), and frequently introduced words such as "allurement" and "fascination." Robie spoke of "quaint stuff" that "casts a spell." The fullest expression of the desire to be brought into a saturated state was expressed by Esther Singleton in 1926:

> China is a world of its own. Into this strange, beguiling, dream-like realm the china-lover is transported. It is a place very real indeed, to those who have imagination—a place of gleaming surfaces; a place of rich, deep, lustrous, and also delicate colors; a place of tea-houses with lattice screens; of pagodas with turned-up roofs; of flowering peach trees and trees with fountain-like foliage; of neat, little gardens and bright meadows; . . . and of rivers thickly sprinkled with tiny, fairy boats. . . . Tea-Cup Land . . . [is] an imaginative Pleasure Ground, a kind of Lotus-land, where, having once entered, [people] dwell forevermore. . . . One little plate . . . is quite enough. Your fancy is engaged; your eyes are charmed;—and off you go![31]

Fairyland was often comprised of small things; "fairy boats" worked best as transports to other worlds when they were really tiny. It is not surprising that women collected miniatures in disproportionate numbers, given previous discussion that linked women with fairies, miniaturization, and women and small "fussy" things. Electra Webb told friends her husband liked the big things—buildings, primarily, and carriages. She appreciated those, but unlike him was drawn even more to the more intimate objects. Almost all the studies I have found of small antiques or decorative arts, furthermore, were written by women. It is true that small objects would usually be most affordable and many women did not have access to great amounts of money, and it is true that collectors who lived in modest homes would most easily be able to house little items, but this would not explain why wealthy collectors such as Electra Webb and Margaret Strong, who could buy anything they wanted, gravitated to them. In fact, women of means

182 had long been involved with miniatures; wealthy individuals were outfitting the first doll ("baby") houses as early as the seventeenth century. Arrangement of miniatures, as we shall soon see, was the source of great delight. Bowles waxed lyrical in *About Antiques* about the joy created by wee furniture "surrounded by flower-sprigged tea sets, tiny brass candlesticks, bits of sandwich glass, and nail-studded trunks." Her words call forth a clear image of a saturated world.[32]

Women's collecting experiences were also characterized by a strong sense of personal connection. First, as Carrick's reference to "L" implies, women liked to go on collecting trips with others, especially with other women. They often did this with relatives; my impression, in fact, is that there were a disproportionately large number of sisters and even mother-daughter pairs who built collections together.[33] Women often talked about parts of their collections that had been received as gifts, or about collections that began, like those of the girls in Burk's study, because they had received a special object as a gift and went on to find others like it.[34] Women forged extremely strong friendships, also, with nonrelated fellow collectors, and letters in Maxine Waldron's files indicate how some of these friendships evolved. Several of her correspondents were at first complete strangers, who called each other "Mrs.___." Over time, their mutual interest led to close relationships and intimate discussions about everything from children to health concerns. A few of them worked up to almost daily correspondence. Even when they were less closely bonded, the paper doll collectors often worked cooperatively to understand their objects; for example, members of a collecting group might send dolls to each member in turn so that they could piece together their stories. It is worth noting, too, that those who collected dolls and other women-identified objects such as textiles often operated almost exclusively in a female world characterized by this cooperative quality. They found advice and encouragement in books written by people such as Virginia Robie—another woman, with like interests—and they dealt with female shop owners and dealers who specialized in the same items.[35]

The Colonial Revival sentiment that pervaded turn-of-the-century collecting also emphasized family relationships. Authors such as Alice Morse Earle and Ella Shannon Bowles were interested in documenting and preserving objects that were connected to their "grandmothers." In *About Antiques*, Bowles explained she was concerned with the home life of her ancestors—with what they thought and why. This was a personal sense of connection, in other words; a "face to face history based on family networks." Even if there was no such relationship, however, collectors could still claim a sense of connection with the makers or users of their objects. Carrick stated that she "counted the people of the past as her intimates"

because her collecting pursuits had taught her so much about their times; working with her objects "placed her in close kinship with the long-ago [owners]."
Hughes spoke of antiques providing a "particularly vivid sense of contact" with
people of the past. Waldron also spoke about how much she liked the idea that
her paper dolls had been well-loved in the past; she could feel the energy of the
girls who once owned them. At meetings of Waldon's doll collector's clubs,
women talked about their dolls as members of their present-day families as well
(fig. 6.4). They presented their dolls' stories as life histories.[36]

FIG. 6.4.
These women, posing with their favorite dolls, were attending a doll collector's conference in Florida, ca. 1950.
The image illustrates the kind of personal connection that women collectors often had with their objects, and it
shows the embodied nature of some of their collections. The photograph was in the papers of Maxine Waldron,
who was a doll collector herself. Courtesy, The Winterthur Library, Joseph Downs Collection of Manuscripts
and Printed Ephemera, Collection 121.

It is easy to understand dolls as "friends and playmates," but women spoke of
all kinds of objects as if they were embodied and alive. Robie stated, "To many
collectors, particularly in this country, the personal history of each article counts
almost half. One of the undoubted joys of hunting old china lies in this personal,
human side which each object possesses. To one who has never gathered together
old teapots, bowls, mugs, etc., this livable, live quality of inanimate objects is
quite unknown." Hooked rugs "aren't merely still life," Waugh and Foley claimed;
they are alive because they embody and express the feelings of the women who

184   made them. In giving instructions to an assistant who was helping her arrange a showcase, Electra Webb told her to use a particular frame because it "would give [the object] more life." Webb felt intimate with many objects that had no semblance of human form. She was most able to "go wild," she said, with patterned bandboxes and similar objects with "strong personalities."[37]

If they were not heavy, collected objects could sometimes travel with their owners; Nellie Maclochlan actually spoke of one of her paper dolls as "a constant companion." More often, owners engaged in vicarious travel. Mary Kramer wrote about a paper doll that had originally been used by a girl who tragically died while moving to Kansas in a covered wagon. "Sometimes I choke up when I tell this story," she said. "It's so easy to climb up in that wagon and travel with [her]." Imaginary travels were stressed in much of the doll-collecting literature, in particular, and the dolls were touted as a way of connecting with "people of other lands." Collectibles of all kinds could also connect one with pleasant memories of actual trips (including some of those happy collecting expeditions that had been taken with friends). Elizabeth Zenorini stated this strongly when she remarked that collected objects "become so full of our memories that they are a part of the fiber of our hearts." Tellingly, this very same phrase had been used by Margaret Sangster in an 1898 discussion of the reason that women cling to "their things." "Any woman can understand" why we become so attached to inanimate things, she said. Things are "so interwoven with the very woof of our memories and the very fibre of our hearts, that they seem as if endowed with sense and emotion." On another occasion, key collector Marie Overton Corbin wrote about the iron of her keys "entering her soul." Collected objects were animated by the sheer power of association, then, and by the personal attention their owners paid to them.[38]

I have mentioned Maxine Waldron a number of times, and before we go further, we will look more closely at her life and experience. Waldron embodies the kind of collector I am talking about, and her story, the first of several brief collector profiles, clearly illustrates the themes of aestheticization and personal connection.[39] Waldron, born in Iowa in 1898, grew up during the time when the scrapbooks, dress-up parties and theme teas, pageants, staged photographs, and other amusements that we have been examining were at their peak and when women's culture was steeped in a saturated sensibility. Waldron's family was not well off. Her father was a shop teacher, and the family had to move repeatedly during her childhood. At one point finances were so strained that her parents could not afford to buy her a teddy bear, but she was nevertheless well-educated and grew up with an appreciation for the arts. Waldron appears to have fully experienced the popular turn-of-the-century emphasis on fairyland. The East

High Minstrels she sang with as a teenager performed a song about "little flowers nodding their heads," for example, and one of the performances she went to while at school was a "Dance of the Elements" (see fig. 1.6). She also kept scrapbooks containing mementoes of activities such as the YWCA Halloween party, artistically arranged posed photographs of her friends and herself (she was usually pictured next to an easel), and clippings on a photographer whose work she admired. As a young adult, Waldron went to Columbia Teacher's College to study art under Arthur Wesley Dow. She had a strong interest in Japonisme and participated fully in the New York art scene. She made drawings, prints (primarily woodcuts), pottery, and later, miniature crèche figures, and, like von Bachellé, she hoped to write and illustrate children's books. These books did not materialize, but Waldron worked throughout her life as an art instructor. She taught for a time at the Metropolitan Museum of Art, but after she married, she followed her husband to Delaware when he went to work for the du Pont Company. She was employed there for many years as a high school teacher.

Waldron started collecting as a young woman, well before she was married. Her first purchases appear to have been Neapolitan crèches (groupings of miniature figures), and these so intrigued her that she eventually wrote a book on the subject. She later collected art books and prints, as well as ephemera. By the time she donated the latter collection to the Winterthur Museum in 1982, it included over ten thousand paper dolls, as well as games and toys, children's books, valentines, scrapbooks, and extensive correspondence and personal papers. While these materials convey a strong sense of Waldron's intellectual prowess and scope, the most striking thing about them is their saturated, fairyland quality. There are books such as *The House That Glue Built*, filled with imaginative worlds within worlds; a "Game of the Five Senses"; and lovingly worked paper doll outfits complete with tiny lace collars and dresses made of as many as nine layers of crepe paper (fig. 1.8). Waldron's husband collected too, although his interests seem to have been more prototypically male. He focused on stamps and sets of cups and saucers. The latter, again, were touted by his contemporaries as products of science and industry, and thus fitting for men's collections.[40]

Waldron brought the aesthetic elaboration of her childhood into adulthood, unabashedly embracing the same paper dolls, brightly colored picture books, and fairytale reality. She approached them, however, with well-trained artistic sensitivity and great intelligence. Although she exhibited a childlike playfulness, she was not childish—on the contrary, her organizational and research skills shine through every letter she wrote. Waldron fit the profile of the early-twentieth-century collector in many other ways as well. She was solidly middle class and highly educated, and many of the items in her collection were the very kinds suggested by women giving advice in the antiques and collectibles literature of the period. She also was concerned with relationships and connectedness. She went on collecting expeditions with other women and was embedded in a strong network of other collectors. Her pastime—which came to almost completely fill her days when she was retired—seems to have become ever more meaningful because of her growing community. For the most part, Waldron approached collecting cooperatively rather than competitively. She rarely expressed concern with the resale value of her items, and although many of her collectibles were commercial products, she was not very interested in their industrial history. Rather, she liked their prettiness and ability to charm. In sum, Waldron's concerns did not conform to Gelber's workplace values, but she was still a serious collector who had clear criteria and intention for everything she did.

Other Forms of Intimacy

Most studies of collecting concentrate on the collecting process and pay relatively little attention to what happens once the items have been procured. What is slighted, in other words, is a look at what might be called the curatorial aspect of collecting—how the objects are organized or displayed, what is done with them, and what roles they have in the collector's everyday life.[41] If we look closely at typical ways that women lived with their collections, we see still more forms of intimacy.

In addition to the idea that women had "up-close" relationships with their "precious treasures" (the fact that many were small meant they were handled and seen from intimate proxemic distances), we must credit the kind of intimacy that came from utility. I have mentioned collectors C. Alice Baker and Edna Greenwood, who lived in restored or re-created historic homes, but even those who lived in ordinary houses and collected just a few objects were likely to put them to use. Antiques were touted in the women's literature as items that would enhance the quality of everyday living. *The Charm of the Antique* stated, "the highest form of collecting is for the furnishing of the home." The advice was applied to objects of different types. Bowles claimed "one of the jolly things about glass collecting" was that glass was usable, for example, and Robie talked about china collecting as a way of effectively filling a corner cupboard and enlivening one's home. Carrick even explained that she decided against buying an exceptional counterpane with a strong provenance because it did not fit her bed. Although she found this a "tragedy of the third dimension," her conviction that collected objects should be functional overrode her disappointment. Functional and contextual need sometimes also led collectors from one type of object to another. As Robie pointed out, "if you begin with china you must sooner or later find a cupboard to house it, or, if you first have the cupboard, you end by hunting for something to fill it."[42]

Notably, even the wealthiest women liked to see objects in functional, in situ contexts. Individuals such as Electra Webb and Louise Crowninshield had to outfit multiple houses and were thus given even more reason to collect. Long before she created the Shelburne Museum, Webb was busy with three homes (in an inventory of just one of these, I counted 130 hooked rugs). She later stated that her collecting began in earnest when she found how much she loved furnishing her houses, and she spoke about the Shelburne buildings in the same terms, as when she said she was outfitting "her" bedroom in the Prentis House.[43]

Because of their interest in contextual placement, women who collected antiques were not always against reproductions; if a particular item were needed to finish in an arrangement and an original could not be found, a well-made modern example might be acceptable. Mary Northend, whose writings on colonial-looking interiors were widely read, felt a handmade copy of an original piece was adequate if it met aesthetic criteria; the "spirit of the environment" might be enough. Where C. R. Clifford devoted an entire chapter of The Junk Snupper to warnings about being taken in by reproductions, Ella Bowles proclaimed that although many collector's pocketbooks would not allow them to purchase genuine old Wedgwood, they could still joyfully benefit from reproductions made by good potters. We are also reminded of Slosson's story of the demise of the China Hunters Club, which was linked to men's insistence on authenticity; Slosson implied that the women in the club did not share their concern. Parenthetically, the less elitist female approach and the women's interest in functional ordinary items meant that women were among the first collectors to be interested in what we now consider folk objects—objects made by informally trained artisans for use in their own communities. Privileged individuals such as Webb and Strong were sometimes even accused of collecting "down" for these preferences. We are brought back to the concept of gift relations introduced in the first chapter. To these collectors, objects were seen less as commodities than as conduits to emotional states and other people. Authenticity and pedigree did not matter as much when one was not operating under the constraints of marketplace values.[44]

Contextual placement also relates to the tableaux or vignettelike display that many women favored. Such arrangement would make an observer look even more closely at the collection—at both the individual objects and the totality. So grouped, the objects were given an even deeper, collective voice. Vignettelike arrangements also increased the quality of aliveness, or embodiment. After Margaret Woodbury

188 Strong's death, those who came to her mansion to look at her myriad glass cabinets full of doll vignettes spoke of "intra-doll sociability," and "family" or "discussion" groupings. As Mia Boynton described it, "Two would be bending toward a third, or one listening in on two who seemed unaware of her presence. . . . One doll would seem to be in a sort of story teller's attitude, the others gathered round; or small scale, fully adult dolls would be seated—like children—on the laps of larger, more babyish-looking dolls. . . . These were people in those cases, not dolls."[45]

Another way that women established an intimacy with their collections was to relate to them from the position of the maker. Many spent time repairing their objects or fashioning mounting devices for them. Elizabeth McCormick was constantly at work on her textile and costume collection, even toward the end of her life. She sewed on her pieces for short periods four times a day and felt deprived when she could no longer see well enough to do so. Waldron made repairs on her paper dolls. Sallie Casey Thayer so enjoyed mending shawls and matting prints that she wrote a friend, "I don't mind the rain—I'm busy working with my collection." Gelber also writes of Eva Earl, a woman who would have horrified "scientific" stamp collectors interested in authenticity if they had known what she did with her pieces. In an 1894 article about her activities, she "wrote of pleasure she found in 'cleaning the backs [of her stamps], the brightening up of their faces, mending little tears, adding here and there, a missing perforation.'" Some women even learned the techniques their pieces were made with in order to understand them from an "inside" perspective. Carrick said she learned to do candlewicking and hook rugs so she might be "really intelligent about" her textiles; she wanted to keep her words about them from being "pure theory." When she talked about mending coverlets in her collection, she stated, "Today I have been very happy . . . darning. . . .The task becomes apotheosized, glorified, [and] it placed me in close kinship" with the ancestress who first made it.[46]

Male collectors rarely had this kind of intimate maker's involvement with their collections, in part because it was only possible to achieve such closeness with certain types of objects. The women were working with "soft" media and techniques that did not involve elaborate or expensive equipment. Their beloved pieces had typically been made by anonymous "amateurs" in domestic settings—in conditions similar to their own. Given their training in handwork and home arts, these collectors could easily repair textiles and paper goods. They probably would not have been able to do more than a simple cleaning of silver or other "hard" objects made in professional workshops. Ironically, then, the very objects that were largely dismissed by those interested in workplace values and authenticity were often the ones that women felt most connected with by virtue of this maker's identification.

Additional Collector Profiles

Having established a context for women's collecting experience, I return now to a closer look at the way this was played out in the lives of particular individuals, with a focus on relatively well-off people for a number of reasons. They are the ones who have left records about their lives, for one thing, so we can reconstruct their stories. Equally important is the fact that because they had the means to collect in any way they saw fit, there were few external limitations on their activities. As I have pointed out, their attitudes and activities was not very different from that of women of more modest means, but they did everything on a grander scale. These profiles should thus make the qualities I have been writing about come even further alive and underline the saturated nature of women's collecting in this period.

Sallie Casey Thayer (1856–1925) was the oldest of the individuals I am profiling.[47] She was raised in the height of the Victorian era, steeped in its rhetoric about the importance of the home and women's role as the molder of artistic and moral temperament, and its assumptions about women learning handwork. She grew up an upper-middle-class southern belle in Kentucky and attended an "institute for young ladies." In 1880 she married a prominent businessman and moved to Kansas City, where she spent most of her life. As a leader in that city's society, she gave a number of entertainments and was involved in home and civic beautification projects. She was also a founding member of the Kansas City Fine Arts Club and the local chapter of the DAR. When her husband died in 1907, she moved to Chicago for three years to study at the Art Institute. Like Waldron, she studied Japanese art, and her interests were not limited to the fine arts. She was heavily influenced by Bessie Bennett, who taught design classes and later became curator of decorative arts at the museum. (We do not know exactly what she learned from Bennett, but the focus certainly must have on three dimensional, useful objects.) It was during this Chicago sojourn that Thayer started her highly eclectic collection. It included some prints, paintings, and sculpture, but they were outnumbered by antique housewares and other Americana, books, enamels, porcelains, pewter, glass, quilts and textiles, fashion plates, crèche figures, and other dolls. After traveling to Central America and California, she added Guatemalan textiles and American Indian baskets to her passions. She claimed her diverse items could "show the history of design in everyday ware from all over the world" and hoped they would eventually be shown in a museum that would infuse local designers with "ideas and inspiration."[48]

Thayer also procured her objects eclectically. She bought them at dealers' shops, department stores, and archeological sites, or, like the adventurers of the China Hunter's Club and the antiques "questers" featured in contemporary books, she knocked on farmhouse doors to "beg, borrow and (almost) . . . steal them from their owners." Her collecting interests led her to other design-related activities, such as organizing contests for the best fashion posters and shop window displays and lecturing on historic costumes, housewares, and crèche traditions. Thayer particularly liked objects with strong stories of their own (probably apocryphally, her Indian dolls were said to each have been made by a chief's wife), and she delighted in the way that they evoked recollections of "adventurous purchases." She also used her objects to create contextual vignettes. Her house included a "praying room," complete with temple replicas, shrines, and Japanese armor and embroidered robes hanging from the walls. She set up thematic exhibitions in her home, which she opened to the public as a temporary museum in 1916. Her first exhibit featured glass and china (the *Kansas City Post* reported on her "dazzling arrays" of "objects gleaned from the farthest corners of the world that created the air of a fairy palace"); the second featured textiles. These too were diverse and nonhierarchical, ranging from European and Oriental luxury fabrics to American samplers, Indian baskets, and dolls.

Thayer eventually convinced the University of Kansas to accept her collection but did not approve of they way it was treated there. Consequently, she moved to Lawrence to act as its curator. She went to the university daily to work with her objects and organize displays. She lined exhibit halls with rugs, for example, and filled the rooms with pull-out cabinets and drawers of textiles and small objects. Unfortunately, after she died, the collection was moved to a new building, and the museum was recast completely. The first curator, a woman, remained true to Thayer's vision, but John Maxson, the director hired after World War II, wanted to create a "real" art museum. Inculcated with the hierarchies of traditional art history, Maxson kept Thayer's two-dimensional prints and paintings, but pointedly "got rid of" many of her "curios." He moved most of the remaining design collection to the basement (sadly, poor conditions there actually ruined some of the materials), although the Indian objects went to the university's anthropology department. Many of Thayer's pieces, especially the textiles, were said to be sorely missed by the public.

Electra Havemeyer Webb (1888–1960)[49] also liked everyday things. She grew up in a family that was concerned with aesthetic matters; her parents were not only avid collectors of fine European art—they were among the first patrons of Impressionists such as Renoir and Degas—but lived in a Tiffany-designed house.[50]

Electra considered her own first collection to be the dolls she received when she was about ten. Her grandmother usually gave her a doll for Christmas and on her birthday, and Electra was so taken by them that she asked if she might have more. She still had all of these beloved pieces at the end of her life. Her first actual purchase, however, was the cigar-store Indian she found when she was eighteen. She promptly named the figure after her nurse, Mary Conner. Electra married into another wealthy family (her husband's mother was a Vanderbilt) and raised five children. She was a capable, active woman who ran multiple houses, participated in sports (including hunting), and even drove an ambulance in France during World War I. She appears to have been a happy individual with a strong sense of humor. She said she "inherited sunshine"—a positive attitude—from her parents, and she tried to pass it on to others. She often used words like "fun" and "wonderful" when talking about her life.

Webb started collecting in earnest when she inherited a sizeable sum of money from her father. She was drawn to "objects made for utilitarian reasons,

FIG. 6.5.

Electra Webb (left) posed with her friend, the actress Zazu Pitts, for this lighthearted image that played with scale and made a seemingly ordinary object seem particularly interesting. The outsized chair was actually a trade sign in Webb's collection. The photo appeared with a feature article on the Shelburne Museum in *American Heritage* magazine in 1982, and it represents the kind of humor and "sunshine" Webb found in her collecting activities. Courtesy, Shelburne Museum, Shelburne, Vermont.

but fashioned in a unique or beautiful manner." She particularly liked surface detail. Among the items that interested her were quilts, hooked rugs, wallpaper, toys, dolls and doll houses, hats and hat boxes, ship figureheads, circus animals, trade signs, and decoys. These, like her initial cigar store Indian, are now often classified as either Americana or folk art. Webb accepted those terms, but she started collecting before such labels were codified, and they did not capture the way she thought about her things. Most of her items were from the United States (and where possible, from Vermont or nearby New England), but she was not interested in their colonial pedigree or rigid about their provenance; she freely mixed in English items, for example, if they appealed to her aesthetically. She acquired some "folk art paintings" but did not like them as much as the three-dimensional sculptural objects and soon stopped pursuing them. When she later created Shelburne Museum to share her collection with the public, she said she hoped to foster an appreciation for the people (notice she did not say an *era*) of the past. Historical accuracy was not the point as much as "human instinct."

In one of her reminiscences, Webb says the beginnings of the museum lay in her need to find storage for a large collection of carriages and sleighs that had belonged to her beloved in-laws. She remembered how splendid these convey-ances looked when in use and wanted to both preserve and get others to appreci-ate them. This was in 1948. By the time the museum opened in 1952, Webb had placed two hundred thousand objects in thirty-seven buildings. This was not a restored or pseudo-historical village, but an idiosyncratic assemblage, a "collec-tion of collections" or "collection of enthusiasms." She liked to think of the build-ings in terms of "personalities," and whimsy guided the way she set them up. The Vermont House, for example, was arranged as the home of an imagined wealthy sea captain, and she placed her collection of decoys in an imagined "woodcutter's home." (Remember, too, that her first sculptural purchase was immediately named and given a personality.) Her sons remarked that the museum gave Webb "unsul-lied spaces in which to indulge her decorator's zest," and this quality was even evident in the way she restocked an old general store with everything from biscuits to hair tonics. A number of collections that wound up in the museum, including tools and stuffed trophy animals, had come to Webb as gifts, but even these more "serious" items were playfully displayed. Little was linear, and Webb liked to "make special" by playing with scale and juxtaposing surprising objects and patterns.

Webb also valued interpersonal connection. She was fiercely loyal to friends and family. Her initial impulse for the museum was her in-laws' collection, and she later insisted that the institution was "not Electra Webb," but the product of the entire staff. (On another occasion she called the staff her "best collection.")

She also cared about the people who made the things she collected, and she approached objects as extensions of those who had used them. Many of the structures she moved to Shelburne were important to her because of their past associations and meanings; even her most unlikely additions, including a Lake Champlain steamboat and lighthouse, were there for that reason.[51]

Webb had enough money to create her museum as she saw fit, and she completed it while she was still alive. Margaret Woodbury Strong's[52] (1897–1969) equally idiosyncratic vision of a "Museum of Fascination" was never realized; like Thayer's, her collection was posthumously taken apart and recast. Strong's father was a successful manufacturer and an early investor in Eastman Kodak stock, and she too was able to spend large sums on her collecting passion. Like Webb, she liked highly decorated objects that others considered trivial; she was said to have "egalitarian taste." Although she had been interested in dolls and miniatures throughout her life, her three hundred thousand objects were primarily acquired when she was in her sixties and had no remaining living family. She applied for a New York state museum charter, and she left the bulk of her estate to establish an institution in her own name. With this legacy in mind, she bought furiously during her final decade. Strong intended the museum to be housed in her mansion home and even added three floors to accommodate it. However, the "professionals" hired by her estate decided to build a new building in downtown Rochester and reshaped the institution as a history museum documenting Victorian life. The curators bought furniture and examples of other more traditional decorative arts in order to make this work, and, to pay for them, sold off many of Strong's newer items and other things that did not fit their vision. They dedicated the museum to education rather than mere "enjoyment."[53] (Interestingly, the Strong Museum recently reinvented itself as the "national museum of play," thus in some senses returning to Strong's images and ideas.)

Strong was a shrewd collector—she had a discerning eye, waited for specific pieces for years, and always knew exactly what she owned—but as her chosen name for the museum indicates, collecting was her creative outlet, and her major motivation was play. One of her dealers said she was "positing universes" with her objects, an idea we can understand when we recall the description of her doll tableaux. Her items came primarily from America and Western Europe, but she was not at all interested in heritage or history, and since effect mattered to her more than pedigree, she freely mixed valuable old pieces and contemporary "junk." A survey of the categories she collected reiterates the familiar profile of saturated domestic objects: a partial list would include doll-related material, toys, door knobs, buttons, inkwells, paperweights, shells, kitchen utensils, Victorian

194 home crafts (see fig. 6.3), vases, pipes, shaving mugs, advertising cards, canes, circus artifacts, minerals, bookplates, nineteenth- and twentieth-century children's literature (she had complete sets of Kate Greenaway and Palmer Cox, who did the Brownies series), and popular prints by Audubon and Currier and Ives. Strong's life also exemplifies the pattern of the proverbial woman I am writing about. She too kept scrapbooks as a child, and she went to an enormous number of teas, luncheons, and other entertainments. She met frequently with other women, as she belonged to numerous art, garden, and doll clubs. Her husband, like Waldron's, was a collector of male-identified objects, including stamps and agricultural products.

Our last "case study" is actually a brief comparative look at a brother and sister, Henry Francis du Pont (1880–1960) and Louise du Pont Crowninshield (1877–1958). During a residency at Winterthur Museum, I started thinking about the way women's collecting has been made invisible. I saw that despite all the attention given to du Pont, his sister, who was involved in very similar pursuits, had largely fallen out of public view. Stillinger, one of the few to acknowledge her at all, labeled Crowninshield an "antiquarian" and portrayed her as a decorator rather than a serious collector.[54] In fact, Louise and "Harry" were equally passionate about antiques, and both collected; Louise is even said to have gotten her brother interested in collecting. They appreciated one another's taste and consulted one another on purchases throughout their lives. (Harry asked her to select pieces for him on numerous occasions.) However, they did have different attitudes and relationships to their objects; Louise *would* have been comfortable with the decorator label. Because they grew up in the same household and were near contemporaries, I realized this pair provided an interesting opportunity to look at gender differences in collecting.

Louise and Harry, the children of a U.S. senator (fig. 6.6), were raised in Delaware in a privileged household. Following social norms of the day, Harry was sent away to boarding school and then to Harvard, while Louise was educated at home. Included among her papers are vestiges of a saturated childhood: Kate Greenaway books; ornate cotillion programs and dance cards; a sea moss album; and a personal history of her ancestral home with lovingly rendered illustrations. She was a debutante with a formal coming-out party, and she spent time in the turn-of-the-century social whirl at Newport. After marrying Francis Crowninshield in 1900, her energy was directed toward tending her houses—she operated four or five separate residences during much of her married life, and one of those was actually a compound, with multiple buildings. She also spent a great deal of time engaged in charitable activities and "good works." She was

FIG. 6.6.
Louise du Pont Crowninshield and her brother, Henry Francis du Pont, ca. 1910.
Louise had already started collecting at this point, but her brother had not. Courtesy, The Winterthur Library, Winterthur Archives, No. P120.

heavily involved in preservation, particularly with restoring historic houses and landscapes, and with museum interpretation. Given her seasonal migrations, she left her mark in many states.[55]

All of this was done on a voluntary basis, and it was primarily visible only to those who worked with her behind the scenes. Louise's collecting was integral to the rest of her life. Much of the time she looked for objects that could be used in particular places; like Virginia Robie or other early-twentieth-century women writing about collecting, she thought about objects in contextual terms. She did a great deal of entertaining and delighted in serving guests on the china she had collected and in having them walk on her hooked rugs. She did not hesitate to move things around for convenience or comfort or to mix the rare with the ordinary. Louise also put a great deal of energy into collecting for *others'* houses; she procured untold numbers of objects for the many historic homes she was involved in and then helped arrange them as she saw fit. She was interested in showing how people of the past lived their lives. Her preservation efforts, in other words, were completely personalized and were built on the same idea of creating contextual tableaux.[56] She did have a "good eye" but was more concerned with attractive, inviting presentation than with the pedigree of the objects. Connoisseurship was not her goal; she wanted the rooms she worked on to "sing with beauty," to look lived in and "feel good."[57]

FIG. 6.7.

This undated photograph represents a room in Kenmore, a home that belonged to George Washington's sister, Betty Lewis. Louise Crowninshield was instrumental in its restoration: she collected suitable antique furnishings and helped arrange the rooms. Note the contextual placement of the dresses in the closet and the rug by the hearth. Crowninshield's notes on this installation shot include information about colors in the different fabrics. Courtesy, the Hagley Museum and Library, Wilmington, Delaware, 71.MSS.471.145.

Louise's brother, who is considered the American decorative arts collector *extraordinaire*, treated his objects differently. He too filled a very large house with antiques, but his collections were not used or lived with in the same sense. Winterthur had been his family home, but Harry kept on adding rooms to accommodate his ever-growing collection, and eventually he moved his family out of the building so it could function solely as a museum. (Many visitors are confused by the structure; they expect it to be a house, but it makes little sense as a living space.) Harry was a perfectionist—he went so far as to put marks on the floor to indicate where every object had to be and was disturbed if anything was moved even an inch. He limited the number of people who could come to Winterthur and discouraged children from coming at all. Because he wanted the rarest and best in his collection, he was constantly upgrading his pieces. In keeping with his concern for his objects' pedigree, he went to great lengths for authenticity. Once he even went so far as to give a church a very large donation in order to be allowed to take a wax impression of a piece of its hardware. He wanted to both under-stand how it worked and have it among his possessions. Unlike Louise, who built memorials to others, Winterthur was Henry du Pont's shrine to his own taste and "greatness." He did not furnish other people's houses—rather, he incorporated walls and parts of other people's houses into his own. Like Louise, he was con-cerned with visual effect, but, unlike her, he was not concerned with personal comfort or happiness.[58]

Again, the two are remembered quite differently. Harry's collection is in one place and easy to understand. Louise's collecting was more diffuse, and because her collected objects were either used or dispersed, often into others' homes or museums, she is not even credited at all. Harry's antiques expertise is often illus-trated by the fact that he was asked to help refurnish the White House under Jacqueline Kennedy. Louise had been asked to help refurnish the White House much earlier, during the Truman administration, but her contribution is largely dismissed or forgotten.

The Marginalization of Women's Vision

Louise and the other women I have been writing about were intelligent, deter-mined individuals who were often at the forefront of the intellectual and artistic movements of their day. They knew what they wanted and acted with agency and direction.[59] Their activities have remained underappreciated because they did not fit the prevailing understanding of collecting or paradigm of what was important. Men often treated women collectors condescendingly. Gelber writes of a French author quoted in the *New York Times* in 1921 who said that women could never be serious collectors; he had the "same indulgent respect for them that one had for 'children devoted to a hard game beyond their strength.'" Gelber also describes the way men dismissed women's button collecting as mere play, claiming their aesthetically driven displays (for example, grouping the buttons together by material or style) indicated something less than a real hobby.[60] Women *did* often think of collecting as play, of course, but did not think that was

198 pejorative. The men could not accept the idea that collections could be educational and worthwhile while still serving as "playmates," and they were no doubt also uncomfortable with women's personification of their objects and intimacy with them.[61] Even in more recent years, women's agency as collectors has been ignored or simply not seen. For example, there are several instances in *The Collector in America* (1969) where the contribution of the wife in a husband-and-wife collector team was essentially dropped away. The chapter on the John Hay Whitney collection is a case in point. This was a joint endeavor, but Mrs. Whitney was not listed in the chapter heading and was not even identified with a first name. There are many other profiles, also, where the text alludes to the wives' involvement, but readers cannot assess the synergy of the partnerships.[62]

It was the male approach that set the standards not only for the objects that were valued, but the very definition of a collection. An educator from Columbia University proclaimed in 1932 that an object "valued primarily for the use, or purpose, or aesthetically pleasing quality, or other inherent value" could not be the subject of a collection. It would "count" only if it were "valued because of its relationship to other objects 'such as being one of a series, part of a whole, a specimen of a class.'" Women's aesthetic criteria thus remained largely invisible, so much so that even a laudatory article on Webb maintained that she collected with "no particular purpose in mind." Her "enthusiasms" were not linear enough to be understood as purposeful.[63] Pomian Krzysztof's more recent definition of a collection also precludes objects used in any way. He refers to a "set of natural or artificial objects, kept permanently out of the economic circuit, afforded special protection in enclosed spaces adapted specially for that purpose and put on display." This view privileges the untouchable Henry du Pont kind of display over Louise Crowninshield's contextual use; she did not protect her items or display them in special places. A similar bias is evident in Arthur Danto's philosophy of collecting. Danto assumes that collections imply hierarchies—"the moment there is collecting," he says, "there are connoisseurs and forgers." If women collect items with little concern for pedigree and provenance, they cannot by Danto's definition really be collecting at all.[64]

Even Gelber, who tries to be fair and sympathetic to the female point of view, perpetuates these attitudes. He describes those whose hobby was "aesthetic or sentimental" as "stealth-collectors who simply disappeared from the historical radar." This is a curious and perhaps inadvertently demeaning statement. Gelber acknowledges that women stayed out of the "self-aggrandizing cycle of male collecting," but they did so openly, without stealth. Since his thesis is that hobbies

reproduce workplace values, it seems he cannot quite take any activities that do
not fit this model seriously on their own terms.[65]

The way that women's aestheticized, contextual vision was erased has already been explored in relation to Margaret Woodbury Strong and Sallie Casey Thayer. It was also seen in another well-known woman's installation, the Isabella Stewart Gardner Museum (Fenway Court) in Boston. Gardner (1840–1924) is best known for her collection of fine paintings, but she too created a "house museum" filled with household objects. Although her collecting activity took place in the nineteenth century, slightly earlier than most of the other women I am writing about, her story is instructive because it clearly demonstrates the same dynamic. Gardner identified herself as a homemaker and hostess, and creating Fenway Court was a way of extending this role into a dramatic public setting. Her goal was to make it look like an Italian villa that an imagined family had lived in for generations. Gardner saw the house as a single entity, an "overall composition," and designed every detail to create the desired effect. For example, she set personal mementoes and objects d'art out on tables so that visitors would have an intimate feeling when they walked through the space. She paid close attention to the way each object related to its architectural setting, and she chose paint and upholstery material with care. In fact, she made great use of fabric: she lined the walls with it and draped it behind paintings like a medieval "cloth of honor." In some cases, she even used the same fabric that went into her garments, meaning that "great" paintings by Titian were literally framed by cloth from her own skirts. Many of the furnishings in the museum had originally been purchased for her family home, but Gardner brought them over if they "felt" right. Her playful and generous attitude was embodied in the Fenway Court seal, which was inscribed "c'est mon plaisir" ("it's my pleasure"). Gardner's vision was holistic. She stipulated in her will that nothing ever be altered; if things were moved out of place, she wanted the building to be sold. Sadly, her wishes were not heeded, and the villa was changed to more closely approximate a traditional museum. Much is made of her prowess as a painting collector, but few even remember the rest of her vision or the experience she wanted to create for others.[66]

The irony is that this same kind of holistic vision has sometimes been appreciated when it was put forth by an already-successful man; collections are received differently, in other words, depending on who has collected them. Designer Alexander Girard was drawn to textiles, folk art sculptural objects, dolls, and miniatures—that is, the same sort of objects that delighted Margaret Woodbury Strong—but his collection never met with the kind of bemused tolerance or embarrassment that hers did. He too created out-of-scale vignettes and object-filled tableaux, but when he installed them at the Museum of International Folk Art in Santa Fe, he was applauded for his whimsical vision.[67] Girard was a successful professional, so his "play" seemed less domestic, less tied to what he did at home and more to the world of work.

While it is not my intention in this book to document the history of the decorative arts, I feel it is important to point out here how women's contributions to that field have been similarly obscured. Stillinger states in *The Antiquers* that the first decorative arts exhibit in America was a show of silver at the Museum of Fine Arts in Boston in 1906. In fact, there had been a number of women-organized exhibitions of samplers and other textiles in the 1890s, notably at the Philadelphia Museum of Art, but they did not "register" as important decorative arts. Stillinger also claims that du Pont was inspired to create his massive Winterthur Museum by the installation at the American Wing at the Metropolitan Museum of Art, but du Pont himself credited the inspiration of Electra Webb.[68]

The reference to a silver exhibition brings us to a final point about men's and women's collecting and the way it has been received. I maintain that men have been disproportionately involved with objects made of hard, permanent, and valuable materials, and women with soft, often fragile, and inherently inexpensive materials such as paper (men certainly collected works on paper, but their focus was typically the imagery rather than the object itself). This reflects further hierarchies within the decorative arts, and it helps us understand why silver exhibitions were remembered while textile exhibitions were not. Silver generally "counts" (is valued) more than pewter, pewter more than clay, and clay more than fiber. Although silver was made into household objects, it was an expensive material and was used on special rather than everyday items. This was compounded by the fact that silver goods were produced by professional craftsmen with specialized equipment. Silver thus had attributable "authorship" or provenance, which further increased its value. I indicated earlier that women felt particularly close to objects that were produced in more domestic settings. Robie expressed this attitude in 1912, when she remarked that silver and other rare metals might be ten times more valuable than china, but they lacked its "personal charm." Given these ingrained associations, it is easy to understand why male silver collectors outnumbered female silver collectors almost four to one in the early part of the twentieth century.[69]

The hierarchies of importance in collecting reflected the same paradigmatic beliefs that were being codified in the divisions of expressive objects in museums and universities at the turn of the twentieth century. They are for the most part still with us today. Art museums typically established separate departments of fine (major) and decorative (minor) arts, and even within the latter, some types of objects were considered more significant than others.[70] Objects made by non-European peoples were labeled "ethnic" or "primitive" and were housed in separate ethnological and historical institutions. (Later, museums devoted to folk and craft art were established as well.) We continue to see these divisions in universities, where ethnic art is studied in departments of anthropology, folk art in departments of folklore, and textile art in home economics-based units. These categories reflected many post-Renaissance assumptions about what and who is important. The "lesser" forms are primarily those associated with or women and individuals of nondominant (and/or nonaffluent) racial, cultural and ethnic groups; with community rather than individualistic norms; or with everyday life and the domestic domain or environment.

It has been necessary to unpack the norms and underlying beliefs about women's collecting and the visual arts in general in order to fully understand why they have been looked at (or ignored) as they have. There is no inherent reason why playfulness, emotional connection, or objects associated with the private or domestic sphere should be valued less than seriousness, emotional distance, and objects associated with the public arena. These are conventions that result from historical developments and power relationships. But while the hierarchies that exist in the visual arts are arbitrary, they are deeply ingrained, so taken for granted that they seem necessary. The labels that we grow up with—the way things are defined and presented—colors our experience and indeed affects our very perception. Sensitivity to these issues is slowly increasing, and a wider range of expressive forms are appreciated. Nevertheless, they are still separately categorized (as "traditional," "ethnic," "outsider" art, and so on), and remain as something "other." The basic hierarchical structure is not challenged. I believe that women's background approach must not only be made visible, but validated. In time this will help shift or even fundamentally alter our paradigmatic cultural beliefs. In turn our lives will be enriched, enlivened, and steeped in an even deeper appreciation of the world we live in.

PARTING WORDS

The final statement in the last chapter bring us nicely back to the beginning of the book. In the introduction, I said I hoped *The Saturated World* would help us reclaim something of the affective experience of the women of the late nineteenth and early twentieth centuries and help us appreciate their imagination, intelligence, creativity, and agency. I wanted to explore the saturated, or aesthetically charged or heightened, quality they cultivated in their domestic amusements, I claimed, because it might help all of us learn how to better infuse our own lives with a greater sense of richness, playfulness, and emotional satisfaction. I wanted us to understand the importance of "enchantment," "making special," and "deep play."

While the discussion in this book has not been exactly linear, it has followed a progressive, chronological logic. The first type of amusement we looked at was the paper doll or scrapbook house that was most popular in the last two decades of the nineteenth century. Such houses were intended for and at least partly worked on by children. I positioned this subject first in order to give the reader a feeling for girls' childhood training and experience, including its focus on the domestic and its overlay of amusement and work. We then explored the parties, entertainments and dress-up occasions that were held at the same time that the book houses were made, as well as in succeeding decades. These entertainments involved children and young people, but they were also fully identified as grown up activities—so much so, in fact, that one of the prototypical party occasions was the bridal shower that marked the passage into adulthood. Such pastimes also overlaid work and play and were built around a domestic model, but most of them were social or community activities, so this topic allowed us to more

204   deeply explore the quality of interpersonal connection in women's amusements. An examination of the entertainments also allowed us to look at the issue of embodiment and the different forms that playfulness might take.

The chapter on iconic dolls covered the whole range of the period under consideration. We looked at the kind of needlework "toys" that were popular in the nineteenth century and then, once women's roles had shifted to incorporate different kinds of household tasks, at the sorts of playthings they made for early-twentieth-century parties and showers. The important point here was that while women's domestic work and projection of self varied over time, they still chose to amuse themselves with self-referencing, embodied figures. This chapter also reminded us once again of the close identification of childhood and adult pastimes (dolls are quintessential toys), and the ways that objects could function as intimates.

The latter theme also permeated the final chapter, that focused on collecting. I positioned this topic last because it made sense in terms of chronological progression; most of the collecting activity under consideration took place in the twentieth century. Collecting too was an adult pastime that referenced childhood memories and reproduced childhood training. More importantly, however, the subject tied together all of the other themes. Women's collections functioned as extensions of their domestic roles but were experienced as "enchantments" imbued with a sense of aesthetic richness and good feeling. This discussion brought us back to the gestalt of the saturated world and its characteristic qualities.

In sum, I hope these explorations will generate interest in the subject of domestic amusements and restore our understanding of women's choices and experience. I am interested in creating a widened historical lens and in pushing our discourse about history, objects, leisure pastimes, and art to a more intimate level. I am interested too in elucidating a different model of adult play—one that is not really separable from daily experience. An appreciation of the many ways that turn-of-the-century women "made special" and cultivated the quality of saturation can help this come about. It is important to remember that it is precisely because women were outside the paradigm of workplace values that they could do this. They did not have as much of a professional identity as men, so their time, like children's, did not "count," and it could be "wasted." For much of the twentieth century, the response to gender inequity and prejudice was an insistence on women's rights in political arena and the professional workplace. That was necessary and important, but it has not been enough. The solution is not only to allow women to do what men do or reproduce male, foreground values; instead, we must look more closely at the alternate model of the background. I am happy to note, as discussed in the introduction, that our postindustrial, postmodern society is beginning to recognize this and move past workplace values altogether. The time is now ripe for us all to embrace the aesthetic paradigm and find new ways to create a more saturated world. We are aesthetic, embodied, sensual beings who are inextricably interconnected with one another. We all deserve to live more enchanted, playful lives and, like Electra Webb, find "zest" and "enthusiasm" in our everyday experience.

NOTES

1. The Meaning of the Saturated World

1. Rilke's statement appeared in a letter to Clara Rilke and is quoted in Gaston Bachelard, *The Poetics of Space* (1958; trans. John R. Stilgoe, Boston: Beacon P, 1994), 220; Bachelard's comment appears in *The Poetics of Space* on 227; Yi-Fu Tuan, *Passing Strange and Wonderful: Aesthetics, Nature and Culture* (Washington, DC: Island P, 1993), 29; Thomas Moore, *The Re-enchantment of Everyday Life* (New York: HarperCollins, 1996).

2. For discussion of gift relations, see James G. Carrier, *Gifts and Commodities: Exchange and Western Capitalism since 1700* (London: Routledge, 1995); Genevieve Vaughan, *For-Giving: A Feminist Criticism of Exchange* (Austin: Plain View P, 1997).

3. William Leach, "Strategists of Display and the Production of Desire," in Simon Bronner, ed. *Consuming Visions: Accumulation and Display of Goods in America, 1880–1920* (New York: W. W. Norton for Winterthur Museum, 1989), 99–132. Dreiser quoted on 99; Culin quoted on 106. Leach echoed Culin, stating, "The new strategies of display and decoration produced a radiant sensual center at the heart of American cities, attracting thousands . . . to the sensual, fluid and radiant density of the center." Leach also wrote on this topic in "Transformations in a Culture of Consumption: Women and Department Stores, 1890–1925," *Journal of American History* 71 (Sep. 1984): 319–42, and he later expanded many of his ideas in *Land of Desire: Merchants, Power and the Rise of a New American Culture* (New York: Pantheon Books, 1993).

4. Jean-Christophe Agnew, "The House of Fiction: The American Interior and the Rise of a Commodity Aesthetic," paper presented at the symposium Accumulation and Display: The Development of American Consumerism, 1880–1920, Henry Francis du Pont Winterthur Museum, Wilmington, Delaware, Nov. 7, 1986. See also T. J. Jackson Lears, *No Place of Grace: Anti-Modernism and the Transformation of American Culture 1880–1920* (New York: Pantheon, 1981), esp. 55, 300; Miles Orvell, *The Real Thing: Imitation and Authenticity in American Culture 1880–1940* (Chapel Hill: U of North Carolina P, 1989), 34–36.

5. The shift into this strong aesthetic consciousness in America has often been associated with the 1876 Centennial Exhibition in Philadelphia, where the public was exposed

to new ideas and images. It became a mark of cultural sophistication to be well versed in artistic precepts, and much of popular culture was soon dominated by aesthetically saturated imagery. While many of the leaders and iconic figures of these artistic movements were men—Oscar Wilde, John Ruskin, William Morris, and Gustav Stickley come immediately to mind—women embraced the movements with gusto. For discussion of these and women's role in them, see William Hosley, *The Japan Idea: Art and Life in Victorian America* (Hartford, CT: Wadsworth Atheneum, 1990), esp. 161–64; Jane Converse Brown, "'Fine Arts and Fine People': The Japanese Taste in the American Home, 1876–1916," in Marilyn Ferris Motz and Pat Browne, eds., *Making the American Home: Middle-Class Women and Domestic Material Culture 1840–1940* (Bowling Green, OH: Bowling Green State U Popular P, 1988), 121–39; Eileen Boris, *Art and Labor: Ruskin, Morris and the Craftsman Ideal in America* (Philadelphia: Temple UP, 1986); Virginia Gunn, "The Art Needlework Movement: An Experiment in Self-Help for Middle-Class Women, 1870–1900," *Clothing and Textiles Research Journal* 10 (Spring 1992): 54–63; *In Pursuit of Beauty: Americans and the Arts and Crafts Movement* (New York: Metropolitan Museum of Art and Rizzoli, 1986); Gillian Naylor, *The Arts and Crafts Movement: A Study of Its Sources, Ideals, and Influence on Design Theory* (Cambridge: MIT P, 1971); Kathleen D. McCarthy, *Women's Culture: American Philanthropy and Art, 1830–1930* (Chicago: U of Chicago P, 1991); Mary Warner Ballard, *Oscar Wilde's America: Counterculture in the Gilded Age* (New Haven and London: Yale UP, 1998).

Katherine C. Grier described one measure of the sharply increased concern with aesthetic matters. She stated that household advice books written earlier in the nineteenth century, from about 1830 to 1880, focused on educating their readers to be good consumers and social citizens; they were taught what a parlor was, how to use it, and what it should be like. In contrast the books published from the late 1870s through the 1920s emphasized the importance of appropriate aesthetic choices and the role of household art. See Katherine C. Grier, *Culture and Comfort: Parlor Making and Middle-Class Identity, 1850–1930* (Washington: Smithsonian Institution P, 1997), esp. 90–95 (abridged ed. of *Culture and Comfort: People, Parlors and Upholstery, 1850–1930* [Rochester, N.Y.: Margaret Woodbury Strong Museum, 1988]).

6. This argument was epitomized in a speech given by Rev. John Anderson, the president of Kansas Agricultural College, when he was outlining his institution's interest in gender-specific education. Woman superseded man in matters of "perception and effect," he maintained, and were better attuned to matters of form and color. "No man can arrange the furniture of a room as tastefully as a woman of equal education." See "Policy of the Regents" in *State Board of Agriculture: Third Annual Report to the Legislature of Kansas for the Year 1874* (Topeka: George W. Martin, State Printing Works, 1985), 259–319.

7. Letter from Milwaukee, *Critic* (Jan. 30, 1897): 4.

8. Frances Willard's famous phrase "make the whole world home-like" succinctly captures the prevalent turn-of-the-century attitude toward domesticity. See Frances Willard, *What Frances E. Willard Said*, ed. Anna A. Gordon (Chicago: Fleming H. Revell, 1905), 78.

At least in the middle and upper classes, most women still functioned primarily outside of the work economy (the "foreground"); while many were heavily involved in public-

sphere activities through women's clubs, social campaigns and the like, they usually
worked predominantly with other women in gender-segregated groups. For information
on women's homosocial focus, see Patricia R. Hill, *The World Their Household: The
American Women's Foreign Mission Movement and Cultural Transformation, 1870–1920*
(Ann Arbor: U of Michigan P, 1985); Karen J. Blair, *The Clubwoman as Feminist: True
Womanhood Redefined, 1868–1914* (New York: Holmes and Meier, 1980); Sophonisba P.
Breckenridge, *Women in the Twentieth Century: A Study of their Political, Social and Eco-
nomic Activities* (1933; reprint, New York: Arno P, 1972).

9. Nellie Mustain, *Popular Amusements for Indoors and Out-of-Doors* (Chicago, 1902).
The illustration is of a "Days of the Week Social." The gingham party is discussed in
Mary Mckin Marriott, "Social Affairs for March Evenings," *Ladies' Home Journal* (Mar.
1908): 47.

10. In her book *Home Comforts: The Art and Science of Keeping House* (New York:
Scribner's, 1999), 3, Cheryl Mendelson explains, "being perceived as excessively domestic
can get you socially ostracized."

11. Rodris Roth, "Scrapbook Houses: A Late Nineteenth Century Children's View
of the American Home," presentation at Henry Francis du Pont Winterthur Museum
and Library Conference on Collecting, Oct. 31, 1992. A later version of this material
was printed under the same title in Eleanor McD. Thompson, ed., *The American Home:
Material Culture, Domestic Space, and Family Life* (Winterthur, DE: Henry Francis du
Pont Winterthur Museum, 1998), 301–23.

12. This is the position taken by Josephine Donovan, "Toward a Women's Poetics,"
Tulsa Studies in Women's Literature 3 (Spring/Fall 1984): 100–103.

13. A definition of the "middle class" has always been difficult to pin down in America;
even today individuals with widely divergent financial resources self-identify with this
group. Katharine C. Grier helps us understand the historical roots of this issue. She
explains that the far-reaching, rapid social change fostered by unbridled industry and
urbanization of the nineteenth century allowed Americans to believe in the possibility
of upward social mobility. Mobility was not guaranteed, but it was common enough to
support the popular belief that status was no longer ascribed as much as achieved. Grier
writes about the particular middle class "vernacular" that sought a balance between the
"conventions of gentility" (an aristocratic sensibility) and domesticity, or a type of modest coziness she labels as "comfort" (*Culture and Comfort*, esp. x). Regarding the issues of
defining class, see also Jean Gordon and Jan McArthur, "American Women and Domestic
Consumption, 1800–1920: Four Interpretive Themes," in Motz and Browne, *Making the
American Home*, 27–47; Warren I. Susman, *Culture as History: The Transformation of
American Society in the Twentieth Century* (New York: Pantheon Books, 1984), 107–11.
Note also that Ethel von Bachellé, maker of the "Vegetable Folk" dolls, was an educated
woman who certainly identified with the middle class but who was nearly destitute by
the end of her life.

14. Recent scholarship has shown that slaves who sewed for their mistresses had an
important role in the production of many of the quilts of the antebellum age; see Gladys-
Marie Fry, *Stitched from the Soul: Slave Quilts from the Ante-Bellum South* (New York:
Dutton Studio Books, 1990). Although we are dealing with a later period and hired

210   maids rather than indentured slaves, it is likely that a parallel situation was operative
        here. I have not studied ethnic variations or the attitudes of specific minorities toward
        these amusements. *The Saturated World* should provide the framework for a future
        researcher to do so.

        15. Beverly Gordon, *Bazaars and Fair Ladies: The History of the American Fundraising
        Fair* (hereafter, *BFL*) (Knoxville: U of Tennessee P, 1998), xviii; Ann Powers, "Mary,
        Quite Contrary," *New York Times*, Nov. 7, 1999, Education and Life section, p. 32. See
        also Kenneth L. Ames, "Anonymous Heroes: Background History and Social Responsi-
        bility," *Museum News* (Sept./Oct. 1994): 34–35. Donovan, "Toward a Women's Poetics,"
        101, characterizes traditional female tasks as "non-progressive, repetitive, and static."
        Women make objects for family use rather than for exchange, and personalize them
        through their touch.

        16. I hope this articulation will contribute to the broader project of feminist scholarship,
        which "undertakes the dual task of deconstructing predominantly male paradigms and
        reconstructing a female perspective and experience in order to change" the way people
        think. Gayle Greene and Coppelia Kahn, eds. *Making a Difference: Feminist Literary Crit-
        icism* (London: Methuen, 1985), 1. Since the 1970s, when feminist writers first pointed
        out that women's activities had not only been taken lightly, but were in many cases liter-
        ally made invisible, thousands of voices have been raised to address that dual task and
        thereby effect this important change. See, for example, Germaine Greer, *The Obstacle
        Race: The Fortunes of Women Painters and Their Work* (New York: Farrar, Straus and
        Giroux, 1979; Patricia Mainardi, "Quilts: The Great American Art," *Feminist Art Journal* 1
        (Winter 1973): 18–23.

        17. Steven Gelber, *Hobbies: Leisure and the Culture of Work in America* (New York:
        Columbia UP, 1999), 2, 74, 184, 104.

        18. In "Beyond Touch: The Body as a Perceptual Tool," *Fiberarts* 26 (Summer 1999): 44,
        Polly Ullrich stated that this Western (Platonic) philosophy of art "identified the 'inner
        mind' and its ideas as the primary and most important mode of human perception and
        denigrated the manual, the material, and the bodily senses as authentic ways of perceiv-
        ing the world. In fact, those sensuous aspects were not thought to be cognitive at all. . . .
        Enlightenment philosophers subsumed and dematerialized the material universe under
        theoretical and analytical models [and] isolated art from everyday life." See also Melvin
        Rader and Bertram Jessup, *Art and Human Values* (Englewood Cliffs, NJ: Prentice-Hall,
        1976), esp. 54–62; Naomi Schor, *Reading in Detail: Aesthetics and the Feminine* (New
        York: Methuen, 1987), 3–25.

        19. Denigrations of the bodily experience and the physical (which reflect Christian
        precepts that posit the natural world as "lower" than the noncorporeal spirit) abound in
        Western art theory. In his *Discourses on Art*, for example, Sir Joshua Reynolds declared
        that only a second-rate artist would "lose himself" in nature and its imperfections (quoted
        in Schor, *Reading in Detail*, 11–18). It is interesting to note that women who theorized
        about aesthetics in the period I cover in this book sometimes held a divergent view. For
        example, in her 1907 U of Chicago dissertation, *The Aesthetic Experience: Its Meaning in
        Functional Psychology*, Elizabeth Kemper Adams insisted that aesthetic experience with
        any object involves an intimate, emotional, even bodily relationship. Women educators

of the early twentieth century were also particularly insistent on the fact that art and aesthetic experience cannot be removed from everyday experience. See Harriet and Vetta Goldstein, *Art in Everyday Life* (New York: Macmillan, 1925); Helen Gardner, *Understanding the Arts* (New York: Harcourt, Brace, 1932); Beverly Gordon, entry on Helen Gardner in *American National Biography* vol. 8 (New York: Oxford UP, 1999), 704–5.

20. Robert Ginsberg, "Experiencing Aesthetically, Aesthetic Experience, and Experience in Aesthetics," in Michael H. Mitias, ed., *The Possibility of Aesthetic Experience* (Dordrecht, Boston, and Lancaster: Martinus Nijhoff, 1986), 63–65.

21. As recently as 1959, Arnold Hauser wrote that "country folk" could not experience things aesthetically because they lacked aesthetic standards. Deprecatingly, he dismissed folk art as "hardly more than play" and popular art as mere entertainment. Arnold Hauser, *The Philosophy of Art History* (New York: Knopf, 1959), 285.

22. Mike Featherstone, *Consumer Culture and Postmodernism* (London: Sage Publications, 1991), 7; Tuan, *Passing Strange and Wonderful*, 100, 113.

23. Michael Owen Jones, "The Concept of 'Aesthetic' in the Traditional Arts," *Western Folklore* 30 (Apr. 1971); Michael Owen Jones, *Exploring Folk Art: Twenty Years of Thought on Craft, Work, and Aesthetics* (Ann Arbor: UMI Research P, 1987), 122–23.

24. Crispin Sartwell, *The Art of Living: Aesthetics of the Ordinary in World Spiritual Traditions* (Albany: State U of New York P, 1995).

25. Ellen Dissanayake, *What Is Art For?* (Seattle: U of Washington P, 1988); Ellen Dissanayake, *Homo Aestheticus: Where Art Comes from and Why* (New York: Free P, 1992). Dissanayake says her work builds on that of many before her who talked about play as something outside normal life that is able to take us into another reality, but she takes it further by giving it an etological basis (*What Is Art For?* 43). Dissanayake's latest book is *Art and Intimacy: How the Arts Began* (Seattle: U of Washington P, 2000.)

26. Diane Ackerman, *A Natural History of the Senses* (New York: Vintage Books, 1991), xvii–xviii.

27. "This American Life" edition airing on Wisconsin Public Radio on Sunday, Jun. 17, 2000; Catherine Bailly Dunne, *Interior Designing for All Five Senses* (New York: Golden Books, 1998), 3, 5; Johanna Putnoi, *Senses Wide Open: The Art and Practice of Living in Your Body* (Berkeley: Ulysses P, 2000); Karen Olson, "Tasting the Wind, Hearing the Water," *Utne Reader* Nov.–Dec. 2001, 52. (*Utne Reader* has subsequently changed its name to *Utne*). Podeswa's *Five Senses* film was theatrically released on Jan. 1, 1999.

28. Edward T. Hall, *The Hidden Dimension* (Garden City, NY: Doubleday, 1969), esp. 119; Edward T. Hall, *The Silent Language* (Garden City, NY: Doubleday, 1959).

29. Ackerman, *A Natural History of the Senses*, 289.

30. Ashley Montagu, *Touching: The Human Significance of the Skin* (New York: Columbia UP, 1971). The cited review, which appears on the book jacket of the Perennial Library paperback edition (1972), is from the *Journal of Individual Psychology*.

31. Paul Stoller, *The Taste of Ethnographic Things: The Senses and Anthropology* (Philadelphia: U of Pennsylvania P, 1989), 9, 29; Paul Stoller, *Sensuous Scholarship* (Philadelphia: U of Pennsylvania P, 1997), xv; Peter Charles Hoffer, *Sensory Worlds in Early America* (Baltimore: Johns Hopkins UP, 2003), esp. 17. Henry J. Drewal won a 2004 Guggenheim Fellowship to study sensiotics. In describing his prize-winning project, he decried the

212 "mind-body split which devalues the senses and bodily experiences in the processes of understanding . . . and appreciat[ing] the arts" (http://news.wisc.edu/releases/9678.html [accessed Dec. 23, 2005]). The geographer Yi-Fu Tuan has also written about the way our culture discounts and undervalues the importance of the proximate senses. See Tuan, *Passing Strange and Wonderful,* 23, 36–41.

32. Beverly Gordon, "Intimacy and Objects: A Proxemic Analysis of Gender-Based Response to the Material World," in Katherine Martinez and Kenneth Ames, eds., *The Material Culture of Gender/The Gender of Material Culture* (Winterthur, DE: Winterthur Museum with the UP of New England, 1997), 237–52.

33. Jane Przybysz, "Quilts and Women's Bodies Dis-eased and Desiring," in *Bodylore,* ed. Katharine Young (Knoxville: U of Tennessee P, 1993), 165–84; Mary Field Belenky, et al, *Women's Ways of Knowing: The Development of Self, Voice and Mind* (New York: Basic Books, 1986), 18.

34. Ullrich, "Beyond Touch," 46; Jerry H. Gill, *Merleau-Ponty and Metaphor* (Atlantic Highlands, NJ: Humanities P, 1991), 11, 20, 57–58.

35. See Jose Luis Bermudez, Anthony Marcel, and Naomi Eilan, eds., *The Body and the Self* (Cambridge: MIT P, 1995); Thomas J. Csordas, ed., *Embodiment and Experience* (Cambridge: Cambridge UP, 2001); George Lakoff and Mark Johnson, *Philosophy in the Flesh: The Embodied Mind and Its Challenge to Western Thought* (New York: Basic Books, 1999); Donn Welton, ed., *Body and Flesh: A Philosophical Reader* (Liphook, UK: Blackwell P, 1998); Mary Douglas, *Natural Symbols: Explorations in Cosmology* (London, Barrie, and Rockliff, UK: Cresset P, 1970); Gail Weiss and Honi Fern Haber, eds., *Perspectives on Embodiment: The Intersections of Nature and Culture* (New York: Routledge, 1999); Kathy Davis, ed., *Embodied Perspectives: Feminist Perspectives on the Body* (London: Sage Publications, 1997); Stoller, *Taste of Ethnographic Things,* 29; Katharine Young, "Whose Body? An Introduction to Bodylore," *Journal of American Folklore* 107, 423 (1994): 9–22. The quote from Young is from *Bodylore,* vii.

36. Ullrich, "Beyond Touch," 46; Dissanayake, *Homo Aestheticus,* xv, 44–47.

37. *Oxford English Dictionary* (2001) online version, s.v. "embody," http://dictionary.oed.com/ (accessed Apr. 12, 2003).

38. Beverly Gordon, "Woman's Domestic Body: The Conceptual Conflation of Women and Interiors in the Industrial Age," *Winterthur Portfolio* 31 (Winter 1996): 281–30. Young noted in her introduction to *Bodylore* (xix) that when women present themselves publicly, they often either suppress evidence of the grotesque or "lower" body (the part involving sex, death, life, filth), or they create an image of an ethereal, ideal body. Although the turn-of-the-century entertainments and other amusements were more private than public, the ethereal image remained, but some elements of the grotesque (food, drink, and laughter) were characteristic. On the grotesque body see Mikhail Bakhtin, *Rabelais and His World* (Bloomington: Indiana UP, 1984), 318.

39. Diane Ackerman, *Deep Play* (New York: Random House, 1999), esp. 6, 12–14, 31.

40. Dissanayake, *What Is Art For?* 78; Grosse and Schiller discussed in Jones, *Exploring Folk Art,* 27; Johan Huizinga, *Homo Ludens: A Study of the Play Element in Culture* (1944; trans. R. F. C. Hall, London: Routledge and Kegan Paul, 1949), 23; Austen Fox Riggs, *Play: Recreation in a Balanced Life* (Garden City: Doubleday, Doran, 1935). For a discussion of

Dewey's approach, see Jay Shivers, *Leisure and Recreation Concepts: A Critical Analysis*
(Boston: Allyn and Bacon, 1981), 147. This book provides an excellent summary of the
development of play theory.

41. Huizinga, *Homo Ludens*, 173; Rebecca Abrams, *The Playful Self: Why Women Need
Play in Their Lives* (London: Fourth Estate, 1997), 22; Gene Quarrick, *Our Sweetest Hours:
Recreation and the Mental State of Absorption* (Jefferson, NC, and London: McFarland,
1989), 1–4, 30, 33.

42. For a good discussion of these dichotomies, see John Bowman, "Making Work
Play," in Gary Alan Fine, ed. *Meaningful Play, Playful Meaning* (Champaign, IL: Human
Kinetics Publishers, 1985), 61–71. The work ethic value system is, of course, what lay
behind Steven Gelber's discussion of leisure-time hobbies.

43. Richard Kraus, *Recreation and Leisure in Modern Society* (New York: Appleton-
Century Crofts, 1971), 179, 188, 264. I must acknowledge that the situation was not
really as polarized as it may sound here. Some of the amusements I write about, including theme parties or dress-up, were part of the organized Recreation movement endeavors. Nevertheless the impetus for the playful attitude and its purest expressions were still
manifest in more spontaneous activities in domestic settings.

44. Writing about historical amusements in 1955, Iris Brooke offhandedly expressed
these differences when she stated that women used amusements "just" to pass the time
and their activities were not purposeful. Iris Brooke, *Pleasures of the Past: A Lighthearted
Commentary on the Enjoyments of Past Generations* (London: Odhams P, 1955), 40, 43.

45. I also discuss the overlay between work and play and the way women "played" with
domesticity in *BFL*, esp. 5–7, 74–76.

46. Abrams, *The Playful Self*, esp. 86–116, 141, 152, 154.

47. George Kneller, *The Art and Science of Creativity* (New York: Holt, Rinehart and
Winston, 1965), esp. 77–78; Silvano Arieti, *Creativity: The Magic Synthesis* (New York:
Basic Books, 1976), esp. 4.

48. Gordon, *BFL*, esp. 16–18. I drew from historical commentary as well as contemporary observation and interviews to come to this conclusion. Significantly, *every person* I
interviewed talked about the sense of fellowship involved in working for a fair.

49. Joyce Ice, "Women's Aesthetics and the Quilting Process," in Hollis, Pershing, and
Young, eds., *Feminist Theory and the Study of Folklore* (Urbana and Chicago: U of Illinois
P, 1993), 166–77, quotations on 169; Beverly Gordon, "Embodiment, Community Building, and Aesthetic Saturation in 'Restroom World,' a Backstage Women's Space," *Journal
of American Folklore*, 116 (Fall 2003): 444–64.

50. For a good overview and discussion of relational theory, see Christina Robb, "A
Theory of Empathy," *Boston Globe Magazine* (Oct. 16, 1988). Primary sources include
Jean Baker Miller, *Toward a New Psychology of Women* (Boston: Beacon P, 1976); Carol
Gilligan, *In a Different Voice: Psychological Theory and Women's Development* (Cambridge:
Harvard UP, 1982); and Belenky et al., *Women's Way of Knowing*.

51. Linda A. Hughes, "Girls' Games and Girls' Gaming," in Hollis, Pershing, and Young,
eds., *Feminist Theory and the Study of Folklore*, 130–48; Marjorie Harness Goodwin, "Ac-
complishing Social Organization in Girls' Play: Patterns of Competition and Cooperation
in an African American Working-Class Girls' Group," in Hollis, Pershing, and Young, eds.,

214   *Feminist Theory and the Study of Folklore*, 149–65. In my study of "Restroom World," I observed a kind of playful one-upsmanship in "call and response" guest book commentary, but these remarks too were never mean or insulting. It is interesting, given the kind of creative, task-oriented activities I am documenting in this book, that Goodwin found the most egalitarian activities were the ones that involved making things together. I do find it necessary to state that these studies present a suspiciously rosy picture of girls' play; and most of us can relate incidents about cruelty among girls, particularly at the middle school level. We must certainly be careful not to romanticize one sex over another. Nevertheless the described patterns point up significantly different operational strategies.

52. Hughes, "Girls' Gaming," 131. Kay Turner and Suzanne Seriff, who studied the celebrations of a Sicilian American St. Joseph's Day feast, pointed out that while women did not overtly seem to have any control or authority in male-dominated cultures, they actually had a different kind of kin-based power manifest in the domestic realm. Cited in M. Jane Young and Kay Turner, "Challenging the Canon: Folklore Theory Reconsidered from Feminist Perspectives," in Hollis, Pershing, and Young, eds., *Feminist Theory and the Study of Folklore*, 14.

53. Jack Santino, *New Old-Fashioned Ways: Holidays and Popular Culture* (Knoxville: U of Tennessee P, 1996), 159; Jack Santino, *All around the Year: Holidays and Celebrations in American Life* (Urbana and Chicago: U of Illinois P, 1994), 34, 39.

54. Michael Owen Jones, *Studying Organizational Symbolism: What, How, Why?* (Thousand Oaks, CA, and London: Sage Publications, 1996), 29; Ice, "Women's Aesthetics and the Quilting Process," 174.

55. Mihaly Csikszentmihlyi and Eugene Rochberg-Halton, *The Meaning of Things: Domestic Symbols and the Self* (Cambridge: Cambridge UP, 1981); Marketing Science Institute, *Deep Meanings in Possessions: Qualitative Research from the Consumer Behavior Odyssey* (video, Boston: Audvid Productions for the Marketing Science Institute, 1988); Russell Belk, Melanie Wallendorf, et al., "Collectors and Collecting," *Advances in Consumer Research* 15 (1988): 27–32; Russell Belk and Melanie Wallendorf, "Of Mice and Men: Gender Identity and Collecting," in Martinez and Ames, *The Material Culture of Gender/The Gender of Material Culture*, 7–26. See also Mary Cantwell, "The Magic of Objects Trailing through Time," (Madison, WI) *Capital Times*, Jun. 28, 1990; Mihaly Csikszentmilhalyi, "Why We Need Things," in *History from Things: Essays on Material Culture*, S. Lubar and W. D. Kingery, eds. (Washington: Smithsonian Institution P, 1993).

56. Bachelard, *The Poetics of Space*, 67–68; Anthony Lawlor, *A Home for the Soul: A Guide for Dwelling with Spirit and Imagination* (New York: Clarkson Potter, 1997), 19; Shaun McNiff, *Earth Angels: Engaging the Sacred in Everyday Things* (Boston: Shambhala, 1995), 3.

57. Ralph Pomeroy, "Navaho Abstraction," *Art and Artists* (1974): 30, cited in Rozsika Parker and Griselda Pollock, *Old Mistresses: Women, Art and Ideology* (New York: Pantheon Books, 1981), 68. There were actually several levels of bias here: Pomeroy could not see the blankets as art because of their functional nature and because they were made by "non-artists," that is, American Indian women.

58. Belenky et al., *Women's Way of Knowing*, 134, 141.

59. Bachelard, *Poetics of Space*, 6–10, 12, 149–50, 154–55, 163; Susan Stewart, *On Longing: Narratives of the Miniature, the Gigantic, the Souvenir, the Collection* (Baltimore:

Johns Hopkins UP, 1984), 46, 60, 65, 66; Alton J. DeLong, "Phenomenological Space-Time: Toward an Experiential Relativity," *Science* 213 (Jul. 1981): 681–83.

60. In some cases we are in fact talking about the same activities, but we see them through this very different filter.

61. Donna R. Braden, *Leisure and Entertainment in America* (Dearborn, MI: Henry Ford Museum and Greenfield Village, 1988); Foster Rhea Dulles, *America Learns to Play: A History of Popular Recreation 1607–1940* (New York: Appleton-Century, 1940), esp. vii.

62. Kathy Peiss, *Cheap Amusements: Working Women and Leisure in Turn-of-the-Century New York* (Philadelphia: Temple UP, 1986), 5. Ironically we know that contemporary women who have access to high-powered jobs are not necessarily happier because of them either; their ability to play and feel joy in everyday experience often suffers considerably.

63. Quarrick, *Our Sweetest Hours*, 19. Some observers believe we now have an increasing acceptance—even glamorization of—nonwork and we allow casualness, formerly associated with leisure, almost everywhere. The lack of dress codes in many offices would be one example of this.

64. Carrier, *Gifts and Commodities*, esp. 11, 117, 172, 175. See also Vaughan, *For-Giving: A Feminist Criticism of Exchange*.

65. Featherstone even quotes from the French writer Jean Braudillard, who goes so far as to call postmodern culture an "aestheticized hallucination of reality." Featherstone, *Consumer Culture and Postmodernism*, 7, 98–100, 109; Edwin L. Wade, "Neo-Primitivism and the Sacred," in Marcia and Tom Manhart, eds., *The Eloquent Object: The Evolution of American Art in Craft Media since 1945* (Tulsa, OK: Philbrook Museum of Art, 1987) 14, 257–78.

66. Rachel Blau Du Plessis, "For the Etruscans," in Elaine Showalter, ed. *The New Feminist Criticism* (New York: Pantheon Books, 1985), 274; see also Elaine Showalter, "Piecing and Writing," in Nancy K. Miller, ed., *The Poetics of Gender* (New York: Columbia UP, 1986), 222–47; Todd Gitlin, "Postmoderism Defined, at Last!" excerpted from Winter 1989 *Dissent*, in *Utne Reader* (Jul./Aug. 1989): 52.

2. The Paper Doll House

1. An earlier version of this chapter appeared as "Scrapbook Houses for Paper Dolls: Creative Expression, Aesthetic Elaboration and Bonding in the Female World," in Katherine Ott, Susan Tucker and Patricia Buckler, eds., *Scrapbooks in American Life* (Philadelphia: Temple University P, 2006), 206–41.

2. The first house I encountered in the Winterthur collection is accessioned as fol. 144, no. 8290.

3. Hartigan, "House That Collage Built"; Rodris Roth, "Scrapbook Houses: A Late Nineteenth-Century Children's View of the American Home," lecture at the Henry Francis du Pont Winterthur Museum Conference on Collecting, Oct. 31, 1992. A later version of this lecture was printed under the same title in Eleanor McD. Thompson, ed., *The American Home: Material Culture, Domestic Space, and Family Life* (Winterthur, DE: Henry Francis du Pont Winterthur Museum, 1998), 301–23.

4. Any study based predominantly on prescriptive literature is certainly open to criticism, for how are we to know if people actually followed published advice? My response is that the artifacts and articles reflect one another quite closely. Based on this evidence

and my previous studies of related advice literature, I am convinced that there was an intimate, interactive, and intertwined relationship between the advice articles and what actual people did—each continually influenced the other. Jessie Ringwalt and others who wrote about this genre, for example, drew on already-extant examples when they talked about what one might do; they were not so much inventing the genre as articulating what was already happening. In turn, of course, their instructions further reinforced those practices as the norm. I address this same issue in *BFL*, xxii.

5. I have set the 1875 start date for the paper doll house phenomenon because it corresponds with the first dated examples I have found, and because the conventions of the genre were already said to be "familiar" in 1880 in the first printed article I have found on the subject (Jessie E. Ringwalt, "Fun for the Fireside: A Help to Mothers—the Paper-doll's House," *Godey's Lady's Book* [Aug. 1880]: 160). I have seen one book house with figures dressed in fashions of the 1860s, but I believe these were taken from an already out-of-date magazine or catalog, because other furnishings suggest a later date. A few extant books appear to have been made in the late 1870s (again, this is based on the styles of the furnishings and fashions in the cut-out images). Roth said the scrapbook house seems to have been particularly prevalent in the eastern and mid-Atlantic states ("Scrapbook Houses" lecture), but I suspect that this may reflect the sample she was familiar with rather than a true geographic distribution. Instructions appear in national magazines, and some known examples are from Chicago (see discussion of Anita Blair's albums, below). I believe the scrapbook house, much like the scrapbook in general, was probably popular nationwide.

6. I use the terms interchangeably throughout the chapter. Usually the specific term is chosen for stylistic reasons, but sometimes I make use of its more specific connotation.

7. See Katherine Ott and Susan Tucker, "An Introduction to the History of Scrapbooks," in Katherine Ott, Susan Tucker, and Patricia Buckler, eds., *Scrapbooks in American Life* (Philadelphia: Temple UP, 2006), 1–46.

8. Ephemera Society Web site, http://www.ephemerasociety.org/ (accessed July 25, 2000); Steven M. Gelber, *Hobbies: Leisure and the Culture of Work in America* (New York: Columbia UP, 1999), 169–70; E. W. Gurley, *Scrapbooks and How to Make Them* (New York: Author's Publishing, 1880). Regarding differential advice given to female scrapbook makers, see also Ellen Gruber Garvey, *The Adman in the Parlor: Magazines and the Gendering of Consumer Culture 1880s–1910s* (New York: Oxford UP, 1996), 26. Regarding girls' predilection for aesthetic arrangement, see Caroline Frear Burk, "The Collecting Instinct," *Pedagogical Seminary* 7 (Apr. 1900): 179–207. Note that other aestheticized and sentimental varieties of scrapbooks were also disproportionately associated with women. They created seaweed and moss albums, for example, where natural specimens were artistically arranged as individual compositions. Working with paper and cardboard had been something women did throughout the nineteenth century—it was cheap, readily available, and easy to manipulate. Pasting preprinted paper scraps or cards into albums was a new variation on the theme.

9. L. Frank Baum, *The Wonderful Wizard of Oz* (Chicago and New York: George M. Hill, 1900), and thirteen subsequent *Oz* titles. Baum also wrote other stories expressly referred to as "fairy tales." James Barrie, *Peter and Wendy* (New York: Charles Scribner's

Sons, 1911). The first book to feature Peter Pan was Barrie's 1902 work, *The Little White* **217**
Bird. Peter Pan was the name of the stage play. Crane's ideal is discussed on www.speel.
demon.co.uk/artists/crane.htm; Burne-Jones statement cited in *The Victorian Cult of Beauty* (Toronto: Art Gallery of Toronto, 1989), 3; John Ruskin, "Fairyland" lecture, 1893, cited by Stella Beddoe, "Fairy Writing and Writers," in Jane Martineau, ed., *Victorian Fairy Painting* (London: Royal Academy of Arts [Merrell Holberton], 1997), 31.

10. Esther Singleton, *The Collecting of Antiques* (New York: Macmillan, 1926), 2–3. I deal at length with the topic of fairyland in Beverly Gordon, "Crazy Quilts as an Expression of the Fairyland Ideal," *Uncoverings* (American Quilt Study Group) 27 (2006): in press. I first addressed the subject in *BFL*, esp. 107–8, 117–18, 135.

11. Charlotte Gere, "In Fairyland," in *Victorian Fairy Painting*, 63; "The Hahnemann [Hospital] Fair, *New York Times*, Apr. 12, 1880; Hubert Howe Bancroft, *The Book of the Fair* (Chicago and San Francisco: Bancroft, 1893), 401; Hubert Howe Bancroft, ed., *The Great Republic by the Master Historians*, vol. 3 (1902), cited on www.publicbookshelf.com/public_html/The_Great_Republic_By_the_Master_Historians_Vol_III/; *BFL*, 107–8.

12. Ringwalt, "Fun for the Fireside," 160.

13. The "Kenilworth Inn," a paper doll house in the Winterthur collection, includes an envelope of cut-outs from the Pan American Exposition, held three years before the book was put together. The pattern of collecting and saving scraps for eventual use was typical for scrapbooks of all types. In commenting on the process, Deborah A. Smith, "Consuming Passions: Scrapbooks and American Play," *Ephemera Journal* 6 (1993): 70, identified the scrapbook a "collector's ultimate achievement." I believe this would have been even more so for a completely realized scrapbook house. The Smith article was also published as the Proceedings of the Ephemera Symposium III, "The American Play Ethic: Ephemera and Recreation," held by the American Antiquarian Society in Worcester, Mass., Oct. 22–23, 1993.

14. Maude Cushing Nash, *Children's Occupations* (Boston and New York: Houghton Mifflin, 1920), 127; Carolyn Wells, "A Paper Doll's House," *Puritan* (Feb. 1901): 273. Wells's article was reprinted in Nash's book *Pleasant Day Diversions* (New York: Moffat, Yard, 1909), 63–73.

15. Emily Hoffman, "Homes for Paper Dolls," *Harper's Bazar* (Jan. 1904): 84–85.

16. Ringwalt, "Fun for the Fireside," 160–62.

17. Ibid.

18. Regarding papers on the market at the turn of the century, see Beverly Gordon, "'One of the Most Valuable Fabrics': The Seemingly Limitless Promise of Crepe Paper, 1890–1935," *Ars Textrina* 30 (1999): 1–30.

19. Such visual density was characteristic of the turn-of-the-century aesthetic. For a discussion of this, see for example Clay Lancaster, *The Japanese Influence in America* (New York: Walton H. Rawls, 1963).

20. Accession number 90.2559, Margaret Woodbury Strong Museum, Rochester, NY.

21. Ringwalt, "Fun for the Fireside," 161.

22. Folder 36 (85 x 41.3), Downs Collection, Henry Francis du Point Winterthur Museum, Winterthur, DE; accession number 90.2559, Margaret Woodbury Strong Museum, Rochester, N.Y.

218   23. Gaston Bachelard, *Poetics of Space* (1958; trans. John R. Stilgoe, Boston: Beacon P, 1994), 174; Anthony Lawlor, *A Home for the Soul: A Guide for Dwelling with Spirit and Imagination* (New York: Clarkson Potter, 1997), 19; Shaun McNiff, *Earth Angels: Engaging the Sacred in Everyday Things* (Boston: Shambhala, 1995), 3.

24. Bachelard, *The Poetics of Space*, 7, 8, 12, 15, 78, 149–50, 154–55, 163. Bachelard is concerned with "topoanalysis," or the study of the "sites of our intimate lives" (8). Bernard Mergen, "Children's Play in American Autobiographies, 1820–1914," in Kathryn Grover, ed. *Hard at Play: Leisure in America* (Amherst: U of Massachusetts P and the Margaret Woodbury Strong Museum, 1992), 172; E. Nesbitt, *Wings and the Child; or, The Building of Magic Cities* (London and New York: Hodder and Stoughton, 1913), 124–25.

25. Bachelard, *The Poetics of Space*, 7, 8, 15; Emily Hoffman, "Homes for Paper Dolls," *Harper's Bazar* (Jan. 1904): 84–87. Bachelard's analysis is, of course, heavily Eurocentric. Individuals who grew up in tents or round huts might have had a different response.

26. Ringwalt, "Fun for the Fireside," 162; Eloise Kruger, "The Dollhouse Multiplied," in Elizabeth Andrews, ed., *Miniature Stuff* (Middletown, CT: by the author, 1964); Susan Stewart, *On Longing,* 61.

27. Hoffman, "Homes for Paper Dolls," 84–87; Wells, "A Paper Doll's House," 273.

28. The Bennington maker wrote her name in the book, but it is unfortunately illegible. It is in the Strong Museum collection. Regarding taking books to friend's houses, see Nash, *Children's Occupations,* 127. See also Marian Dudley Richards, "Fun with Paper Dolls," *Ladies' Home Journal* (Sept. 1902): 41.

29. Mary White, *The Child's Rainy Day Book* (New York: Doubleday, Page, 1905), 13; Richards, "Fun with Paper Dolls," 41; Katherine C. Grier, personal correspondence, Nov. 1998.

30. After I came to this conclusion, I found Roth's written version of "Scrapbook Houses," in which she expressed the same idea (316).

31. Harriet Brown's album, like Edith Washburn's, is in the Domestic Life Division of the Smithsonian Institution. Brown's, like the Grier example at the Strong Museum, was donated by the granddaughter of the recipient. Anita Blair's books are in the Chicago Historical Society. They are discussed in Barbara Chaney Ferguson, *The Paper Doll: A Collector's Guide with Prices* (Des Moines, IA: Wallace-Homestead, 1982), 54–55. Emilie Hickey's book is also in the Strong Museum. Grier, personal correspondence. Note that the Grier/Ross collaboration is unusual in that the furnishings are all painted rather than pasted in.

32. Regarding crepe paper, see Gordon, "'One of the Most Valuable Fabrics." Jan Jennings discussed the perceived relationship between women and wallpaper in "Controlling Passion: The Turn-of-the Century Wallpaper Dilemma," *Winterthur Portfolio* 31 (Winter 1996): 243–64.

33. The suggestion that such male retreats might be included was specifically indicated in *Harper's Bazar* in 1904. Hoffman, "Homes for Paper Dolls," 85.

34. Patricia P. Buckler and C. Kay Leeper, "An Antebellum Woman's Scrapbook as Autobiographical Composition," *Journal of American Culture* 14 (Spring 1991): 4, quoting Dominic Ricciotti, "Popular Art in *Godey's Lady's Book:* An Image of the American Woman, 1830–1880," *Historical New Hampshire* 27 (Spring 1972): 3–26.

35. Ruutz Rees, *Home Occupations,* 97. The role of sentimentality in nineteenth-century women's lives is explored in Ockenga Starr, *On Women and Friendship: A Collection of Victorian Keepsakes and Traditions* (New York: Stewart, Tabori, and Chang, 1995). Starr illustrates what she calls a "house album" on p. 76.

36. Roth, "Scrapbook Houses," presentation and personal conversation, Aug. 1998; Hoffman, "Homes for Paper Dolls," 85. Deborah Smith of the Strong Museum was responsible for dating the Ivory Soap advertisement.

37. Hoffman, "Homes for Paper Dolls," 85.

38. Smith, "Consuming Passions," 69; Hoffman, "Homes for Paper Dolls," 84, 86.

39. Richards, "Fun with Paper Dolls," 41. Further supporting this thesis is the fact that Christine Grier's paper doll house included no commercial material at all; its furnishings were completely hand drawn and painted, and it represented her actual home.

40. Smith, "Consuming Passions," 70; Wells, "A Paper Doll's House," 273; White, *Child's Rainy Day Book,* 13. Significantly, none of the broader nineteenth-century literature on scrapbooks made an overt connection between scrapbooks and consumer training.

41. Kenneth L. Ames discusses the way material items could help further bonding across the generations. He reiterated that in Victorian America, fostering this kind of social bonding was women's responsibility. See "When the Music Stops" in Kenneth L. Ames, *Death in the Dining Room and Other Tales of Victorian Culture* (Philadelphia: Temple UP, 1992), 150–84. For more on paper doll houses as social training *and* amusement, see M.E.W.S. [probably Mary Sherwood], *Home Amusements,* Appleton's Home Books Series (New York: D. Appleton, 1881), 151–52; Lina and Adelia Beard, *The American Girl's Handy Book: How to Amuse Yourself and Others* (New York: Charles Scribner's Sons, 1893), 396–97.

42. Richards, "Fun with Paper Dolls," 41; Nash, *Children's Occupations,* 122; Hoffman, "Homes for Paper Dolls," 85.

43. The fact that such pride and satisfaction was inextricably tied to aesthetic pleasure would have made it an even more satisfying experience. Hoffman talked about the child who had a conception of the "house beautiful" for whom paper doll house–making was "pure joy." Hoffman, "Homes for Paper Dolls," 85.

44. Richards, "Fun with Paper Dolls," 41. Rodris Roth and I discussed this possibility (personal conversation, 1998), and she agreed that it was plausible.

45. Flora Gill Jacobs, *A History of Doll Houses: Four Centuries of the Domestic World in Miniature* (New York: Charles Scribner's Sons, 1953), 229, 220–24.

46. Jacobs discusses a number of the commercial paper houses in *A History of Doll Houses,* 29, 225. Examples of newspaper supplements with dollhouse imagery, including ones from the *Boston Globe* on Sep. 29, 1895, and Apr. 26, 1896, are in the Strong Museum library. Both of those supplements were copyrighted by Armstrong and Co. One of the Mcloughlin Brothers folding houses is housed there as well (accession number 79.1340). Barbara Whitton Jendricks, *Paper Dollhouses and Paper Dollhouse Furniture* (N.p.: by the author, 1975).

47. Clara Andrews Williams, *The House That Glue Built* (New York: Frederick Stokes), discussed in Jendricks, *Paper Dollhouses,* 8; Edith A. Root, *A Paper Home for Paper People* (Saalfield, 1909), discussed in Jendricks, *Paper Dollhouses,* 10–11. Other examples of the

220   printed-book genre include Jane Eayre Fryer, *The Mary Frances Housekeeper: Adventures among the Doll People* (Philadelphia: John C. Winston, 1914); Clara Andrews Williams, *Children's Store* (New York: Frederick Stokes, 1910). There were also books that folded into three-dimensional forms, including *Dolly Blossom's Bungalow* (Chicago: Reilly and Britton, 1917).

48. Doris Davey (After Helen Waite), *My Dolly's Home* (London: Simpkin, Marshall, Hamilton, Kent for the Arts and General Publishers, 1921) (in the collection of the Strong Museum). I am not sure what the "After Helen Waite" phrase means, but it is possible that Ms. Waite made a scrapbook house that inspired Davey to publish the book. I have found no other English examples of scrapbook houses, but since I was not expressly looking for them, I cannot come to any conclusions about their prevalence in England.

49. Ringwalt, "Fun for the Fireside," 162; Hoffman, "Homes for Paper Dolls," 84; *Merriam-Webster Online,* s.v. "Ephemera," http://www.m-w.com/ (accessed Jan. 25, 2006). A more positive definition of ephemera is provided by the Ephemera Society of America, which refers to a "wide range of minor, everyday documents and artifacts, most intended for one-time use." See the Web site, http://www.ephemerasociety.org (accessed July 25, 2000). I was delighted to read the Ephemera Society's explanation of why these often-dismissed paper items appeal to its members, because it echoes my description of items made with saturated consciousness: "Today, the mundane items from earlier times which somehow survived delight our eyes, feed our minds, and offer unique windows into the details and realities of the past."

50. *Oxford English Dictionary,* 2nd ed., s.v. "Toy"; Sidney Brower, "Tools, Toys, Masterpieces, Mediums," *Landscape* 19 (Jan. 1975): 29.

51. Charles Baudelaire, *Le Monde Litteraire,* 1853, quoted in Ian Starsmore, *English Fairs* (London: Thames and Hudson, 1975), 9.

52. Diane Waldman, *Collage, Assemblage and the Found Object* (New York: Harry N. Abrams, 1992), 10; Harriet Janis, *Collage: Personalities, Concepts, Techniques* (Philadelphia: Chilton, 1967), 3; Hartigan, "The House That Collage Built."

53. Waldman, *Collage, Assemblage and the Found Object,* 17; Hartigan, "The House That Collage Built."

3. Parties and Party Givers

1. Ellye Howell Glover, *"Dame Curtsey's" Art of Entertaining for All Occasions* (Chicago: F. G. Browne, 1913; A. C. McClurg, 1918, 1920), cover, foreword.

2. Corinne Wentworth, *Entertainment for All Occasions: Parties Completely Planned for Evenings, Luncheons, Afternoons, Holidays and Other Occasions* (New York and Newark: Barse and Hopkins, 1921), 204–8.

3. The blurring of different types of events is discussed in Gordon, *BFL,* esp. 50–51. Note that a kermiss involved folk rather than ballroom dancing. See *BFL,* 132.

4. See Katherine C. Grier, "Dishes and More Dishes: Tableware in the Home," in Charles L. Venable, ed., *China and Glass in America* (Dallas: Dallas Museum of Art, 2001), 30, 34. Grier reminds us (20) that "when someone asks where the work of many nineteenth century women artists is, remember to [reply] that a lot of it was eaten!" A "dinner" almost always implied a mixed group of men and women.

5. *Hints on Entertaining* (Minneapolis: Young Women's Christian Association, 1897), **221** 19. The word "dainty" appeared a great deal in turn-of-the-century references to women's entertainments. *Dainty Dining* is the title of a 1908 book with luncheon recipes written by Mary Alice Bown (Lexington, ME, 1908). Grier remarks that this kind of "gendered cuisine" reflected the increasingly visual culture of turn-of-the-century America ("Dishes and More Dishes," 41).

6. M. E. W. Sherwood, *Manners and Social Usages* (New York, 1884), 247, accessed on "American Memory" Web site, http://memory.loc.gov/ (accessed Jan. 25, 2006). Paul Pierce, *Breakfasts and Teas: Novel Suggestions for Social Occasions* (Chicago: Brewer, Barse, 1907), 44, concurs that teas originated in English homes where guests returning from driving or field sports would require light refreshments before preparing for dinner.

7. Sherwood, *Manners and Social Usages*, 248; Anna. R. White, *Youth's Educator for Home and Society* (N.p.: L. W. Walter, 1896), chap. 9, reproduced on http://www.history. rochester.edu/ehp-book/yefhas/chap9.htm (accessed Jan. 25, 2006). An Americanized version of the officer's wives story was recently included in a story in the Fort Hays University newspaper. According to a press release provided by a Michigan couple who were inviting the public to a "kettle drum tea" as part of a historic reenactment, the name came from "the spartan living conditions in the west, [when] a military drum was often used as a table." Brandie Elliott, "Spend a Day with Gen., Mrs. Custer," *University Leader* 1 (Apr. 23, 1999).

8. Emily Rose Burt, *Entertaining Made Easy* (New York: Edward J. Clode, 1919), 107– 8. The time frame for card parties is included in Glover, *"Dame Curtsey's,"* 20. Card parties often had intentionally simple repasts, especially by the 1920s. Edna Sibley Tipton, *Table Service for the Hostess* (New York: D. Appleton, 1926), 77, noted that many card clubs had instituted rules that only two things might be served at any given gathering.

9. I discuss the rise of women's organizations at length in Gordon, *BFL*, 119. For a general history of home economics, see Sarah Stage and Virginia B. Vincenti, *Rethinking Home Economics: Women and the History of a Profession* (Ithaca: Cornell UP, 1997). Regarding cooking schools, see Laura Shapiro, *Perfection Salad: Women and Cooking at the Turn of the Century* (New York: Farrar, Straus, and Giroux, 1986).

10. Mark C. Carnes, *Secret Ritual and Manhood in Victorian America* (New Haven: Yale UP, 1989), 1. See also Barbara Franco, "The Ritualization of Male Friendship and Virtue in Nineteenth Century Fraternal Organizations," paper presented at Winterthur Conference on the Material Culture of Gender, Winterthur, DE, Nov. 10, 1989; Mary Ann Clawson, *Constructing Brotherhood: Class, Gender and Fraternalism* (Princeton: Princeton UP, 1989). Note that fraternal and benevolent society groups cut across class and race, although in any given organization, members tended to be homogeneous.

11. Certain types of parties, such as showers, continued to be exclusively for women after the war, but the heyday of these events had passed.

12. *Hints on Entertaining*, 49–50; Adele Mendel, *Indoor Merrymaking and Table Decorations* (Boston and Chicago: W. A. Wilde, 1915), 7; Grier, "Dishes and More Dishes," 34.

13. Regarding women's magazines, see Kathleen L. Endres and Therese L. Lueck, eds. *Women's Periodicals in the United States: Consumer Magazines* (Westport, CN: Greenwood P, 1950); Frank Luther Mott, *History of American Magazines* (Cambridge: Harvard

UP, 1942), vol. 4., 1885–1905; vol. 5., 1905–1930; Salme Harju Steinberg, *Reformer in the Marketplace: Edward W. Bok and the Ladies' Home Journal* (Baton Rouge: Louisiana State UP, 1979). In the introduction (p. 3) to *Breakfasts and Teas* in 1907, Pierce said, "no school teacher of the world has such a large class to instruct as [the editor of the woman's page]. Her pupils are numbered by the thousands and tens of thousands and hundreds of thousands. The knowledge she must impart . . . is the knowledge of the day, which is constantly changing."

14. There was a real interchange between most of these magazines and their readers. *Woman's Home Companion* went so far as to query a panel of two thousand readers on a monthly basis, bringing them to New York for two weeks every summer to get their input.

15. *Day Entertainments and Other Functions,* Metropolitan Handwork Series, vol. 2, no. 3 (New York: Butterick Pub., 1896), 104, 85; Gordon, *BFL,* 21.

16. The cited examples come from Winnifred Fales and Mary H. Northend's *The Party Book* (Boston: Little, Brown, 1926), 29. The authors mention reference works such as Katherine Wood's *Quotations for Occasions* (New York: Century Co., 1903), and Elisabeth Luther Cary and Annie M. Jones's *Books and My Food: Quotations and Original Recipes for Every Day in the Year* (New York: Rohde & Haskins, 1904). Thirty years earlier, the fictional recipient of an invitation to the "Literary Leaves Tea" expressed some concern that she had little time to read and was not well versed on literary matters. Her friend laughingly told her, "don't you know it is to be only a burlesque?" (*Day Entertainments,* 104).

17. Mrs. Hamilton Mott, ed., *Home Games and Parties* (Philadelphia: Curtis, 1891), 146.

18. Gordon, *BFL,* 129; Louise Dew, "A College Fair," *Entertainments for All Seasons* (New York: S. H. Moore, 1904), 114–15. Florence Hull Winterburn, author of *Novel Ways of Entertaining* (New York: Harper and Bros., 1914), 64–66, commented that "one result of college life for women has been a more intimate knowledge of one another," and a new, mutual appreciation for one another's intelligence. "College life has given birth to [a new] condition," she explained. "Culture has become so wide-spread . . . that women are delighted to meet one another to have talks on all sorts of subjects and find immense enjoyment in the interchange of wit and fancy. They sharpen their minds upon one another." She noted that even a "colored woman" who worked as a "visiting servant by the hour" was found to be up-to-date on "politics, social progress, international questions, the last public scandal, [or] the newest society topic."

19. Myrtle Jamison Trachsel, "A Plantation Party," *Parties* (Jul.–Aug. 1927): 11–12; Fales and Northend, *The Party Book,* 170. The earliest reference I have seen to a plantation party was in Lillian Heath, *80 Pleasant Evenings* (Boston and Chicago: United Society of Christian Endeavor, 1898), 45–46. See Gordon, *BFL,* 145, for an image of a "reproduction of Mt. Vernon" that featured "pickaninnies" (I cite varied original spellings of this word) serving tea. It was staged at Milwaukee's 1896 "Bazar of All Nations" by the Daughters of the American Revolution. See chapter 4 on men's dress-up.

Sarah Leavitt, who wrote about domestic advice literature more generally, also concluded that a white middle-class audience was assumed. She pointed out that throughout the literature immigrants appear as servants. See Sarah A. Leavitt, *From Catharine Beecher to Martha Stewart: A Cultural History of Domestic Advice* (Chapel Hill: U of North Carolina P, 2002), 20.

20. For a good discussion of cultural shifts at this time, see Michael Kammen, *Mystic* **223** *Chords of Memory: The Transformation of Tradition in American Culture* (New York: Alfred A. Knopf, 1991); Karal Ann Marling, "From the Quilt to the Neocolonial Photograph: The Arts of the Home in an Age of Transition," in Jessica H. Foy and Karal Ann Marling, eds., *The Arts and the American Home, 1890–1930* (Knoxville: U of Tennessee P, 1994), 1–13. Also relevant is the discussion of periodization in my article "Spinning Wheels, Samplers and the Modern Priscilla: The Images and Paradoxes of Colonial Revival Needlework," *Winterthur Portfolio* 33 (Summer/Autumn 1998): 163–94. Leavitt concurs that there was a new tone to domestic advice after World War I, with an increasing assumption that it should be made available to all (*From Catharine Beecher*, 40, 55). A comment made by Anna Wentworth Sears in a column entitled "Midwinter Entertainments," *Harper's Bazar* (Jan. 1904): 88, alludes to the idea of fun in another context. Sears talked about the boredom in small communities where people all knew one another and were tired of each others' company. Hostesses faced with the prospect of another such gathering were anxious to "enliven their afternoons" with something novel and entertaining, and Sears assured them that there were "ways of making time pass pleasantly even in this strenuous age."

21. Editorial, *Hostess* (Nov. 1923): 2, 5; *Dennison Party Magazine* (Jan.–Feb. 1927): 1. Regarding the influences of the Recreation movement, see Richard Kraus, *Recreation and Leisure in Modern Society* (New York: Appleton-Century Crofts, 1971); Steven Gelber, *Hobbies: Leisure and the Culture of Work in America* (New York: Columbia UP, 1999), esp. chap. 1. Books written by recreation leaders bore titles such as *The Church at Play: A Manual for Directors of Social and Recreational Life* (written by Norman E. Richardson, a professor of religious education) (New York: Abingdon P, 1922). Renee Stern, author of *Neighborhood Entertainments* (New York: Sturgis and Walton, 1913), said her book was designed to help make rural life more enjoyable, in part "to keep people on the farm." She felt such recreation advice was especially important for the women of the community, since others were able to get out more (ix–xi).

22. There were new resorts catering to upwardly mobile segments of the population, including recent immigrants. See Barbara A. Schreier, *Becoming American Women: Clothing and the Jewish Immigrant Experience, 1880–1920* (Chicago: Chicago Historical Society, 1994). Golf, too, became accessible through the institution of public courses. My own parents, both from poor immigrant families, were avid golfers in the late 1920s and 1930s. They met on a municipally run golf course in New York City. Regarding the wealthy going out to entertain in the 1920s, see Grier, "Dishes and More Dishes," 48.

23. Tipton, *Table Service for the Hostess;* "Landscape Dinner Party," *Entertainment for All Occasions,* 108. Instructions for table decorations, party favors, and the like were especially highly detailed in Fales and Northend's *The Party Book.*

24. Grier ("Dishes and More Dishes," 41) goes so far as to say that, with their emphasis on decoration, women's parties became identified with the fashion system.

25. Mrs. Herbert [Hilda] Linscott, *Bright Ideas for Entertaining* (Philadelphia: George W. Jacobs, 1905), 180; Mendel, *Indoor Merrymaking,* 91–95. Party suggestions were closely tied to changes in women's culture. Turn-of-the-century feminists were willing to make fun of themselves at New Woman or Suffragette parties, but by the interwar years the

tone was more conservative. In describing suitable activities for a Valentine's Day party, for example, Corinne Wentworth echoed contemporary sentiments when she used the heading "Home Keeping Hearts Are Happiest" (*Entertainment for All Occasions*, 33). "Home Keeping Hearts" came from Longfellow's poem, "The Courtship of Miles Standish," which was frequently quoted and illustrated during this period. See Gordon, "Spinning Wheels, Samplers and the Modern Priscilla."

26. Fairyland was associated with both women and children (prepubescent boys as well as girls) at the end of the nineteenth century. I discuss a similar progression—a "juvenilization" of fundraising entertainments—in *BFL*, 128–29, 162–63.

27. Leavitt, *From Catharine Beecher*. Leavitt mentions (10–11) influential advice givers and fiction writers such as Lydia Maria Child and Helen Hunt Jackson and profiles (19) Emma Church Hewitt, author of a manual entitled *Queen of the Home: Her Reign from Infancy to Age, from Attic to Cellar* and associate editor of *Ladies' Home Journal*, who was also known as a poet and nonfiction writer. Jean Gordon and Jan McArthur have written a number of articles looking at the advice genre in relation to interior design; see "Interior Decorating Advice as Popular Culture: Women's Views Concerning Wall and Window Treatments, 1870–1920," in Marilyn Ferris Motz and Pat Browne, eds., *Making the American Home: Middle Class Women and Domestic Material Culture, 1890–1940* (Bowling Green, OH: Bowling Green State U Popular P, 1988), 105–20. See also Lisa M. Koenigsberg, *Professionalizing Domesticity: A Tradition of American Writers on Architecture, 1848–1913* (Ph.D. dissertation, Yale University, 1987).

28. Information on Emily Rose Burt available on http://www.mtholyoke.edu/~dalbino/letters/women/eburt.html (accessed Jan. 25, 2006) and on Louise Dew at http://www.albionmich.com/history/histor_notebook/940130.shtml (accessed Jan. 25, 2006). Fales's article "The Fire on the Hearth" appeared in *Good Housekeeping* (Oct. 1919): 32–33. Regarding Northend, see Leavitt, *From Catharine Beecher*, 166. The Mary Harrod Northend archive is at the Massachusetts Historical Society, Boston, MA; her photographic archive is at the Winterthur Museum and Library. Information on Bowles, Bradley, Hoffman and Irish comes from Web searches of their names, yielding primarily bibliographic information.

29. These statements are based on my own content analysis and observation of these sources. The idea that women were more likely to stress lighthearted fun than men was echoed by Mary E. Moxcey, *Good Times for Girls* (New York: Methodist Book Concern, 1920), 9, who indicated that girls-only parties could be "nonsense affairs" much more easily than coed events.

30. Carrie May Ashton, "Home Entertainments" section of *Goodform: A Magazine for the People* (Jan. 1893): 125–26.

31. In *BFL*, 146, I reported on an actual event indicating the speed with which magazine suggestions were put into effect.

32. Ashton, "Home Entertainments," 125.

33. Mendel, *Indoor Merrymaking;* "A Rosebud Tea," *Day Entertainments*, 7. I believe the author of this book was probably Lillian Pascal Day, who went on to publish *Social Entertainments: A Book of Practical Suggestions for Entertaining* (New York: Moffat, Yard, 1914).

34. Leavitt, *From Catharine Beecher,* 2–3. The same point was made by Janet Theophano, a University of Pennsylvania professor, who argued that cookbooks enable a would-be cook to "indulge her senses in imaging how food will taste, feel, smell and appear." "Among the Slices of Pie, a Slice of Life," *Pennsylvania Gazette* (Mar. 1996): 19.

35. Mary Dawson and Emma Paddock Telford, *Book of Frolics for All Occasions* (New York: William Rickey, 1911), 143.

36. During the Depression, *Good Housekeeping* featured an "employment party" that played on the very idea of unemployment. Guests were invited to a "labor meeting" at the home of "employment agent Beverley Stewart." Jobs open to the unemployed included gaming and bridge contracting as well as darning and "waiting on table." According to the author of this feature, a hostess could "exercise her ingenuity no end," depending upon the guests' choices. Her challenge "was to provide happy entertainment for each one." Elaine, "An Employment Party," *Good Housekeeping* (Aug. 1932): 104.

37. Day, "A Snow Fete," *Social Entertainments,* 118; "Literary Leaves: An Autumn Entertainment," *Day Entertainments,* 104. Remember that, given available technology, it was not a simple matter for a hostess to provide music—at least until late in the period I am concerned with, one could not casually play a record for background ambience.

38. Mrs. L.[izzie] C. Stocking, *How to Entertain* (Salt Lake City: L. C. Stocking, 1903), n.p.

39. Novel decorations were first seen on aristocratic European tables after the Crusades. Charles V, for example, had an ornament in the shape of a ship that symbolized fair sailing on the seas of life (Smith, *Table Decorations,* 48). Even the idea of a place card was carried over from the time when hierarchical seating prevailed. Another example of the tamed version of the once-fierce displays was provided in Marie Biossat, "A Colonial Supper," *Hostess* (Mar. 1925): 15. One of the suggested amusements for this event was a "cockade battle," where players used palm leaf fans to "battle" with crepe paper cockades. This was described as a version of the "Rose War." Georgiana Reynolds Smith, *Table Decorations: Yesterday, Today and Tomorrow* (Rutland, Vt.: Charles E. Tuttle, 1968), 26, maintains that table decoration was primarily done by men until the end of the nineteenth century; by the twentieth it had become women's domain.

It would not very much matter who sat where at a round table, but place cards were still de rigueur at turn-of-the-century parties, primarily, I believe, because they afforded another opportunity for aesthetic display in the form of color and theme-related imagery. The only exception to the equitable nature of the favors was at a shower, when a bride-to-be might get an unusual gift. At one party featured in *How to Entertain at Home,* 94, everyone else received a "wee gold wish-bone pin" when they opened their favor boxes, but the guest of honor found a (mock) engagement ring.

40. Jack Santino, *All around the Year: Holidays and Celebrations in American Life* (Urbana and Chicago: U of Illinois P, 1994), 34, 39.

41. Day, "A Snow Fete," *Social Entertainments,* 117.

42. Linscott, *Bright Ideas for Entertaining,* 124. Twenty-one years later Linscott was still offering sample rhyming invitations in her book *Up-to-Date Social Affairs* (Philadelphia: George W. Jacobs, 1924). Those asked to come to a "Vegetable Garden Party" were told, for example, "And we'll really be delighted / If you'll come and be our guest. / Please wear some article to suggest / A vegetable of some kind" (118).

43. *How to Entertain at Home* (Boston: Priscilla Publishing, 1928), 264.

44. Linscott, *Bright Ideas*, 97; *How to Entertain at Home*, 167; Wentworth, *Entertainment for All Occasions*, 113; Winterburn, *Novel Ways of Entertaining*, 8.

45. Day, "A Snow Fete," *Social Entertainments*, 124; Stocking, *How to Entertain*, 17–18. Guessing games at some of the earlier aristocratic entertainments had a strong edge. Enigmas could be interpreted only by the most in-the-know upper crust who were privy to court secrets, for example, or they might consist of rather nasty rhymes implying cuckolding or the like. See Betsy Rosasco, "Masquerade and Enigma at the Court of Louis XIV," *Art Journal* 48 (Summer 1989): 144–49.

46. Fales and Northend, *Party Book*, 295–98; 304; Day, "A Snow Fete," 120–22. The potato animals were the forerunners of the familiar contemporary game "Mr. Potato Head."

47. *Day Entertainments*, 32; Burt, *Entertaining Made Easy*, 148; "The Christmas Announcement Party," *Hostess* (Christmas 1925): 23; Glover, "Favors for an Engagement Luncheon," *"Dame Curtsey's,"* 236. Favors were not always handmade. *A Catalogue of Favors* published by B. Shackman and Co. in 1910 runs more than two hundred pages (this includes not only favors, but party supplies such as confetti, tally cards, and card markers). Its "favors" section is introduced by the statement "new, dainty, odd, unique and effective designs in miniatures and delightful conceits" (67). In addition to tiny boxes, novelty tape measures and match safes are offered, as well as miniatures relating to specific party themes. A pair of 4" wooden shoes, a 5" windmill, or 2.5" china Dutch boy and girl figures were among the offerings for a Holland-theme party (147). This catalog is in the Winterthur Library Trade Catalogue Collection, item 719.

48. "Literary Leaves Tea," 104.

49. Day, "A Snow Fete," 117–24; Effie W. Merriam, *Modern Entertainments* (New York: F. M. Lupton, 1898), 80.

50. Linscott, *Bright Ideas*, 54, 97, 140–41; Mary Elizabeth Ford, "The Cross Word Puzzle Party," *Hostess* (Jan. 1925): 13; Wentworth, *Entertainment for All Occasions*, 29; Winterburn, *Novel Ways of Entertaining*, 121, 134; "A Colonial Tea," *Dennison's Party Magazine* (Jan.–Feb. 1927): 9; Day, *Social Entertainments*, 88.

51. See Beverly Gordon, "'One of the Most Valuable Fabrics': The Seemingly Limitless Promise of Crepe Paper, 1890–1935," *Ars Textrina* 31 (1999): 107–44. The white tablecloth originally connoted wealth; it was difficult to keep clean and implied the presence of servant labor. See Sarah Paston-Williams, *The Art of Dining: A History of Cooking and Eating* (London: National Trust, 1993), 131, 249. Fine linens were expensive, and if they were white, they had to be washed especially often, indicating an abundant labor pool to take care of them. Damask, with white-on-white patterning, was the essence of a prestige cloth. In the mid–nineteenth century, multiple layers of white cloth were expected on a fine dinner table; each course would have its own cloth, which was successively removed. Guests also used large napkins on their laps.

52. Merriam, *Modern Entertainments*, 113. Doilies were named after a Mr. Doyley, a seventeenth-century English linen draper who introduced a relatively inexpensive fringed mat for dessert service. For more on the popularity of doilies, see Beverly Gordon, "Cozy, Charming and Artistic: Stitching Together the Home Environment," in Jessica Foy and Karal Ann Marling, eds., *The Arts and the American Home, 1890–1930* (Knoxville: U of

Tennessee P, 1994), 124–48. Edna Sibley Tipton wrote in *Table Service for the Hostess* (New York: D. Appleton, 1926), 92, that men disliked doilies; some of them felt the bare spaces visible behind the doilies reminded them of "quick-lunch counters" and were not very "homey." She also noted that hostesses were dipping linen tablecloths in fugitive dyes "in order to match the color scheme of the occasion" (93).

53. Sara Sedgwick, "Our House Affairs," *Goodform: A Magazine for the People* (Jan. 1893): 113; *Day Entertainments*, 7; Mary Dawson, "A Snow Luncheon for Warm Days," *Hostess* (Jul. 1905): 55 Linscott, *Bright Ideas*, 97; Carrie May Ashton, "Practical Amusements," *Goodform* (Dec. 1892): 46; Linscott, *Up-to-Date Social Affairs*, 118. Smith, *Table Decorations*, 30–32, explains that the centerpiece tradition was in full swing by the eighteenth century.

54. Mendel, *Indoor Merrymaking*, 108–11, 117; Glover, *"Dame Curtsey's,"* 245; *How to Entertain at Home*, 92.

55. Stern, *Neighborhood Entertainments*, 186; *How to Entertain at Home*, 91–92, 334; Pierce, *Breakfasts and Teas*, 67; Glover, *"Dame Curtsey's,"* 97, 245; Mendel, *Indoor Merrymaking*, 27, 43, 108–11, 117; Wentworth, *Entertainment for All Occasions*, 62–63, 67–68.

56. Jean Latham, *The Pleasure of Your Company: A History of Meals and Manners* (London: Adam and Charles Black, 1972), 31, 152; Patricia Easterbrook Roberts, *Table Settings, Entertaining and Etiquette: A History and Guide* (London: Thames and Hudson, 1967), 135; Roy Strong, *Splendor at Court: Renaissance Spectacle and the Theater of Power* (Boston: Houghton Mifflin, 1973), 56–63, 198. The mirror lake idea was introduced to aristocratic tables by the early eighteenth century; often these were set up to reflect porcelain figures and temples (Smith, *Table Decorations*, 136). In 1700 a Mr. Canade of France invented a so-called artificial frost (actually a sugar concoction) that would melt in the warmth of the room, meaning that banquet guests could witness a changing vignette of winter turning into spring (Smith, *Table Decorations*, 52). In the eighteenth and nineteenth centuries, table decoration emphasized verticality and architectural-looking structures. Pyramids of food were common, sometimes stabilized with caramel or set on tiered dishes called epergnes, and there might be molded jellied dishes and puddings that looked like castles. (This historical reference was acknowledged in Paul Pierce's discussion of a "Grandmother's Tea Party" in *Breakfasts and Teas*, 70.)

57. Fales and Northend, *Party Book*, 134–40, 146–65; Linscott, *Bright Ideas*, 54, 82, 152; Mendel, *Indoor Merrymaking*, 117; Linscott, *Up-to-Date Social Affairs*, 118; Pierce, *Breakfasts and Teas*, 14; *Day Entertainments*, 15. Brentano's *Original and Artistic Novelties for Table Decoration* (New York and Washington, ca. 1908) featured "original and artistic menus and place cards" and a range of paper "ice or souffle" holders in various "saucy figure" forms. Would-be customers were assured that they looked good from all sides of the table, as they were finished on both sides. The catalog is in the Winterthur Library.

58. Mary Dawson, "A Snow Luncheon for Warm Days," *Good Housekeeping* (Jul. 1905): 55.

59. Fales and Northend, *Party Book*, 63; Burt, *Entertaining Made Easy*, 109.

60. Day, *Social Entertainments*, 54; Wentworth, *Entertainments for All Occasions*, 62–63.

61. Wentworth, *Entertainments for All Occasions,* 39–40; Claire Wallis and Nellie Ryder Gates, *Parties for All Occasions* (New York: Century, 1925), 174.

62. That rhyme had itself been based on an actual aristocratic conceit where oversized pielike shapes were filled with birds or other small animals; in some versions we are told that the birds were still living. See Bryan Holme, *Princely Feasts and Festivals: Five Centuries of Pageantry and Spectacle* (London: Thames and Hudson, 1988), 10; Reay Tannahil, *The Fine Art of Food* (S. Brunswick and New York: A. S. Barnes, 1968), 70; Paston-Williams, *The Art of Dining,* 112; "Little Jack Horner," http://www.grovepublishingco.uk/index/page5e.htm (accessed February 1, 2006). The earliest reference I have found for a surprise pie links it to an English Christmas tradition: Caroline Smith's *American Home Book of Indoor Games, Recreations and Occupations* (Boston: Lee, Shephard and Dillingham, 1871), 229–31 refers to a "bran pie" filled with little gifts such as sugar hearts or mock rings. Lina and Adelia Beard, *What a Girl Can Make and Do* (New York: Charles Scribner's Sons, 1913), chap. 3, also speak of Christmas gift pies. By the 1890s, however, such pies were used on other types of occasions. I have found one 1905 description of a surprise pie that called for an actual pie crust (Linscott, *Bright Ideas for Entertaining,* 20), but most speak of tin pie pans covered with paper. An 1898 reference spoke of "pies" that were simply napkins filled with popcorn. There the amusement was referred to as a "Plum Pudding or Jack Horner's Pie," and the guests pulled out humorous quotations. See Heath, *80 Pleasant Evenings,* 14–15.

63. Mott, *Home Games and Parties,* 12; Linscott, *Bright Ideas for Entertaining,* 20; Burt, *Entertaining Made Easy,* 111–12.

64. Burt, *Entertaining Made Easy,* 129; Fales and Northend, *Party Book,* 84–119.

65. "Jack Horner Pies for Grown-Ups and Children," *Parties* (Feb. 1930): 31; *A Catalogue of Favors,* 42–50. Fales and Northend discussed variations on the standard tradition, such as Jack Horners placed on a separate table instead of used as a centerpiece or attaching the ribbons to the handles of nut cups rather than place cards.

66. Glover, "Dame Curtsey's," 250, 257; *How to Entertain at Home,* 327, 141.

67. Wentworth, *Entertainments for All Occasions,* 40; Glover, "Dame Curtsey's," 235, 347; Linscott, *Up-to-Date Social Affairs* 111; Linscott, *Bright Ideas,* 11, 174; Pierce, *Breakfasts and Teas,* 18–19. A social recommended in 1898 actually used a menu as an organizing device for the entire entertainment. Listed courses referred to activities rather than foods. "Consomme a la Galop," for example, referred to a piano selection; "Pressed Tongue" consisted of short excerpts from current literature; "Roast Turkey" was a debate on the war between Turkey and Greece; "Saratoga Chips" were readings from a book about Saratoga, and "Scotch Marmelade" was a cue for the singing of a Scotch song. See Heath, *80 Pleasant Evenings,* 14–15.

68. Linscott, *Bright Ideas,* 8; *How to Entertain at Home,* 316–18; Tipton, *Table Service for the Hostess,* 79; Glover, "Dame Curtsey's," 63, 315; Wentworth, *Entertainments for All Occasions,* 157; Fales and Northend, *Party Book,* 228; Linscott, *Up-to-Date Social Affairs,* 199; Mildred Olson Woodward, "Christmas Announcement Party," *Hostess* (Christmas 1925): 23; *Hints on Entertaining,* 143; Shapiro, *Perfection Salad,* 98. Shapiro traces such novelties as chicken or duckling-shaped foods to Fanny Farmer and her cooking school (121–22).

69. Linscott, *Up-to-Date Social Affairs*, 120–21; "Bridge Luncheon Menus," *Hostess* **229** (Mar. 1925): 12; Glover, *"Dame Curtsey's ,"* 80, Dawson and Telford, *Book of Frolics*, 187.

70. The "Jolly Roger Cake" that concluded the Captain Kidd meal had baked into it the "key" to the captain's chest. See *How to Entertain at Home*, 316–18; Day, *Social Entertainments*, 95; "Little Things for Pretty Tables," *Ladies' Home Journal* (Oct. 1905): 52. According to Dena Attar in "Keeping Up Appearances: The Genteel Art of Dining in Middle-Class Victorian Britain," in C. Anne Wilson, ed., *'The Appetite and the Eye: Visual Aspects of Food and its Presentation Within Their Historic Context* (Edinburgh UP, 1991), 129, croquettes were an excellent type of food for the aspiring middle class. They looked genteel or dainty but could be made from relatively cheap ingredients.

71. Heath, *80 Pleasant Evenings*, 46; Linscott, *Bright Ideas*, 98; *Day Entertainments*, 85; Burt, *Entertaining Made Easy*, 123; Glover, *"Dame Curtsey's ,"* 35; *How to Entertain at Home*, 268, 274; Dawson and Telford, *Book of Frolics*, 187; Woodward, "Christmas Announcement Party," 23. Richard J. Hooker, *Food and Drink in America* (Indianapolis/ New York: Bobbs-Merrill, 1981), 242 notes that salads weren't eaten at all until the 1880s, and were then considered an "American dainty." The Knox Gelatin company offered a booklet entitled *Dainty Desserts for Dainty People* in 1893 (Shapiro, *Perfection Salad*, 99). Shapiro claims (84) a wholly color-coordinated meal was the pinnacle of decorative cooking and represented "a high degree of control over the mess and unpredictability of the kitchen." She traces this kind of color coordination to the 1897 graduation ceremonies of the Boston Cooking School (67).

72. Shapiro, *Perfection Salad*, 90–94; Mary McKim Marriott, "Midsummer Social Affairs," *Ladies' Home Journal* (Jul. 1908): 29; Pierce, *Breakfasts and Teas*, 92.

73. Pierce *Breakfasts and Teas*, 91–94; *Hints on Entertaining*, 57; Woodward, "Christmas Announcement Party," 23; Glover, *"Dame Curtsey's,"* 339; Shapiro, *Perfection Salad*, 102.

74. Shapiro, *Perfection Salad*, 43. Shapiro quotes from *New England Kitchen Magazine*, (Mar. 1898): 240.

75. Tipton, *Table Service for the Hostess*, 120; Shapiro, *Perfection Salad*, 72, 100; Mendel, *Indoor Merrymaking*, 7. A rose petal cake with whipped cream filling, featured in *Hostess* (Christmas 1925): 23, would have met many criteria of daintiness: it was sweet, filled with a light, white substance, and referred to the delicacy of flowers.

76. A pheasant, for example, could be carefully skinned in one piece so that the skin and feathers were intact, and restuffed with its own cooked meat. The same combination of appearance and taste was also part of medieval and Renaissance pageantry. According to Bridget Ann Henisch, *Fast and Feast: Food in Medieval Society* (University Park: Pennsylvania State UP, 1976), 106, hosts had to "pass the test" of pleasing both eye and palate.

77. P. W. Hammond, *Food and Feast in Medieval England* (Phoenix Mill, England, and Dover, NH: Alan Sutton, 1993), 137–38, 142; George B. Carroll, *Art of Dinner Giving and Usages of Polite Society* (New York: Dempsey and Carroll, 1880), 16; Sidney W. Mintz, *Sweetness and Power: The Place of Sugar in Modern History* (New York: Viking/Penguin Books, 1985), 77, 87–88, 90, 95; Simon R. Charsley, *Wedding Cakes and Cultural History* (London and New York: Routledge, 1992), 33; *For the Tabletop* (New York: American Craft Museum of American Crafts Council, 1980), 6–8; Smith, *Table Decorations*, 51. Cake icing was originally a lavish display in itself. See Charsley, *Wedding Cakes*, 69;

230 Paston-Williams, *The Art of Dining*, 260, 287. One renowned example of the aristocratic conceit was a confectionary stag that was brought to the table with an arrow in its flank. When the arrow was removed, the stag "bled" red wine. When a guest ate from this dessert, he was symbolically affirming the impressive power of the banquet giver.

78. Moxcey, *Good Times For Girls*, 9; "Entertainments" column, *Woman's Home Companion* (Feb. 1914): 27; Merriam, *Modern Entertainments*, 18; Wentworth, *Entertainments for All Occasions*, 156; Mary Mckim Marriott, "Social Affairs for March Evenings," *Ladies' Home Journal* (Mar. 1908): 47.

79. *How to Entertain at Home*, 334; Pierce, *Breakfasts and Teas*, 89; Mendel, *Indoor Merrymaking*, 51.

80. Winterburn, *Novel Ways of Entertaining*, 131. For a "super-dainty" meal Winterburn suggested filets of sweetbreads, veal cutlets, and chicken timbales, as well as parfaits and sherbets. The "Barnyard Party" was described in *Parties for the Bride-Elect* (Boston: Priscilla Publishing, 1924), 15. The guests at that event were first served a mock lunch consisting of corn, oyster shells, and grit (a real lunch followed).

81. Glover, "*Dame Curtsey's*," 233, 237, 242.

82. Helen Emily Webster, *Shower Parties for All Occasions* (New York: Woman's P, 1949), 8. Burt provides essentially the same story in her *Shower Book*, ix, although it is not set in Holland. The same story is recounted on "The Bridal Shower," http://oldhawaii weddingchapel.com/shower.com (accessed July 2005). There it is credited to Lilian Eichler's book *The Customs of Mankind*.

83. Webster, *Shower Parties for All Occasions*, 10; Burt, *Entertaining Made Easy*, 99. Note that occasionally there were showers given for grooms to be. See Glover, "*Dame Curtsey's*" 248–49.

84. *How to Entertain at Home*, 96 (reprinted in *Parties for the Bride-Elect*, 13); Webster, *Shower Parties for All Occasions*, 69.

85. Burt, *Entertaining Made Easy*, 121–24; Burt, *The Shower Book*, 25; Wentworth, *Entertainments for All Occasions*, 70–71.

86. Glover, "*Dame Curtsey's*," 253–54.

87. Burt, *Entertaining Made Easy*, 108; Burt, *Shower Book*, 45; Olive F. Wooley Burt, "A Rainbow Shower for Luck," *Hostess* (Spring 1925): 16; *How to Entertain at Home*, 96, 384–6. Some of these were reprinted in *Parties for the Bride-Elect* (Boston: Priscilla Publishing, 1924).

88. *How to Entertain at Home*; Webster, *Shower Parties for all Occasions*, 31–32; Burt, *Shower Book*, 3–4.

89. Webster, *Shower Parties*, 31–32; *Dennison's Party Magazine* (Jul.–Aug. 1928): 16.

90. Burt, *Entertaining Made Easy*, 108; Glover, "*Dame Curtsey's*," 245, 247, 257.

91. The favors served as tangible reminders, or "concretizers," of that time out of time, and they were given as gifts to people moving from this extraordinary space/time back into their ordinary lives. This fits with the model of souvenirs that I developed in "The Souvenir: Messenger of the Extraordinary," *Journal of Popular Culture* 20, no. 3 (1987): 136–46.

4. Dressing-Up as Embodied Amusement

1. The period sources I have drawn on most often used the words "costume" or "dress-up" rather than the phrase "fancy dress," which commonly implies a rather formal type of costumed portrayal, especially associated with dances or balls. The term is no longer in common usage in the United States. Thus "costume" and "dress-up" are my preferred terms.

2. Emily Rose Burt, *Entertaining Made Easy* (New York: Edward J. Clode, 1919), 59; Ellye Howell Glover, *"Dame Curtsey's" Art of Entertaining for All Occasions* (Chicago: A. C. McClurg, 1920), 43, 58.

3. "En Masque," *Delineator* (Feb. 1881): 92; Helen Hoover Santmeyer, *Ohio Town* (1956; reprinted, New York: Berkley Books, 1985), 215; *How to Make Paper Costumes* (Framingham, MA: Dennison Manufacturing, ca. 1920), 4–5.

4. Ruth Davies Champenois, "Let's Dress Up," *Good Housekeeping* (Feb. 1925): 101.

5. Clara Hasseltine Fair, "The Quilt Make," *Modern Priscilla* (May 1902): 17. At this event, uncostumed men joined the ladies when they finished quilting. Burt, *Entertaining Made Easy*, 96. Martha Banta, author of *Imaging American Women: Idea and Ideals in Cultural History* (New York: Columbia UP, 1987), 648, 650, criticized turn-of-the-century women's love for colonial costuming, dismissing it as reflective of conservative, small-town values. "The lives of Martha Washington [and] Abigail Adams . . . [were] reduced to a matter of costume and wigs," she claimed; women were reduced to weak romantic figures, or wives and mothers. Romanticized wives and mothers were indeed typical characterizations, but women were not in any way "reduced" to these portrayals; they were having fun and playing with their own role and image. See Beverly Gordon, "Gendered Identity in Historical Dress-Up in America, 1850–1940," *Dress* 30 (2003): 3–20.

6. "Ingle Nook" column, *Farmer's Advocate* (Oct. 27, 1927): 1547; see also *Farmer's Advocate* (Jan. 7, 1932).

7. Cynthia Brandimarte, "Tea Rooms and the Colonial Revival in New England," paper presented at the Historic Deerfield conference, Colonial Revival in New England: New Voices/New Themes, Deerfield, MA, Nov. 1995; Beverly Gordon, "Spinning Wheels, Samplers and the Modern Priscilla: The Images and Paradoxes of Colonial Revival Needlework," *Winterthur Portfolio* 33 (Summer/Autumn 1998): 177–84; Robert Kiracofe, *The American Quilt: A History of Cloth and Comfort 1750–1950* (New York: Clarkson Potter, 1993), 225–50; Thomas K. Woodard and Blanche Greenstein, *Twentieth Century Quilts 1900–1950* (New York: Dutton, 1988), 11.

8. For further discussion of the way women embodied abstract concepts and objects, see Beverly Gordon, *BFL*, esp. 32, 134–5, 148, 151. For more about the overlay between women's bodies and environments, see Beverly Gordon, "Woman's Domestic Body: The Conceptual Conflation of Women and Interiors in the Industrial Age," *Winterthur Portfolio* 31 (Winter 1996): 281–30. For a description of the way costume was used to help women bond at a bridal shower, see Day, *Social Entertainments*, 53.

9. Ardern Holt, *Fancy Dresses Described, or What to Wear to Fancy Balls*, 6th ed. (London: Debenham and Freebody, 1896), xiii; "En Masque," *Delineator* (Feb. 1881): 92; R. Barry Blackburn, ed., *Art, Society and Accomplishments: A Treasury of Artistic Homes, Social Life and Culture* (Chicago: Blackburn, 1891), 158; Cynthia Cooper and Linda Welters, "Brilliant

232 and Instructive Spectacles: Canada's Fancy Dress Balls, 1876–1898," *Dress* 22 (1995): 3, 13; "Six Crepe Paper Costumes," *Good Housekeeping* (Aug. 1925): 109.

10. Sara Stevenson and Helen Bennett, *Van Dyck in Check Trousers: Fancy Dress in Art and Life 1700–1900* (N.p.: Scottish National Portrait Gallery, 1978), 81; *Good Housekeeping* (Jan. 1930): 70–71; Caroline Grey, "If Life Has Forced You from Your Fate Afar—In Fancy Dress Be What You Really Are!" *Good Housekeeping* (Oct. 1927): 66.

11. Barbara Burman Baines, who studied British dress-up, came up with four categories of fancy dress: dress based on historic themes, dress in the classical (that is, Greek and Roman) mode, dress drawn from rural life, and "exotic" dress. See Baines, *Fashion Revivals from the Elizabethan Age to the Present Day* (London: Anchor P, 1981), 13. I consider rural dress-up to be a part of more general exotic category, and I have added an additional allegorical/fairyland category that incorporates classical dress.

12. Gordon, "Spinning Wheels, Samplers and the Modern Priscilla;" Gordon, "Gendered Identity in Historical Dress-Up in America."

13. "A Colonial Tea," *Dennison's Party Magazine* (Jan.–Feb. 1927): 9, 31. Even the logo adopted by *Vogue* magazine during the 1920s was a colonially dressed figure. See Virginia Gunn, "Quilts for Milady's Boudoir," *Uncoverings* 9 (1989): 81–101.

14. Laurel Thatcher Ulrich, *The Age of Homespun: Objects and Stories in the Creation of an American Myth* (New York: Alfred A. Knopf, 2001), 30–32, 417.

15. Helen Landon, "The Church Sociable," *Harper's Bazar* (Oct. 1905): 1051.

16. Confusingly, it was sometimes referred to at the time as "national" dress, since it was associated with the different nations of the world.

17. See Gordon, *BFL*, 136; *Entertaining with Cards* (Cincinnati: U.S. Playing Card, 1900), for example, 44, 45; Blackburn, *Art, Society and Accomplishments* (Chicago: Blackburn, 1891). *The Milton-Bradley Catalogue of Games, Toys and Novelties* (Springfield, MA, ca. 1885), n.p., even included a card game of "costumes and fashions," where the cards were to "serve as patterns for fancy dress, tableaux and parlor dramas."

18. "Let Fancy Dress Release Your Dream and Be Just What You'd Like to Seem," *Good Housekeeping* (Jan. 1930): 70–71; "Six Crepe Paper Costumes," 109.

19. Theresa Wolcott, "The Fair of the Good Fairies," *Ladies' Home Journal* (Oct. 1916): 28.

20. "En Masque," 93.

21. Harriet Adams Ganahl, "The Story of a Paper Ball," *Puritan* ([Jan.?] 1901): 120; Champenois, "Let's Dress Up," 101–2; Blackburn, *Art, Society and Accomplishments*, 164, 180; Baines, *Fashion Revivals*, 133.

22. Rodney Engen, *Kate Greenaway: A Biography* (New York: Shocken Books, 1981); Ina Taylor, *The Art of Kate Greenaway: A Nostalgic Portrait of Childhood* (Gretna, LA: Pelican, 1991). Greenaway outfits may have been worn by children, but we must remember it was their mothers who made them and organized the parties where they appeared.

23. Entry on Walter Crane on http://www.speel.demon.co.uk/artists/crane.htm (accessed Feb. 2003); Colin White, *The World of the Nursery* (New York: E. P. Dutton, 1984), 119–29; Walter Crane, *Flora's Feast: A Masque of Flowers* (London: Cassell, 1895).

24. Mary Dawson, "A Wonderland Bazaar," *Ladies' World* (May 1911): 25; *Directions for Making Tissue Paper Flowers and Fancy Articles* (New Haven: Yale Silk Works, ca. 1885),

11–12; *Dennison's Dictionary* (Framingham, MA: Dennison, ca. 1908), 99; Jonreau,   **233**
"Novelties in Fancy Dress," 653 (Jonreau also enthused about a "head of lettuce" outfit,
built up with a graduated series of tiny paper leaves); Maie Parke Coyne, *New York Home
Journal*, reprinted in *Household Companion* (Feb. 1892): 41.

25. See Gordon, *BFL*, 118–99; John Neubauer, *The Fin-de-siecle Culture of Adolescence*
(New Haven: Yale UP, 1992); Mrs. Herbert [Hilda] Linscott, "Childhood Party for Grown-
ups," in *Bright Ideas for Entertaining* (Philadelphia: George W. Jacobs, 1905), 62. Note,
however, that when women reached a certain age, it no longer seemed appropriate for
them to take on these particularly picturesque roles. When older, according to the advice
literature, they might more suitably wear "old fashioned" (in my typology, historic)
costumes.

26. David Glassberg, *American Historical Pageantry: The Uses of Tradition in the Early
Twentieth Century* (Chapel Hill: U of North Carolina P, 1990), 27; "Pictures from the
'Realm of the Rose,'" *Puritan* ([Dec.?] 1898): 25.

27. Those dressed as advertisements were actually peddling the products. Gordon,
BFL, 30; Jonreau, "Novelties in Fancy Dress," 653.

28. Emily Rose Burt, *Planning Your Party* (New York and London: Harper and Bros.,
1927), 3; Linscott, *Bright Ideas for Entertaining*, 234.

29. See Stevenson and Bennett, *Van Dyck in Check Trousers*, 87, 95.

30. During the Centennial era, when the term "calico party" was first in common usage,
it was largely synonymous with a patriotic or colonial tea; the term was (inaccurately)
associated with the homespun American past. By the turn of the century, the connotations of the term shifted to the picturesque. Jonreau, "Novelties in Fancy Dress," 651;
Ganahl, "The Story of a Paper Ball," 122; *Art, Society and Accomplishments*, 159–60;
Arden Holt, *Fancy Dresses Described, or What to Wear at Fancy Balls* (London: Debenham
and Freebody, 1879, 6th ed., 1896); Arden Holt, *Gentlemen's Fancy Dress: How to Choose It*
(London: Wyman and Sons, 1882, 3rd ed., 1898); "En Masque," 92–93.

31. Jonreau, "Novelties in Fancy Dress," 651; Ganahl, "The Story of a Paper Ball," 122;
Dennison's Dictionary, 8; *Art and Decoration*, 48; *Directions for Making Tissue Paper Flowers and Fancy Articles* (New Haven, CT: Yale Silk Works, ca. 1885), 12. On crepe paper, see
Beverly Gordon, "'One of the Most Valuable Fabrics': The Seemingly Limitless Promise
of Crepe Paper, 1890–1935," *Ars Textrina* 30 (1999): 1–30.

32. Stevenson and Bennett, *Van Dyck in Check Trousers*, 87, 95; Ganahl, "The Story of
a Paper Ball," 118, 119, 122.

33. *How to Make Paper Costumes* (Framingham, MA: Dennison Manufacturing Company, ca. 1920 [note that there several editions of this, but all are undated]). For a thorough
description of a slipover costume, see also "When Serving a Patriotic Crowd," *Dennison's
Party Magazine* 1 (Jan.–Feb. 1927): 22, 31, and *The Party Book* (Framingham, MA: Dennison Manufacturing, 1922), 23. Because they were most adaptable, the most favored
foundation slips in the 1920s were those that buttoned in the back. On the history of
crepe paper, see Beverly Gordon, "One of the Most Valuable Fabrics," 1–30.

34. Karen Halttunen, *Confidence Men and Painted Women: A Study of Middle Class
Culture in America 1830–1870* (New Haven: Yale UP, 1982), 174–77, 181; Jack W.
McCullough, *Living Pictures on the New York Stage* (Ann Arbor: UMI Research P, 1981).

35. *Boston Post,* Dec. 15 and 21, 1858; Laurel Thatcher Ulrich, *The Age of Homespun: Objects and Stories in the Creation of an American Myth* (New York: Alfred A. Knopf, 2001), 26. Sanitary fairs raised money for the Sanitary Commission, the government agency in charge of hospitals, supplies, and other nonmilitary aspects of the war. Kitchen exhibits were staged (sometimes in locally modified guises) in thirteen of twenty fairs during the Civil War. See Gordon, *BFL,* chap. 3.

36. Fancy dress balls had long been associated with the aristocracy, who could afford to indulge in leisure pastimes that called for a significant financial outlay. Queen Victoria sponsored such balls in the 1840s, helping popularize them for the nineteenth-century public. Baines, *Fashion Revivals,* 129.

37. "Centennial Ball," *Boston Evening Transcript,* Feb. 25, 1876; *Boston Evening Transcript,* Feb. 24, 1876; "Centennial Tea Party," 189–90; Rodris Roth, "The New England, or 'Old Tyme" Kitchen Exhibits at Nineteenth Century Fairs," in Alan Axelrod, ed., *The Colonial Revival in America* (New York: W.W. Norton, 1985), 177–81; Gordon, "Gendered Identity in Historical Dress-Up in America."

38. For a discussion of fundraising fairs and costume, see Gordon, *BFL;* Beverly Gordon, "Dress and Dress-up at the Fundraising Fair," *Dress* 12 (1986): 61–72. Note that terms such as "kirmiss" could be used loosely. Michael Cleary's *Hometown USA* (La Jolla, CA: San Diego Poets P, 1992), includes a picture of a kirmess with women in classical Greek robes rather than European folk dress. This was sponsored by the Odd Fellows and the Woman's Auxiliary of the YMCA in Burlington, VT.

39. Mrs. G. R. Skies, *American Heroines: An Entertainment for Churches and Church Societies, Secular Societies and Lodges* (Dayton, Ohio: Lorenz, 1900); Edna J. Witherspoon, *Fancy Drills for Evening and Other Entertainments* (New York: Butterick, 1894), esp. 25, 49; Lewis O. Saum, "The Broom Brigade, Colonel Donan and *Clementine,*" *Missouri Historical Society Bulletin* 25, no. 3 (1969):192–200; verses from Lucretia Hale and Margaret E. White, *300 Decorative and Fancy Articles for Presents, Fairs, etc.* (Boston: S. W. Tilton, 1885), 166–68.

40. Kathy Peiss, *Cheap Amusements: Working Women and Leisure in Turn of the Century New York* (Philadelphia: Temple UP, 1986), 106–7.

41. Regarding calico parties, see Blackburn, *Art, Society and Accomplishments,* esp. 158–60; Ganahl, "The Story of a Paper Ball," 117–22. Children's costumes *could* still be made by professionals. The Chippewa Valley Museum in Eau Claire, WI, has in its collection a number of "colonial suits" and other outfits from costume parties held in the 1890s. The documentation that accompanied George Shaw's suit indicates that his parents paid someone to make it for him. Because several families had saved their costumes and thought them worthy of donation to the museum, we can surmise that they must have been perceived as rather special.

42. Glassberg, *American Historical Pageantry,* esp. 38, 105; Naima Prevots, *American Pageantry: A Movement for Democracy* (Ann Arbor: UMI Research P, 1990). Note that pageants changed significantly after World War I. "War masques" were common during the war itself, and after it smaller-scale pageants, often sponsored by single groups or schools, or focusing on specific stories, became common.

43. Glassberg, *American Historical Pageantry*, 105; Prevots, *American Pageantry*, 29; Trudy Baltz, "Pageantry and Mural Painting: Community Rituals in Allegorical Form," *Winterthur Portfolio* 15 (Autumn 1980): 212–13.

44. Glassberg, *American Historical Pageantry*, 38; Karen J. Blair, *The Torchbearers: Women and Their Amateur Art Associations in America, 1890–1930* (Bloomington: Indiana UP, 1994), 118–42.

45. Glassberg, *American Historical Pageantry*, 71, 77.

46. Alice Beard, "Historical Origins of Camp Fire," and excerpt from 1914 edition of the *Camp Fire Handbook*, http://members.aol.com/alicebeard/campfire/book/03.html (accessed Dec. 20, 2005); Mary Ann Clawson, *Constructing Brotherhood: Class, Gender and Fraternalism* (Princeton: Princeton UP, 1989), 195. The *Camp Fire Handbook* noted that the ceremonial gown could not be worn in suffrage or other "partisan" parades, as the Camp Fire organization could not take sides, but it was acceptable to wear it in pageant floats.

47. Gordon, *BFL*, 117–19; McCullough, *Living Pictures*, 107, 120–21; Glassberg, *American Historical Pageantry*, 27; Robert W. Rydell, *All the World's a Fair: Visions of Empire at American International Expositions, 1876–1916* (Chicago: U of Chicago P, 1984); Edo McCullough, *World's Fairs Midways* (N.p.: Carnivaland Enterprises, 1966; reprint, n.p.: Arno P, 1976), 38–41; John F. Kasson, *Amusing the Million: Coney Island at the Turn of the Century* (New York: Hill and Wang, 1978); Miles Orvell, *The Real Thing: Imitation and Authenticity in American Culture 1880–1940* (Chapel Hill: U of North Carolina P, 1989); Peiss, *Cheap Amusements*, 115.

48. Burt, *Entertaining Made Easy*, 67, 112; Day, *Social Entertainments*, 18, 23, 28. Regarding costumed hosts and hostesses at coed parties: I believe that setting the hosts off this way may echo the dinner party tradition, wherein the graciousness and prosperity of the hosting family had to be shown off. I have also found one reference (Linscott, *Bright Ideas for Entertaining*, 97) to dressing actual servants in thematic costume. This would strengthen the argument about the outfits serving as a symbolic livery.

49. Day, *Social Entertainments*, 33; Beatrice Plumb, *Here's for a Good Time: A Collection of Parties for Holidays and All Kinds of Miscellaneous Social Occasions* (Minneapolis: T. S. Denison, 1929), 88–90.

50. Mrs. Herbert [Hilda] Linscott, *Bright Ideas for Entertaining*, rev. ed. (New York: Grosset & Dunlap with Macrae, Smith, 1935), 246–50. An earlier (1905) edition of this book is much sketchier about the "Poverty Sociable," although the same costumes and playful language were included on the invitation (156). "Come in your rags, come in your tags," stated the invitation; "but not in velvet gowns, or you will be fined the usual, some 25 sents [*sic*]."

51. Cecil H. Bullivant, *Home Fun* (New York: Dodge, 1910); *Novelties That Create Fun*, catalogue no. 33 (Chicago: Rainbo Paper Favor Works, ca. 1925).

52. Mike Weaver, *Julia Margaret Cameron 1815–1879* (Boston: Little, Brown [NY Graphic Society], 1984).

53. Naomi Rosenblum, *A History of Women Photographers* (New York: Abbeville P, 1994), 55–60; Madelyn Kay Moeller, *Ladies of Leisure: Domestic Photographers in the*

236 *Nineteenth Century* (Master's thesis, University of Delaware, 1989), 18, 48; Peter E. Palmquist, preface to Women in Photography Archive, http://www.sla.purdue.edu/ WAAW/Palmquist/Essays.htm (accessed Sept. 2003).

54. Sarah E. Slater, "Profitable Industries for Women—Photography," *Woman's Magazine* (Feb. 1904): 29; Rosenblum, *A History of Women Photographers*, 60, 64.

55. Rosenblum, *A History of Women Photographers*, 95, 100; Marie Kendall, "An Afternoon with Dolls," *American Amateur Photographer* (Apr. 1992): 143–46; Juan C. Abel, "Women Photographers and Their Work," *Delineator* (Nov. 1901): 750; Moeller, *Ladies of Leisure*, 58; Marjorie L. McLellan, *Six Generations Here: A Farm Family Remembers* (Madison: State Historical Society of Wisconsin, 1997), 73–78.

56. Moeller, *Ladies of Leisure*, 144.

57. Joyce P. Barendsen, "Wallace Nutting, an American Tastemaker: The Pictures and Beyond," *Winterthur Portfolio* 18 (Summer/Autumn 1983): esp. 212.

58. Lisa M. Koenigsberg, *Professionalizing Domesticity: A Tradition of American Women Writers on Architecture, 1848–1912* (Ph.D. diss., Yale U, 1987), 177–226; Suzanne L. Flynt, "The Arts and Crafts Movement in Deerfield," paper presented at Historic Deerfield (MA) symposium "Aspects of the Arts and Crafts Movement in New England," Nov. 1996; Suzanne L. Flynt, *The Allen Sisters: Pictorial Photographers, 1885–1920* (Deerfield: Pocumtuck Valley Memorial Association with UP of New England, 2002); Moeller, *Ladies of Leisure*, 35, 117; Sarah L. Giffen and Kevin D. Murphy, *A Noble and Dignified Stream: The Piscataqua Region in the Colonial Revival, 1860–1930* (York, ME: Old York Historical Society, 1992), esp. 130. Another successful photographer of this type was Chansonetta Emmons, who had trained as an artist in Boston. She too specialized in costumed individuals engaged in rural occupations.

59. Giffen and Murphy, *A Noble and Dignified Stream*, 130.

60. Nellie Mustain, *Popular Amusements for Indoors and Out-of-Doors* (Chicago, 1902), 34, 39, 128.

61. Ann Novotny, *Alice's World: The Life and Photography of an American Original: Alice Austen, 1866–1952* (Old Greenwich, CT: Chatham P, 1976), 51.

62. Burt, *Planning Your Party*, 133; "Six Crepe Paper Costumes"; Cynthia Cooper and Linda Welters, "Brilliant and Instructive Spectacles: Canada's Fancy Dress Balls, 1876–1898," *Dress* 22 (1995):16.

63. See Gordon, "Gendered Identity in Historical Dress-Up in America."

64. When the term "fancy dress" appeared in the entertainment advice literature, it almost always referred to seemingly more formal coeducational events. See for example "A Fancy Dress Party," *Hints on Entertaining* (Minneapolis: Minneapolis Young Women's Christian Association and Minneapolis Tribune, 1897), 95–96.

65. *Atlanta Constitution*, Dec. 10–11, 1900; *Milwaukee Journal*, May 7–9, 15, 1896.

66. *Entertaining with Cards*, 29.

67. Burt, *Entertaining Made Easy*, 61–65; Linscott, *Bright Ideas for Entertaining*, 79, 155–56; Mustain, *Popular Amusements*, 36; Bullivant, *Home Fun*, 56–61.

68. Mark C. Carnes, *Secret Ritual and Manhood in Victorian America* (New Haven: Yale University P, 1989), 1, 43–50; Barbara Franco, "The Ritualization of Male Friendship and Virtue in Nineteenth Century Fraternal Organizations," paper presented at Winter-

thur Conference on the Material Culture of Gender, Wintherthur, DE, Nov. 10, 1989; Mary Ann Clawson, *Constructing Brotherhood: Class, Gender and Fraternalism* (Princeton: Princeton University P, 1989), 175; Foster Rhea Dulles, *America Learns to Play: A History of Popular Recreation 1607–1940* (New York: Appleton-Century, 1940), 254–57.

69. Catalogue, Ihling Brothers Everard Co. (Kalamazoo, MI, n.d.), misc. pages. Other examples include Pettibone Bros., catalogue #791 (Cincinnati, OH, ca. 1910); Henderson-Ames Co. catalogue #8 (Kalamazoo, MI, 1912). Some scholars talk about the way fraternal rituals also helped men express the "softer," feminine side of themselves. See Franco, "The Ritualization of Male Friendship"; Clawson, *Constructing Brotherhood*, 13.

70. Dulles, *America Learns to Play,* 255–56.

71. *Atlanta Constitution,* Dec. 10–11, 1900; *Milwaukee Journal,* May 7–9, 15, 1896.

5. Iconic Dolls and Household Helpers

1. Emma Churchman Hewitt, *Queen of the Home: Her Reign from Infancy to Age, from Attic to Cellar* (Oakland: H. J. Smith, 1889), 253–54. In my article "Woman's Domestic Body: The Conceptual Conflation of Women and Interiors in the Industrial Age," *Winterthur Portfolio* 31 (Winter 1996): 281–30, I quote the 1879 guide *The Complete Home,* which told the story of a sickly, disabled girl named Margaret who was given tasks related to fixing up the house as a form of therapy. On surveying the results of her handiwork, Margaret "lean[ed] back with a sigh of satisfaction," saying, "Don't I look nice! . . . Why I feel almost well." Margaret identified so completely with the room she had worked on that she had literally became one with it. By "fixing" her house, she had fixed herself. See Julia McNair Wright, *The Complete Home: An Encyclopaedia of Domestic Life and Affairs* (Philadelphia: J. C. McCurdy, 1879), 167–68.

2. Beverly Gordon, "Victorian Fancywork in the American Home: Fantasy and Accommodation," in Marilyn Motz and Pat Browne, eds., *Making the American Home: Middle Class Women and Domestic Material Culture, 1840–1940* (Bowling Green, OH: Bowling Green State University Popular P, 1988), 48–68; *Ornamental Toys and How to Make Them* (Boston: Cyrus Cooke, ca. 1870), 3; *Oxford English Dictionary,* s.v. "fancy."

3. Jane Weaver, "Doll Pincushion," *Peterson's Magazine* (Sept. 1865): 209; Jane Weaver, "The Little Companion," *Peterson's Magazine* (Jan. 1865): 79; Caroline Smith (Aunt Carrie) *American Home Book of Indoor Games, Recreations and Occupations* (Boston: Lee and Shepard, 1872), 15; *Godey's Lady's Book* (Mar. 1868), pictured in Katharine Morrison McClinton, *Antiques of American Childhood* (New York: Branhall House, 1970), 199; Eliza Leslie, *The American Girl's Book, or Occupations for Play Hours* (New York: R. Worthington, 1879); Frances E. Lanigan, "Christmas Gifts for Women," *Ladies' Home Journal* (Dec. 1896): 24.

4. LEZA, *Ladies Floral Cabinet and Pictorial Home Companion* (Apr. 1874): 59; *Ornamental Toys and How to Make Them,* 31. Fancywork objects with women's shapes were also sometimes given as gifts to men—see Frances E. Lanigan, "Christmas Gifts for Men," *Ladies' Home Journal* (Dec. 1896): 25. On the abundance of dolls in the last part of the nineteenth century, see Miriam Formanek-Brunell, "Sugar and Spite: The Politics of Doll Play in Nineteenth-Century America," in Elliott West and Paula Petrik, eds., *Small Worlds: Children and Adolescents in America, 1850–1950* (Kansas City: UP of Kansas,

1992), 107–24. So-called peddler dolls—figures outfitted with baskets of miniature "wares"—were also popular toys in the nineteenth century. Peddler dolls usually represented old women, and they had no practical function. See Bea Howe, *Antiques from the Victorian Home* (London: Batsford, 1973), 163–64; Lesley Gordon, *A Pageant of Dolls* (New York: A. A. Wyn, 1949), 30. Note also that the interconnection between dolls and needlework had a long history. "Stumpwork," a type of embroidery popular among aristocratic English women in the sixteenth and seventeenth centuries, for example, involved the stitch-by-stitch construction of miniature well-dressed figures. See Muriel L. Baker, *Stumpwork: The Art of Raised Embroidery* (New York: Scribner, 1978); Thomasina Beck, *Embroidered Gardens* (New York: Viking P), 1979.

5. S. F. A. Caulfeild and Blanche C. Saward, *The Dictionary of Needlework: An Encyclopedia of Artistic, Plain and Fancy Work* (London, L. U. Gill, 1887), supplement; *Our Homes: How to Beautify Them* (New York: O. Judd, 1888), 54, 71–72. Fittingly, in *Household Magazine*, which was published from 1868 to 1903, the fancywork section where this kind of item was discussed was called "The Dressing Room."

6. Smith, *American Home Book of Indoor Games*, 10–12; *Art and Decoration in Crepe and Tissue Paper* (Framingham, MA: Dennison Manufacturing, ca. 1896), 92–95; Raphael Tuck series and other internationally dressed paper dolls in Maxine Madsen Waldron Papers, Downs Collection, Winterthur Library. Specific historic references and further discussion of doll fairs are included in Gordon, *BFL*, 138, 141, 248. We can intuit that dressing dolls was as much an adult pleasure as a child's pastime because the type of doll most consistently recommended for girls' play in this period was a baby—a doll so young that she would not yet wear dress-up costume. See Marilyn Ferris Motz, "Maternal Virgin: The Girl and Her Doll in Nineteenth-century America," in *Objects of Special Devotion: Fetishes and Fetishism in Popular Culture* (Bowling Green, OH: Bowling Green State UP, 1982): 54–68. I was also told by a woman who remembered being in charge of doll booth at a church fair in 1915 that some of the dolls in miniaturized tableaux were dressed by milliners (personal conversation with Evelyn Huggins, Madison, Wisconsin, 1986). The importance of dressing dolls in various outfits has been linked to the idea that the display of fashion was extremely important in Victorian America (see Formanek-Brunell, "Sugar and Spite," 115), but I believe that fantasy and playfulness were more salient motivations, just as they were in full-scale dress-up.

7. Flower-doll making was considered a child's pastime, and since it was children who were most often dressed in this sweet and innocent-looking fashion, the parallel to dress-up is particularly resonant.

8. Smith, *American Home Book of Indoor Games*, 26–27; Margaret Coulson Walker, *Lady Hollyhock and Her Friends: A Book of Nature Dolls and Others* (New York: Baker and Taylor, 1906), 50–52; Joyce Lankester Brisley, *Bunchy* (Philadelphia: David McKay, ca. 1930); Lina and Adelia B. Beard, *Indoor and Outdoor Handicraft Recreation for Girls* (New York: Charles Scribner's Sons, 1904), 323–25. Alternately, clothes pin dolls could be dressed in crepe paper, which draped much like a flower petal. See *Art and Decoration in Crepe and Tissue Paper*, 92–95.

9. Walker, *Lady Hollyhock*, 31.

10. Maude Nash, *Children's Occupations* (Boston: Houghton Mifflin, 1921), 56; Lina and Adelia B. Beard, *New Ideas for Work and Play: What a Girl Can Make and Do* (New

York: Scribner's, 1902), 102–3; *The American Home Book of Indoor Games*, 322–23; Marie Overton Corbin and Charles Buxton Going, "Child's Garden of Vegetables," *Puritan* (1900–1901): 593–97.

11. Alan Meisler, *Vegetable People: 30 Original Victorian Postcards from the World-Class Meisler Collection* (N.p.: SPI Books, Cards Edition, 1998); reproductions of the Rice trade cards are now available from Classic Image Prints, http://www.classicimageprints. com/cip/cipstock/classic.htm (accessed Jan. 25, 2006); L. Frank Baum, Dorothy and the Wizard in Oz, cited in the Online Literature Library, http://www.literature.org/authors/ baum-l-frank/dorothy-and-the-wizard-in-oz/ (accessed Jan. 25, 2006); D. Barton Johnson, "Nabokov's Golliwogs: Lodi Reads English, 1899–1090," http://www.libraries.psu.edu/ nabokov/dbjgo4.htm (accessed Jan. 25, 2006); "Florence Upton . . . Creator of the Golliwog," http://www.teddybears.com/golliwog/issue/10gw2a.htm (Web sites accessed July 2003). Note that the first Golliwog book was called *The Adventures of Two Dutch Dolls and a Golliwog*. Thirteen Golliwog books were published between 1895 and 1909.

12. Bertha Johnston, *Home Occupations for Boys and Girls* (Philadelphia: George W. Jacobs, 1908), 5.

13. Walker, *Lady Hollyhock*, 11, 50–52, 95.

14. Ibid., 61; *American Home Book of Indoor Games, Recreations and Occupations*, 332–33.

15. I have been unable to find an actual birth date and am approximating based on the time she began teaching. The scanty biographical information I do have comes from accession records to *The Garden Party of the Vegetable Folks* at the Wisconsin Historical Society. This is also the source of other statements about von Bachellé's life, below.

16. Jeanne Madeline Weimann, *The Fair Women: The Story of the Woman's Building, World's Columbian Exposition, Chicago, 1893* (Chicago: Academy Chicago, 1981), vii; Lionel Lambourne, *Utopian Craftsmen: The Arts and Crafts Movement from the Cotswolds to Chicago* (Salt Lake City, UT: Peregrine Smith, 1980); http://www.cl.utoledo.edu/canaday/ artsandcrafts/midwest.html (accessed Dec. 20, 2005); http://www.craftsmanperspective. com/docs/history-1920.html (accessed Dec. 20, 2005). "Miss Jenks," who was mentioned in chap. 2 (she was the Art Institute student who made one of Anita Blair's paper doll houses), would have been part of this same arts community.

17. The sunflower seems to have functioned here as a symbol for African Americans. *Good Housekeeping* featured a paper doll called "Little Louise" in 1909, for example, that was draped in sunflowers. Original found in Maxine Madsen Waldron Papers, Downs Collection, Winterthur Library.

18. Mrs. Herbert [Hilda] Linscott, *Up-To-Date Social Affairs* (Philadelphia: George W. Jacobs, 1924), 118–21; advertisement for Farmer Boy doll, *Needlecraft* (Dec. 1931): 22; *Needlecraft* (Jul. 1932): p. unclear; Christine Ferry and E. Marion Stevens, *Needlecraft* (Apr. 1933): 7; Marian Hagen Schieff, "Stuffies You Can Make," *Ladies' Home Journal* (Jan. 1938): 62. Note that cutesy, alliterative names of this sort had been common in the women's press for some time. In 1874 contributors to the *Ladies Floral Cabinet and Pictorial Home Companion* used pseudonyms such as "Winnie Wiseacre," "Daisy Chain," and "Birdie Wren." Popular paper dolls that appeared in the women's magazines also bore names such as "Dorothy Dimple," "Dolly Della," and "Dottie Darling." Stuffed animal toys were popular in the 1930s; there was even a whole book on the subject: Edith Moody, *Dressed*

240   *Soft Toys* (New York: Dryad P, 1937). For more about happy, escapist imagery in the interwar years, see Beverly Gordon, "Spinning Wheels, Samplers and the Modern Priscilla: The Images and Paradoxes of Colonial Revival Needlework," *Winterthur Portfolio* 33 (Summer/Autumn 1998): 163–94.

19. Dream cottage cushion design by Marie Hawthorne, *Needlecraft* (May 1931): 28–9; "Easter Gift Whimsies," *Needlecraft* (Apr. 1933): 7.

20. *The Only True Mother Goose* (Boston: G. W. Cotrell, 1833), n.p.

21. For more on the new housewifely roles and the needlework that reflected it, see Beverly Gordon, "Cozy, Charming and Artistic: Stitching Together the Home Environment," in Jessica Foy and Karal Ann Marling, eds., *The Arts and the American Home, 1890–1930* (Knoxville: U of Tennessee P, 1994), 124–48.

22. "Pottery Lady," in "On the Feminine Side," *Good Housekeeping* (Nov. 1927): 65; "Ribbon Displays Its Facile Beauty in These Dainty Trifles That May Be Easily Made at Home," *Good Housekeeping* (Feb. 1923): 56; Junia, "Snipping and Stitching," *Farmer's Advocate* (Dec. 8, 1927): 1782; "Lace and Fine Linens," *Good Housekeeping* (Dec. 1925): 66.

23. *Needlecraft* (Feb. 1923), 10; Carolyn Wells, "Christmas Presents," *Puritan* (Dec. 1900): 439; Patricia A. Turner, *Ceramic Uncles and Celluloid Mammies: Black Images and Their Influence on Culture* (New York: Anchor Books, 1994), 49–51. There was also a fad for "topsy-turvy dolls," rag dolls made so that turned one way, they had a white face, but turned upside-down, they had an African American face (the long skirt would cover the face in whichever direction the doll was turned).

Note that African-American figures were certainly popular before the turn of the century—for example, images that recalled the characters of *Uncle Tom's Cabin* were familiar at the time of the Civil War. A "Dinah Penwiper" pictured in *Godey's Lady's Book* in 1861, reproduced in McClinton's *Antiques of American Childhood* (199), is an example of this longstanding black helper. These Civil War–era figures were not generally referred to overtly as "mammies," however, and this particular Dinah is slightly dressier-looking than the typical mammy figure of the turn of the century.

24. The accession number of this object is 258257; its catalog number is T.16203.

25. Turner, *Ceramic Uncles and Celluloid Mammies*, 49–51; *Hostess* (Mar. 1924): 14; Myrtle Jamison Trachsel, "A Plantation Party: Memories of the 'Old South'," *Dennison's Party Magazine* (Jul.–Aug. 1927): 12. Note that string holders were easy to make, but they could also be purchased ready-made; *Good Housekeeping* offered one in 1926 in an attractive box with an extra ball of twine for a dollar. ("Important Christmas Trifles," *Good Housekeeping* (Nov. 1926): 88.) The last instruction I have seen for an Aunt Jemima twine holder was in *Home Arts* (formerly *Needlecraft*) (Dec. 1938): p. unclear. (This magazine claimed more than seven hundred thousand readers at this time, so we can assume this kind of object was still widespread.)

26. Anna G. Bailey, "First Aid in the Laundry," *Needlecraft* (Nov. 1923): 17. Interestingly, while the description refers to "Bridget" in a bonnet, the illustration that accompanies Bailey's description sports a turban and a very dark complexion; she looks more like a mammy than an Irish maid.

27. Handwritten note to the author, Mar. 1988. The doll was given to me by Marian DeLong Merill's son, who provided the contextual information about the wedding shower.

28. L.S.C., "Centerpiece for a Kitchen Shower," sent into Betty Somerville, "And the Way That We Did It Was This: An Exchange of Party Ideas," *Dennison's Party Magazine* (Jul.–Aug. 1928): 16–17.

29. Ellye Howell Glover, *"Dame Curtsey's" Art of Entertaining for All Occasions* (Chicago: A. C. McClurg, 1913), 258–59.

30. Adele Mendel, *Indoor Merrymaking and Table Decorations* (Boston and Chicago: W. A. Wilde, 1915), 50.

31. *Legacies: Collecting America's History at the Smithsonian* (Washington, DC: Smithsonian Institution P, 2001), 222; also see http://www.smithsonianlegacies.si.edu/object description.cfm?ID=245 (accessed Dec. 15, 2005).

32. Helen Emily Webster, *Shower Parties for All Occasions* (New York: The Woman's P [National Board of the YWCA], 1949), 31–32; http://www.allsands.com/Misc4/bridal showergi_uko_gn.htm (accessed Apr. 12, 2004).

33. Trachsel, "A Plantation Party," 12; "Piccaninny [*sic*] Licorice Doll," *Dennison's Party Magazine* (Jul.–Aug. 1928): 28; Mendel, *Indoor Merrymaking,* 57; Corinne Wentworth, *Entertainment for All Occasions: Parties Completely Planned for Evenings, Luncheons, Afternoons, Holidays and Other Occasions* (New York and Newark: Barse and Hopkins, 1921, 1926), 55. To contemporary readers, the description of the 1927 Plantation Party is particularly offensive, as it was to be "fashioned after the rollicking, happy-go-lucky revels of the cotton pickers" of old.

34. Shackman's Favors (New York: B. Shackman, 1910); *Novelties That Create Fun,* catalogue no. 33 (Chicago: Rainbo Paper Favor Works, ca. 1925); *Art and Decoration in Crepe and Tissue Paper,* 92–95; 142–43; *Dennison's Dictionary* (Framingham, MA: Dennison, ca. 1908), 122–25; *Let's Make Whoopie! Favors and Decorations for Hallowe'en, Armistice Day, Christmas, and Other Celebrations* (Chicago: Slack Manufacturing, ca. 1925).

Before World War I, Dennison seemed to expect its customers to make their own paper doll dresses, but soon after, it offered printed sheets, ready to be cut out. These premade versions were aimed more pointedly at children. By the mid-1930s, the company had already arrived at the presentation of simple tabbed dresses that is familiar to us today. An edition of the company's Little Tot's Crepe Paper Doll Outfit that dates from this time included international characters such as "Eileen from Ireland," "Cecile from France," and "Franz from Switzerland."

35. *How to Entertain at Home* (Boston: Priscilla Pub., 1928), 96–97.

36. Elisabeth L. Cameron, *Isn't S/he a Doll? Play and Ritual in African Sculpture* (Los Angeles: U.C.L.A. Fowler Museum, 1996), esp. 12, 18–19.

37. Cited in Cameron, *Isn't S/he a Doll?,* 22.

38. In our own time, such "holders" are used to cover up toilet paper rolls.

39. Agnes Hooper Gottlieb, *Women Journalists and the Municipal Housekeeping Movement 1868–1914* (N.p.: Edwin Mellen P, 2001); "Charming Samplers for the Little House," (designs by Eveline D. Johnson, verse by Grace Noll Crowell), *Needlecraft* (Jan. 1933): 19; Grace Noll Crowell, "The Sampler," *Good Housekeeping* (Feb. 1933): 94. In relation to von Bachellés creation, note that during the 1930s there was a new rage for rag dolls and stuffed animals with names such as "Snuggle Pussy" and "Jolly Johnnie Bullfrog."

40. With this assertion, I am not including the commercially produced figures such as the Smithsonian's pincushion sent as through the mail as a gag gift; I am referring only to those handmade dolls in which women invested their own time and energy.

41. Cameron, *Isn't S/he a Doll?*, 14.

42. In a study of women's tradition of doll making in Maine, Margaret R. Yocum concluded that women particularly value the period of childhood and childhood play that teaches children to be nurturing. See "'Awful Real': Dolls and Development in Rangeley, Maine," in Joan Newton Radner, ed., *Feminist Messages: Coding in Women's Folk Culture* (Urbana and Chicago: U of Illinois P, 1993), 147.

43. Iconic dolls made by members of separatist societies (for example, the Shakers) or groups of outsiders or "others" (for example, American Indians) may mark the exception to this statement. Shaker women dressed dolls in their own image in a way that was serious rather than comical; it projected a sense of pride and strength. See Beverly Gordon, "Victorian Fancy Goods: Another Reappraisal of Shaker Material Culture," *Winterthur Portfolio* 25, nos. 2/3 (1990): 111–29.

44. Cameron, *Isn't S/he a Doll?*, 27. Making and dressing dolllike figures is still part of popular culture today. Few women regularly dress up themselves, but many still enjoy embellishing ready-made human and animal figures.

6. Collecting

1. Papers of Maxine Maxson Waldron, Waldron Collection, Joseph Downs Collection of Manuscripts and Printed Ephemera, Winterthur Library, Winterthur, Del. The article was not clearly dated and might have been from either 1919 or 1920.

2. While the overall cut-off date for *The Saturated World* is about 1940, some of the individuals I am profiling continued their collecting activities after that date. All of them, however, began before World War II, and all developed their collecting attitudes in the earlier period. This is significant because collecting began to be seen as a much more "serious" pastime after World War II; it became less of a hobby and more of an avocation.

3. The arenas of collecting and amusement also overlapped for male advice-givers. Cecil Henry Bullivant, author of *Home Fun* (New York: Dodge, 1910), also wrote *Every Boy's Book of Hobbies* (New York: Dodge, 1912).

4. In today's terms some of the objects would now be categorized as antiques, others collectibles, others art. While hierarchies certainly existed, these categories were not codified in the collecting period I am concerned with and were of little concern to the women I am writing about. Categorizations *have* made a great difference in the way that women's collecting activities have been understood and received, however, and are taken up later in this chapter.

5. Fittingly, *The China Hunter's Club* follows the same format; each chapter is written as an individual's story. The tales are peppered with a liberal use of colorful dialogue. This literary presentation is akin to the presentation of entertaining advice discussed in chap 3.

6. Annie Trumbull Slosson, *The China Hunter's Club* (New York: Harper and Bros., 1878), quotes from 13, 243; Elizabeth Stillinger, "Edna Greenwood," presentation at Per-

ceptions of the Past—Private Collections, Public Collections conference, Winterthur **243** Museum and Gardens, Oct. 7, 1994.

7. Steven Gelber, *Hobbies: Leisure and the Culture of Work in America* (New York: Columbia UP, 1999), 130; Richard Henry Saunders, *American Decorative Arts Collecting in New England 1840–1920* (Master's thesis, U of Delaware, 1973); Karal Ann Marling, *George Washington Slept Here: Colonial Revivals and American Culture, 1876–1986* (Cambridge: Harvard UP, 1988), 39.

8. Gustav Stickley, "From Ugliness to Beauty," *Craftsman* 7 (Dec. 1904): 315; Suzanne L. Flynt, *The Allen Sisters: Pictorial Photographers, 1885–1920* (Deerfield, MA: Pocumtuck Valley Memorial Association with UP of New England, 2002).

9. Alice Morse Earle, *Colonial Dames and Good Wives* (Boston: Houghton Mifflin, 1895); Saunders, *American Decorative Arts Collecting*, esp. 8, 29, 82; Elizabeth Stillinger, *The Antiquers* (New York: Alfred A. Knopf, 1980), xi–xiii. For more on the domestic vision promulgated by turn-of-the-century women, see Susan Williams, "In the Garden of New England: Alice Morse Earle and the History of Domestic Life" (Ph.D. diss., U of Delaware, 1992); Beverly Gordon, "Spinning Wheels, Samplers and the Modern Priscilla: The Images and Paradoxes of Colonial Revival Needlework," *Winterthur Portfolio* 33 (Summer/Autumn 1998): 163–94. The latter article also provides information on the collecting of textiles.

10. Caroline Frear Burk, "The Collecting Instinct," *Pedagogical Seminary* 7 (Jan. 1900): 179–207.

11. Ibid, 196, 204.

12. Gelber, *Hobbies*, 102.

13. Chelsea Curtis Fraser, *Every Boy's Book of Handicraft, Sports and Amusements* (Boston: Dana Estes, 1913), 253; Janet E. Ruutz-Rees, *Home Occupations* (New York: Appleton, 1883), 95; Mrs. Henry Mackarness, *The Young Ladies' Book: Amusements, Exercises, Studies & Persuits* (London: Routledge, 1872); Lilla Elizabeth Kelley, *Three Hundred Things a Bright Girl Can Do* (Boston: Page, 1903), 523; Beard, *New Ideas for Work and Play*, 69–88.

14. Emma Churchman Hewitt, *Queen of the Home: Her Reign from Infancy to Age, from Attic to Cellar* (Oakland: H. J. Smith, 1889), 253; E. Landells, *The Boy's Own Toymaker: A Practical Illustrated Guide to the Useful Employment of Leisure Hours* (Boston: Shepard, Clark and Brown, 1859), vii; E. Landells and (his daughter) Alice Landells, *The Girl's Own Toymaker and Book of Recreation* (London: Griffin and Ferran, 1860) Edna A.[bigail] Foster, *Something to Do—Girls!* (Boston and Chicago: W. A. Wilde, 1916), n.p.; Edna A. Foster, *Something to Do—Boys!* (Boston and Chicago: W. A. Wilde, 1916), n.p. Tellingly, even the very audience the latter books were aimed at differed, and this indicated the more relational expectations for females. The *Boy's Own Toymaker* was written for the boys themselves—anyone who was "old enough to use a penknife" could follow it. The girls' volume was directed toward mothers, who would teach their daughters what to do.

15. Louis H. Hertz, *Antique Collecting for Men* (New York: Galahad Books, 1969), 3–7; Major H. Byng Hall, *The Bric-A-Brac Hunter; or, Chapters on Chinamania* (Philadelphia: J. B. Lippincott, 1875), 21–22; Donna Gail Rosenstein, "'Historic Human Tools': Henry Chapman Mercer and His Collection, 1897–1930" (Master's thesis, U of Delaware, 1977), 8, 27, 33, 46; Stillinger, *The Antiquers*, 255. Note that Mercer had originally hoped to

244   open an outdoor museum—the very opposite of the "domesticated" interior space he abhorred. Ford's Greenfield Village is in part a realization of this outdoor vision.

16. Gelber, *Hobbies,* 115–17; Werner Muensterberger, *Collecting: An Unruly Passion, Psychological Perspectives* (Princeton: Princeton UP, 1994), 138; Slosson, *The China Hunter's Club,* last chap.

17. Saunders, *American Decorative Arts Collecting,* 104–11; Hall, *The Bric-A-Brac Hunter,* 16; details on Rebecca Gratz from a letter sent by Henry Francis du Pont to Philip Spalding, Jan. 13, 1933, in the Henry Francis du Pont Winterthur Library archives, Winterthur, DE; other observations about the Walpole Society are from the Society Notebooks and miscellaneous materials in du Pont's papers. See also Stillinger, *The Antiquers,* 165–70. As Stillinger points out (169), the Walpole Society never admitted Henry Ford because he did not have the right ancestry.

18. George Blake Dexter, *The Lure of Amateur Collecting* (Boston: Little, Brown, 1923); C. R. Clifford, *The Junk Snupper: The Adventures of an Antique Collector* (New York: Macmillan, 1925), esp. 31, 132, 147, 165; Ramsay and Mackail cited in Gelber, *Hobbies,* 82.

19. Rupert Sargent Holland, "Boy's Hunt for Big Game," *St. Nicholas* (Dec. 1925): 156–59; Gelber, *Hobbies,* 84, 92. Bibliophiles Reginald Brewer, William Dana Orcutt, and Gabriel Wells are cited in Gelber, *Hobbies,* 64, 72.

20. Diana Jean Schemo, "For Musical Appreciation, Sexes Go Their Own Way," *New York Times,* Nov. 15, 1994, C1. For another recent study showing the same gender attitudes in contemporary collecting, see Russell Belk and Melanie Wallendorf, "Of Mice and Men: Gender Identity and Collecting," in Katherine Martinez and Kenneth L. Ames, eds., *The Material Culture of Gender/The Gender of Material Culture.* (Winterthur, DE: Henry Francis du Pont Museum with UP of New England, 1997), 7–26.

21. We might say that, effectively, their hunts were often really gathering expeditions.

22. Even a wealthy woman such as Abby Aldrich Rockefeller was known for her interest in Indian art as well as folk and modern art. She was reportedly the first collector of blackware pottery made by Maria Martinez of San Ildefonso Pueblo. See Bernice Kert, *Abby Aldrich Rockefeller: The Woman in the Family* (New York: Random House, 1993), 232.

23. Mame A. Keene, "A Plea for the Ladies," *Pennsylvania Philatelist* (Oct. 1893): 20, and Maud Charlotte Bingham, "My Stamp Album," *Pennsylvania Philatelist* (Jun. 1894): 334, cited in Gelber, *Hobbies,* 117; Ruutz-Rees, *Home Occupations,* 97–98.

24. Henry Mercer, who was especially virulent in his derogatory comments, seems to have gone to an opposite extreme: his collection of the "important tools that men had devised" included horrifying torture devices (personal observation at Mercer Museum, 1994). They represented a pointed counterpoint to the saturated fairyland image the women were promoting.

25. Louise Paine Benjamin, "Do Men Have the Most Fun?" *Ladies' Home Journal* (Oct. 1939): 74, cited in Gelber 103–4; Ruutz-Rees, *Home Occupations,* 92; Helen Bowen, "The Quilting Quest," *House Beautiful* (Jan. 1924): 48.

26. Stephen Birmingham, *The Grandes Dames* (New York: Simon and Schuster, 1982), 76; Electra Webb, "Mrs. Webb's Williamsburg Speech," (typescript of presentation given Jan. 30, 1958), 3; Betsy Brayer, *Margaret Woodbury Strong and the Origins of the Strong*

Museum (Rochester: Strong Museum, 1982), 2, 5, 15; Ella Shannon Bowles, *About Antiques* (Philadelphia: J. B. Lippincott, 1919), 65; Letter from Frieda E. Smith to Maxine Waldron, Jan. 22, 1962, in Waldron Collection; Catherine Collison commentary on a page from mimeographed notes of doll club meeting, unidentified date (based on context, it might be Oct. 28, 1947), in Waldron Collection. In her presentation at the 1994 Winterthur collecting conference, "Printed Ephemera Collectors and Collections: A Case Study of the Maxine Waldron and Thelma Mendsen Collections," Mary-Elise Haug observed that much of what twentieth-century women collected was material that was part of girls' childhood training in the nineteenth century. It is interesting to note, also, that many of the wealthier women collectors I am considering in this study had traveled extensively in their youth and were exposed to unfamiliar daily customs and activities. Later they collected items that reflected those same kinds of activities.

27. Alice Kent Trimpey, *The Story of My Dolls* (Racine, WI, and Poughkeepsie, NY: Whitman, 1935), 16; Alice Van Leer Carrick, *Collector's Luck; or, A Repository of Pleasant and Profitable Discourses of the Household Furnishings and Ornaments of Olden Time* (Boston: Atlantic Monthly, 1919), 1, 4. A sense of pride about overcoming elemental difficulties for the sake of the collection comes through in a number of women's writings. In *Collecting Hooked Rugs* (New York: Century, 1927), 109–22, Elizabeth Waugh and Edith Foley write of a trip to Cape Breton that involved having to find someone to take them to remote areas in howling winter storms and then, because the sea was ice-blocked, being forced to wait for so long that the food supply on the boat was getting low.

28. Letter from Alberta Anderson to Nellie Maclochlan, Mar. 21, 1951, in Waldron Collection; Carrick, *Collector's Luck*, 8; Amy Lyman Phillips, "Hitting the Trail of the Antique: Adventures in the King's Domain," *House Beautiful* (Apr. 1925): 474–75.

29. Mary Harrod Northend, "Hunting for Antiques," unpublished manuscript in the files of the Society of the Preservation of New England Antiquities, cited in Saunders, *American Decorative Arts Collecting*, 155; Georgia Dickinson Wardlaw, *The Old and Quaint in Virginia* (Richmond: Dietz P, 1939); Virginia Robie, *Bypaths in Collecting* (New York: Century, 1912), intro.; Mrs. Willoughby Hodgson, *The Quest of the Antique* (London: Herbert Jenkins, 1924), 7.

30. Letter from Avis Gardiner to Maxine Waldron, Aug. 16, 1960, Waldron Collection; Nina Fletcher Little, *Little by Little: Six Decades of Collecting American Decorative Arts* (New York: E. P. Dutton, 1984), 38; Letter from Elizabeth Day McCormick to G. Harold Edgell, Dec. 7, 1938, Boston Museum of Fine Arts [hereafter, MFA] Archives; Letter from Marian Howard to Maxine Waldron, Feb. 17, 1960, Waldron Collection.

31. Robie, *By-Paths in Collecting*, 60, 49; Electra Webb, "Museum Notes," Mar. 17, 1961 (penciled notes copied and typed by Lilian Carlisle), Shelburne Museum Archives; Zona Gale, introduction to Trimpey, *The Story of My Dolls*, n.p.; Letter from Elizabeth Day McCormick to G. Harold Edgell, Feb. 19, 1944, MFA Archives; Robert and Elizabeth Shackleton, *The Charm of the Antique* (New York: Hearst International Library, 1912), 1; Esther Singleton, *The Collecting of Antiques* (New York: Macmillan, 1926), 2–3.

32. Webb, "Museum Notes;" Bowles, *About Antiques*, 211; Susan Stewart, *On Longing: Narratives of the Miniature, the Gigantic, the Souvenir, the Collection* (Durham: U of North Carolina P, 1993), 46, 112; Beverly Gordon, "Intimacy and Objects: A Proxemic

246   Analysis of Gender-Based Response to the Material World" in Katherine Martinez and
        Kenneth Ames, eds., *The Material Culture of Gender/The Gender of Material Culture*
        (Winterthur, DE: Winterthur Museum with the UP of New England, 1997), 237–52. On
        small items for collectors, see Robie, *By-Paths in Collecting*, 277. For more on the history
        of doll houses and miniature rooms, see Flora Gill Jacobs, *A History of Dolls Houses: Four
        Centuries of the Domestic World in Miniature* (New York: Scribners, 1953; Leonie von
        Wilckens, *Mansions in Miniature: Four Centuries of Doll Houses* (New York: Viking, 1980).

        33. Some of these collecting "teams" became quite well known. Eleanor and Sarah
        Hewitt, for example, scoured Europe for examples of textiles and other examples of good
        design and donated their collection to the institution they founded (with some assistance
        from their mother and sister Amy) in 1896, the Cooper Union Museum for the Arts of
        Decoration. Their intention was to provide free resources for those in the design profes-
        sions. It is interesting to note that, at some of the entertainments they gave in the 1890s,
        the Hewitts had guests come dressed as vegetables and flowers, or as minstrels. Harriet
        and Vetta Goldstein also collected examples of good design for their students in the
        Department of Home Economics at the University of Minnesota. They were the authors
        of the popular textbook *Art in Everyday Life* (New York: Macmillan, 1925). See Russell
        Lynes, *More Than Meets the Eye: The History and Collections of the Cooper-Hewitt Museum*
        (Washington: Smithsonian Institution, 1981), esp. 16; Beverly Gordon, "Related Art: Aes-
        thetic Education by and for Women," paper presented at the College of Human Ecology,
        Cornell University, Ithaca, New York, Feb. 1994.

        34. Russell Belk, Melanie Wallendorf, et al., "Collectors and Collecting," *Advances in
        Consumer Research* 15 (1988): 27–28, demonstrate that even today most personal collec-
        tions begin with a "seed object," which was often something received as a gift.

        35. Letter from Marian Howard to Maxine Waldron, Mar. 13, 1959, Waldron Collection.
        In "Spinning Wheels," my article on Colonial Revival needlework, I discuss the way some
        women were able to carve out a professional niche for themselves as historical experts.
        According to Mia Boynton, a folklorist who studied Margaret Woodbury Strong, many
        doll dealers were well-to-do women (Boyton, unpublished monograph notes, 1990, file 6).

        36. Susan Williams, "Alice Morse Earle and the Culture of Collecting," presentation at
        the American History through the Collector's Eye conference sponsored by the Museum
        of Fine Arts–Houston and Bayou Bend, Oct. 1, 1994; Bowles, *About Antiques*, 21; Hughes,
        Small Decorative Antiques, 111; Carrick, *Collector's Luck*, preface; Mimeographed notes
        from unidentified Philadelphia doll club meeting, Oct. 28, 1947, Waldron Papers, Waldron
        Collection.

        37. Letter from Mary Louise McCaughy to Maxine Waldron, Jan. 31, 1958, Waldron
        Collection; Robie, *By-Paths in Collecting*, 317; Waugh and Foley, *Collecting Hooked Rugs*,
        27; Letter from Electra Havemeyer Webb to Helen Bruce, Jun. 10, 1952 and Webb,
        Williamsburg Speech, 17, Shelburne Museum Archives. Aline Bernstein Saarinen wrote
        in *The Proud Possessors: The Lives, Times and Tastes of Some Adventurous American Art
        Collectors* (New York: Random House, 1958), 300, that Webb "shop[ped] for *life-giving*
        props in the giant supermarket of her personal collections" (italics added).

        38. Mary Kramer, typed statement in what appears to be a circular to doll collectors
        from Elsie Clark Krug of Krug Chinese Imports and International Doll House, Balti-
        more, Waldron Papers; Mary Margaret Blaine, "From the Land of 'Mama Ocllo,'" "Doll-

ology" column *Hobbies* (Jan. 1942), in Waldron Papers; Elizabeth Zenorini, "One Family's Hobbies," "Doll-ology" column, *Hobbies* (Jul. 1949), Waldron Papers; Margaret Elizabeth Sangster, *The Art of Homemaking in City and Country, in Mansion and Cottage* (New York: Christian Herald Bible House, 1898), 305; Marie Overton Corbin, "Key Collecting As a Fad," *Puritan* 1 (1897): 712. As World War II was approaching (1938), the Christmas Bulletin of Waldron's doll club commented, "dolls can help stimulate interest in people of other lands in this sad time."

39. The information on Waldron is compiled from various materials in the Waldron collection, including letters, clippings, flyers, photos, and bulletins; a high school yearbook (1917) and personal scrapbook; books and magazine articles; actual dolls and doll-related matter; an obituary in the *Wilmington Evening Journal,* Mar. 29, 1982; notes from an interview with Beatrice Taylor, Nov. 18, 1979; and Margaret N. Coughlan, "The Maxine Waldron Collection of Children's Books and Paper Toys," in Carol Field, ed., *Special Collections in Children's Literature* (Chicago: American Library Association, 1982), 62.

40. Waldron gave only certain items to Winterthur. She had also collected art books and prints but donated those to the Wilmington, Delaware Art Museum. Clara Andrews Williams, *The House That Glue Built* (New York: Frederick Stokes, 1905). I have no information on the extent or quality of Mr. Waldron's collection.

41. The one exception I am familiar with is Brenda Danet and Tamar Katriel, "No Two Alike: Play and Aesthetics in Collecting," *Play and Culture* 2, no. 3 (1989): 253–77 (reprinted in Susan M. Pearce, ed., *Interpreting Objects and Collections* [London and New York: Routledge, 1994], 220–39). I find it significant that this study was the result of a research project conducted by women.

42. The endearment "precious treasures" comes from Elizabeth Day McCormick, who was talking about embroideries and other items in her costume collection. Letter from McCormick to Gertrude Townsend, Feb. 28, 1943, MFA Archives. Shackleton, *Charm of the Antique,* 288–89; Robie, *By-Paths in Collecting,* 302, 322; Bowles, *About Antiques,* 89–90; Carrick, *Collector's Luck,* 157. Regarding proxemic distances, see Gordon, "Intimacy and Objects."

43. Celia Oliver, "Electra Havemeyer Webb: Quilts at the Shelburne Museum," typescript of talk presented at the Shelburne Symposium on Collecting, Nov. 4, 1993; Webb, Williamsburg speech. When Henry Francis du Pont wrote to Webb on Oct. 5, 1954, he too spoke of her "doing" the houses in her museum, also as if she were outfitting a home (letter in Shelburne Museum Archives). Webb had loved decorating so much that she kept adding rooms on her houses. At Shelburne she kept adding buildings.

44. Webb's egalitarian impulses were clear in a letter she wrote to Lew Wiggins (Nov. 10, 195?) after learning of du Pont's activities. She said, "I think it is a pity to stress wealth [in one's collection.]" Letter in Shelburne Museum Archives. On Northend, see Saunders, *American Decorative Arts Collecting,* 152. Clifford, *Junk Snupper;* Bowles, *About Antiques,* 129. Regarding collecting "down": when Electra Webb brought her cigar-store Indian home, her mother made a horrible face and told her it was "perfectly dreadful." On another occasion she said, "It's hard for a mother to raise a child with Rembrandts and Manets and Corots, and see what taste she's fallen to now" (Webb, Williamsburg speech, 4, 17).

45. Boynton, unpublished monograph notes, file 12.

46. Letters from Elizabeth Day McCormick to Gertrude Townsend, Jul. 6, 1943, Jul. 23, 1944, MFA Archives; Carol Shankel, *Sallie Casey Thayer and Her Collection* (Lawrence, KS: University of Kansas Art Museum, 1976), 65–66; Gelber, *Hobbies,* 122; the article by Eva Earl that Gelber discusses was published as Eva Earl, "A Lady's Experience," *Pennsylvania Philatelist* (Jun. 1894): 337; Carrick, *Collector's Luck,* 46, 145. Some of the women who collected antiques at the turn of the century were also involved in self-help craft projects. For example, the individuals who organized the Deerfield (Massachusetts) Blue and White Society, which gave employment to village women, also collected historic needlework. See Gordon, "Spinning Wheels."

47. The profile of Thayer is taken from Shankel's full-length study, *Sallie Casey Thayer.* Quotes come from pages 48, 49.

48. She had the same idea as the Hewitt sisters, founders of the Cooper Union Museum (see note 34).

49. The profile of Webb is compiled from a number of sources: letters and miscellaneous papers in the Shelburne Museum Archives; Electra H. Webb, "Folk Art in the Shelburne Museum," *Art in America* (May 1955): 15–22, 60–63; Webb, Williamsburg speech; Electra Webb, penciled notes copied and typed by Lilian Carlisle, Mar. 17, 1961; Mrs. J. Watson (Electra) Webb, "Americana at Shelburne," East Side House Winter Antiques Show catalog, 1957; Oliver, "Electra Havemeyer Webb"; Walter Karp, "Electra Webb and Her American Past," *American Heritage* (Apr./May 1982): 16–29; *Collecting American Folk Art: The Shelburne Museum,* video recording hosted by John Wilmerding and produced by Byron McKinney Associates (Washington, DC: National Gallery of Art, 1988); *An American Sampler: Folk Art from the Shelburne Museum* (Washington, DC: National Gallery of Art, 1987); Saarinen, *The Proud Possessors* (Webb's sons quoted on 301); Frances Weitzenhoffer, *The Havemeyers: Impressionism Comes to America* (New York: Harry N. Abrams, 1986).

50. Interestingly, Electra's mother was also very taken with contextual presentation. She was quite concerned with appropriate backgrounds for her paintings, for example, and at times she dressed her servants in costumes that fit the art on display.

51. Saarinen, *The Proud Possessors,* 305. It is worth noting that Webb's husband, Watson, had an architectural eye and taught her to appreciate buildings soon after they were married. She "caught" his interest, although she seems to have cared less about their form and more about their meaning and what could be put inside.

52. Although Strong began collecting in earnest after the period I am primarily concerned with in this book, she spent her formative years in that time. In Betsy Brayer's words, she "collected with the exuberance of the Victorian and Edwardian ages, and to a large extent in categories dating from these periods." Her father had collected coins and stamps; her mother had collected fans, parasols, and Japanese items. See Brayer, *Margaret Woodbury Strong,* 3, 5. My profile of Strong is taken from Brayer's work as well as Barbara Moynehan, "The Legacy of Margaret Woodbury Strong," *Americana* (Sept.-Oct. 1982): 82–86; and Mia Boynton, unpublished monograph notes.

53. The staff tried to distance themselves from Strong, who many saw as a frivolous old lady. They tried to erase her personal image as much as possible. When Director H. J. Swinney visited local schools, he avoided taking any of her dolls and toys, for fear that the museum would not be taken seriously (Moynehan, "Legacy of Margaret Woodbury Strong," 86).

54. Stillinger, *The Antiquers,* 245. Much of the information in my profiles is taken from materials (letters, account books, newspaper clippings, childhood memorabilia, and so on) in the personal papers of du Pont and Crowninshield in the archives of the Winterthur and Hagley museums. I spent so much time looking at this material during research trips in 1994 and 1996 that I felt personally involved with these individuals, and thus I take the liberty of referring to them as they referred to one another—as "Louise" and "Harry." For more information on the history of du Pont and Winterthur Museum, see Walter Karp, "Henry Francis du Pont and the Invention of Winterthur," *American Heritage* 34 (Apr./May 1983): 87–97; Ruth du Pont Lord, *Henry F. du Pont and Winterthur: A Daughter's Portrait* (New Haven: Yale UP, 1999).

55. Among the restoration projects she was involved in were Gore Place, Waltham, MA; Lee Mansion, Marblehead, MA; Wayside Inn, Sudbury, MA; Pierce-Nichols House, Derby House and Gardner-Pingree House, Salem, MA; Mission House, Stockbridge, MA; Kenmore, Fredericksburg, MD; Wakefield National Memorial (Washington's birthplace near Fredericksburg, VA). She was also a trustee of the Peabody Museum and Essex Institute, Salem, MA; president of the Salem Maritime [preservation] Trust; board member of the Boston National Historic Sites Commission; director of the Old Dutch House, New Castle, DE; director of the First Iron Works, Saugus, MA; director of the Arnold Arboretum, Boston, MA; and vice president of the Garden Club of America.

56. She reconstructed her husband's yacht, *Cleopatra's Barge;* worked for the establishment of Princeton Battle Park and the restoration of Independence Hall and Society Hill in Philadelphia; and was on the redecorating committee of the Truman White House.

57. In a handwritten note, Louise proclaimed the chandelier she installed at Kenmore was "singing with beauty." The "feel good" statement is from an interview with her gardener, Walter Biddle, conducted by Debra Hughes and Robert Howard, Oct. 4, 1994, and by Debra Hughes and Alisha Palmer, Jan. 27, 1995, typescripts in Hagley Museum Archives, Wilmington, DE.

58. While outside the scope of this discussion, it is also interesting to note that while Louise was personally involved with her charitable groups—she was active in the day-to-day operations of Children's Island in Marblehead and the Boston Lying-In Hospital, for example, and she routinely invited Girl Scout troops to visit her home—Harry donated money but kept his distance from the institutions he supported.

59. There are many other stories about these women's perseverance in collecting, as my references to braving storms in order to go on collecting expeditions may illustrate. Even for those profiled in these case studies, there are other illustrative tales. One particularly impressive image is that of Electra Webb pulling off the "impossible" task of moving the SS *Ticonderoga,* a full-sized, nine-hundred-ton steamboat, two miles over land to her museum. This took eight months and $250,000 from Webb's pocket.

60. Walter Nelson Durost, "Children's Collecting Activity Related to Social Factors," Contributions to Education no. 535 (New York: Columbia U Teacher's College, 1932), 10, cited in Gelber, *Hobbies,* 74; Gelber, *Hobbies,* 103.

61. Many of the men who talked about the educational value of their collections seemed relatively humorless. Henry Ford set out to create an educational experience with his museum, for example, and bought up whole shops, schools, taverns, and workshops in order to outfit Greenfield Village. Webb also talked about the educational value of the

schoolhouses, shops and other buildings she created at Shelburne, but she did not procure objects in a wholesale fashion as much as choose and arrange them as "individuals." She was also thoroughly amused by the processing of arranging the buildings. Louise Crowninshield, similarly, was always willing to talk about having a good time, far more so than her brother. I believe the women's playful attitude also may have made them less possessive about their objects. Webb said that when an item was gone from one of her houses (for example, was taken by one of her children), she thought that was great fun—it gave her the excuse to go and find a replacement (typed notes, Shelburne Archives). This calls to mind the fact that in much of the advice literature on women's pastimes, it is difficult to tell if described activities are meant for children or adult women. To a great extent, the intended audience seems to have been interchangeable.

62. Jean Lipman and the eds. of *Art in America, the Collector in America* (New York: Viking P, 1961). In situ context is generally also ignored in this book. Typically the objects and artworks are profiled as if they stand alone; they are isolated and treated as individual pieces. This is particularly true for paintings. Interviews with the collectors and some of installation shots often tell a different story, however, and many of the collections were apparently conceived of more holistically. One place the woman's role is identified in this book is in a chapter on the collection of Mrs. and Mrs. Jack Glenn. Because this includes self-conscious, pop-art type commentary on traditional decorative arts (for example, a Chippendale revival settee outfitted with cushions advertising Schlitz beer and Campbell soup), their objects can literally be seen differently. The pattern of primarily focusing on male collectors was also evident in Saarinen's *Proud Possessors*. Webb was included, but an undue amount of attention was given to her folk art paintings, even though they were of minor interest to her. In the dominant paradigm, paintings "counted" more than the three dimensional objects she loved.

63. Gelber, *Hobbies*, 104; Moynehan, "Legacy of Margaret Woodbury Strong," 82.

64. Pomian Krzysztof, *Collectors and Curiosities: Paris and Venice, 1500–1800,* trans. Elizabeth Wiles-Portier (Cambridge: Polity P, 1990), 9; Arthur C. Danto, "From Matchbooks to Masterpieces: Toward a Philosophy of Collecting," *Aperture* 124 (Summer 1991): 2–3. Scholars such as Kathleen D. McCarthy, *Women's Culture: American Philanthropy and Art,* Chicago: U of Chicago P, 1991), have shown that women's work in the arts has often fallen outside or beyond the dominant paradigms. Interestingly, Webb's mother, Louisine Havemeyer, was one of the first to appreciate the aesthetic of the Impressionists and collect their works, much as her daughter was one of the first to appreciate and collect folk art. Again, the exception to the dominant male bias in evident in Danet and Katriel, "No Two Alike." The collections they are concerned with sometimes include "mundane recycled items such as corkscrews or Coca Cola paraphernalia," and they find that the meanings of the collecting experience are not dependent on the item collected.

65. Gelber's inadvertent biases appear in many subtle ways. In discussing psychiatrist William Menninger's belief that collecting could create a feeling of satisfaction because it allowed one to impose order "on a small corner of the chaotic world of manufactured goods," Gelber says Menninger "symbolically affirmed continuing human mastery over factory production" (*Hobbies,* 76). In reality one could equally well impose order on

handmade goods. He sometimes also fails to recognize women's divergent criteria for their collections. For example, in comparing the way women approached scrapbooks with men's systematic organization of stamp albums, he takes Ruutz-Rees's advice out of context. She is quoted as saying that the scrapbook "has no legitimate arrangement" since everything that strikes ones fancy could "promiscuously" go into it (*Hobbies*, 62). The quote is accurate, but Ruutz-Rees only means to imply that there was no preordained or absolute organizational method. Individuals could still impose order—they could decide what went on which page according to their own aesthetic criteria.

66. The profile of Gardner is taken from miscellaneous papers in the archives of the Isabella Stewart Gardner Museum, Boston, MA; Birmingham, *The Grandes Dames,* 57–92; and Anne Higonnet, "Where There's a Will . . . ," *Art in America* 77 (May 1989): 65–75. Higonnet writes of the phenomenon of the house museum, which was especially associated with women. As she put it, this kind of museum functioned simultaneously as a public and private domain, and domesticized the aesthetic experience. Many of the women who founded these museums continued to live in them even after they were open to the public. While Gardner did not live at Fenway Court, she did intend that the (female) director would live on the upper floor. The most recent change in the structure took place in the 1980s, when that space was transformed into museum offices. Higonnet argues (65, 73) this destroyed the domestic character of the villa.

This same holistic, contextual approach to art and objects was made invisible in the case of a popular art history textbook. Helen Gardner's *Art through the Ages* was posthumously recast, much as the museums were. In the first two editions of the text (1926, 1936), Gardner stressed repeatedly that no arts were more "minor" than any other. She devoted as much attention to pottery, textiles, and similar items as she did to painting and sculpture. The book was essentially rewritten by male art historians after Gardner died, and those sections and her proclamations about equal worth were eliminated in later editions. For more on Gardner, see Beverly Gordon, entry in *American National Biography,* vol. 8 (New York: Oxford UP, 1999), 704–5.

67. Henry Glassie, *The Spirit of Folk Art: The Girard Collection at the Museum of International Folk Art* (New York: Abrams, 1991). Girard, like Strong, only began his collection after World War II.

68. Stillinger, *The Antiquers,* 125; letter from du Pont to Webb, Oct. 6, 1958, Shelburne Archives. Saunders, *American Decorative Arts Collecting,* notes that most nineteenth-century collectors were professional men (doctors, lawyers, and so on) who were particularly interested in silver and furniture (that is, those products that were made by crafts*men*). He also treats decorative arts scholarship as a kind of male territory, completely ignoring women's contributions. Gelber, *Hobbies,* 103, also states that "the only women collectors taken seriously by men were those who collected on male terms." For a discussion of the history of women's scholarship in relationship to textiles, see Gordon, "Spinning Wheels," 175–78.

69. Robie, *By-Paths in Collecting,* 235; Charles A. Montgomery and Catherine Maxwell, *Early American Silver: Collectors, Collections, Exhibitions, Writing* (printed in the Walpole Society *Notebook,* reprinted 1969). I acknowledge that women could generally not produce china at home, but they could easily understand its construction, and they could

252   repair it. Textiles, which were rarely collected by men, also were rarely included in the early antiquing literature. Even Shackleton's 1913 work, *The Charm of the Antique,* which proclaimed the highest form of collectibles to be furnishings for the home (298–99), omitted them completely. The volumes that did discuss textiles were all written by women. Because samplers were attributable (their maker's names were worked into them) and could be used as genealogical evidence, it makes sense that they were the first American textiles to be exhibited and actively collected. The first exhibition took place in 1894 at the Philadelphia Museum of Art. See Gordon, "Spinning Wheels," 175.

70. We also generally distinguish today between antiques and collectibles. An "antique" is understood to be something older (technically, one hundred years) or more valuable— a piece of nineteenth-century furniture, for example, or a silver teapot. A collectible is thought of as a more "trivial" item and would typically be considerably newer. It might derive from popular culture. The category thus includes objects as diverse as salt shakers, walking sticks, metal lunch boxes, or even black "mammy" figures of the type discussed in the previous chapter. The objects that women collected in the period under consideration would thus often fall into the collectible category today.

SELECTED BIBLIOGRAPHY

Books, Articles, and Scholarly Presentations

Abrams, Rebecca. *The Playful Self: Why Women Need Play in Their Lives.* London: Fourth Estate, 1997.

Ackerman, Diane. *Deep Play.* New York: Random House, 1999.

———. *A Natural History of the Senses.* New York: Vintage Books, 1991.

Ames, Kenneth L. "Anonymous Heroes: Background History and Social Responsibility," *Museum News* (Sept./Oct. 1994): 34–35.

———. *Death in the Dining Room and Other Tales of Victorian Culture.* Philadelphia: Temple UP, 1992.

Arieti, Silvano. *Creativity: The Magic Synthesis.* New York: Basic Books, 1976.

Bachelard, Gaston. *The Poetics of Space.* 1958; new ed., trans. John R. Stilgoe, Boston: Beacon P, 1994.

Baines, Barbara Burman. *Fashion Revivals from the Elizabethan Age to the Present Day.* London: Anchor P, 1981.

Barendsen, Joyce P. "Wallace Nutting, an American Tastemaker: The Pictures and Beyond," *Winterthur Portfolio* 18 (Summer/Autumn 1983): 187–212.

Baltz, Trudy. "Pageantry and Mural Painting: Community Rituals in Allegorial Form," *Winterthur Portfolio* 15 (Autumn 1980): 212–13.

Beard, Lina, and Adelia. *The American Girl's Handy Book: How to Amuse Yourself and Others.* New York: Charles Scribner's Sons, 1893.

———. *What a Girl Can Make and Do.* New York: Charles Scribner's Sons, 1913.

Belden, Louise Conway. *The Festive Tradition: Table Decorations and Desserts in America, 1650–1900.* New York: W. W. Norton, 1983.

Belenky, Mary Field, et al. *Women's Ways of Knowing: The Development of Self, Voice and Mind.* New York: Basic Books, 1986.

Belk, Russell, Melanie Wallendorf, et al. "Collectors and Collecting," *Advances in Consumer Research* 15 (1988): 27–32.

254

Belk, Russell, and Melanie Wallendorf. "Of Mice and Men: Gender Identity and Collecting." In Katherine Martinez and Kenneth Ames, ed. *The Material Culture of Gender/ The Gender of Material Culture.* Winterthur, DE: Winterthur Museum with the UP of New England, 1997, 7–26.

Bermudez, Jose Luis, Anthony Marcel, and Naomi Eilan, eds. *The Body and the Self.* Cambridge: MIT P, 1995.

Birmingham, Stephen. *The Grandes Dames.* New York: Simon and Schuster, 1982.

Blackburn, R. Barry, ed. *Art, Society and Accomplishments: A Treasury of Artistic Homes, Social Life and Culture.* Chicago: Blackburn, 1891.

Blair, Karen J. *The Torchbearers: Women and Their Amateur Art Associations in America 1890–1930.* Bloomington: Indiana UP, 1994.

Bowles, Ella Shannon. *About Antiques.* Philadelphia: J. B. Lippincott, 1919.

———. *Practical Parties.* Philadelphia: J. B. Lippincott, 1919.

Bowman, John. "Making Work Play." In Gary Alan Fine, ed., *Meaningful Play, Playful Meaning.* Champaign, IL: Human Kinetics Publishers, 1985, 61–71.

Braden, Donna R. *Leisure and Entertainment in America.* Dearborn, MI: Henry Ford Museum and Greenfield Village, 1988.

Brayer, Betsy. *Margaret Woodbury Strong and the Origins of the Strong Museum.* Rochester, NY: Strong Museum, 1982.

Bronner, Simon, ed. *Consuming Visions: Accumulation and Display of Goods in America, 1880–1920.* New York: W. W. Norton for Winterthur Museum, 1989.

Bullivant, Cecil H. *Home Fun.* New York: Dodge, 1910.

Burk, Caroline Frear. "The Collecting Instinct." *Pedagogical Seminary* 7 (Apr. 1900): 179–207.

Burt, Emily Rose. *Entertaining Made Easy.* New York: Edward J. Clode, 1919.

———. *Planning Your Party.* New York and London: Harper and Bros., 1927.

———. *The Shower Book: 77 Showers for the Engaged Girl.* New York: Harper and Bros., 1928.

Cameron, Elisabeth L. *Isn't S/he a Doll? Play and Ritual in African Sculpture.* Los Angeles: U.C.L.A. Fowler Museum, 1996.

Carnes, Mark C. *Secret Ritual and Manhood in Victorian America.* New Haven: Yale UP, 1989.

Carrick, Alice Van Leer. *Collector's Luck, or a Repository of Pleasant and Profitable Discourses of the Household Furnishings and Ornaments of Olden Time.* Boston: Atlantic Monthly, 1919.

Carrier, James G. *Gifts and Commodities: Exchange and Western Capitalism since 1700.* London: Routledge, 1995.

Chalmers, Lillian H. "The Collecting Instinct." *Pedagogical Seminary* 6 (Jul. 1900): 179–207.

Clawson, Mary Ann. *Constructing Brotherhood: Class, Gender and Fraternalism.* Princeton: Princeton UP, 1989.

Csikszentmilhalyi, Mihaly. "Why We Need Things." In S. Lubar and W.D. Kingery, eds., *History from Things: Essays on Material Culture.* Washington: Smithsonian Institution P, 1993.

Csikszentmilhalyi, Mihaly, and Eugene Rochberg-Halton. *The Meaning of Things: Domestic Symbols and the Self.* Cambridge: Cambridge UP, 1981.

Csordas, Thomas J., ed. *Embodiment and Experience.* Cambridge: Cambridge UP, 2001.   *255*

Davey, Doris (After Helen Waite). *My Dolly's Home.* London: Simpkin, Marshall, Hamilton, Kent for the Arts and General Publishers, 1921.

Davis, Kathy, ed. *Embodied Perspectives: Feminist Perspectives on the Body.* London: Sage Publications, 1997.

Dawson, Mary, and Emma Paddock Telford. *Book of Frolics for All Occasions.* New York: William Rickey, 1911.

Day, Lillian Pascal. *Social Entertainments: A Book of Practical Suggestions for Entertaining.* New York: Moffat, Yard, 1914.

Day Entertainments and Other Functions. New York: Butterick Publishing, 1896.

Deep Meanings in Possessions: Qualitative Research from the Consumer Behavior Odyssey (video). Boston: Audvid Productions for the Marketing Science Institute, 1988.

Dennison's Dictionary. Framingham, Mass.: Dennison, n.d. [ca. 1908].

Dew, Louise. *Entertainments for All Seasons.* New York: S. H. Moore, 1904.

Dexter, George Blake. *The Lure of Amateur Collecting.* Boston: Little, Brown, 1923.

Directions for Making Tissue Paper Flowers and Fancy Articles. New Haven: Yale Silk Works, [ca. 1885].

Dissanayake, Ellen. *Homo Aestheticus: Where Art Comes from and Why.* New York: Free P, 1992.

———. *What Is Art For?* Seattle: U of Washington P, 1988.

Dolly Blossom's Bungalow. Chicago: Reilly and Britton, 1917.

Dulles, Foster Rhea. *America Learns to Play: A History of Popular Recreation 1607–1940.* New York: Appleton-Century, 1940.

Engen, Rodney. *Kate Greenaway: A Biography.* New York: Shocken Books, 1981.

Entertaining with Cards. 3rd ed. Cincinnati: U.S. Playing Card, 1900.

Fales, Winnifred, and Mary H. Northend. *The Party Book.* Boston: Little, Brown, 1926.

Featherstone, Mike. *Consumer Culture and Postmodernism.* London: Sage Publications, 1991.

Ferguson, Barbara Chaney. *The Paper Doll: A Collector's Guide with Prices.* Des Moines, IA: Wallace-Homestead, 1982.

Foy, Jessica H., and Karal Ann Marling, eds. *The Arts and the American Home, 1890–1930.* Knoxville: U of Tennessee P, 1994.

Fraser, Antonia. *A History of Toys.* New York: Delacorte P, 1966.

Fryer, Jane Eayre. *The Mary Frances Housekeeper: Adventures among the Doll People.* Philadelphia: John C. Winston, 1914.

Garvey, Ellen Gruber. *The Adman in the Parlor: Magazines and the Gendering of Consumer Culture 1880s–1910s.* New York: Oxford UP, 1996.

Gelber, Steven. *Hobbies: Leisure and the Culture of Work in America.* New York: Columbia UP, 1999.

Giffen, Sarah L., and Kevin D. Murphy. *A Noble and Dignified Stream: The Piscataqua Region in the Colonial Revival, 1860–1930.* York, ME: Old York Historical Society, 1992.

Gill, Jerry H. *Merleau-Ponty and Metaphor.* Atlantic Highlands, NJ: Humanities P, 1991.

Gilligan, Carol. *In a Different Voice: Psychological Theory and Women's Development.* Cambridge: Harvard UP, 1982.

256   Glassberg, David. *American Historical Pageantry: The Uses of Tradition in the Early Twentieth Century.* Chapel Hill: U of North Carolina P, 1990.

Glover, Ellye Howell. *"Dame Curtsey's" Art of Entertaining for All Occasions.* Chicago: F. G. Browne, 1913.

Gordon, Beverly. *Bazaars and Fair Ladies: The History of the American Fundraising Fair.* Knoxville: U of Tennessee P, 1998.

———. "Costumed Representations of Early America: A Gendered Portrayal, 1850–1940." *Dress* 30 (2003): 3–20.

———. "Cozy, Charming and Artistic: Stitching Together the Home Environment." In Jessica Foy and Karal Ann Marling, eds. *The Arts and the American Home, 1890–1930.* Knoxville: U of Tennessee P, 1994, 124–48.

———. "Dress and Dress-up at the Fundraising Fair." *Dress* 12 (1986): 61–72.

———. "Embodiment, Community Building, and Aesthetic Saturation in 'Restroom World,' a Backstage Women's Space." *Journal of American Folklore* 116 (Fall 2003): 444–64.

———. "Intimacy and Objects: A Proxemic Analysis of Gender-Based Response to the Material World." In Katherine Martinez and Kenneth Ames, eds., *The Material Culture of Gender/The Gender of Material Culture.* Winterthur, DE: Winterthur Museum with the UP of New England, 1997, 237–52.

———. "'One of the Most Valuable Fabrics': The Seemingly Limitless Promise of Crepe Paper, 1890–1935." *Ars Textrina* 30 (1999): 1–30.

———. "Related Art: Aesthetic Education by and for Women." Paper presented at the College of Human Ecology, Cornell U, Ithaca, New York, Feb. 1994.

———. "Spinning Wheels, Samplers and the Modern Priscilla: The Images and Paradoxes of Colonial Revival Needlework." *Winterthur Portfolio* 33 (Summer/Autumn 1998): 163–94.

———. "Victorian Fancy Goods: Another Reappraisal of Shaker Material Culture." *Winterthur Portfolio* 25 (1990): 111–29.

———. "Victorian Fancywork in the American Home: Fantasy and Accommodation." In Marilyn Motz and Pat Browne, eds., *Making the American Home: Middle Class Women and Domestic Material Culture, 1840–1940.* Bowling Green, OH: Bowling Green State U Popular P, 1988, 48–68.

———. "Woman's Domestic Body: The Conceptual Conflation of Women and Interiors in the Industrial Age." *Winterthur Portfolio* 31 (Winter 1996): 281–30.

Gordon, Lesley. *A Pageant of Dolls.* New York: A. A. Wyn, 1949.

Grier, Katherine C. *Culture and Comfort: Parlor Making and Middle-Class Identity, 1850–1930.* Washington: Smithsonian Institution P, 1997.

———. "Dishes and More Dishes: Tableware in the Home." In Charles L. Venable, ed., *China and Glass in America.* Dallas: Dallas Museum of Art, 2001.

Grover, Kathryn, ed. *Hard at Play: Leisure in America.* Amherst: U of Massachusetts P and the Margaret Woodbury Strong Museum, 1992.

Hall, Edward T. *The Hidden Dimension.* Garden City, N.Y.: Doubleday, 1969.

———. *The Silent Language.* Garden City, N.Y.: Doubleday, 1959.

Hall, Major H. Byng. *The Bric-A-Brac Hunter; or, Chapters on Chinamania.* Philadelphia: J. B. Lippincott, 1875.

Hartigan, Lynda Roscoe. "The House That Collage Built." *American Art* 88 (Summer 1993): 88–91.

Heath, Lillian. *Eighty Pleasant Evenings.* Boston and Chicago: United Society of Christian Endeavor, 1898.

———. *Enjoyable Entertainments.* Boston: United Society of Christian Endeavors, 1913.

Hertz, Louis H. *Antique Collecting for Men.* New York: Galahad Books, 1969.

Hewitt, Emma Churchman. *Queen of the Home: Her Reign from Infancy to Age, from Attic to Cellar.* Oakland: H. J. Smith, 1889.

Higgonet, Anne. "Where There's a Will . . ." *Art in America* 77 (May 1989): 65–75.

Hints on Entertaining. Minneapolis: Young Women's Christian Association (and Minneapolis Tribune), 1897.

Hodgson, Mrs. Willoughby. *The Quest of the Antique.* London: Herbert Jenkins, 1924.

Hollis, Susan Tower, Linda Pershing, and M. Jan Young, eds. *Feminist Theory and the Study of Folklore.* Urbana and Chicago: U of Illinois P, 1993.

Holloway, Laura C. *The Hearthstone; or, Life at Home: A Household Manual.* Chicago and Philadelphia: L. P. Miller, 1888.

Holt, Arden. *Fancy Dresses Described, or What to Wear at Fancy Balls.* 1879. Sixth ed., London: Debenham and Freebody, 1896.

Hosley, William. *The Japan Idea: Art and Life in Victorian America.* Hartford: Wadsworth Atheneum, 1990.

How to Entertain at Home. Boston: Priscilla Publishing, 1928.

How to Make Paper Costumes. Framingham, MA: Dennison Manufacturing, [ca. 1920].

Huizinga, Johan. *Homo Ludens: A Study of the Play Element in Culture.* German ed. 1944. New ed., trans. R F. C. Hall, London: Routledge and Kegan Paul, 1949.

Irish, Marie. *Novel Notions for Nifty Entertainments.* N.p.: L. M. Paine, 1925.

Jacobs, Flora Gill. *A History of Doll Houses: Four Centuries of the Domestic World in Miniature.* New York: Charles Scribner's Sons, 1953.

Jendricks, Barbara Whitton. *Paper Dollhouses and Paper Dollhouse Furniture.* N.p.: by the author, 1975.

Jones, Michael Owen. "The Concept of 'Aesthetic' in the Traditional Arts." *Western Folklore* 30 (Apr. 1971): 77–104.

———. *Exploring Folk Art: Twenty Years of Thought on Craft, Work, and Aesthetics.* Ann Arbor: UMI Research P, 1987.

Kelley, Lilla Elizabeth. *Three Hundred Things a Bright Girl Can Do.* Boston: Page, 1903.

Kneller, George. *The Art and Science of Creativity.* New York: Holt, Rinehart and Winston, 1965.

Kraus, Richard. *Recreation and Leisure in Modern Society.* New York: Appleton-Century Crofts, 1971.

Lakoff, George, and Mark Johnson. *Philosophy in the Flesh: The Embodied Mind and Its Challenge to Western Thought.* New York: Basic Books, 1999.

Latham, Jean. *The Pleasure of Your Company: A History of Meals and Manners.* London: Adam and Charles Black, 1972.

Lawford, Louisa, ed. *Every Girl's Book: A Compendium of Entertaining Amusement for Recreation in Home Circles.* London: George Routledge and Sons, n.d. [ca. 1860].

Leavitt, Sarah A. *From Catharine Beecher to Martha Stewart: A Cultural History of Domestic Advice*. Chapel Hill: U of North Carolina P, 2002.

Linscott, Mrs. Herbert [Hilda]. *Bright Ideas for Entertaining*. Philadelphia: George W. Jacobs, 1905.

———. *Up-to-Date Social Affairs*. Philadelphia: George W. Jacobs, 1924.

McCullough, Jack W. *Living Pictures on the New York Stage*. Ann Arbor: UMI Research P, 1981.

McNiff, Shaun. *Earth Angels: Engaging the Sacred in Everyday Things*. Boston: Shambhala, 1995.

Mendel, Adele. *Indoor Merrymaking and Table Decorations*. Boston and Chicago: W. A. Wilde, 1915.

Mendelson, Cheryl. *Home Comforts: The Art and Science of Keeping House*. New York: Scribner's, 1999.

Merriam, Effie W. *Modern Entertainments*. New York: F. M. Lupton, 1898.

Miller, Jean Baker. *Toward a New Psychology of Women*. Boston: Beacon P, 1976.

Miller, Nancy K., ed. *The Poetics of Gender*. New York: Columbia UP, 1986.

Moore, Thomas. *The Re-enchantment of Everyday Life*. New York: HarperCollins, 1996.

Montagu, Ashley. *Touching: The Human Significance of the Skin*. New York: Columbia UP, 1971.

Mott, Mrs. Hamilton, ed. *Home Games and Parties*. *Ladies Home Journal* Girl's Library. Philadelphia: Curtis, 1891.

Motz, Marilyn Ferris, and Pat Browne, eds. *Making the American Home: Middle-Class Women and Domestic Material Culture 1840–1940*. Bowling Green, OH: Bowling Green State U Popular P, 1988.

Moxcey, Mary E. *Good Times for Girls*. New York: Methodist Book Concern, 1920.

Muensterberger, Werner. *Collecting: An Unruly Passion, Psychological Perspectives*. Princeton: Princeton UP, 1994.

Mustain, Nellie. *Popular Amusements for Indoors and Out-of-Doors*. Chicago, 1902.

Nash, Maude Cushing. *Children's Occupations*. Boston and New York: Houghton Mifflin, 1920.

———. *Pleasant Day Diversions*. New York: Moffat, Yard, 1909.

Nesbitt, E[dith]. *Wings and the Child, or the Building of Magic Cities*. London and New York: Hodder and Stoughton, 1913.

Novotny, Ann. *Alice's World: The Life and Photography of an American Original: Alice Austen, 1866–1952*. Old Greenwich, CT: Chatham P, 1976.

Ott, Katherine, Susan Tucker, and Patricia Buckler, eds. *Scrapbooks in American Life*. Philadelphia: Temple UP, 2006.

Parties for the Bride-Elect. Boston: Priscilla Publishing, 1924.

Paston-Williams, Sarah. *The Art of Dining: A History of Cooking and Eating*. London: National Trust, 1993.

Peiss, Kathy. *Cheap Amusements: Working Women and Leisure in Turn-of-the-Century New York*. Philadelphia: Temple UP, 1986.

Phillips, Amy Lyman. "Hitting the Trail of the Antique: Adventures in the King's Domain." *The House Beautiful* (Apr. 1925): 474–75.

Pierce, Paul. *Breakfasts and Teas: Novel Suggestions for Social Occasions.* Chicago: Brewer, Barse, 1907.

———. *Suppers: Novel Suggestions for Social Occasions.* New York: Barse and Hopkins, 1907.

Plumb, Beatrice. *Here's for a Good Time: A Collection of Parties for Holidays and All Kinds of Miscellaneous Social Occasions.* Minneapolis: T. S. Denison, 1929.

"Policy of the Regents." In *State Board of Agriculture: Third Annual Report to the Legislature of Kansas for the Year 1874.* Topeka: George W. Martin, State Printing Works, 1985, 259–319.

Powers, Ann. "Mary, Quite Contrary," *New York Times,* Nov. 7, 1999, Education and Life section.

Prevots, Naima. *American Pageantry: A Movement for Democracy.* Ann Arbor: UMI Research P, 1990.

Robb, Christina. "A Theory of Empathy," *Boston Globe Magazine,* Oct. 16, 1988.

Robie, Virginia. *Bypaths in Collecting.* New York: Century, 1912.

Rook, Lisele J., and Mrs. E. J. H. Goodfellow. *Money-Making and Merry-Making Entertainments.* Philadelphia: Penn Publishing, 1903.

Rosenblum, Naomi. *A History of Women Photographers.* New York: Abbeville P, 1994.

Rosenstein, Donna Gail. "'Historic Human Tools': Henry Chapman Mercer and His Collection, 1897–1930." Master's thesis, U of Delaware, 1977.

Roth, Rodris. "Scrapbook Houses: A Late Nineteenth Century Children's View of the American Home." Presentation at Henry Francis du Pont Winterthur Museum and Library Conference on Collecting, Oct. 31, 1992.

Ruutz-Rees, Janet E. *Home Occupations.* New York: Appleton, 1883.

Saarinen, Aline Bernstein. *The Proud Possessors: The Lives, Times and Tastes of Some Adventurous American Art Collectors.* New York: Random House, 1958.

Santino, Jack. *All around the Year: Holidays and Celebrations in American Life.* Urbana and Chicago: U of Illinois P, 1994.

Sartwell, Crispin. *The Art of Living: Aesthetics of the Ordinary in World Spiritual Traditions.* Albany: State U of New York P, 1995.

Saunders, Richard Henry. American Decorative Arts Collecting in New England 1840–1920. M.A. thesis, U of Delaware, 1973.

Schor, Naomi. *Reading in Detail: Aesthetics and the Feminine.* New York: Methuen, 1987.

Seeger, Frederica. *Entertainments for Home, Church and School.* New York: Christian Herald Bible House, 1912.

Shackleton, Robert and Elizabeth. *The Charm of the Antique.* New York: Hearst International Library, 1912.

———. *The Quest for the Colonial.* New York: Century, 1920.

Shankel, Carol. *Sallie Casey Thayer and Her Collection.* Lawrence: U of Kansas Art Museum, 1976.

Shapiro, Laura. *Perfection Salad: Women and Cooking at the Turn of the Century.* New York: Farrar, Straus, and Giroux, 1986.

Sherwood, Mary [identified as M.E.W.S.]. *Home Amusements.* New York: D. Appleton, 1881.

260   Showalter, Elaine, ed. *The New Feminist Criticism.* New York: Pantheon Books, 1985.

Singleton, Esther. *The Collecting of Antiques.* Macmillan, 1926.

Slosson, Annie Trumbull. *The China Hunter's Club.* New York: Harper and Bros., 1878.

Smith, Caroline ("Aunt Carrie"). *American Home Book of Indoor Games, Recreations and Occupations.* Boston: Lee and Shepard, 1871.

Smith, Deborah A. "Consuming Passions: Scrapbooks and American Play." *Ephemera Journal* 6 (1993): 70. Also printed as "The American Play Ethic: Ephemera and Recreation." In American Antiquarian Society, *Proceedings of the Ephemera Symposium* 3 (Oct. 22–23, 1993).

Starr, Ockenga. *On Women and Friendship: A Collection of Victorian Keepsakes and Traditions.* New York: Stewart, Tabori and Chang, 1995.

Stern, Renee. *Neighborhood Entertainments.* New York: Sturgis and Walton, 1913.

Stevenson, Sara, and Helen Bennett. *Van Dyck in Check Trousers: Fancy Dress in Art and Life 1700–1900.* Scottish National Portrait Gallery, 1978.

Stewart, Susan. *On Longing: Narratives of the Miniature, the Gigantic, the Souvenir, the Collection.* Baltimore: Johns Hopkins UP, 1984.

Stocking, Lizzie. *How to Entertain.* Salt Lake City: L. C. Stocking, 1903.

Stillinger, Elizabeth. *The Antiquers.* New York: Alfred A. Knopf, 1980.

Stoller, Paul. *The Taste of Ethnographic Things: The Senses and Anthropology.* Philadelphia: U of Pennsylvania P, 1989.

Susman, Warren I. *Culture as History: The Transformation of American Society in the Twentieth Century.* New York: Pantheon Books, 1984.

Tipton, Edna Sibley. *Table Service for the Hostess.* New York: D. Appleton, 1926.

Trimpey, Alice Kent. *The Story of My Dolls.* Racine, WI: Whitman, 1935.

Tuan, Yi-Fu. *Passing Strange and Wonderful: Aesthetics, Nature and Culture.* Washington, DC: Island P, 1993.

Ullrich, Polly. "Beyond Touch: The Body as a Perceptual Tool." *Fiberarts* 26 (Summer 1999): 43–48.

Vaughan, Genevieve. *For-Giving: A Feminist Criticism of Exchange.* Austin: Plain View P, 1997.

Waldman, Diane. *Collage, Assemblage and the Found Object.* New York: Harry N. Abrams, 1992.

Walker, Margaret Coulson. *Lady Hollyhock and Her Friends: A Book of Nature Dolls and Others.* New York: Baker and Taylor, 1906.

Wallis, Claire, and Nellie Ryder Gates. *Parties for All Occasions.* New York: Century, 1925.

Waugh, Elizabeth, and Edith Foley. *Collecting Hooked Rugs.* New York: Century, 1927.

Weaver, Mike. *Julia Margaret Cameron 1815–1879.* Boston: Little, Brown (NY Graphic Society), 1984.

Welton, Donn, ed. *Body and Flesh: A Philosophical Reader.* Liphook, UK: Blackwell P, 1998.

Weiss, Gail, and Honi Fern Haber, eds. *Perspectives on Embodiment: The Intersections of Nature and Culture.* New York: Routledge, 1999.

Wentworth, Corinne. *Entertainment for All Occasions: Parties Completely Planned for*   *261*
    Evenings, Luncheons, Afternoons, Holidays and Other Occasions. New York and
    Newark: Barse and Hopkins, 1921.
White, Mary. *The Child's Rainy Day Book.* New York: Doubleday, Page, 1905.
Winterburn, Florence Hull. *Novel Ways of Entertaining.* New York and London: Harper
    and Brothers, 1914.
Witherspoon, Edna J. *Fancy Drills for Evening and Other Entertainments.* New York:
    Butterick, 1894.
Wright, Julia McNair. *The Complete Home: An Encyclopaedia of Domestic Life and Affairs.*
    Philadelphia: J. C. McCurdy, 1879.
Young, Katharine, ed. *Bodylore.* Knoxville: U of Tennessee P, 1993.

Popular Magazines Consulted

Delineator
Dennison's Party Magazine (also known as *Parties*)
Farmer's Advocate
Farmer's Journal
Godey's Lady's Book
Good Housekeeping
Goodform: A Magazine for the People
Harper's Bazar (later *Harper's Bazaar*)
Hobbies
Home Comfort
Hostess
House Beautiful
Household Companion
Ladies Floral Cabinet and Pictorial Companion
Ladies' Home Journal
Ladies World
Modern Priscilla
Needlecraft
Peterson's Magazine
Puritan
Woman's Home Companion

Archives and Collections Consulted

Bayou Bend, Houston, TX
Chicago Historical Society, Chicago, IL
Cooper Union Archives, New York, NY
Hagley Museum and Library (including Eleutherian Mills), Wilmington, DE
Helen Louise Allen Textile Collection, U of Wisconsin–Madison
Henry Ford Museum and Greenfield Village, Dearborn, MI

262   Historic Deerfield, Deerfield, MA

Historic New England (formerly Society for the Preservation of New England
    Antiquities), Boston, MA

Isabella Stewart Gardner Museum, Boston, MA

Lee Mansion, Marblehead, MA

Margaret Woodbury Strong Museum, Rochester, NY

Mercer Museum, Doylestown, PA

Museum of Fine Arts, Houston, TX

Museum of Our National Heritage, Lexington, MA

National Museum of American History, Smithsonian Institution, Washington, DC

Philadelphia Fine Arts Museum, Philadelphia, PA

Shelburne Museum, Shelburne, VT

Winterthur Museum, Library and Archives, Winterthur, DE

Wisconsin Historical Society, Madison, WI

INDEX

Page numbers in **boldface** refer to illustrations.

A

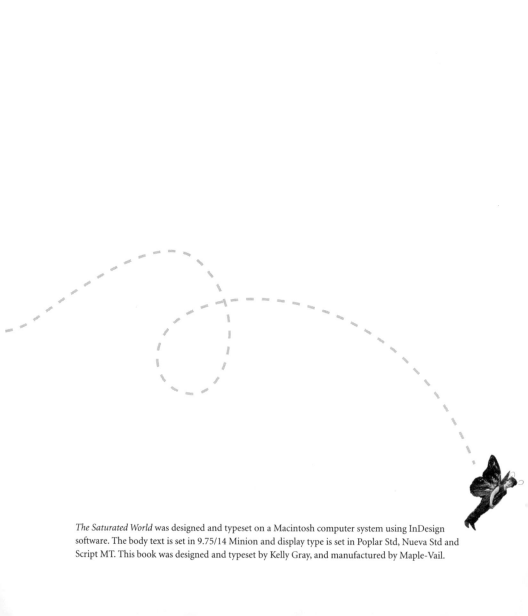

The Saturated World was designed and typeset on a Macintosh computer system using InDesign software. The body text is set in 9.75/14 Minion and display type is set in Poplar Std, Nueva Std and Script MT. This book was designed and typeset by Kelly Gray, and manufactured by Maple-Vail.